The
I Love to Cook
Book

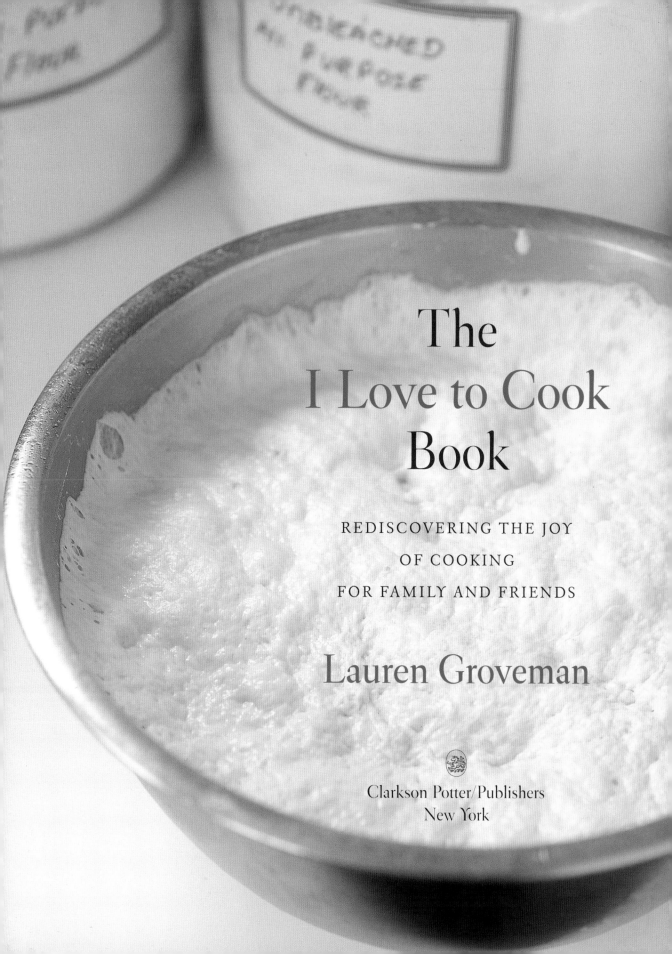

The
I Love to Cook
Book

REDISCOVERING THE JOY
OF COOKING
FOR FAMILY AND FRIENDS

Lauren Groveman

Clarkson Potter/Publishers
New York

Copyright © 2004 by Lauren Groveman
Photographs by Mark Ferri

Published by Clarkson Potter/Publishers, New York, New York,
Member of the Crown Publishing Group, a division of
Random House, Inc.
www.crownpublishing.com

CLARKSON N. POTTER is a trademark and POTTER and
colophon are registered trademarks of Random House, Inc.

Printed in Singapore

Design by Marysarah Quinn

Library of Congress Cataloging-in-Publication Data
Groveman, Lauren
  The I love to cook book : rediscovering the joy of cooking for
family and friends / Lauren Groveman. — 1st ed.
      p.   cm.
1. Cookery.   I. Title.
TX714 .G79   2004
641.5—dc21   2003007634

ISBN 0-609-61087-2

10 9 8 7 6 5 4 3 2 1

FIRST EDITION

To my kitchen, a most magic room. Thank you for providing me with a consistent, lifelong way to please my favorite people, so intimately. Thank you, too, for helping me to physically construct the type of home life I've always wanted and will forever cherish.

To my favorite people: Jon, Ben, Julie, Jessie, and Rosebud (who's like a person). Thank you for being such a constant source of love and support and for always acknowledging and appreciating how much my ability to please you has meant to me. I love you all, more than I can say.

CONTENTS

INTRODUCTION

To me, cooking has never been just something to do and meals are not just something to eat. When I was growing up, my mother didn't cook, but Mabel, a large, rather stern Southern woman employed by my parents, cooked for us daily. Although I'd never call her "sweet," she did have a way with simple home cooking, particularly evident by the way her concoctions made our home smell good. Especially memorable were the aromas that would meet me at the door when I came home from school each afternoon. I remember how safe and calm those aromas made me feel. I also remember a truly defining day, in my seven-year-old life, when I sat on the front steps in the foyer of our house, after what felt like a long day out in the world. I sat there, alone, for many minutes, breathing in the smell of Mabel's simmering meatballs, drenched in a vat of marinara sauce, and I thought to myself that I had discovered a valuable secret: "Good smells are important." It dawned on me that day that good food aromas made me feel better and less alone. Along with this revelation I also vowed that, no matter what I chose to do, when I grew up I wanted to be the one who would provide this safe, healing feeling for my children, as often as I could.

I first fell in love with the act of cooking when I wanted desperately to be a mother, but life threw me a curve. About a year after I got married, Jon and I decided to try to make a baby, but it wasn't happening. I was determined to change careers because my original dream of being a successful actress required that I relocate to Los Angeles, which would have separated me from my husband, whose work was based in New York. (Not much chance of making a baby that way, even under the best of circumstances . . .) Anyway, while I waited (for several years) to conceive, I tried different types of work, none of which made me happy. Feeling more than a bit lost, I finally asked myself, "Lauren, what would you do, without payment if necessary, just because you enjoyed it that much?" That was how I always felt about being an actress. The only image that surfaced, vividly, was the picture of my husband, Jon, enjoying the food that I prepared just for him. That image is what initiated my enrollment in my first cooking class, with Gilda Latsky, at The Epicurean Gallery, a tiny cooking school in Manhattan. After just one daylong class I went wild. At night I devoured cookbooks, reading until I fell asleep from exhaustion. On weekends I went to the markets, then came home and made all of the new recipes I learned in class. Eventually, I started to experiment, to concoct and construct different dishes, trusting that my individual sense of what was delicious would make my husband and friends happy, and it did. I was clearly on to something. At an incredibly frustrating time in my life, when I was longing to care for someone as wholly as a mother cares for her child, I found that preparing delicious food created the aromas and tastes that soothed me and those I cared about. This helped me to feel able to nurture, with or without a baby. But that was just the beginning.

After the first baby came, the next two arrived in close succession. With three kids, all two years apart, we moved to the suburbs, where my days and nights revolved around the needs of my children. There was no time to take cooking classes and, as happy and grateful as I was to have been blessed with my beautiful children, my desire to feel creatively challenged and able to build something tangible in the world felt as much like my birthright as did mothering. So, once again, I turned to cooking as an easily accessible and "at-home" way to feel better and more able.

From the time they were babies, several times a week, I would pile all my kids into the car and we'd trek to the markets where we'd traipse around together, touching, sniffing, and selecting a variety of ingredients that I would tote home, anxious to build them into something aromatic, texturally diverse, and, ultimately, soothing to eat. For the first time in my life I used my hands to knead a yeast dough, destined to be baked into either big crusty chewy rounds or plump tender sandwich loaves. I made fresh pasta, intricate pastries, homemade candies, and flavored custards that I would churn into different types of ice cream. As far as I was concerned, cooking provided me with infinite creative possibilities.

The best news was that although I used cooking first as a personal outlet, I saw that the results made my family really happy, too. The more I cooked, the better I got. The better I got, the more my family loved my food. The more my family loved my food, the quicker they'd run to the table, helping me to feel both appreciated and more and more confident as a cook. It was a win-win situation. Unlike most hobbies affecting only the participant, no one balked at the time I spent cooking, since I didn't have to leave home to do it and everyone in the house got to experience the benefits as a good cook got even better.

Eventually, people began to ask me to teach them what I knew. Maybe it was the discerning way I selected one type of vegetable over another, but strangers seemed to gravitate toward me in the markets, asking for ways to get something tasty out of some type of food. Then, one night at our family dinner table, Jon suggested that I start to write my recipes down so I could easily share them with others. That was all the encouragement I needed. Not only did I start to write, but it wasn't long before I began teaching weekly cooking classes in my home. As the kids became older and more independent, I joined a few culinary organizations so I could interact with others who loved to cook as much as I did. Each year, I took on more and more outside commitments in the culinary world, until ultimately things busted loose and I began to regularly contribute to national "foodie" magazines. I started teaching cross-cultural cooking classes, each consisting of a wide variety of demographic groups. I raised the funds and gathered the materials to build a teaching kitchen in a New York correctional facility, where I now teach—men and women—as often as possible. I've hosted two different cooking series on television and I produce and host a weekly "live" radio program, all about the intrinsic benefits of living a life filled with homemade tastes.

All throughout my adult journey, cooking has proved to be a bridge that's supported my personal life as my goals expanded. Cooking made me feel better about myself when I was home raising my kids and is still helping me to feel better and more empowered now that my work no longer stems just from my home kitchen. For the last several years, my days have been filled with rigorous writing assignments, out-of-home cooking classes, and extensive travel as a television host, leaving me just as conflicted as any other parent who's made the choice to weave both professional and personal accomplishments into his or her life. As my career took off, I continued to use cooking to help stay connected to my family so my outside aspirations wouldn't preclude my ability to provide the satisfying existence that we were all accustomed to. I just had to cook in a more efficient way.

Today, when I'm not working I'm really home. I dedicate parts of my downtime to filling my house with the same cooking and baking scents that we all love. I maximize my "take" on designated cooking days by making big batches of the components that will help me arrive at my family's favorite dishes more easily. I'll make four times the amount of barbecue sauce and teriyaki sauce and put them in the fridge. I'll make an assortment of pestos, homemade spice blends, and a big weekly batch of the garlic confit oil that I use every day, to flavor meats or vegetables and also as a dip for bread. I make bread crumbs, puff pastry, and different types of stocks ahead and freeze them, since, when time is scarce, their presence makes from-scratch sweet or savory foods much easier to accomplish while still providing me with the creative ownership of the words "This is delicious." And because mixing and sifting is time-consuming, I use leisurely Sunday afternoons to concoct large batches of dry mixes, each producing a variety of wonderful things. For instance, I use my homemade pancake mix that my children were raised on to make truly luscious cupcakes and layer cakes (chocolate and vanilla). And since my kids were accustomed to having their dinners feel big and abundant, I decided to make large mixes for some of their favorite dinnertime embellishments, like tender cornbread and biscuits. While experimenting to find more ways that these mixes could perform for me, I found that the biscuit mix also makes outrageously delicious scones, which the kids love either first thing in the morning or as a quick bite as they run in and out of the house. The cornbread mix also makes wonderful corn muffins; and speaking of muffins, my assorted muffin mix makes (at last count) five different types of gorgeous muffins. As a busy person, I'm truly grateful to have these mixes on hand, since they make me that much closer to getting something great tasting into a pan and out of the oven.

So, from personal and professional experience, I've seen that cooking can help people to feel better on every level. The recipes in this book are the ones I cook for my family, the food that has helped me sustain the type of home life that's made me and my family very happy. If you're single or newly married and you want to make a cozy existence for yourself or your spouse, and feel able to entertain your friends, this book can help you. If you're either home raising your kids or retired and searching for a daily way to feel more tactile and creatively proficient, this book can help you. If you're a working parent who wants to stay connected to your children, making them feel that they're a priority in your life, this book can help you. If you're a single father and you're tired of going to take-out pizza and Chinese food on alternate weekends with the kids, this book can help you. And if thirty years ago, you deemed something else more important and you'd like to finally be able to gather your friends and family in a "homemade way" so you feel personally proud, this book can help you. I truly love to cook. I hope this book helps you to love it, too.

CHAPTER ONE
STOCK UP!
With a Better-Than-Basics
Homemade Pantry

THIS FIRST CHAPTER is very special to me. It's been con-
structed to help busy people fulfill their desire to provide
wholesome, delicious foods for themselves and their favorite people, easily and consistently, even with a hectic weekday agenda.
Actually, it's usually when we're the busiest that we feel the need to
reconnect and reaffirm our priorities, embracing the comforts of
family and home. So, in this first chapter, you'll learn how to set up
your kitchen to, at the drop of a hat, fortify your home with luscious
tastes, soothing textures, and wonderful aromas.

You can use an occasional "down day" (or the closest you get to that) to
make a few different dry mixes for things like cornbread and corn muffins or
tender biscuits and scones, and one that makes everything from buttermilk
pancakes to the most tender and delicious cupcakes and layer cakes. You can
make spice blends to quickly perk up grilled or roasted chicken, steaks,
shrimp, fish, and even cookies and pastries. Or cook up a rich, robust homemade barbecue sauce that's good enough to use as a table condiment; or a
variety of stocks to be used later to enrich your rice, bathe your stews, or serve
as the base for your soups.

My hope is that the recipes in this chapter will enable you to take away
more creative ownership from the act of cooking and baking.

What Defines a Pantry?
To many, the term "pantry" refers to shelves that are stacked with canned items
or a cabinet full of extra sugar, flour, and aluminum foil. To me, a pantry's purpose can be much more far-reaching. A truly useful "better-than-basics"
pantry is filled with concoctions that will enable a busy person to either scoop
from a canister of this, or go into their refrigerator and spoon from a jar of that,
and to thaw from the freezer a tub of something else, all in order to quickly
come up with something delicious. To do this, you'll need to have certain containers so your efforts on one day can provide you with long-lasting benefits.

CANISTERS

Whether or not these are see-through, all canisters must be airtight. For larger pancake, cornbread, and muffin mixes, I suggest owning several 5-pound canisters and one or two 10-pound canisters. Smaller ones are great for storing salts, leavening, nonfat dry milk, cornstarch, unsweetened cocoa powder, confectioners' sugar, and so on. Make sure they all have nice wide mouths to accommodate easy entry and exit when using either a measuring spoon or a big scoop. I suggest dedicating an entire cabinet in your kitchen to "better-than-basics" concoctions. Choose a cabinet within close reach, making it easier to use mixes. Clear jars and canisters are my first preference, since the sight of homemade dry mixes is so homey and reassuring that something tasty is never far away. However, try not to put jars and canisters in direct sunlight or in an excessively warm area. Cool, dry, dim, and airtight are always preferable for best longevity.

GLASS JARS

Jars of assorted sizes (½ pint, pint, and quart), all with screw tops and wide mouths, are great for storing homemade barbecue sauce, teriyaki sauce, fruit butters, sweet and savory spice blends, and so on. If you buy canning jars that use lids, be sure to get extra lids, since these can be used only once when canning, and also deteriorate after a while. Also, see page 15 to learn an inexpensive way to create your own shaker-top jars, with holes as big or little as you like. For extra protection, regardless of the contents, lay a small doubled layer of plastic wrap snugly over the jar opening before applying the lid and attaching the screw band.

FREEZER CONTAINERS

Have lots, in a wide variety of sizes, made of heavy, thick plastic with tight-fitting lids. To eliminate confusion, stack containers of the same size in one spot and place their lids directly behind or underneath them. When filling containers for freezing, it's a good idea to list the measured amount on a sticky label (to remind you of how many servings that container will provide, when thawing). Also, remember to allow enough room for the natural expansion that occurs when a liquid becomes frozen. For example, don't put more than 3⅔ cups liquid in a quart container. And remember to list the contents of the containers (along with the amount and the date), since when frozen, different things can look remarkably alike.

HEAVY-DUTY PLASTIC BAGS

Pint, quart, gallon, and jumbo (2-gallon) bags are a must in any house that has a freezer. I prefer ones that pinch shut, without the "zipper," since zippers usually let air in at one end. It's also a good idea to double your bags when freezing (especially things like bread crumbs), and make sure that both seals are secure with a minimum of air trapped in either bag. If you don't own lots of plastic containers, or if freezer space is an issue, use a freezer container that is low and long (stackable) to freeze your food. After your food is frozen solid, pop out the contents and place the block in a doubled jumbo freezer bag. As always, it's a good idea to attach a label with the contents, date, and amount.

STICKY LABELS

I couldn't live without these. I use sticky labels every day, whether to tag my bowl of yeast dough to remind me when I should punch it down, or to identify a frozen item before freezing, or to label my canisters with a freshly made dry mix. When labeling your canister, don't attach a date to the front (since every time you replace your mix, you'll have to cross out that date to put on another). Instead, place a separate sticky label on the bottom of the canister, and before refilling with a new batch, re-enter a new date.

HERE'S THE SCOOP:
To Create Your Own Shaker-Top Jars

Go to a hardware store and pick up a small hammer, a center punch with a 5/16-inch broad point, a small plain cutting board that you'll devote just to this purpose, a wide-mouth funnel for filling jars, and several pint-size glass jars with screw-top lids. You'll also need to purchase an extra box of lids to keep your spice blend sealed and fresh.

Set aside two lids for each jar. Place one lid on the wooden board, metal side up, and position the point of the center punch on the lid. Using a small hammer, hit the top of the center punch to puncture the lid many times. The larger you want the holes to be, the more times you'll have to hit the hammer in that one spot. For the poultry blend, make the holes nice and big so you can apply the seasoning evenly and liberally. After filling your jar, place the perforated lid on the opening. Place a plain (nonperforated) lid on top of the first, and attach the screw band to secure it shut. To use, unscrew the jar and remove the solid lid. Re-attach the screw band to secure the perforated lid in place. After each use, unscrew the top, replace the solid lid over the perforated one, and affix it using the screw band as before.

LIQUID GOLD ... CHICKEN STOCK

If I were looking for the first thing to make when creating a homemade pantry, something that could be counted on to provide countless opportunities to quickly concoct something soothing and delicious, I would absolutely vote for homemade stock. Whether you want to make a pot of soup, or simmer a rice pilaf, or throw together a quick yet full-flavored pan sauce, or slow-cook a classic roux-based gravy, homemade stock is one of those components that is truly pivotal to the quality of a finished dish. When making chicken stock, I like to use a large stewing hen that's been sawed in half by my butcher. Although it's not necessary, because the flesh is more mature, the hen naturally adds more depth of flavor. I also recommend using the bigger 16-quart pot and the larger amount of ingredients, since this will leave you with the most amount of stock. ❧ YIELD: 3 TO 7 QUARTS

3 to 8 pounds assorted bony chicken parts, skin left intact (backs, necks, wing tips, feet, etc.) and, if available, a cooked chicken or turkey carcass

Salt, as needed

8 to 16 cups assorted scrubbed and cut-up aromatic vegetables: large unpeeled yellow onions, root ends removed, leeks, carrots, celery, unpeeled garlic cloves

One 4- to 10-pound chicken (optional; I use the larger stewing hen) with neck and gizzard (no liver), well rinsed

1 tablespoon black peppercorns

A few parsley sprigs

Generous pinch of crumbled dried thyme (optional)

PREHEAT THE OVEN TO 450°F. Sprinkle the rinsed and well-dried bony chicken parts lightly with salt and toss them with some of the chopped onions. Place the chicken (skin side up) and the onions on one or two shallow baking sheets and roast in the hot oven until the onions and chicken are deeply golden and caramelized, about 30 minutes. (If roasting on two racks, position the racks to the upper and lower thirds of the oven and switch the baking sheets halfway through the roasting time.)

Remove the baking sheets from the oven and scrape the browned ingredients into a tall 8- to 16-quart stockpot. Working with one at a time, place a baking sheet directly on the stove burner and pour on some boiling water. Turn the heat to low and, using the flat edge of a wooden spatula, scrape any caramelized bits of chicken and onions off the bottom of the sheet. Carefully pour this liquid into the stockpot and add the remaining ingredients, along with enough cold water to generously cover the solids by at least 2 inches. Bring the mixture to a boil, then reduce the heat and simmer gently, with the cover ajar, for 2 hours, occasionally skimming off any scum that rises to the surface. Carefully remove the hen (if using) and allow it to become cool enough to handle. Remove the meat, set aside for another use, and return the skin and bones to the simmering broth along with some more fresh vegetables, if desired. Continue to simmer with the cover ajar for 1 more hour. Uncover the pot and simmer for another 1 to 3 hours to reduce and concentrate the flavors. During this time, occasionally press down on the solids to extract any remaining goodness.

Allow the stock to cool with the solids, off the heat. Place a large sturdy triple-mesh sieve over an extra-large bowl and strain the stock into the bowl. Discard the solids from the colander. Clean the stockpot and pour the stock through a fine-mesh sieve back into the pot. Clean the bowl, pour the strained stock back into the bowl, and cover well with plastic wrap. Refrigerate the stock for 48 hours to allow all the fat to solidify and rise to the top of the bowl.

Use a large shallow spoon to scoop off the thick yellow layer of congealed fat on top of the chilled gelatinous stock. At this point you can either season the stock with salt and pepper to taste and use it now, or divide it among labeled heavy-duty freezer containers and freeze it for future use. (Don't season the stock until you know its ultimate use.) You can also reduce it further, which will concentrate the flavors even more, but taste after reducing to determine the need for salt.

Chicken stock will freeze perfectly for at least six months. Stock can also be refrigerated for up to three days before using, if kept very cold. Always boil thawed stock for a solid minute before eating. (And yes, you can refreeze stock once it's been thawed, reboiled, and cooled.)

BEEF, VEAL, OR LAMB STOCK

For a beef, veal, or lamb stock with maximum body, ask your butcher for a bunch of different meaty bones and do use the meat from the more connective cuts, like neck, shoulder, or shank meat. Have the bones sawed into manageable pieces so it's easier to brown more, occasionally slipping them into the simmering liquid, which will add enrichment to the broth. The simmering process can be accomplished almost completely unsupervised—you show up only sporadically to feed the pot—so please don't be aghast when you read my instructions to simmer veal and beef stock for anywhere between 8 and 36 hours (lamb is just 4 to 8 hours). Once (I learned this in France) I actually simmered my veal stock for three days, occasionally feeding the pot more browned bones and crisp fresh vegetables. That time produced the richest, most wonderful batch I've ever made. (And my family never complained about the fabulous aromas that continually wafted throughout my house.) Again, as with the chicken stock recipe, I highly recommend using the larger 16-quart pot and the increased amount of ingredients, so you can make the benefits of a stock-making day last longer. ❧ YIELD: 2 TO 7 QUARTS

FOR BEEF STOCK

4 to 8 pounds (or more) beef short ribs, oxtails, meaty slices from the shank, beef knuckles, and/or meaty beef bones hacked into medium-size pieces (ask your butcher to do this for you)

FOR VEAL STOCK

4 to 8 pounds (or more) meaty veal bones from the shank, knuckles, and/or tails, with some cubed shoulder meat

FOR LAMB STOCK

4 to 8 pounds (or more) meaty lamb bones from the neck and shoulder, including cubed shoulder or neck meat

REMAINING INGREDIENTS
FOR ALL THREE STOCKS

One or two 6-ounce cans tomato paste, depending on quantity of meat
10 to 20 cups assorted scrubbed and cut-up aromatic vegetables: large unpeeled onions (root ends removed), carrots, leeks, unpeeled garlic cloves
1 to 4 whole tomatoes, coarsely chopped
1 tablespoon black peppercorns
½ to 1 cup dry red wine, depending on the size of your pot (optional)
Bouquet garni: 4 fresh thyme sprigs or 1 teaspoon crumbled dried thyme leaves, 1 small bunch of parsley with stems intact, 1 imported Turkish bay leaf, all wrapped in a double thickness of dampened cheesecloth and tied with kitchen twine
1 to 2 teaspoons salt

PREHEAT THE OVEN TO 450°F. Dry the meat and place the pieces on a large shallow baking sheet. Spread a thin layer of tomato paste over some of the exposed meat and bones, then scatter some onions and carrots around it. Roast the meat and vegetables until deeply caramelized (the tomato paste will darken considerably), 30 to 35 minutes. Scrape the browned mixture into a nonreactive 8- to 16-quart stockpot and discard any rendered fat that remains on the baking sheet. Deglaze the baking sheet as described for Chicken Stock (see page 16). Pour this meaty liquid into the stockpot.

ADD THE REMAINING RAW VEGETABLES (including the tomatoes), the peppercorns, wine, if using, and the bouquet garni. Add enough cold water to cover the contents by 2 inches, and add the salt. Bring the liquid to a bubble. Reduce the heat to very low and simmer the stock, with the cover ajar, occasionally skimming off any scum that rises to the surface, for 8 to 36 hours (simmer lamb stock for 4 to 8 hours). During this time, occasionally press on the solids to extract as much flavor from them as possible. If some evaporation occurs while the stock is simmering, add enough boiling water to keep the solids submerged. As the broth simmers, if desired, occasionally remove some of the old solids and add more raw vegetables and browned meat and bones.

Cool, strain, chill, and defat the stock as you would when making Chicken Stock (page 17).

HERE'S THE SCOOP:
On Creating Richness in Canned Broth

Soups, stews, and sauces taste infinitely better when made with homemade stock. If you don't have homemade, you can doctor the store-bought stuff. Use a low-sodium brand since the others are salty. Bring the canned chicken stock to a full simmer (uncovered) with some chopped aromatic vegetables like carrots, yellow onions, celery, and leek. When fixing canned beef broth, also add some whole garlic cloves, along with some browned stew beef and one or two slices of browned oxtail. Adding a chopped fresh tomato with a few sprigs of fresh thyme will enhance the beef broth even more. Simmer for an hour or so, or until the additions have rendered all of their goodness and the broth is more fragrant of tangible things.

To make up for any evaporation that will naturally occur when simmering, start out with twice as much broth as is required in your recipe. And when adding fresh meat, allow time to remove the fat before making your sauce. (To speed this up, after straining, put the hot liquid into a heatproof bowl and submerge the bottom into another bowl that has a generous layer of ice, mixed with a little water and a tablespoon of kosher salt.) After simmering, straining, and defatting the liquid, you'll have a mini-stock to use in any recipe calling for stock.

SHRIMP STOCK

It always amazes me how quick and easy it is to make shrimp stock. You can collect a stash of shells in your freezer or ask your fishmonger for some; he probably has plenty. You don't have to make stock on the day that you find yourself with shrimp shells. They'll freeze really well in a doubled, securely sealed freezer bag. However, don't rinse the shells before freezing unless you dry them impeccably, or they'll develop ice crystals that will damage their flavor potential. Thaw the shells overnight in the refrigerator, in their original bag. Then rinse, drain well, and use as directed below. Use shrimp stock for soup, rice, and sauces that complement a seafood entree. Although the butter is optional, it does add a level of richness that I love. ❧ YIELD: ABOUT 1 QUART

1 tablespoon unsalted butter (optional)

Shrimp shells from 2 to 3 pounds raw shrimp

About 2 generous cups assorted scrubbed and cut-up aromatic vegetables: yellow onions, celery, carrots

Cold water or chicken stock (or a combination of both) as needed

1 tablespoon black peppercorns

Kosher or sea salt and freshly ground black pepper to taste

IF USING THE BUTTER, melt it in a 2½-quart heavy-bottomed saucepan over medium heat until bubbling. If not using the butter, heat the dry pan until hot. Either way, add the shells to the heated saucepan and cook them, stirring frequently, until their color deepens and they become wonderfully fragrant, 2 to 3 minutes. Add the onion, celery, and carrots, along with enough cold water or stock to cover the solids by about 2 inches. Add the peppercorns and bring the whole thing to a brisk bubble. Turn the heat down low and simmer the liquid for about 45 minutes. You'll know it's done when the color becomes a beautiful amber.

Remove the saucepan from the stove and let the stock cool with the solids. Season with salt and pepper. Strain and discard the solids before using or just freeze it for another day (no need to defat). Shrimp stock can also remain refrigerated (well covered) for up to two days before using.

HERE'S THE SCOOP:
To Shell and Devein Shrimp

It's the easiest thing in the world to shell and devein shrimp, and it can be done quickly and efficiently using a short serrated knife, preferably with a thin, somewhat flexible blade.

To shell shrimp, hold the shrimp rounded side up (legs down and head toward you) in your nonworking hand. Use your working hand to insert the blade of the knife underneath the shell (blade side up). As you continue to drive the blade in, toward the tail, lift the knife handle in an upward motion, releasing the shell. Just peel the shell off. If you want to keep the tails on, only insert the blade to the point where it reaches the beginning of the tail.

To devein shrimp, run the blade over the thin crevice created after removing the shell (still working on the outer rounded part of the shrimp), deepening it slightly. Rinse out the dark intestinal vein and you're ready to cook. To butterfly shrimp so they will stand, tails up, just cut a little deeper when deveining.

FISH STOCK

The bones, heads, skin, and tails of mild white fish such as flounder, striped bass, halibut, catfish, or red snapper make the most flavorful fish stock. And, like shrimp and vegetable stock, the process is very quick in comparison to stock made from chicken, beef, or veal, since oversimmering fish remnants can turn your stock bitter. Use a low, wide pot instead of the more traditional tall, narrow one; this way, more of the liquid will be continually exposed to the heat, helping to quickly pull more flavor out of the solids and into the broth. Sometimes I sweat the vegetables gently, under close cover, while other times I opt to roast half the vegetables and use the remaining ones raw. Sweating encourages the vegetables' sweetness to come to the forefront, while roasting lends a toasted flavor. Both are great. Remember to make sure that any blood or bits of organs (especially the gills—the red, fan-shaped tissue that's attached to both sides of the throat) are removed first, since their presence will make the stock bitter tasting. You'll need good kitchen scissors for that or just ask your fishmonger to do it.

§ YIELD: ABOUT 4 QUARTS

2 tablespoons flavorless vegetable oil

About 8 generous cups assorted scrubbed and cut-up aromatic vegetables: yellow onions, celery, carrots, parsnips

2 to 3 pounds fish frames, heads, tails, broken skeletons, etc., rinsed

1 tablespoon black peppercorns

4 quarts cold water or chicken stock, or a combination of both

1 teaspoon crumbled dried thyme

Kosher or sea salt and freshly ground black pepper to taste

To SWEAT THE VEGETABLES on the stove, heat the oil in an 8-quart short, wide-bottomed pot over medium heat and, when hot, stir in the vegetables. Place a piece of oiled waxed paper directly over the vegetables and reduce the heat to low. Sweat the vegetables this way, just until softened and fragrant, about 7 minutes. Alternatively, to roast the vegetables, toss half of them with the oil and spread them out on a shallow baking sheet. Roast them in a pre-heated 450°F. oven for 15 minutes, or until wilted and fragrant, then scrape the vegetables into the pot.

Add the fish bones along with the raw vegetables, if using, and pepper-corns. Cover generously with liquid and bring to a boil over medium-high heat. Reduce heat to low, add the thyme, and simmer the broth, with the cover ajar, for 30 minutes, occasionally using a skimmer to remove any gray scum from the top. Season with salt and pepper. Remove from the heat and let sit for about 20 minutes. Strain and either use immediately, or chill until cool and freeze for up to three months. Fish stock can also remain refrigerated (well covered) for up to two days before using.

ROASTED VEGETABLE STOCK

Ever since my father-in-law announced that he no longer eats meat, I've kept a stash of this wonderful vegetable stock in my freezer. My family loves it (and most of us are devout carnivores). Roasting half the vegetables definitely gives this brew extra dimension in both taste and color, as does leaving the skins on the onions. And when making this stock for those who I know don't have dietary restrictions, I drizzle melted butter on the vegetables before roasting, even though you can use vegetable oil, too. Remember, in any stock, stay away from vegetables that are overly pungent, like broccoli, cabbage, asparagus, and cauliflower.

❧ YIELD: ABOUT 4 QUARTS

About 24 cups (or more) assorted scrubbed and cut-up aromatic vegetables: large unpeeled yellow onions (root ends removed), carrots, parsnips, celery, leeks, a few whole heads garlic cut in half through the middle

4 tablespoons (½ stick) butter, melted, or flavorless vegetable oil

Kosher or sea salt to taste
2 teaspoons black peppercorns, coarsely cracked
2 bay leaves, preferably Turkish (optional)
A few parsley sprigs
Generous pinch of crumbled dried thyme (optional)

PREHEAT THE OVEN TO 425°F. In a large bowl, toss about half of the chopped vegetables with the melted butter or vegetable oil and place them on a greased shallow baking sheet. Roast the vegetables until tender and turning golden, 30 minutes to 1 hour, then scrape them into a short, wide 8-quart pot along with the rest of the raw vegetables and the remaining ingredients. Deglaze your baking sheet with a thin layer of boiling water over direct heat. As the water bubbles, use the flat edge of a wooden spatula to scrape up any browned bits of caramelized vegetables from the bottom of the pan and add this flavorful liquid to your pot.

Add enough cold water to the pot to cover the solids by 2 inches. Bring the liquid to a boil through the center, then reduce the heat and simmer with the cover ajar for 1 to 2 hours, pressing on the solids occasionally to help them render all their goodness. If desired, feed the pot more raw and/or cooked vegetables after the first hour and continue to simmer until you are satisfied with the color and richness of the broth. Strain the stock and either use immediately, or let it cool and freeze for up to four months. Vegetable stock can also remain refrigerated (well covered) for up to three days before using.

GARLIC CONFIT
with Cracked Pepper and Herbs and Garlic Confit Oil

This is one recipe that I prepare every week (without fail) and use almost every day. Whole garlic cloves, still in their papery skins, simmer away at the barest bubble in extra-virgin olive oil that's laced with red pepper flakes and cracked black peppercorns, and are finished with some crumbled herbes de Provence. *I use the oil to brush on meat, fish, poultry, and vegetables before (and even after) grilling, roasting, or pan-searing. I also serve the garlic-scented oil with the tender nuggets of cooked garlic (still in their skins) in small bowls, at the table. We squeeze out the garlic meat onto slices of crusty bread, drizzle some of the oil on top, and top it off with a light sprinkle of kosher salt.* ❧ YIELD: ABOUT 1½ CUPS

2 heads of garlic (or more), broken into individual cloves but not peeled (remove any excess papery skins)

Extra-virgin olive oil as needed

1 tablespoon black peppercorns

½ rounded teaspoon red pepper flakes (optional)

Pinch of *herbes de Provence,* crumbled (optional)

PLACE THE GARLIC CLOVES in a 1-quart heavy-bottomed saucepan and add enough olive oil to cover by 1 inch. Crack the peppercorns using a mortar and pestle; or lay the peppercorns on a sturdy work surface, cover with a clean kitchen towel, and give the peppercorns several swift whacks until most are split open. Add the cracked peppercorns and red pepper flakes, if using, to the oil and place the pan over very low heat.

After about 5 minutes you'll see the oil begin to bubble. Let the oil and garlic simmer gently for 10 to 15 minutes, uncovered. Don't let the oil simmer too briskly or the garlic might burst (I once found a few cloves clinging to my kitchen ceiling). When the garlic is tender, remove the pan from the stove and add the crumbled *herbes de Provence,* if using. Let the garlic confit cool and, after you've used what you need for that day, store the rest in the refrigerator, in tightly covered containers, to use throughout the week. For best flavor and ease of use, bring the oil to room temperature before using.

GARLIC-SCENTED
ROASTED PEPPERS

At least once a week, my family dinner includes a large platter of roasted red and yellow peppers, partnered with slices of fresh mozzarella cheese, sliced ruby-red beefsteak tomatoes, and thin wedges of sweet red onions, topped with a scattering of my favorite olives and a small handful of drained capers. Often I add a bunch of cleaned baby arugula or basil leaves that I either park on one side of the peppers or tuck neatly in between the tomatoes or peppers.

Whether sliced and tossed into a simmering sauce or a succulent stew, chopped and incorporated into a rice pilaf, or used as a piquant topping for hot slices of garlic toast that accompanies a soup meal or cocktails, roasted peppers in your refrigerator enable you to quickly embellish your meals. And don't limit this to sweet bell peppers since the roasting process also works well on jalapeños.

❧ YIELD: DEPENDS ON HOW MANY PEPPERS ARE USED

As many red and yellow bell peppers as desired
Garlic Confit Oil (page 23) or extra-virgin olive oil as needed
Freshly ground black pepper to taste

Thinly sliced or minced fresh garlic to taste (optional)
Kosher or sea salt to taste

TIMING IS
EVERYTHING

❧ *The peppers can be roasted, skinned, seeded, flavored with oil and ground pepper, and stored in the refrigerator, securely covered, several days ahead and used throughout the week. The addition of fresh garlic, however, reduces their longevity, so avoid adding garlic more than one or two days before serving.*

STICK A STURDY METAL SKEWER into the stem end of a red or yellow bell pepper and place the pepper over and into a direct flame. Let the skin blister and become blackened, turning frequently. When blackened all over, slide it off the skewer directly onto a clean kitchen towel or into a paper lunch bag. Enclose the pepper completely in the towel (or scrunch the bag shut) and let it steam until it becomes tender and cool enough to handle. Repeat for the remaining peppers.

Alternatively, preheat the broiler with the rack as close as possible to the heating element. Halve the peppers and lay them on a cold broiler pan, skin side up. Broil the peppers until the skins are blackened and blistered, then remove them from the oven and let them cool as described above.

UNWRAP THE PEPPERS (they will look somewhat shriveled and feel limp), and rub the blackened skins off, revealing the flesh. If little stubborn bits of the blackened skin bother you, just rinse them off, though this will remove a bit of their smoky flavor. Cut the peppers in half through the stem end (if not already halved), and pull out their veins and seeds. Again, feel free to lightly rinse out any stray seeds; then dry the peppers meticulously and place them in a clean wide-mouth jar or in a sturdy plastic tub. Drizzle the peppers with the garlic oil or olive oil and grind in some black pepper. If serving within 24 hours, you can layer several thinly sliced (or minced) garlic cloves within the halved peppers. If serving that day, keep the peppers at room temperature. If planning to refrigerate, for best flavor, bring the peppers close to room temperature before serving. In a pinch, zap them in the microwave (uncovered) for 30 seconds to 1 minute on high, just to help loosen any congealed oil and to take off their chill. Sprinkle the peppers lightly with kosher salt just before serving.

HERE'S THE SCOOP:
On Roasting Peppers Perfectly

In my cooking classes, I'm often asked "Can you overroast a pepper?" The answer is yes. The secret to obtaining perfectly roasted peppers is to not overcook them, since retaining their fresh texture is part of the reason for making them at home in the first place (and not resorting to the jarred variety, which are softer). Once they are blackened, continued exposure to heat will just leave the peppers overcooked. Also, keep in mind that when the pepper is cooling, the flesh will become even more tender. So, for perfect roasted peppers, rotate the pepper as it blackens and remove the skin it as soon as it's cool enough to handle.

GARLIC CONFIT page 23

GARLIC-SCENTED
ROASTED PEPPERS

A Trio of Pestos

Having an assortment of pestos in the refrigerator is a terrific way to satisfy a busy person's need for homemade "fast food." Use the pesto to liberally flavor boneless chicken breasts before grilling, or to add flavor to a whole gutted fish before roasting. Mix it into softened cream cheese for a savory spread. You'll also be able to whip up pasta pesto, using any of the three following mixtures or a combination.

ROASTED TOMATO PESTO

❧ YIELD: ABOUT 3½ CUPS

20 Oven-Roasted Tomatoes (page 100), seeds and all liquid reserved

A pinch of red pepper flakes (optional)

4 sun-dried tomatoes packed in olive oil, minced

4 cooked garlic cloves from Garlic Confit (page 23; optional but highly recommended)

5 garlic cloves, minced

½ cup toasted pine nuts (see page 271)

1 cup Garlic Confit Oil (page 23) or extra-virgin olive oil, plus more as needed

Freshly ground black pepper to taste

½ cup freshly grated Parmagiano-Reggiano cheese

Kosher or sea salt

RUB THE SEEDS, reserved from the tomatoes, in a fine-mesh sieve placed over another bowl to extract as much of the tomato flavor as possible. Discard the seeds and simmer the resulting liquid in a small dry skillet (with a pinch of red pepper flakes, if you want it spicy) over medium heat until the water evaporates and all that's left is a thick tomato concentrate. Put the roasted tomatoes, along with the tomato concentrate, sun-dried tomatoes, cooked garlic (if using), minced raw garlic, and pine nuts in the bowl of a food processor fitted with the steel blade. Pulse to chop everything small. Add 1 cup of oil and a generous amount of black pepper, and process until the ingredients are very finely chopped but still retain some texture. If not planning to freeze, add the cheese, a generous amount of black pepper, and salt to taste. Process just to combine.

Remove as much pesto as needed and, before storing the rest in the refrigerator, pour a generous layer of olive oil over the top. Keep refrigerated in a well-sealed sturdy container. Bring the pesto to room temperature before each use. See Basil Pesto (page 27) for do-ahead instructions.

BASIL PESTO

❧ YIELD: ABOUT 4 CUPS

4 cups packed basil leaves (from 2 large, very full bunches)

6 to 8 garlic cloves, minced

⅔ cup toasted pine nuts (see page 271)

1 teaspoon red pepper flakes (optional)

2 scant cups olive oil (preferably a combination of Garlic Confit Oil, page 23, and pure olive oil), plus more for topping

Freshly ground black pepper to taste

1¼ cups freshly grated Parmigiano-Reggiano cheese

Kosher or sea salt

PLACE THE BASIL LEAVES in the bowl of a food processor fitted with the steel blade and, using the pulsing button, chop the leaves until reduced in volume. (Depending on the size of your workbowl, you might need to add half the amount of leaves at first, and when reduced, add the remaining leaves.) Add the garlic, pine nuts, red pepper flakes (if using), 2 cups olive oil, and a generous amount of black pepper. Process until the pesto is finely chopped but still retains some texture. If not planning to freeze the pesto, add the cheese and salt to taste. Process just to combine. (See the note at right for instructions on freezing pesto.)

Remove as much pesto as needed and, before storing the rest in the refrigerator, pour a generous layer of olive oil over the top. Keep pesto refrigerated in a well-sealed sturdy container. Bring the mixture to room temperature, before each use.

TIMING IS EVERYTHING

❧ *Refrigerate pesto for several weeks in a well-sealed container, completely covered with a layer of good olive oil. To use, uncover and tilt the container to let the oil run to one side. Scoop out the pesto and cover the remaining pesto with the olive oil.*

To freeze pesto, combine all the ingredients, except the cheese and salt. Separate out the portion you'd like to freeze. For this portion, add salt sparingly and omit the cheese. (For remaining portion, add regular amounts of cheese and salt.) Freeze the pesto, covered with a generous layer of olive oil, for up to three months. Add the cheese and more salt after thawing.

ROASTED RED PEPPER
PESTO page 28;
BASIL PESTO; AND
ROASTED TOMATO PESTO

ROASTED RED PEPPER PESTO

🍃 YIELD: ABOUT 4 CUPS

5 large red bell peppers, roasted, skinned, seeded, and halved (see page 24)
2 canned chipotle chiles in adobo, with 1 tablespoon sauce for a slightly smoky flavor (optional)
6 large garlic cloves, minced
5 cooked garlic cloves from Garlic Confit (page 23; optional but highly recommended)

¾ cup toasted pine nuts (see page 271)
1 cup Garlic Confit Oil (page 23) or extra-virgin olive oil, plus more as needed
Freshly ground black pepper to taste
1 cup freshly grated Parmigiano-Reggiano cheese
Kosher or sea salt

PLACE THE ROASTED PEPPERS and chiles and sauce (if using) in the bowl of a food processor fitted with the steel blade. Add the minced fresh garlic, cooked garlic (if using), and the pine nuts and pulse to chop everything small. Add 1 cup of the oil and a generous amount of black pepper and process until the pesto is almost pureed but still retains some texture. If not planning to freeze, add the cheese and some salt to taste. Process just to combine.

Remove as much pesto as needed and, before storing the rest in the refrigerator, pour a generous layer of olive oil over the top. Keep refrigerated in a well-sealed sturdy container. Bring the pesto to room temperature before each use. See Basil Pesto (page 27) for do-ahead instructions.

HERE'S THE SCOOP:
On Storing Fresh Basil

If you don't grow your own basil, try to purchase bunches with the roots attached and fully intact. Fill a tall glass with cool water and stand the bunch up in the water, completely submerging the roots. The basil can stay out, at room temperature, for days this way (it's actually a beautiful and aromatic addition to your kitchen!). Change the water daily. (If your basil starts to quickly wilt, it probably wasn't fresh, so clean and dry the leaves and use them as soon as possible.) To store basil of average freshness, wrap the roots with a very damp paper towel and store the bunch in the refrigerator in a loose-fitting perforated plastic bag.

MAKE DRIED CRUMBS
and Cubes from Fresh Bread

By definition, store-bought bread crumbs are old and stale. So why use them (or worse, serve them to guests)? For the best bread crumbs, regardless of their ultimate use, always purchase the freshest bread possible and, within 24 hours of purchase, if the bread's not eaten, make dried bread crumbs or croutons. The good news is that homemade dried bread crumbs and cubes freeze perfectly when stored in doubled, well-sealed freezer bags. And there's no need to thaw them—just scoop them straight from the freezer as you need them. Whether you are making croutons or stuffings, or need crumbs to cover fish, chicken cutlets, or shrimp, or want a savory topping for freshly cooked pasta or a bubbling gratin, the flavor and aroma of bread crumbs and cubes made at home are unbelievably better than the store-bought stuff. ❧ YIELD: 2 TO 3 CUPS CRUMBS OR CUBES (RECIPE MAY BE DOUBLED)

1 large, fresh loaf Italian bread (preferably with
    sesame seeds on top), crust kept intact

To MAKE CRUMBS, preheat the oven to 375°F. Cut the bread into 1-inch slices and lay them in a single layer on a wire cooling rack set on a shallow baking sheet. Bake for 10 minutes or until light golden all over. Turn off the heat and let the bread remain there until dry and very crisp, about 15 minutes. (If your oven runs hot, leave the door ajar while drying.) Remove from the oven and, when the slices are cool, crush them and drop into the bowl of a food processor fitted with the steel blade. Process the bread until the crumbs are coarse or fine, depending on which type you want. Transfer the crumbs to a bowl and use as directed in your recipe or store them in an airtight canister for one week at room temperature.

To make cubes, preheat the oven to 375°F. Cut the bread (including the crust) into ½-inch slices, then stack two slices and cut them lengthwise into ½-inch strips. Cut these strips into ½-inch cubes. Continue until you've cut the entire loaf this way. Place the bread cubes on a shallow (not-too-dark) baking sheet in a single layer and bake until the cubes are dry and light golden all over, about 10 minutes. (If still somewhat soft, leave the cubes in a turned-off oven for 10 to 15 minutes with the door ajar. When done, the cubes should feel dry and hard.) Remove the baking sheet from the oven and use bread cubes as desired or allow them to cool completely before storing them in an airtight canister for one week at room temperature.

TIMING IS
EVERYTHING
❧ *Bread cubes and crumbs can be frozen for at least two months in doubled securely sealed plastic bags. To use, just scoop them from the freezer.*

THE BEST BARBECUE SAUCE
(I'm Not Kidding)

Yeah, I know that other people say that their barbecue sauce is the best, but I mean it! Seriously, whether I use this rich, red, and robust mixture to dress a pair of succulent butterflied chickens or on pork ribs, it's always a huge success, clearly indicated by the hefty pile of bare bones left on people's plates. This sauce doubles perfectly and keeps well for ages, so I usually make a really big batch and store it in the refrigerator to use throughout the year. Unlike most barbecue sauces, which are too assertive for my family, this one tastes so great that we also use it as a table condiment. Try it spooned alongside a simple roast loin of pork and even grilled mushrooms. And if you want to make a friend for life, give a quart-size jar of this sauce to that special someone any time of the year.

 ❧ YIELD: ABOUT 4½ CUPS (RECIPE MAY BE DOUBLED)

2 cups ketchup
2 cups bottled chili sauce (I use Heinz)
1 generous cup minced yellow onion
8 large garlic cloves, minced
⅓ cup dark brown sugar
⅓ cup unsulphured molasses
¼ cup mild-flavored honey
2 rounded tablespoons Dijon mustard
2 teaspoons Worcestershire sauce
¼ cup soy sauce, preferably tamari

½ cup apple cider vinegar
2 generous tablespoons Bovril (beef extract), available in well-stocked supermarkets and Asian grocery stores (optional)
1 or 2 fresh habanero chiles (also called Scotch Bonnets) or jalapeños, pierced several times with a fork, or 1 to 2 teaspoons hot pepper sauce (optional)
Freshly ground black pepper to taste

TIMING IS
EVERYTHING
 ❧ *This sauce can be fully assembled and stored in the refrigerator for six months.*

COMBINE ALL THE INGREDIENTS except the black pepper in a 2½-quart, heavy-bottomed, nonreactive saucepan. Stir well to combine and place the pan over medium heat with the cover ajar. Bring the mixture to a full simmer, then turn the heat to low. Simmer until the sauce is thickened and the color deepens considerably, about 30 minutes, stirring occasionally (see right). Uncover, stir in a generous amount of black pepper, and remove the saucepan from the heat. Let the sauce cool, uncovered, until just warm. (While cooling, lay a clean kitchen towel over the pan to prevent debris from falling into the sauce.)

Pour the sauce through a triple-mesh wire sieve that's positioned over another bowl and, using the flat edge of a wooden spatula, force the sauce through, leaving the onions, garlic, and chiles behind. Discard the solids, pour the sauce into jars, and affix their lids. Store the sauce in the refrigerator.

About "Blip, Blap, Bloop"

Often, I'm asked by my students, "How will I know when a sauce [or any mixture] has thickened enough to be removed from the stove?" It's a good question, since insufficient cooking limits flavor development, while letting a sauce simmer too long causes it to overreduce and scorch on the bottom. The best way to understand when your sauce has thickened enough is to be aware of the sounds of your sauce as it bubbles. When a sauce starts to simmer, the bubbles quickly rise to the surface and pop abruptly, saying "blip, blip, blip." As this continues, natural evaporation eliminates more of the water content, so the bubbles rise more slowly, with a "blap, blap, blap" sound. More simmering means even more evaporation of water, leaving your sauce with a considerably deeper color and a sluggish voice that says "bloop, bloop, bloop." It's this evaporation of water that helps intensify and meld flavors and also gives body to a sauce. Unless your recipe instructs you otherwise, keep the heat low and stir occasionally to prevent scorching. And pay attention to the position of the lid. Covering a sauce completely as it simmers will cause too much condensation, diluting flavors and inhibiting reduction. Simmering uncovered, or with the cover ajar, is always better.

"KILLER" MARINARA SAUCE

Don't worry, this awesome sauce certainly won't hurt you—but the intense aroma from all the savory garlic might having you swooning a little. Adding flour at the front of the cooking process makes the texture extra velvety and not watery. I really suggest doubling this sauce, since it's just so good. If the thought of peeling so many tomatoes is daunting, just put on the music and ask the kids to help (just get the tomatoes all blanched and pile them in a big bowl), or substitute all or half the amount with whole canned tomatoes. When purchasing canned tomatoes, look for brands from the San Marzano region of Italy—they're renowned for having the best taste and meatiest texture. You'll find them in most Italian grocery stores and in many well-stocked supermarkets. ❦ YIELD: ABOUT 7 CUPS

5 pounds ripe plum (Roma) tomatoes, or four
    28-ounce cans peeled plum tomatoes, drained
3 tablespoons extra-virgin olive oil
1 tablespoon unsalted butter
2 tablespoons unbleached all-purpose flour
1 teaspoon red pepper flakes
10 garlic cloves, minced
1 cup chopped fresh basil

1 teaspoon crumbled dried oregano
One 28-ounce can tomato puree
2 rounded tablespoons tomato paste
Strip of rind from Parmigiano-Reggiano cheese
    (about 1 inch wide by 4 inches long; optional)
Kosher or sea salt and freshly ground black pepper
    to taste

BRING A LARGE POT of water to a rapid boil and, working in small batches, put some tomatoes into the water and count to 10. Remove them from the water and place in a large bowl. Use your thumbnail or a small paring knife to remove the stem end and cut the tomato in half through the waist. Squeeze the seeds out and coarsely chop the tomatoes. If using canned tomatoes, use kitchen scissors to snip them in half and gently squeeze out the seeds. Snip them all into smallish irregular pieces.

Heat a 6-quart nonreactive, heavy-bottomed saucepan over medium heat and, when hot, add the olive oil and butter. When the butter is bubbling, stir in the flour. Let it bubble for about 15 seconds, then stir in the red pepper flakes, half the minced garlic, ½ cup chopped basil, and the oregano. When fragrant (about 15 seconds), stir in the chopped tomatoes, tomato puree, and tomato paste. Stir well, then push the cheese rind if using, deep into sauce, and bring the sauce to a brisk simmer. Reduce the heat to low and cook the sauce gently, with the cover ajar, for 35 minutes. Add the remaining garlic, the remaining ½ cup chopped basil, and a generous amount of salt and black pepper.

A Heartier Variation

Use a food processor fitted with the steel blade to finely chop 1 medium yellow onion, 1 trimmed celery stalk, 1 medium carrot, and 5 garlic cloves. Increase the butter to 3 tablespoons and, together with the olive oil, gently sweat these vegetables, directly covered with a piece of greased waxed paper, for 10 minutes or until fragrant and starting to soften. Discard the paper and stir in the flour, red pepper flakes, and half the basil, as directed in the original recipe. Raise the heat to medium and cook for a minute or so, just to fully incorporate everything. Follow the remaining sauce instructions.

A Quick Marinara Sauce

By just changing the type of tomatoes you can have a quicker version of marinara sauce that's still great tasting. Heat a 4-quart heavy-bottomed saucepan over medium heat, and when hot, add 3 tablespoons extra-virgin olive oil. When the oil is hot, add half the minced garlic, half the basil, and the red pepper flakes. When fragrant (about 10 seconds), add a 28-ounce can each of tomato puree and crushed tomatoes. Bring to a full simmer through the center, then add two 28-ounce cans drained canned plum tomatoes, snipped into irregular pieces using kitchen scissors. Bring back to a full simmer, then reduce the heat to low and cook the sauce gently for 15 minutes with the cover ajar. Add a generous amount of freshly ground black pepper, the remaining garlic, and the last dose of basil, and simmer 5 minutes more. When time is scarce, this is a perfect sauce for Loaded-with-Vegetables Lasagna (page 162).

An Ultra-Speedy Version

When time feels nonexistent, substitute your favorite prepared marinara sauce for all of the tomatoes. Heat a 3-quart heavy-bottomed saucepan over medium heat and, when hot, add a few tablespoons extra-virgin olive oil. When the oil is hot, add half the minced garlic, half the basil, and the red pepper flakes. When fragrant (about 10 seconds), add about 8 cups of your favorite prepared tomato or marinara sauce (I use four 15-ounce containers of the refrigerated Buitoni Marinara Sauce). Stir to combine, then bring to a full bubble through the center. Reduce the heat to low and simmer 15 minutes with the cover ajar. Add a generous amount of freshly ground black pepper, the remaining garlic, and the remaining basil, and simmer 5 minutes more. This sauce is perfect on pizza (page 240).

TIMING IS EVERYTHING
All of the marinara sauce variaions can be stored, when cool, in the refrigerator for up to four days or frozen for three months.

HERE'S THE SCOOP
On Peeling and Seeding Tomatoes

I'm frequently asked two questions about the process of peeling and seeding tomatoes. One of them is, "When blanching tomatoes in order to release their skins, how will I know how long to keep them in boiling water?" You'll need to go by feel. Gather all of your tomatoes and separate the heavier, less firm ones from the rest. Really ripe tomatoes need just 10 seconds in rapidly boiling water and firmer ones need up to 20 seconds. Your best bet is to work in small batches (no more than four tomatoes at a time), all with the same feel. And use a large slotted spoon to remove them quickly, since every extra second counts. Remember, you're not cooking the tomatoes, just skinning them.

The second question is, "Do I really have to take the seeds out of the tomatoes?" To me, there aren't many "have-tos" in cooking (as opposed to baking). There are a couple reasons most people remove the seeds in tomatoes. First, some people find them hard to digest. Second, the seeds are suspended in a water-rich substance that can dilute the sauce. This means that, in order to get your sauce to the proper consistency, you'll need to cook it longer, which can remove some of the fresh tomato taste from your sauce. If removing the seeds feels like too much of a bother, omit this step and see how you like the sauce. That's the beauty of home cooking.

HOMEMADE TERIYAKI SAUCE

This savory sauce not only makes a perfect baste to slather on grilled shrimp, chicken, fish, and beef during cooking, but also can be served at the table to flavor cooked rice. If you have kids, you might as well double this concoction, since it's destined to get lots of action. It's fine if you don't use the sauce constantly, since it keeps really well in the fridge for up to six months. Please don't be put off by the number of ingredients, since they're all available in well-stocked supermarkets and Asian grocery stores. ❧ YIELD: ABOUT 3 CUPS

3 tablespoons cold-pressed peanut oil
1 cup minced scallions (white and 1½ inches of
    the green)
¼ cup minced fresh ginger
1 large shallot, minced
4 garlic cloves, minced
¼ cup dehydrated minced onions
1½ cups soy sauce, preferably tamari

1 cup water
¼ cup mirin (Japanese sweet wine)
¼ cup medium-dry sherry
2 generous tablespoons honey
1 tablespoon cornstarch
2 tablespoons unseasoned rice wine vinegar
2 tablespoons toasted sesame oil
Up to 1 tablespoon wasabi paste (optional)

TIMING IS
EVERYWHERE

❧ *This sauce can be fully assembled and stored in the refrigerator for three months.*

HEAT A 2½-QUART NONREACTIVE heavy-bottomed saucepan over medium heat, and when hot, add the peanut oil. When the oil is hot, stir in the scallions, ginger, shallot, garlic, and dehydrated onions. Cook the vegetables, stirring occasionally, until softened and very fragrant, about 3 minutes. Stir in the soy sauce, water, mirin, sherry, and honey and bring the liquid to a brisk bubble through the center. Turn the heat down to low and simmer the sauce for 10 minutes with the cover ajar.

Meanwhile, mix the cornstarch and vinegar in a small bowl. After the sauce has simmered for 10 minutes, stir in the dissolved cornstarch. Bring it back to a bubble, then let it simmer, uncovered, for 5 minutes. Stir in the toasted sesame oil and the wasabi paste, if using. Remove from the heat and let the flavors meld until completely cool. Strain the cooled sauce through a fine-mesh sieve that's positioned over another bowl, pressing hard on the solids. Store in the refrigerator in a clean, securely sealed jar.

CINNAMON SUGAR

Why would anyone want to purchase cinnamon sugar when it's so easy and so much more cost-effective to make it yourself? Feel free to make a larger batch and store it in a quart jar. One of the real benefits of making this homemade blend is that you can adjust the amount of cinnamon to your own taste. Cinnamon sugar gets a lot of action in my house. It's sprinkled on French toast, lavished on muffins before baking, and used to perk up the flavor of hot chocolate, whipped cream, and hot cereal. And homemade applesauce just wouldn't be the same without it.

YIELD: ABOUT 1¾ CUPS

1½ cups granulated sugar

3 tablespoons ground cinnamon, or more to taste

1 long supple vanilla bean, split lengthwise, seeds removed and reserved for another purpose

USE A WHISK TO COMBINE the sugar with the cinnamon. Spoon the cinnamon sugar into a pint jar, using a wide-mouth funnel. Stick the seeded vanilla bean deep into the sugar and attach a generously perforated lid along with another solid lid and screw band, to shut securely (see page 15). Shake the jar well to distribute and let sit for a few days before using. Store on a cool pantry shelf, away from direct sunlight, for up to one year.

Vanilla Sugar

For a vanilla-flavored sugar that dissolves easily in cold drinks, use superfine sugar. Omit the cinnamon and use 2 seeded vanilla beans per each 2 cups of sugar. Replenish the sugar as you use it and shake the jar to redistribute. Every six months or so, discard the old vanilla beans and replace with fresh seedless ones. If superfine sugar is unavailable, whirl granulated sugar in a food processor fitted with the steel blade until finely ground.

POULTRY SEASONING

Spice blends not only are easy to make but really do make the process of season-ing a lot less messy. Before I decided to assemble this mixture, which contains all of my favorite savory flavors for cooked poultry, every time I wanted to season my chicken I had to locate all the ingredients and apply them individually. Then, after rubbing the chickens with oil and applying more seasoning, everything was always a sticky mess. Now I just grab one jar and shake away. If you can't find a shaker jar with holes that allow you to season your birds liberally, make your own shaker top (see page 15).

As with all spice blends, remember to keep the jars out of direct sunlight, since both light and heat will encourage both the distortion and the dissipation of flavor. And while I have your attention, turn to page 168 to learn how to make the best roast chicken you've ever had. ❧ YIELD: ABOUT 1⅔ CUPS

⅓ cup plus 1 tablespoon (6 tablespoons) minced dehydrated garlic chips, or 3 tablespoons garlic powder

⅓ cup plus 1 tablespoon (6 tablespoons) minced dehydrated onions, or 3 tablespoons onion powder

1½ teaspoons red pepper flakes, or ½ rounded teaspoon chili powder

2 tablespoons freshly ground black pepper

2 tablespoons Lawry's seasoned salt

1 tablespoon kosher or sea salt

¾ cup sweet Hungarian paprika

IF YOU HAVE A SPICE GRINDER, one by one, finely grind the garlic chips, dehydrated onions, and red pepper flakes and place the powdered ingredients in a food processor fitted with the steel blade. If not using a spice grinder, place the garlic, onion, and chili powders directly into the workbowl of the food processor. Add the black pepper, seasoned salt, kosher salt, and paprika and process until the ingredients are thoroughly blended and more finely ground, about 2 minutes. Store in a generously perforated shaker-top jar, tightly shut, on a cool pantry shelf away from direct sunlight, for up to one year.

FAJITAS SEASONING

Since my kids love to order fajitas when we go out for a Mexican meal, I decided to create a fajita spice blend that could easily be added to steak, chicken, shrimp, or even a whole fish (see page 188). This way, it's really easy to pull together a truly savory and delicious meal at a moment's notice. ❧ YIELD: 1½ CUPS

3 teaspoons cumin seeds (use ground cumin if you don't have a spice grinder)

3 tablespoons minced dehydrated garlic chips (use garlic powder if you don't have a spice grinder)

3 tablespoons freshly ground black pepper

3 tablespoons kosher or sea salt

3 tablespoons chili powder

2 teaspoons aromatic dried oregano, crumbled

3 tablespoons packed light brown sugar

HEAT A 10-INCH SKILLET over high heat. While the pan is heating, place a plate next to your work surface. When the pan is hot, add the cumin seeds and toast them, stirring constantly, until the seeds are fragrant and take on a visibly deeper hue, about 2 minutes. Immediately pour the seeds onto the plate and set them aside until they become cool.

Transfer the seeds to a spice grinder and process until finely ground. Put the ground cumin in the bowl of a food processor fitted with the steel blade. Use the spice grinder to finely grind the garlic chips and add to the food processor. Add the pepper, salt, chili powder, oregano, and brown sugar to the workbowl and process until everything is evenly distributed and finely ground. Store the blend in a generously perforated pint shaker-top jar (see page 15), securely sealed, on a cool pantry shelf away from direct sunlight, for up to one year.

SPICE BLEND
for Quick Breads, Cookies, and More

Ready and waiting to be used as a flavor-packed addition to your quick breads and cookies, this dry spice blend is a real comfort, especially when you want to get something sweet and aromatic in and out of the oven in a hurry. In addition to the uses mentioned above, this mixture tastes great when sprinkled on sautéed apples, in applesauce, in fresh apple or pear pies, in whipped cream, and even on sweet potatoes or winter squash, either mashed or drizzled with a little melted butter and maple syrup. ❧ YIELD: GENEROUS ⅔ CUP

½ cup ground cinnamon
¼ cup nutmeg, preferably freshly grated
1 tablespoon ground ginger

1 teaspoon ground allspice
½ teaspoon ground cloves
Pinch of salt

USE A WHISK to combine all of the listed ingredients, then sift them into another bowl. Position a wide-mouth funnel over a ½-pint jar and spoon the spice mix into the jar. Store on a cool pantry shelf, away from direct sunlight, for up to one year.

Double Your Pleasure
BUTTERMILK PANCAKE
and Cake Mix

Of all the recipes in this book, I think this one gives me the most sense of comfort and support. An incredibly easy and thoughtful gift is to assemble a canister of this mix and give it to a friend or family member who loves pancakes along with the recipe on page 56. Or turn to pages 290 and 294 and learn how to use this same dry mix to bake a generous batch of chocolate or vanilla cupcakes, or tender and delicious layer cakes, for one of your children's birthday parties.

❧ YIELD: MIX FILLS A 5-POUND CANISTER (ABOUT 9 DOZEN PANCAKES)

14 cups plain (not self-rising) cake flour
6 tablespoons baking powder
1 tablespoon plus 2 teaspoons baking soda

1 tablespoon plus 1 teaspoon salt
1 cup plus 2 tablespoons sugar

USE A WHISK to thoroughly combine the flour, baking powder, baking soda, salt, and sugar in an extra-large mixing bowl. Sift this into another large bowl of equal capacity. Whisk again thoroughly, then spoon the mix into a 5-pound canister with a tight-fitting lid. Store the canister on a cool, dry pantry shelf.

ASSORTED MUFFIN MIX

Don't think it's easy to be a cookbook writer. I used this mix so many times to test the muffin recipes in the breakfast chapter that my family started calling me "The Muffin Lady!" It was worth all the effort when I could finally deem them perfect.

🍴 YIELD: MIX FILLS A 5-POUND CANISTER (ABOUT 5 DOZEN MUFFINS)

15 cups bleached all-purpose flour (see page 42)
1 tablespoon plus 1 teaspoon salt

5 tablespoons baking powder
1 tablespoon plus 1 teaspoon baking soda

USE A WHISK to thoroughly combine all of the ingredients in an extra-large mixing bowl. Sift the muffin mix into another large bowl. Whisk again thoroughly, then spoon into a 5-pound capacity canister with a tight-fitting lid. Store the canister on a cool dry pantry shelf.

CORNBREAD MIX

Cornbread is another one of those soothing recipes that I turn to often to embellish my weeknight meals. Having this mix on my shelf is a real lifesaver, especially when we're all tired and really hungry. ❧ YIELD: MIX FILLS A 5-POUND CANISTER (ABOUT FIVE 10-INCH ROUNDS OR 5 DOZEN MUFFINS)

9 cups finely ground yellow cornmeal

6 cups bleached all-purpose flour, preferably White Lily or Martha White brand (see page 42)

3 tablespoons salt

4 tablespoons baking soda

1 tablespoon plus 2½ teaspoons baking powder

¾ cup plus 2 tablespoons sugar

USE A WHISK to thoroughly combine all of the ingredients in an extra-large mixing bowl, then sift into another large bowl. Whisk again thoroughly, then spoon into a 5-pound canister with a tight-fitting lid. Store the canister on a cool, dry pantry shelf.

HERE'S THE SCOOP:
For Best Texture in Quick Breads

For tenderness, I mix my pancake, muffin, and quick bread batters using a batter whisk. A batter whisk is a strange-looking tool, available in well-stocked kitchenware shops and in home-baking catalogs (see the Source List on page 313). It's a thin piece of metal coil wound into an irregular circular shape that sits at the end of a long wooden handle. It allows you to stir a batter more assertively (and thus more thoroughly) without creating elasticity in your batter, which could cause your baked bread to be tough. If you don't have a batter whisk, you can also use a wide fork with three or four prongs (it's similar to a large serving fork).

If you accidentally overbake a quick bread, simply wrap it securely while still warm (not hot) in plastic wrap. The trapped steam will become reabsorbed and the texture will regain some lost moisture.

BAKING POWDER BISCUIT MIX

If you live with finicky eaters, this recipe is for you! Ever since my children were little, whenever I chose to serve an entree that could be perceived by kids as "iffy," like fresh fish for dinner, I'd avoid getting the evil eye by always having these delicious biscuits parked strategically at the table. If you don't want to fuss with measuring tools and bags of flour on a hectic weekday (which is when we could all use a good biscuit), why not use a few minutes on a leisurely weekend or on an unoccupied evening to quickly put together this mix. That way, a fresh batch of tender biscuits is always just minutes away. ❧ YIELD: MIX FILLS A 5-POUND CONTAINER (ABOUT 7 BATCHES OF BISCUITS)

14 cups all-purpose flour

⅓ cup plus 2 tablespoons sugar

2 tablespoons plus 2 teaspoons salt

½ cup plus 1½ teaspoons baking powder

USE A WHISK to thoroughly combine all the ingredients in an extra-large mixing bowl, then sift this into another large bowl. Whisk again thoroughly, then spoon the mix into a 5-pound canister with a tight-fitting lid. Store the canister on a cool, dry pantry shelf for up to six months.

HERE'S THE SCOOP:
On Bleached All-Purpose Flour

For most of my quick breads, I use a bleached all-purpose flour that's milled in the South from soft red winter wheat. It's lower in protein than regular unbleached flour, which is milled from hard winter wheat. Soft wheat makes lighter and more tender quick breads because it absorbs less liquid than the hard wheat varieties and works best with batters using baking powder and baking soda leaveners, like quick breads. Because people in the South are known to make more quick breads and fewer yeast breads than northerners, the flour milled there reflects this preference. If you don't have access to either White Lily or Martha White plain low-protein flours, see my Source List on pages 313–314. You can also use regular bleached flour, which although not exactly the same, will yield perfectly good results.

Butta, Butta, Butta! An Assortment of Savory
COMPOUND BUTTERS

To give store-bought butter some extra sass, work in some of the ingredients suggested below to make a compound butter. Be sure to use unsalted butter (it's always fresher), and season it yourself before folding in your flavoring ingredients. These combinations are especially delicious as an instant flavoring for grilled or broiled fish, boneless chicken, and lean cuts of pork, steak, veal, and lamb.

The shelf life of both refrigerated and frozen compound butters will vary, depending on the way you flavor them. It's best to make a small batch and use it within 48 hours if refrigerated and within one month if rolled into logs, wrapped in plastic wrap, encased in doubled freezer bags, and frozen.

For every 8 tablespoons (1 stick) of butter that's softened but not oily, use a sturdy rubber spatula, a fork, or the pulse function on a food processor fitted with a steel blade to work in one of the following flavoring combinations. For each serving of butter, slice off a 1/2-inch round from a firm log, and let it sit at room temperature for 20 minutes if the butter was refrigerated and 40 minutes if it was frozen. Place the softened slice directly on top of piping hot food just before serving, and allow it to melt into a creamy puddle, then serve right away.

FOR EACH 8 TABLESPOONS OF SOFTENED BUTTER, ADD:

- 2 tablespoons strained fresh lemon juice and 2 generous tablespoons minced flat-leaf Italian parsley
- 1 tablespoon each minced drained capers, pitted and minced oil-cured or Kalamata olives, and minced roasted red peppers or pimientos
- 4 raw garlic cloves mashed to a wet paste with a little kosher salt (omit the salt when seasoning the butter)
- Roasted garlic cloves (see page 45), 2 tablespoons minced flat-leaf Italian parsley, and 2 tablespoons strained fresh lemon juice
- 4 tablespoons minced scallions (white part and 1½ inches of the tender green), 4 minced garlic cloves, and 1 tablespoon minced flat-leaf parsley
- 4 tablespoons Dijon mustard, 2 teaspoons strained fresh lemon juice, and 1 generous tablespoon minced drained capers
- 2 generous tablespoons any variation of pesto (see pages 26–28)
- 2 tablespoons minced shallots and 2 tablespoons minced fresh mint (with lamb only)
- 2 teaspoons curry powder (preferably Madras), 2 teaspoons strained fresh lemon juice, and 2 tablespoons minced flat-leaf Italian parsley
- 2 teaspoons ground cinnamon, ½ teaspoon freshly grated nutmeg, and 2 generous tablespoons maple syrup (for cooked sweet potatoes, winter squash, and sautéed apples and/or pears)

FIG BUTTER

SPICED-BANANA
BUTTER

APRICOT BUTTER

GARLIC BREAD BUTTER

PRUNE
BUTTER

WHIPPED FRUIT-SCENTED
BUTTER

GARLIC BUTTERS, BREAD, AND TOASTS

Roasted Garlic Butter

Place 6 unpeeled garlic cloves in a small ovenproof dish and drizzle them with a generous tablespoon of extra-virgin olive oil. Sprinkle on 1½ teaspoons minced fresh thyme and 1 scant teaspoon minced fresh rosemary. Cover the dish with aluminum foil and puncture the foil in several spots with a fork. Roast the garlic in a preheated 425°F. oven for 20 minutes or until the garlic is tender. Let the garlic cool in the herb-infused oil. Squeeze the cooked garlic pulp out of its skin and work it into 8 tablespoons softened butter along with the oil and herbs.

Garlic-Bread Butter

Create a compound butter with 8 tablespoons (1 stick) softened butter, 4 minced raw garlic cloves, 2 generous tablespoons thinly sliced fresh chives or minced flat-leaf Italian parsley, and if using parsley, 1 teaspoon crumbled dried oregano.

Garlic Bread

Slice open lengthwise a fresh loaf of crusty Italian bread with sesame seeds without cutting all the way through. Open the loaf like a book, and spread Garlic-Bread Butter lavishly on both "bready" sides, then sprinkle on some freshly grated Parmigiano-Reggiano cheese. Close the loaf, and using a sharp serrated knife, slice the loaf into horizontal slices, stopping short of the closed spine. Wrap the seasoned bread snugly in aluminum foil (this can be done up to two days ahead and kept refrigerated). To serve, bake the wrapped bread on a shallow baking sheet on the top shelf of a preheated 375°F. oven for 15 to 20 minutes or until hot throughout. Turn on the broiler, open the loaf, and broil the seasoned surface (cheese side up) until golden. Serve hot.

Garlic Toasts

Prepare Garlic-Bread Butter, substituting chopped fresh basil for the chives and stirring in 2 generous tablespoons chopped flat-leaf parsley. Spread a thin layer of the compound butter on both sides of 10½-inch-thick slices of best-quality Italian bread with sesame seeds. Sprinkle the tops only with some freshly grated Parmigiano-Reggiano cheese and grind on some pepper. Position the oven rack close to the heat source and preheat the broiler. A few minutes before you're ready to serve, broil the bread, turning once, until golden on both sides. After broiling the second side, turn the slices over so the cheese side faces up. Serve hot as a bed for a savory topping or as an accompaniment.

SWEET FRUIT BUTTERS

Fruit butters are thick and rich and not only make a perfect filling for pastries but they also taste great, simply spread on toast or biscuits, lavished over a layer of cream cheese. Fresh fruit spreads, although more delicate, are also wonderful. And don't forget about the luscious Fig Butter on page 288.

Whipped Fruit-Scented Butter ❧ YIELD: ABOUT 2 CUPS

¾ cup cold heavy cream
¼ rounded teaspoon salt
½ cup cold very thick crème fraîche, mascarpone or room temperature block-style cream cheese
4 generous tablespoons strawberry or seedless raspberry jam

USING A STAND MIXER fitted with the whip attachment or a food processor fitted with the steel blade, whip the cream with the salt until very thick, but not broken. Add the crème fraîche, mascarpone or cream cheese and beat to combine. Add the jam and beat until a light pink color is consistent throughout. Transfer the whipped butter to a decorative bowl. Chill and serve with warm toast or fresh biscuits.

Prune Butter ❧ YIELD: ABOUT 2¼ CUPS

3 cups (packed) best-quality dried pitted prunes
Water to cover
1 tablespoon strained fresh lemon juice
⅓ cup sugar
¼ cup finely chopped walnuts

TO ASSEMBLE THE PRUNE BUTTER, place the prunes in a 2½-quart heavy-bottomed saucepan with enough cold water to cover them and bring the water to a brisk bubble. Turn the heat down to low and simmer the prunes gently (uncovered) until soft, about 10 minutes (timing will depend largely on their original suppleness). Drain the prunes, reserving 1 tablespoon of the poaching liquid and place the fruit with the lemon juice, poaching liquid, and sugar into the bowl of your food processor fitted with the steel blade. Process until smooth, then use a rubber spatula to transfer the puree to a bowl and stir in the ground walnuts. Let the prune butter cool before storing in the refrigerator, in a well-sealed tub, for up to 2 weeks before using.

Spiced Fresh Banana Butter ❧ YIELD: ABOUT 1½ CUPS

2 cups banana puree (from 3 very large or 4 medium very ripe bananas)
3 tablespoons strained fresh lemon juice
⅓ cup sugar
¼ teaspoon ground nutmeg (preferably fresh)
½ cinnamon stick
½ teaspoon pure vanilla extract
Pinch of salt

BLEND THE BANANA PUREE with the lemon juice, sugar and nutmeg, until smooth. Pour into a 2-quart heavy-bottomed saucepan and add the cinnamon stick. Bring the puree to a brisk bubble, over medium heat, stirring frequently. Reduce the heat to low and simmer it, until thick and somewhat reduced, and the sugar has begun to caramelize, about 15 minutes, stirring occasionally. Remove the saucepan from the stove and remove the cinnamon stick. Stir in the vanilla and the salt, then pour the banana butter into a clean 12-ounce jar. Cover the top with a clean kitchen towel, until it's completely cool. Place a doubled sheet of plastic wrap over the opening, then apply the lid and refrigerate the jar. The banana butter will thicken substantially, once cool.

Apricot Butter ❧ YIELD: ABOUT 1½ TO 2 CUPS

2 cups best-quality dried apricots
Water to cover
¼ cup (firmly packed) light brown sugar
1½ tablespoons Amaretto or lemon juice
¼ cup finely chopped toasted blanched (skinned) almonds (page 271)

PLACE THE APRICOTS in a 2½-quart heavy-bottomed saucepan with enough cold water to cover them and bring the water to a brisk bubble. Reduce the heat to low and simmer apricots gently until soft, 10 to 15 minutes. Drain the apricots and place them into the bowl of the food processor, fitted with the steel blade. Add the brown sugar and the amaretto or lemon juice and process until smooth. Use a rubber spatula to transfer the puree to a bowl and stir in the ground toasted almonds. Let the apricot butter cool before storing in the refrigerator, in a well-sealed tub, for up to 2 weeks.

They'll Never Know It's Quicker . . .
QUICK PUFF PASTRY

Whether it encases a sweet or a savory filling, I think you'll love this pastry. The dough results in a baked pastry that's crisp, light, incredibly flaky, and substantially quicker to pull together than classic puff-stuff. You'll find whole-wheat pastry flour in well-stocked supermarkets and in all health food stores. I suggest making two batches of pastry on one day, so you get more experience using your rolling pin. This way, you'll also have more pastry ready and waiting, in your freezer, for more spur-of-the-moment goodies.

Please don't panic because the dough is so crumbly at the beginning. This initial texture is what ensures that the pastry will be perfectly flaky when baked. With each successive turn, the dough becomes more obedient and beautiful. And if your kitchen is warm or if rolling pastry is new to you, always chill the dough for the maximum time suggested. To learn about how to choose and use the right rolling pin, see page 51. ❧ YIELD: ONE 16 × 11-INCH ROLLED SHEET

1½ cups unbleached all-purpose flour, plus more as needed for dusting

½ cup plain or whole wheat pastry flour

½ cup bread flour

1 rounded tablespoon sugar

1¼ teaspoons salt

1 cup (2 sticks) plus 3 tablespoons unsalted butter, cut into small cubes and frozen for at least 30 minutes

⅔ cup heavy cream

⅓ cup water

1 tablespoon strained fresh lemon juice

Ice cubes as needed

PLACE THE FLOURS, sugar, and salt in the bowl of a food processor fitted with the steel blade and process until combined, about 10 seconds. Mix the cream, water, and lemon juice in a cup with a spout. Add a few ice cubes to the liquid, stir to help facilitate chilling, and set aside. Add the frozen butter cubes to the workbowl and pulse to cut the butter into the seasoned flour until the mixture is granular looking, the pieces of butter are the size of baby peas, and they are visible throughout. Remove the ice from the cream mixture. Uncover the workbowl and pour in about ⅔ cup of the liquid, then pulse just to moisten the ingredients. Lightly pinch the dough in several places to check its consistency (always unplug a food processor before inserting your fingers into the workbowl). The dough should feel cool and moist but not wet. If it's too dry, sprinkle on a bit more liquid and pulse, just to moisten. When finished, the texture should feel like a perfectly prepared pie crust dough. (Be aware that one area might feel a bit too wet, which would make up for drier parts of the dough.)

Lightly flour a cool, smooth work surface and dump the contents of the workbowl on top. Gently gather the mass into a flattened rectangular lump (the mixture will feel very crumbly and not cohesive), rub some flour into a straight wooden rolling pin, and roll the broken dough out into a 9 × 14-inch rectangle about ⅓ inch thick. As you roll, occasionally wipe off the rolling pin with a clean towel to remove any clinging pieces of dough. Also, use your hands to knock the fragmented sides in place, and use your pastry scraper to help lift up the dough to sprinkle flour underneath to prevent sticking.

NEXT, FOLD THE DOUGH using the blade of your pastry scraper to help lift and turn the top portion of dough down to meet the middle of the rectangle. Bring the bottom up to enclose the top (like folding a business letter). Turn the pastry so the bound end is on your left (like a book). This is your first half-turn.

The last three full turns are a bit different. Lightly dust underneath the dough and your clean rolling pin with flour. Roll the dough out as before, only this time roll it out a few inches longer and wider, dusting with flour as necessary, and using the pin to knock the sides into shape, keeping things as even as possible. Fold the top third of dough down and the bottom third up, so the edges meet in the center. Brush off any exposed flour and fold the top half down over the bottom, enclosing it. Brush off any excess flour from the exposed dough and wrap it in plastic. Refrigerate the dough for 30 minutes to 1 hour. (To remind yourself of how many turns you've done and to monitor chilling time, write this information on a sticky label and place it on the plastic wrap.) Unwrap the dough and place it on your floured work surface with the bound side always to the left.

PROCEED WITH THE REMAINING two full turns exactly the same as the first full turn, but roll the dough out into a slightly larger rectangle, approximately 12 × 17 inches, between ¼ and ⅛ inch thick. When the final turn is done, brush off any excess flour and wrap the dough in plastic. Chill the dough for at least 1 hour and up to two days before using, or freeze for up to six months.

TIMING IS EVERYTHING

❧ The pastry can be assembled fully and frozen whole, wrapped in plastic wrap, then in aluminum foil, and stored in a labeled, doubled heavy-duty plastic bag for up to six months

❧ It can also be cut into small or large rounds (for fruit tarts) or squares (for turnovers). Just roll the pastry slightly smaller and thicker than desired, since you'll be rolling this out again just before assembling. Once frozen, stack the pastry separated with sheets of waxed paper and slip the stack into appropriately sized, doubled freezer bags and keep for up to three months.

❧ To thaw pastry, place it in the refrigerator overnight.

PÂTE BRISÉE
Pie and Tart Pastry

Today, most people think a "basic" pie dough is one that's purchased in the frozen section of a supermarket. Well, in about 5 minutes, without the trip to the market, you can create the flakiest pie crust imaginable, with the freshest taste. Perfect for sweet or savory treats, this pastry is a real comfort to have on hand. So if you want to spend only a minimum of time with your rolling pin, but still want a delicious pie or tart pastry, try this.

❧ YIELD: ONE 9-, 10-, OR 11-INCH PIE OR TART CRUST

2 cups unbleached all-purpose flour
½ slightly rounded teaspoon salt
2 rounded tablespoons sugar (for dessert pastry)
    or 1½ teaspoons sugar (for savory pastry)
½ cup (1 stick) unsalted butter, cut into cubes
    and frozen

¼ cup chilled solid vegetable shortening, pulled
    into bits
½ cup ice water as needed

PUT THE FLOUR, salt, and sugar in a food processor fitted with the steel blade. Whirl the dry ingredients together for 30 seconds, until combined. Add the frozen butter cubes along with the bits of shortening. Pulse to cut the fat into the flour until it's well distributed and the pieces are the size of peas. Pour in ¼ cup of the ice water. Pulse until the mixture in the bowl just starts to come together. Stop the machine and test several areas by gently pinching a piece of dough with your fingers (always unplug your food processor before inserting your fingers into the workbowl). The dough should feel moist but not wet, and should hold together when pressed gently between two fingers. If the dough seems overly dry or mealy, drizzle on a little more water *on those dry areas only* and pulse just to incorporate the added moisture. Be sure to check several areas of the dough before adding more liquid. Depending on your bag of flour and the humidity in the air that day, you should need between ⅓ and ½ cup liquid, total.

Dump the dough out onto a large crisscross of plastic wrap and place the exposed ends of the wrap over the dough. Flatten the dough into a disk and after wrapping it securely, chill the dough for 1 hour (or up to two days) before using. This dough also freezes perfectly for two months when wrapped and placed in a labeled heavy-duty freezer bag.

On Choosing and Using a Rolling Pin

Rolling out pastry is like dancing—and you're the leader. And, as when dancing with a partner, the more you do it, the better you get. For me, the best, most comfortable, and most efficient rolling pin is a perfectly smooth wooden one, without ball-bearings. For rolling out pie pastry or flour tortillas, I like tapered ones (those that are wider through the center). Here, the most challenging part is always keeping a round shape around the edges while thinning the dough to an even thickness, and these pins facilitate that.

For puff pastry, I like to use a long wooden pin that's the same thickness throughout, since straight sides and no curves are the goal. Use even pressure, first going up and down, and then side to side. With all pastry (especially puff pastry), you don't ever roll over the edges, like a steamroller, or you'll flatten out your flaky layers. Instead, bring the pin just up to the edges. If it's too thick at one spot, apply a bit more pressure just before reaching that edge, and repeat this until the pastry's even throughout. Also, when cutting off any jagged edges, use the sharp, straight blade of a chef's knife to cut directly down through the layers, and immediately pull the blade up and out.

Spice-Scented Pear-Currant
Muffins page 72

CHAPTER TWO
NOW THAT'S BREAKFAST!

In this chapter you'll find lots of ways to help you (and yours) to start each day in an extra-satisfying and self-fortifying way. Since most weekday mornings are frenetic, and it's almost impossible to get people to gather around a table, I've provided an assortment of muffins and scones that stay in great condition for several days when wrapped securely in plastic and stored at room temperature. And, although in many recipes it's easiest to use one of the mixes in Chapter One, every recipe also lists the ingredients needed to make the muffins without a mix. In several of the hot recipes, you'll notice that I give ingredients for a single serving, which is unusual in cookbooks featuring family food. I thought that, rather than ask you to scale down a recipe, I'd give you a way to quickly put something hot and great-tasting on the table, just for yourself or for your family members. Having said this, these recipes also multiply perfectly, so you can multiply the ingredients as you wish. I truly love the recipes in this breakfast chapter. I hope you find some new favorites that will become trusted morning traditions.

SPICED OVEN-PUFFED PANCAKE

Mornings don't get lovelier than this. A crisp oven-puffed pancake, filled with a mound of assorted fresh berries, all lightly dusted with confectioners' sugar. This recipe promises to please even the pickiest eater.

❦ YIELD: 2 TO 4 SERVINGS

2 extra-large eggs
½ cup milk
¼ cup sugar
¼ teaspoon salt
¼ teaspoon pure vanilla extract
⅔ cup unbleached all-purpose flour, sifted

3 tablespoons unsalted butter
1 teaspoon Spice Blend for Quick Breads, Cookies, and More (page 38), or see the end of this recipe
Suggested accompaniments: assorted berries and confectioners' sugar

PREHEAT THE OVEN TO 400°F. with the rack on the center shelf.

Whisk the eggs with the milk, sugar, salt, and vanilla. Pour the flour over the egg mixture and, using a batter whisk or a regular whisk, combine the ingredients until no large dry pockets remain. Then give the batter a few more brisk stirs to make the mixture come together, but don't overwork it (small lumps will still be visible).

Place the butter in a 9½-inch glass pie plate or a 10-inch well-seasoned cast-iron skillet and place the dish in the preheated oven for 6 minutes, or until the butter is melted and bubbling and the pan is very hot. Pull the rack toward you so the dish is accessible. Working quickly so the oven stays hot, whisk the spice blend into the hot butter. Shut the door and let this heat for 1 minute. Open the door and pour in the pancake batter (don't worry if it seems uneven). Shut the door and bake the pancake for 25 to 30 minutes, or until the sides are very high and golden and the center is irregularly puffed.

REMOVE FROM THE OVEN and use a thin metal spatula to transfer the pancake (which will look like a giant empty pastry bowl) to a serving plate. Use a paper towel to dab off any excess melted butter in the center. Serve the pancake immediately, filled with mixed fresh berries, dusted lightly with confectioners' sugar.

If you don't have the preassembled spice blend: Combine ½ teaspoon cinnamon, ¼ teaspoon nutmeg, ⅛ teaspoon ginger, and ⅛ teaspoon allspice.

TIMING IS EVERYTHING

❦ To enjoy these pancakes first thing in the morning, do this:

❦ If you've made your spice blend ahead of time, you're ahead of the game.

❦ The night before, measure and sift the flour. Leave the dish or pan on your work surface. Measure out the butter and keep it wrapped in the refrigerator. Assemble a bowl of assorted berries and keep chilled. Measure 1 teaspoon of the spice mix and leave this in a small covered bowl. Set the table for breakfast.

HERE'S THE SCOOP:
On Parents, Kids, and Breakfast

As the mother of three children, regardless of their age, I've noticed that mornings—and breakfast foods, in particular—have always helped me to reaffirm and even strengthen my bond with my kids. During those early years, I tried to use breakfast as a time to reassure my kids that I would always take care of them and that doing certain errands without them just wouldn't be any fun.

Our morning talks, usually wrapped around something homemade to eat, seemed to make a discernible difference when they left the house each morning feeling calm, satisfied internally, and knowing how much I loved them.

Now that my kids are teenagers, weekday breakfasts are quite different. Mornings are hectic and everyone has a different schedule. Usually

I only get to kiss them good-bye as they fly into the kitchen, grab something edible, and then disappear. When I'm organized, baked goods like homemade muffins, scones, and pancakes are very doable and still seem to make my kids so happy. Even though we don't get to sit down, eat, and schmooze the way we used to, I can still provide their morning dose of nurturing.

BUTTERMILK PANCAKES,
With or Without Berries

If you like pancakes, you'll adore these. I can't count how many times I've made these tender and truly ethereal pancakes, and each time I hear the same words from those at the table: "These are the best pancakes I've ever had." And feel free to use this same amount of batter to make three crisp standard-size waffles, using ½ cup of batter for each. This could vary, though, depending on your particular appliance. I've written this recipe requiring the use of buttermilk, since, hands-down, buttermilk makes the best-tasting pancakes with the lightest, most tender texture. If you don't always have liquid buttermilk in the house, I suggest keeping a supply of powdered buttermilk in your pantry so you can just reconstitute it. This recipe doubles perfectly. ❧ YIELD: ABOUT TWELVE 3½-INCH PANCAKES

1½ cups Buttermilk Pancake and Cake Mix
   (page 39), or see the end of this recipe
1¼ cups buttermilk
1 extra-large egg
2 tablespoons flavorless vegetable oil, plus more
   for brushing

3 tablespoons water
2 tablespoons melted unsalted butter, cooled to just
   warm
½ rounded cup plump ripe blueberries (optional)

PLACE THE PANCAKE MIX in a large bowl. In another bowl, combine the buttermilk, egg, vegetable oil, water, and melted butter. Gently stir the wet ingredients into the pancake mix, using a batter whisk or a wide blending fork, until thoroughly mixed, being careful not to overwork the batter. (See page 41 for more on batter whisks and blending forks.)

HERE'S THE SCOOP:
On Perfect Pancakes

OK, let's face it—perfectly cooked pancakes wait for no man (or child). Every minute that they wait means a loss of texture, even when kept in a low oven. Because of this, I find it incredibly frustrating when I see a fresh batch of pancakes just sit there, waiting for each member of my family to stroll into the kitchen to eat. The only remedy I've found for this is to assemble the batter and leave it, covered, on the counter next to a small bowl of vegetable oil with a pastry brush, which is used, occasionally, to grease the griddle. The batter can sit out like this for a couple of hours. This way I can cook pancakes as each body becomes visible on lazy mornings.

I also suggest using an electric griddle, since the cooking surface is larger than the stove-top kind; because it's thermostatically controlled, the griddle will remain at the perfect temperature until you're ready to ladle on your next serving. Follow the specific manufacturer's instructions for the suggested setting for pancakes.

Heat a nonstick griddle or a large nonstick skillet, and when hot, brush the surface lightly with vegetable oil. When the oil is hot, pour or ladle several ¼-cup portions of batter onto the hot surface, leaving 1 inch of space between them, and, if desired, scatter several blueberries on top. Cook over medium-high heat until bubbles appear on the surface, 1 to 2 minutes. Using a thin wide spatula, flip each pancake over and cook on the other side until golden, about 1 minute. Remove the pancakes to a warmed platter and repeat with the remaining batter. Serve the pancakes immediately after cooking, in individual stacks, with softened butter and warmed pure maple syrup.

If you don't have the preassembled pancake mix: Per each batch of pancakes, whisk together 1½ cups cake flour, 2 teaspoons baking powder, ½ teaspoon baking soda, ⅓ teaspoon salt, and 1 tablespoon plus 1 teaspoon sugar. Sift this into another bowl and continue with the recipe above.

TIMING IS EVERYTHING

For pancakes on busy weekday mornings, do this:

❧ *The night before, combine all of the wet ingredients except the melted butter and refrigerate the mixture, well covered. Measure your dry mix and place it in a covered bowl on your counter.*

❧ *In the morning, remove the wet ingredients from the refrigerator. Melt the butter and, when just warm, add it to the buttermilk mixture. Combine the wet and dry ingredients using a batter whisk (be gentle, but no dry pockets should remain). Leave the bowl of batter covered, at room temperature, until you're ready to cook. When ready, ladle the batter onto a hot, greased griddle, as directed.*

SERVED WITH GARLIC TOASTS page 45

Pan-Seared
PORTOBELLO MUSHROOM
and Tomato Topped with Chive-laced Scrambled Eggs

This dish is unusually quick and easy, especially considering how elegant and absolutely wonderful it is. Since the mushrooms are seasoned in advance, all you need to do is heat a dry pan and sear away. Usually, I don't cook mushrooms in a nonstick skillet, since that can keep them from caramelizing. I do here, however, since the mushroom liquid that's released is used to flavor the scrambled eggs.

❧ YIELD: 1 SERVING

2 tablespoons extra-virgin olive oil, plus more as needed
1 teaspoon mixed minced fresh thyme and rosemary
Freshly ground black pepper to taste
1 portobello mushroom (between 3 and 4 inches in diameter), stem removed and cap wiped clean on both sides
Kosher or sea salt

One 1-inch-thick slice ripe beefsteak tomato, at room temperature
2 teaspoons butter or olive oil, or nonstick vegetable spray
1 extra-large egg, lightly beaten
2 teaspoons snipped fresh chives, plus more for garnish

MIX THE OLIVE OIL with the herbs and some black pepper, and brush it liberally on both sides of the mushroom. Heat a heavy-bottomed 8-inch non-stick skillet over high heat and, when hot, sprinkle the surface lightly with salt. Add the mushroom to the hot pan and cook, turning several times, until golden and cooked through, about 7 minutes. Remove the mushroom from the pan and keep it on a warmed serving plate, gill side up, covered loosely with aluminum foil. Don't wipe out the pan; just put it back on the stove.

If you'd like to heat the tomato, warm a teaspoon or so of butter or oil in the pan over medium-high heat. When hot, add the tomato slice and sear well on one side only. Sprinkle the top (raw) side with a little salt and pepper. Remove the tomato using a thin spatula and place it, seared side up, on the underside of the cooked mushroom and cover them. Don't wipe out the pan; just put it back on the stove. Alternatively, just lay a beautiful slice of room-temperature raw tomato on top of the mushroom. Melt 2 teaspoons butter or heat more oil in the same skillet over medium heat. When hot, add the beaten egg and let it cook, undisturbed, just until it starts to set on the bottom. Reduce the heat to low and, using a heatproof rubber spatula, stir the egg, incorporating any bits of mushroom and tomato left in the pan. Add the chives and some salt and pepper, and cook, stirring continually, until it's done to your liking. Spoon the scrambled egg over the tomato and garnish with a little more snipped chives. Serve right away.

TIMING IS EVERYTHING
❧ *The mushroom can be seasoned up to two days ahead and kept in the refrigerator, well covered.*

Over Easy and Medium Rare . . .
STEAK AND EGGS

You certainly don't need to be an aspiring bodybuilder to crave this protein-packed breakfast. And if you follow the organizational instructions under "Timing Is Everything," you'll see just how easy it is to make busy weekday mornings just as satisfying as those on leisurely weekends. And don't limit this meal to breakfast—it's also a fabulous midweek supper.

YIELD: 1 SERVING (RECIPE CAN BE DOUBLED)

One 4- to 6-ounce fillet steak (1 inch thick)
Freshly ground black pepper to taste
Extra-virgin olive oil as needed
Kosher or sea salt to taste
2 teaspoons unsalted butter, or vegetable spray
1 or 2 extra-large eggs
2 teaspoons thinly sliced fresh chives (if unavailable, mince the deeper green part of a scallion)

⅓ cup cherry tomatoes, halved and drizzled with a little olive oil, a few droplets of balsamic vinegar, and scattered with a few very thin ribbons of fresh basil
Suggested accompaniment: 2 slices Italian bread, sliced ½ inch thick on the diagonal and toasted just before serving

TIMING IS EVERYTHING

To enjoy this breakfast any day of the week, do this:

The night before, line the baking sheet with foil and place it in the oven. Season the steak and refrigerate, covered. Slice two pieces of Italian bread and wrap them in plastic.

In the morning, preheat the oven. Preheat the toaster. Prepare the cherry tomatoes. Sear and roast the steak. Just before you crack the egg(s) into the pan, place your bread in the toaster. Cook the egg(s) and serve as directed.

LINE A SHALLOW BAKING SHEET or a glass pie plate with aluminum foil (shiny side up) and place it on the center shelf of the oven. If using a baking sheet, preheat the oven to 425°F.; if using glass, preheat to 400°F. Season both sides of your steak generously with black pepper and brush the meat evenly with olive oil. Turn on your exhaust fan now. Heat a well-seasoned cast-iron skillet or an 8- to 10-inch nonstick skillet over medium heat until it's very hot. Turn the heat up to high and wait about 20 seconds. Sprinkle the steak on one side with salt, then sear the meat, salted side down, for 3 minutes. Salt the top of the meat, then sear it well on the other side. Remove the pan from the stove and, using tongs, transfer the meat to the prepared baking sheet in the preheated oven. Roast the meat for 3 minutes (for medium rare) or until done to your liking. Take the meat out of the oven and let it rest on a cool plate while you cook your egg(s).

Wipe out the interior of the pan used to sear the meat. Place the pan over medium heat and melt the butter (or before heating, spray the pan with vegetable spray). When the pan is hot and the butter bubbling, crack one or two eggs directly into the pan and let them cook until the white starts to turn golden on the bottom, about 1½ minutes. Sprinkle the top lightly with salt and pepper. Use a thin nonabrasive turning spatula to carefully turn the egg(s) over.

TRANSFER THE EGGS to a serving plate and scatter the chives over them. Place the steak, whole or sliced, next to the eggs and tomatoes with toasted Italian bread. Serve hot.

Served with Hash-Browned Potatoes page 212

Just Mound Them Up . . .
EGGS, LOX & ONIONS

There are few better or more enticing morning scents, guaranteed to help a person open his or her eyes with a smile, than the seductive aroma of sautéed onions. I think this is because the scent of onions cooking is usually experienced later in the day, before dinner, when people are often tired and needy. I've found that choosing to include them at breakfast is a great way to start the day in an extra soothing way. Actually, on weekends I usually double-up on this great scent and taste by serving the eggs next to a split and toasted Onion Bialy (page 248).

🍴 YIELD: 1 SERVING (RECIPE CAN BE DOUBLED)

2 teaspoons flavorless vegetable oil
½ cup thinly sliced yellow onion
Kosher or sea salt and freshly ground black pepper
   to taste
1 generous tablespoon thinly sliced fresh chives,
   plus more for garnish (if unavailable, mince the
   deeper green part of a scallion)

3 ounces (about 3 thin slices) smoked salmon (use
   belly lox or another very flavorful smoked salmon)
2 teaspoons unsalted butter
2 extra-large eggs, lightly beaten with 1 teaspoon
   water
Suggested accompaniment: hot toast with cream
   cheese

TIMING IS
EVERYTHING
🍴 *For eggs, lox, and onions on busy weekday mornings, do this:*
🍴 *The night before, slice the onions and the salmon and keep them refrigerated, separately, well covered. Cut the chives and put them in a small covered bowl. Beat the eggs in a bowl with 1 teaspoon water and chill, covered. Leave your skillet on the stove on a turned-off burner.*

HEAT AN 8-INCH NONSTICK SKILLET over medium-high heat, and when hot, add the vegetable oil. When the oil is hot, add the onion and cook, stirring frequently, until softened, very fragrant, and golden at the edges. Don't let the onion turn brown, however, or it will be too sweet. Sprinkle the onion with a little salt and black pepper and scrape into a small bowl. Stir the minced chives into the onion. Place the skillet back on the stove.

Stack the slices of smoked salmon and roll them up lengthwise. Slice the roll into ½-inch slices, then unravel the slices and briefly sauté the salmon over medium-high heat, stirring frequently, just until it loses its translucency, about 30 seconds. Add the salmon to the bowl of hot onion.

Place the same skillet back on the stove and melt the butter over medium-high heat. When hot and bubbling, add the beaten eggs and turn the heat to medium. Let the eggs cook, undisturbed, just until they start to set on the bottom, about 1 minute. Give the eggs a good turn with a wooden spoon or a heat-proof rubber spatula, then fold in the salmon and onion. Cook the eggs until they're done to your liking, folding occasionally. Try not to overstir as the eggs cook, as this breaks them down into small curds. The eggs should remain in fluffy clumps, laced with chive-flecked onions and pieces of smoked salmon.

Sprinkle the eggs with salt and pepper to taste, then scrape them onto an individual serving plate. Sprinkle the top with additional minced chives and serve immediately, with your choice of hot toast.

SERVED WITH
ONION BIALYS
page 248

Cinnamon-scented
FRENCH TOAST
with Caramelized Bananas

OK, be brave. There are more ways to serve French toast than drizzled with maple syrup. The creamy texture and candied taste of caramelized bananas are incredible and are also a perfect accompaniment to the inwardly tender, outwardly crisp, pan-fried toast.

See my suggestions at the end of this recipe to help you serve this delicious dish even on a weekday morning. And, please don't limit these quick and easy bananas to just French toast, since they are unbelievable when spooned over ice cream. ❧ YIELD: 2 TO 4 SERVINGS

FOR THE FRENCH TOAST

¾ cup milk

4 extra-large eggs, lightly beaten

1 teaspoon pure vanilla extract

2 tablespoons plus 1 teaspoon Cinnamon Sugar or Vanilla Sugar (page 35)

3 or 4 slices (¾ to 1 inch thick) day-old Country White Bread (page 224) or plain Six-strand Braided Challah (page 226), or another good quality firm-textured white bread

3 tablespoons unsalted butter (preferably Clarified, page 195), plus 1 tablespoon whole butter

FOR THE CARAMELIZED BANANAS

1 tablespoon unsalted butter

2 tablespoons granulated sugar

1 teaspoon strained fresh lemon juice

1 or 2 ripe but firm bananas, peeled and halved lengthwise

Confectioners' sugar

PREPARE THE FRENCH TOAST. Whisk the milk, eggs, vanilla, and 1 tablespoon of the flavored sugar together in a wide shallow bowl (I use a 9-inch pie plate). Place the bread next to the custard mixture. Put a 12- to 14-inch nonstick skillet on the stove and add the 3 tablespoons clarified butter. Don't turn the stove on just yet.

CARAMELIZE THE BANANAS. Melt the butter in a 10-inch skillet over medium-low heat and, when bubbling, add the sugar and lemon juice. Let the sugar dissolve, swirling the pan occasionally. When the mixture starts to bubble, stir just to help evenly distribute the ingredients, then let the sugar turn a light golden brown. (This will happen around the edges first, so swirl the pan, drawing in those edges to help keep the syrup from scorching.) When the color is consistent, add the halved bananas cut-side down to the hot syrup and cook for 2 to 3 minutes, or until the cut sides are golden and luscious looking. Use a thin metal spatula to turn each half and let cook only briefly on the other side, about 30 seconds. Remove the bananas to a warmed plate and cover loosely with aluminum foil.

Turn the heat to medium-high under the larger skillet and heat until nice and hot, but not smoking. As the butter heats, lay the bread in the custard mixture to soak, working with two slices at a time. When well coated, turn each slice and let them absorb more of the custard, until well coated but not overly saturated. Lay the slices in the hot butter, then immediately dip the remaining slices in the remaining custard and add them to the pan. Sprinkle the tops of each slice of bread with 1 teaspoon cinnamon sugar and, when the undersides are golden, use a thin nonabrasive turning spatula to flip each slice over. Add the 1 tablespoon whole butter to the skillet and swirl the pan by its handle to help the freshly melted butter distribute around the bread. Let the bread cook on the second side until golden, then divide the French toast between two warmed serving plates.

Slice the caramelized bananas into 2-inch pieces on the diagonal. Sift some confectioners' sugar lightly over the French toast, then place the bananas on top. Serve immediately.

TIMING IS EVERYTHING

❧ *To enjoy this wonderful meal first thing on a busy morning, do this the night before:*

❧ *Assemble your custard mixture and leave it, covered, in the refrigerator.*

❧ *Leave your bananas (still in their skins) on your work surface with a cutting board and a knife.*

❧ *Strain some lemon juice and leave it in the refrigerator in a small covered bowl.*

❧ *Measure your clarified butter and put it in a small bowl in the refrigerator, covered.*

FRESH ORANGE JUICE

Spiked with Strawberry Puree

Vibrant looking and fresh tasting, the combination of orange juice and strawberry puree is not only classic, it's also a real winner. When choosing oranges, don't let size or color fool you. Small to medium oranges are sweeter than larger ones, and those tinged with green can be just as sweet as those with vibrant orange skin. For the most juice, choose oranges that have thin skins and are heavy for their size.

🍓 YIELD: 8 CUPS

2 cups (1 dry pint) fresh strawberries, stemmed and hulled, plus more for garnish
1 to 2 tablespoon superfine sugar to taste
1 tablespoon Grand Marnier (optional)

7 cups strained fresh orange juice (from approximately 16 room-temperature juicy juice oranges)
Freshly opened bottle of Champagne (optional)

TIMING IS
EVERYTHING
🍓 *The juice can be refrigerated for up to 24 hours, well covered. If including Champagne, don't open the bottle until ready to serve.*

PLACE THE BERRIES in either the bowl of a food processor fitted with the steel blade or a blender, and process until liquefied and smooth. Pour the puree into a bowl and stir in the sugar and the Grand Marnier, if using. Cover and let the mixture sit at room temperature for at least 1 hour and up to 4 hours for the flavors to heighten. Push the puree through a fine-mesh wire sieve positioned over another bowl. Stir the strained strawberry puree into the orange juice and chill well.

Just before serving, stir the juice and pour some into long-stemmed wine or Champagne glasses. If desired, fill each glass half full with the juice and top each serving with some cold Champagne. Either way, garnish each glass with a beautiful fresh strawberry (stem intact) that's been slit in the bottom and attached to the edge of the glass.

ANYTIME FRUIT SMOOTHIE

If it's not the height of fresh fruit season or if you want to quickly concoct something that's incredibly refreshing, fruit smoothies are the way to go. Actually, since I always have an assortment of frozen fruits in my freezer, my kids make their own smoothies, either first thing in the morning or whenever they need a quick pick-me-up. ✿ YIELD: 1 SERVING (RECIPE CAN BE DOUBLED)

About 1 cup orange juice
About 1 cup frozen fruit (mixed assorted berries and peaches)

Optional fortifying additions: ½ cold ripe banana, a few spoonfuls of a favorite yogurt, or some drained silken tofu

WHIRL THE ORANGE JUICE and frozen fruit in a blender until smooth and thick. If too thick, thin with more juice and, if too thin, add a few more pieces of frozen fruit. For a more fortified smoothie, blend in the banana, some of your favorite yogurt, or some drained silken tofu. Serve right away.

Yikes, That's Bubbling!
MELTED CHEESE ON TOAST

There's something about this recipe that, although incredibly simple, is also unusually satisfying: a crisp, hefty piece of toast topped with halved ripe cherry tomatoes that are covered with an abundance of shredded cheese. The really seductive part is, of course, what happens next. The cheese is broiled under intense heat until it completely surrenders into a sea of rapid bubbles, draping lavishly around the tomatoes. ❧ YIELD: 1 SERVING (RECIPE CAN BE DOUBLED)

1 slice best-quality bread like Country White Bread
   (page 224) or rye bread, sliced ¾ inch thick
4 cherry tomatoes, halved
Freshly ground black pepper to taste

Pinch of aromatic dried oregano, crumbled (optional)
⅓ generous cup shredded cheese (Jarlsberg, sharp
   Cheddar, Muenster, Havarti, mozzarella,
   Monterey Jack, or a combination)

PREHEAT THE BROILER with the rack as close as possible to the heat source.

Tear off a sheet of aluminum foil and place it, shiny side up, either on a cold broiler pan or on a shallow baking sheet. Toast the bread in your toaster until golden on both sides. Place the toast on the foil and scatter the cherry tomato halves on top, cut side up. Sprinkle the tomatoes with black pepper and a pinch of oregano, if using. Scatter the cheese generously and evenly over the tomatoes and slide the baking sheet under the hot broiler. Broil until the cheese is melted and bubbling furiously. Bring this briskly to the table, but instruct those eating to "blow" since this stays hot for a while.

TIMING IS
EVERYTHING
❧ *To enjoy this cheesy toast on busy weekday mornings, do this:*
❧ *Shred small amounts of different types of cheese and keep them refrigerated, either together or separately, in sealed plastic bags to use throughout the week.*
❧ *The night before, place the foil on the baking sheet. Leave your cherry tomatoes on a cutting board with a short serrated knife.*

Moist, Wholesome
CORN MUFFINS

If you really love corn muffins but are tired of standing on line at the noisy corner deli, try these. ❧ YIELD: 12 MUFFINS

2¾ cups prepared Cornbread Mix (page 41),
  or see the end of this recipe
1¼ cups bleached low-protein all-purpose flour
  (see page 42)
1½ cups buttermilk

2 extra-large eggs, lightly beaten
1 generous tablespoon mild-flavored honey
⅔ cup sugar, plus extra for sprinkling
1½ teaspoons pure vanilla extract
⅔ cup flavorless vegetable oil

SPRAY THE TOP of a nonstick 12-muffin tin with vegetable spray and line the cups with paper liners. Preheat the oven to 400°F., with the rack on the center shelf. In a large bowl, use a whisk to combine the cornbread mix and flour. In another bowl, mix the buttermilk with the beaten eggs, honey, sugar, vanilla, and vegetable oil. Pour the mixture into the bowl with the dry mixture and, using either a batter whisk or a wide blending fork, combine the mixture gently but thoroughly (check for dry pockets using a rubber spatula).

Divide the batter evenly among the muffin cups, using a medium-size ice cream scoop or a spoon, filling to the top (use all of the batter). Sprinkle the tops with some more sugar and bake for 5 minutes. Reduce the temperature to 375°F. and bake for 15 minutes more, or until the tops are golden and a tester comes out clean. Remove from the oven and place the tin on a wire rack for a few minutes, then carefully lift each muffin out and let them cool on the rack until just warm before eating. To store cooled muffins, wrap each one in plastic and store at room temperature for up to two days. To freeze muffins, see page 74.

IF YOU DON'T HAVE THE PRE-ASSEMBLED CORNBREAD MIX: For each batch of muffins, use a whisk to combine 1½ cups fine or medium corn-meal, 2¼ cups bleached low-protein all-purpose flour, 2 teaspoons baking soda, 2½ tablespoons sugar, and 1½ teaspoons salt. Sift into another bowl. Combine the wet ingredients with the listed ⅔ cup sugar. Then follow the instructions above.

HERE'S THE SCOOP:
When You Run Out of Muffin Batter

Don't panic when you run out of batter and you still have several cups to fill. Just fill the empty ones two-thirds full with very hot water and your muffins will bake perfectly. When the metal cups stay empty, they draw in too much heat, which can cause the muffins to bake unevenly. Most important, don't try to stretch the batter. Fill each cup to the level called for in your recipe before you move on to the next.

TIMING IS
EVERYTHING
❧ *For fresh corn muffins in the morning, do this:*
❧ *The night before, pre-pare your muffin tin. Place your measured dry ingredients in a bowl and leave it on your counter, covered. Mix your wet ingredients (including the sugar) and leave it cov-ered, in the refrigerator.*
❧ *In the morning, preheat the oven to 400°F. Mix the wet and dry ingredi-ents and follow the remaining instructions.*

Spice-scented
PEAR-CURRANT MUFFINS
with Streusel Tops

What a winning combination! Juicy pears, chewy dried currants, and a spice blend that perfectly complements both. Without the currants, the batter will make a dozen big, fat muffins with hefty tops (my daughter Julie's favorite part). When you include the currants, you'll get two extra muffins, but don't worry. See page 71 to learn what to do when you run out of batter before filling your second muffin tin. Feel free to substitute unpeeled, seeded, and chopped Golden Delicious apples for the pears, since they provide yet another way to widen your muffin repertoire. Oh—and don't overlook the blueberry variation at the end of this recipe; they're also truly wonderful. ❧ YIELD: 12 TO 14 MUFFINS

FOR THE TOPPING
⅔ cup unbleached all-purpose flour
⅓ cup sugar (white granulated or packed light brown)
1 teaspoon cinnamon
½ teaspoon pure vanilla extract
½ cup (1 stick) cold unsalted butter, diced

FOR THE BATTER
3½ cups Assorted Muffin Mix (page 40), or see the end of this recipe
2½ teaspoons Spice Blend for Quick Breads, Cookies, and More (page 38), or see the end of this recipe
1¼ cups buttermilk

2 extra-large eggs, lightly beaten
⅔ cup flavorless vegetable oil
⅔ cup firmly packed light brown sugar
⅔ cup granulated sugar
1 teaspoon pure vanilla extract
½ generous cup dried but supple currants (optional)
2 generous cups peeled, cored, and finely chopped pears (about 3 medium)

FOR THE VANILLA GLAZE
1 generous cup sifted confectioners' sugar
Up to 3 tablespoons cool water or milk
¼ teaspoon pure vanilla extract

MAKE THE TOPPING. Combine the flour, sugar, and cinnamon in the bowl of a food processor fitted with the steel blade. Add the vanilla and pulse just a few times to distribute. Add half the cold butter cubes and pulse to break them into the size of peas. Add the remaining butter and do the same (some pieces should appear smaller than others). Transfer the topping to a bowl and refrigerate or freeze it, covered, until needed.

MAKE THE MUFFINS. Spray the tops of a nonstick 12-muffin tin and a 6-muffin tin with vegetable spray and line the cups with paper liners. Preheat the oven to 400°F. with the rack on the center shelf. Whisk together the muffin mix and the spice blend in a 5-quart mixing bowl and set it aside. In another bowl, combine the buttermilk, eggs, oil, sugars, vanilla, and currants, if using. Mix well. Add the wet mixture to the bowl with the dry ingredients and, using either a batter whisk or a wide blending fork, combine the mixtures gently but thoroughly (check for dry pockets using a rubber spatula). Gently fold in the chopped pears using a rubber spatula. Use a medium-size ice cream scoop or a spoon to divide the batter among the muffin cups, filling to the top (you will have two unfilled cups). Sprinkle the tops *very generously* with the topping.

Bake for 20 minutes. Reduce the temperature to 375°F. and bake for 5 minutes. Reduce the temperature to 325°F. and bake 5 to 7 minutes more (a toothpick should come out clean when inserted into the center and the tops should be golden and crisp). Remove the tins from the oven and place on a wire rack for 5 minutes. Use a knife to cut in between the muffins where the edges merged during baking, then carefully lift each muffin out and let them cool further on the rack.

GLAZE THE MUFFINS. Place a large sheet of waxed paper underneath their rack. Use a fork to mix the confectioners' sugar with enough water or milk to make a smooth paste that's thick enough to form a ribbon when lifted from the bowl and allowed to dribble back onto itself. If too thin, add more sugar, and if not thin enough, add more liquid, 1 teaspoonful at a time. Stir in the vanilla. When the muffins are cool, use a fork to lift some of the glaze up (about 8 to 10 inches) above each muffin and drizzle the glaze in a repetitive zigzag motion. When done, let the glaze set. (If the glaze ever becomes too stiff to drizzle, sit the bottom of the bowl in some hot tap water for few minutes.) Once the glaze is set, wrap each muffin in plastic wrap and store at room temperature for up to three days. To freeze muffins, see page 74.

If you don't have the preassembled muffin mix or the spice blend: For each batch of these muffins, you'll need 3½ cups bleached flour, 1 tablespoon baking powder, 1 teaspoon baking soda, ¾ teaspoon salt, 1½ teaspoons cinnamon, 1 teaspoon nutmeg, ½ teaspoon ginger, ¼ teaspoon allspice, and a pinch of ground cloves. Combine these ingredients well, using a whisk, then follow the instructions above.

Blueberry Muffins

For 12 blueberry muffins, omit the currants and instead of the spice blend, add 1½ teaspoons cinnamon and 1 teaspoon nutmeg to the same amount of muffin mix. After combining the wet and dry ingredients as directed, replace the pears with 2 generous cups of blueberries. Fill each cup of the tin to the top. Sprinkle the tops generously with sugar and bake in a preheated 400°F. oven for 20 minutes, then reduce the oven temperature to 325°F. and bake for 5 to 10 minutes more, or until golden and a tester comes out clean. Cool.

TIMING IS
EVERYTHING
❧ *For fresh muffins in the morning, do this:*
❧ *The night before, prepare the muffin tins or loaf pans. Whisk together the dry mix and spices and leave this on your counter, covered. Combine the buttermilk, currants, sugars, oil, eggs, and vanilla. Refrigerate this, covered. Assemble the topping and refrigerate it, covered.*
❧ *In the morning, preheat your oven to 400°F. Remove your wet mixture from the refrigerator and give it a good stir, and continue as directed in the recipe.*

BANANA CRUMB MUFFINS
(or Loaves)

If the word "magnificent" is ever appropriate in the world of muffin-dom, these gorgeous specimens definitely fit the bill. And this recipe gives you a great way to use those really ripe now-or-never bananas.

🍌 YIELD: 12 TO 16 MUFFINS OR TWO 8 × 4-INCH LOAVES

FOR THE TOPPING
Up to ¾ cup walnuts
Up to ¾ cup granulated sugar
Up to 1½ teaspoons cinnamon
Up to ¾ teaspoon nutmeg, preferably freshly grated

FOR THE BATTER
3½ cups Assorted Muffin Mix (page 40),
   or see the end of this recipe
1½ teaspoons cinnamon
1 teaspoon nutmeg, preferably freshly grated
½ cup buttermilk

½ cup flavorless vegetable oil
2 extra-large eggs
⅔ cup each granulated sugar and firmly packed
   light brown sugar
1½ teaspoons pure vanilla extract
2 cups banana puree (from 4 or 5 large, very ripe
   bananas)
Optional additions: 1½ cups diced ripe bananas
   tossed with 1½ teaspoons strained fresh lemon
   juice and ½ cup mini chocolate chips, or 1½ cups
   chocolate chips

ASSEMBLE THE TOPPING. If using the optional additions listed at the end of the ingredients list, place the full amount of nuts, sugar, cinnamon, and nutmeg in the bowl of a food processor fitted with the steel blade. (If not using the additions, or if making loaves, use the following amounts: ½ cup each of sugar and walnuts, 1 teaspoon cinnamon, and ½ teaspoon nutmeg.) Pulse the ingredients until the nuts are finely chopped and well distributed within the sugar. Transfer the topping to a bowl and set it aside for now.

HERE'S THE SCOOP:
On Freezing Muffins or Quick Bread Loaves

Most muffins and quick bread loaves freeze really well for up to three months. To freeze muffins or loaves, let them cool to just barely warm, then wrap in plastic and let them cool completely. The small amount of steam retained in the wrapped muffins or loaves will add moisture, helping them stay moist during their stay in the freezer, which can be dry-ing. When cool, rewrap the muffins in fresh plastic, then place them, in a single layer, in a shallow, rectangular, heavy-duty plastic container (with a tight-fitting lid). After re-wrapping the loaves, cover them securely with aluminum foil and place them in a heavy-duty freezer bag and seal it securely. To thaw, remove the loaf or the number of muffins you want from the container, but leave them wrapped. Let them thaw at room temperature, and by morning they'll be great. If you want to wake up their "just-baked" flavor and aroma, place thawed unwrapped muffins in a 350°F. oven for 5 minutes (loaves for 8), just to warm them.

Preheat the oven to 400°F. Spray the tops of a nonstick 12-muffin tin with vegetable spray, and line the cups with paper liners. If making loaves, preheat the oven to 375°F. and brush two 8 × 4-inch nonstick loaf pans with melted butter or spray them with vegetable spray.

MAKE THE BATTER. Whisk together the dry mix and spices in a 5-quart mixing bowl and set it aside. Combine the buttermilk, oil, eggs, granulated and brown sugars, and vanilla. Add the banana puree to the bowl of wet ingredients and mix well. Add the wet ingredients to the dry and if using the optional additions, fold them in now. Using either a batter whisk or a wide blending fork, combine the mixture gently but thoroughly (check for dry pockets using a rubber spatula).

To bake muffins, use a medium-size ice cream scoop or a spoon to divide the batter among the cups, filling to the top and mounding slightly (use all of the batter). If not using the optional additions, you will fill one 12-muffin tin perfectly. If using additional ingredients, depending on the amount, the batter will yield between 14 and 16 muffins. (See page 71 for instructions on baking partially full muffin tins.) Sprinkle the tops *very generously* with the topping (although it will seem like too much, use all of it). Bake in the center of the oven for 20 minutes. Reduce the temperature to 375°F. and bake for 5 minutes. Reduce the temperature to 325°F. and bake 5 to 7 minutes more (a toothpick should come out clean when inserted into the center and the tops should be golden and crisp).

For loaves, divide the batter between the prepared loaf pans and smooth the tops. Sprinkle the tops with the topping and place in the oven. Turn the heat down to 350°F. and bake for 40 to 50 minutes, or until evenly risen, golden, and a tester comes out clean.

When done, place the pans on a wire rack for a few minutes. Then use a knife to cut in between the muffins (where the edges merged during baking). Carefully lift each muffin out and let them cool further on the rack. To unmold the loaves, place a piece of waxed paper on top of each loaf and invert it onto another wire rack. Invert once more, so the loaf is right side up. Discard the paper. To store cooled muffins or loaves, wrap each in plastic and store at room temperature for up to three days. To freeze muffins or loaves, see page 74.

If you don't have the preassembled muffin mix: Per each batch of these muffins, you'll need 3½ cups bleached flour, 1 tablespoon baking powder, 1 teaspoon baking soda, ¾ teaspoon salt, 1½ teaspoons cinnamon, and 1 teaspoon nutmeg. Combine these ingredients well using a whisk, then follow the previous instructions.

TIMING IS EVERYTHING

* For fresh muffins in the morning, do this:
* The night before, prepare the muffin tins or loaf pans. Whisk together the dry mix and spices and leave this on your counter, covered. Combine the buttermilk, oil, sugars, eggs, and vanilla. Refrigerate this, covered. Assemble your crumb topping and leave this on your counter, covered.
* Measure your chocolate chips, if using, and place them next to the dry mix. If adding diced bananas, strain a little lemon juice and leave this in the refrigerator, covered (you'll need only 1 to 1½ teaspoons).
* In the morning, preheat your oven to 400°F. Remove your wet mixture from the refrigerator and give it a good stir. Continue as directed in the recipe.

PEANUT BUTTER MUFFINS

This muffin definitely talks to the kid in me. As a food writer, it's such fun to take all of my favorite foods and put them together in all sorts of wonderful ways. I suggest you try these chubby muffins with lots of mini-chocolate chips, since they're truly memorable. If you end up with a partially filled muffin tin, see page 71. ❧ YIELD: 12 TO 18 MUFFINS

FOR THE TOPPING
Up to ¾ cup salted cocktail peanuts
Up to ¾ cup granulated sugar
Up to ¾ teaspoon cinnamon

FOR THE BATTER
1½ cups milk
2 cups commercial peanut butter (smooth or chunky)
3½ cups Assorted Muffin Mix (page 40), or see the end of this recipe
1½ teaspoons cinnamon

½ cup buttermilk
½ cup flavorless vegetable oil
2 extra-large eggs, lightly beaten
1 cup firmly packed light brown sugar
½ cup mild-flavored honey
1½ teaspoons pure vanilla extract
Optional additions: 1 rounded cup mini chocolate chips, or a combination of chips and diced ripe bananas not to exceed 2 cups total (toss bananas in a bit of fresh lemon juice to preserve their color)

ASSEMBLE THE TOPPING. If using the optional additions listed at the end of the ingredients list, place the full amount of nuts, sugar, and cinnamon in the bowl of a food processor fitted with the steel blade. If not using the additions, use the following amounts: ½ cup each of sugar and peanuts, ½ teaspoon cinnamon. Pulse the ingredients until the nuts are finely chopped and well distributed throughout the sugar. Transfer the topping to a bowl and set it aside for now.

Preheat the oven to 400°F. Spray the tops of a nonstick 12-muffin tin with vegetable spray and line the cups with paper liners. (Prepare an additional 6-cup tin as described, if using the optional additions.)

MAKE THE BATTER. Heat the milk with the peanut butter over low heat until completely homogenous, stirring frequently with a whisk. (Don't over-heat, however, or the mixture will clump.) When warmed and smooth, remove from the heat. Whisk the muffin mix and cinnamon together in a 5-quart mixing bowl. In another bowl, combine the buttermilk, oil, eggs, brown sugar, honey, and vanilla; when well mixed, whisk in the peanut butter mixture. Add the wet mixture to the bowl of dry ingredients and, using either a batter whisk or a wide blending fork, combine the mixtures gently but thoroughly (check for dry pockets, using a rubber spatula). Now's the time to fold in your optional additions, if using.

Use a medium-size ice cream scoop or a spoon to divide the batter among the muffin cups, filling them to the top (use all of the batter). If not using the optional additions, you will fill one 12-muffin tin perfectly. If using additional ingredients, depending on the amount, the batter will yield between 16 and 18 muffins. Sprinkle the tops *very generously* with the topping. Bake in the center of the oven for 20 minutes. Reduce the temperature to 375°F. and bake for 5 minutes. Reduce the temperature to 325°F. and bake 5 to 7 minutes more (a toothpick should come out clean when inserted into the center and the tops should be golden and crisp).

REMOVE THE MUFFINS from the oven and place the tin(s) on a wire rack for a few minutes, then use a knife to cut in between the muffins (where the edges merged during baking). Carefully lift each muffin out and let them cool further on the rack. To store cooled muffins, wrap each one in plastic and keep at room temperature. The muffins will stay perfectly moist for three days. To freeze muffins, see page 74.

If you don't have the preassembled muffin mix: For each batch of these muffins, you'll need 3½ cups bleached flour, 1 tablespoon baking powder, 1 teaspoon baking soda, ¾ teaspoon salt, and 1½ teaspoons cinnamon. Combine these ingredients well using a whisk, then follow the instructions above.

HERE'S THE SCOOP:
On Choosing Peanut Butter

Personally, I've never been a food snob. I don't mind using commercially prepared peanut butter in my recipes (or on my morning toast), especially since I think the creamy texture is truly soothing. Additionally, because of its emulsified consistency, it really does lend a much better texture to baked goods. As far as the "best" brand of peanut butter, choose the one that makes you remember the best parts of your childhood.

TIMING IS
EVERYTHING

For fresh muffins in the morning, do this:

The night before, prepare the muffin tins. Mix the dry mix with cinnamon and leave this on your counter, covered. Combine the buttermilk, oil, sugar, honey, eggs, and vanilla and refrigerate this, covered. Assemble your crumb topping and leave on your counter, covered.

Place the measured peanut butter in a 1½-quart covered saucepan off the heat. If using diced bananas, strain a little lemon juice and leave this in the refrigerator, covered (you'll need only 1½ teaspoons).

In the morning, preheat your oven to 400°F. Heat the peanut butter with the milk, as directed. Remove your wet mixture from the refrigerator and give it a good stir. Continue as directed in the recipe.

Big, Fat Wedges . . .
ORANGE-SCENTED CURRANT SCONES

This recipe produces scones that are (as far as my family and friends are concerned) unsurpassed. The biscuit mix on page 42 has been specifically designed to make scones that are lighter than most with a very tender, slightly cakelike crumb. If you're having a casual gathering at home, like a midmorning or afternoon tea, why not make two variations of scones? For more information about how to handle biscuit dough, see page 257. ✷ YIELD: 6 TO 8 SCONES

FOR THE GLAZE

1 egg, at room temperature
2 tablespoons heavy cream
2 teaspoons granulated sugar
¼ teaspoon pure vanilla extract

FOR THE SCONES

¾ cup heavy cream
3 tablespoons orange juice or thawed frozen orange juice concentrate
1 extra-large egg

½ teaspoon pure vanilla extract
2 teaspoons minced orange zest (colored part only)
2 cups Baking Powder Biscuit Mix (page 42), or see the end of this recipe
⅓ cup Vanilla Sugar (page 35) or regular sugar, plus more for sprinkling
½ rounded cup dried but supple currants
6 tablespoons cold unsalted butter, cut into small dice
Unbleached all-purpose flour for dusting
Confectioners' sugar for dusting (optional)

PREPARE THE GLAZE. Combine the egg, cream, sugar, and vanilla using a fork. Pour this through a medium-mesh sieve into another bowl, and set it aside. Preheat the oven to 400°F with the rack on the center shelf. Line a flat cookie sheet with parchment paper.

MAKE THE DOUGH. Combine the cream, orange juice, egg, vanilla, and zest in a 1-cup liquid measuring cup. Whirl the biscuit mix and sugar in the workbowl of a food processor fitted with the steel blade to combine well. Add the currants and pulse to distribute evenly. Drop the cold diced butter into the workbowl and use the pulsing button to cut the butter into the flour mixture until it looks like coarse meal. Uncover the bowl and pour in most of the liquid ingredients (reserving only about 2 tablespoons); after attaching the cover, pulse just until the batter seems cohesive (don't overwork it). If the mixture seems at all dry, add the remaining liquid and pulse it in. (Scone dough should be moist, but not overly wet.) Turn the dough out onto a lightly floured surface and knead gently seven or eight times.

Pat the dough out into a 1-inch thick round and transfer it to the prepared baking sheet. Using a sharp chef's knife, cut the dough into six or eight wedges. Wipe off the knife after each cut, and sprinkle the blade with some flour. Repeat this cutting procedure, going into the original lines and, when the blade reaches the bottom, rock the blade (by its handle) back and forth to widen the space between the wedges. Do this several times if necessary until there's between ⅛ and ¼ inch between the wide part of the wedges. Of course, this space will be much narrower at the center.

USE A PASTRY BRUSH to remove any excess flour on the dough, then brush the tops with the prepared glaze. Sprinkle the tops with sugar and bake for 20 minutes. Then remove the sheet from the oven and, using a sharp chef's knife, cut in between the wedges, wiping off the blade after each cut. If necessary, go over your cuts until you are sure that all the wedges are completely separate. One by one, place a narrow metal spatula underneath each wedge and pull it away from the rest, giving them all total exposure to the heat. Place the sheet back in the oven and reduce the temperature to 375°F. Bake for 5 minutes more. Cool the wedges completely on a rack.

Before serving, if desired, give the tops of the scones a light dusting of confectioners' sugar. Store scones at room temperature in an airtight container or individually wrapped with plastic.

Chocolate Chip Scones

Substitute ½ cup mini chocolate chips for the currants. Keep everything else the same.

Dried Cherry Scones

Substitute ½ cup dried cherries (chopped if too big). Omit the orange juice and zest and increase the cream by 3 tablespoons. Add to the cream ¼ teaspoon each pure almond extract and vanilla. All of the remaining directions stay the same.

If you don't have the pre-assembled biscuit mix: Per each batch of scones, mix 2 cups unbleached all-purpose flour with 1 tablespoon plus 1 teaspoon baking powder, 1 tablespoon sugar, and ¾ teaspoon salt. Whisk well and follow the previous instructions

TIMING IS EVERYTHING

For fresh-baked scones first thing in the morning, do this:

The night before, line your baking sheet with parchment paper. Place the biscuit mix and sugar in the bowl of your food processor and leave it there, with the lid on. Cut the butter into dice and leave it in the refrigerator, covered. Mix the cream, orange juice, zest, egg, and vanilla and leave it in the refrigerator, covered. Assemble your glaze and refrigerate it, covered.

In the morning, preheat the oven to 400°F. Cut the butter into the dry mixture, mix in the currants, add the wet ingredients, and follow the remaining instructions.

FRESH FRUIT PARFAIT

These parfaits are as beautiful for breakfast as they are refreshing for dessert. The addition of a few ripe rounds of banana is very strategic, since their creaminess adds a surprising (and very soothing) contrast to the cold, juicy melon.

❧ YIELD: 6 SERVINGS

1 rounded cup (½ dry pint) blackberries, raspberries, or hulled strawberries, plus 2 extra beautiful berries per person for garnish
1 rounded tablespoon seedless raspberry jam
2 large, ripe, but firm bananas
1 to 2 teaspoons strained fresh lemon juice

4 cups melon balls from two or three different types of ripe melon
Two 8-ounce containers vanilla yogurt
Optional additions: your favorite granola or some dry-toasted sliced almonds or walnuts (see page 271)
Fresh mint leaves for garnish

TIMING IS EVERYTHING
❧ *The fruit puree can be prepared up to two days ahead and stored in the refrigerator, well covered.*
❧ *Although the bananas must be scooped close to assembling the parfaits, the melon balls can be scooped one day ahead and stored in the refrigerator, well covered.*
❧ *The parfaits can be assembled (without the granola or nuts) up to 2 hours ahead of serving. Cover them loosely with plastic wrap and refrigerate. If using a topping, add it just before serving.*

PLACE THE BERRIES in the bowl of a food processor fitted with the steel blade or in a blender. Process the berries until thoroughly pureed. Place the jam in a 1-quart saucepan. Position a fine-mesh sieve over the pan and pour the berry puree into the sieve. Using a sturdy rubber or wooden spatula, rub the puree through the sieve, leaving the seeds behind (straining is not necessary if using strawberries). Bring the pureed mixture just to a simmer over low heat, stirring to break up any coagulated jam. Remove this from the stove, pour it into a bowl, and let it cool.

When you're almost ready to serve the parfaits, lay each peeled banana on a flat surface. Use a gentle but firm hand to scoop down into the banana flesh, with a melon baller, making a full clockwise revolution with the scoop. Lift the scoop and, to help the banana ball pop out, knock the stem of the scooper over the rim of a bowl. When you've measured at least 1 cup, toss them with the lemon juice to prevent them from discoloring.

GENTLY FOLD TOGETHER the banana and melon balls. Place 1¼ cups of the fruit balls in each parfait glass and ladle ⅓ to ½ cup of vanilla yogurt over the fruit. Spoon 2 tablespoons of the berry puree on top of the yogurt. Allow the parfait to sit for a few minutes so the toppings can trickle down throughout the fruit. If desired, top each parfait with a tablespoon or so of your favorite granola or some toasted sliced almonds. Garnish each serving with two plump berries and a beautiful sprig of fresh mint.

CHAPTER THREE

More Than a Mouthful . . .

GREAT FOOD
with
COCKTAILS

AS A COOKING TEACHER, I've never had a student (regardless of his or her level of culinary expertise) who wasn't anxious to learn a great new recipe to serve with cocktails. In this chapter I've featured dishes that are both boldly flavorful and enticing to look at.

When you're deciding on a starter for a menu, remember that these are the first scents, sights, tastes, and textures that your guests will experience in your home. Think aroma first, since that's what greets people upon entering. If you choose to serve something great tasting that requires no cooking at all (like a gorgeous platter filled with halved chewy dates stuffed with creamy cheese and wrapped in prosciutto), I'd include a basket full of crisp slices of freshly broiled garlic toasts, since their aroma promises to make even a stoic swoon. The following assortment of dishes run the gamut from piping hot and crisp to chilled, smooth, and spicy. They all continue to make me and my guests very happy.

OH-SO-CHEESY REFRIED BEANS page 84

Oh-So-Cheesy . . .
REFRIED BEANS
with Warmed Corn Chips

Although this creamy bean dish is featured here as a starter for a cocktail party, it's equally satisfying as a side dish, especially with Steak, Chicken, and Shrimp Fajitas (page 188). Either way, always park a basket of warmed yellow and/or blue corn tortilla chips close by.

❧ YIELD: 12 SERVINGS AS A STARTER OR 8 AS A SIDE DISH

1 pound dried pinto beans, rinsed and drained well, and picked over to remove stones (see page 85)

2 large white or yellow onions, chopped

2 large carrots, peeled and sliced

4 large garlic cloves, minced

About 7 cups hot unsalted Chicken, Beef, or Roasted Vegetable Stock (pages 16, 18, and 22) or water

Kosher or sea salt and freshly ground black pepper

4 tablespoons extra-virgin olive oil, plus more as needed

2 fresh jalapeño chiles, roasted, skinned, seeded, and minced (page 24)

Up to 1½ cups grated cheese (combine Monterey Jack and Muenster)

2 tablespoons minced cilantro

Accompaniment: warmed blue and yellow tortilla chips

TIMING IS EVERYTHING

❧ *The refried beans can be fully assembled (without the cheese) one day ahead. Once cool, brush the top with olive oil, then cover the dish with aluminum foil (shiny side down) and refrigerate. Bring close to room temperature before baking in a 375°F. oven, covered, until hot throughout, 30 to 45 minutes. Uncover the beans and scatter the cheese on top. Bake or broil until the cheese is melted and bubbling.*

PLACE THE BEANS in a 4-quart bowl and cover with cold water. Cover the bowl and place it in the refrigerator overnight. Or, for a quick-soak method, pour enough boiling water over the beans to cover them by 2 inches and let them sit, uncovered, at room temperature for 1 to 1½ hours. Either way, drain the beans well, put them into a 3-quart pot, and cover with cold water. Bring the water to a boil, uncovered, and simmer them for 3 to 5 minutes. Drain the beans and rinse them again, before proceeding.

Place the beans in a 4-quart heavy-bottomed saucepan and add half the onions, the carrots, and half the garlic. Pour 6 cups of the hot stock over the beans and bring the liquid to a boil, covered. Turn the heat down to low and simmer the beans until almost tender, about 30 minutes. Stir in some salt and black pepper to taste. Cover the pan and continue to cook until the beans are very tender, 30 to 45 minutes more. As the beans cook, occasionally lift the lid and, if needed, add more stock to continually keep them covered. (You won't need more than 1 additional cup of stock for presoaked beans.)

WHEN THE BEANS ARE DONE, heat a 12-inch, heavy-bottomed, deep-sided skillet over medium heat and, when hot, add the olive oil. When the oil is hot, add the remaining chopped onion, remaining garlic, and the chiles.

Cook the vegetables, stirring constantly, until softened and very fragrant, about 2 minutes. Lightly drain the cooked beans and vegetables over a bowl, and reserve the cooking liquid. Transfer the beans to another bowl. Add a large ladleful of beans to the skillet and, using an old-fashioned potato masher, mash the beans, then add another ladleful of beans and continue until all the beans have been incorporated. Continue to cook the beans, stirring constantly, until they're thick, somewhat smooth, and creamy textured, 10 to 20 minutes. If they seem dry, add some of the reserved cooking liquid to help them achieve the texture of creamy mashed potatoes. (You won't use more than a third of the liquid.) Season the refried beans well with salt and black pepper.

Transfer the bean mixture to a 3-quart shallow, oven-to-table baking dish. Preheat the broiler. Sprinkle the top of the dish with a combination of grated cheese and cilantro, and place the dish under the broiler until the cheese is bubbling and turning golden. Serve the refried beans piping hot, with a basket of mixed blue and yellow tortilla chips that have been heated on a shallow baking sheet in a preheated 375°F. oven for 8 to 10 minutes.

HERE'S THE SCOOP:
On Storing and Cooking Dried Beans

Make sure to date your beans when you get home from the market. You don't want to mix old beans with those that were newly dried, since the old ones will require longer cooking. Old beans also seem to be more likely to cause the unwanted side effects during digestion. Before using dried beans, pour them onto a shallow baking sheet and shimmy the pan to identify and remove any small stones. And be aware that if you decide not to presoak the beans, you'll need an increased amount of stock to rehydrate the beans and make them tender.

It's been well documented not to salt beans in the beginning of the cooking process, since this toughens their skins, making it more difficult for them to absorb moisture and become tender. One point that's rarely mentioned, however, is that for beans to develop a full and satisfying flavor internally, they should be salted toward the end of cooking, *before* they become perfectly tender. When beans are softened but are not yet tender enough to eat, they still have a bit more room to absorb their final dose of moisture. This is the ideal time to absorb seasoning, which will intensify the flavor at their core. This way, your cooked beans will be more than just texturally soothing—they'll be flavorful. However, if you season beans too late in the cooking process, they will already be filled to capacity with moisture and any added flavor will just remain in the surrounding liquid.

STUFFED MUSHROOMS
alla Bolognese (My Way)

Plump, tender, and delectable, these stuffed mushrooms make a perfect first course as part of an Italian meal or as one savory component of a larger hot antipasto. The stuffing, made from ground veal, prosciutto, and sautéed vegetables, also freezes perfectly. So, although this recipe uses only twenty-four mushrooms and serves eight, the filling is purposely generous, either for a big party or simply to tuck half in the freezer for another day. Refrigerate the leftover mushroom stems for a few days, and use them, chopped, in sauces, sautés, and soups.

🍂 YIELD: ENOUGH TO STUFF 40 TO 50 BUTTON MUSHROOMS

FOR THE FILLING

2 large leeks, cleaned and thinly sliced (about 3 cups)
5 garlic cloves, chopped
1 celery stalk, thinly sliced
1 carrot, peeled and thinly sliced
4 tablespoons (½ stick) unsalted butter or extra-virgin olive oil
1 pound ground veal
½ cup Beef or Veal Stock (page 18)
Kosher or sea salt and freshly ground black pepper to taste
1 tablespoon extra-virgin olive oil
¾ pound sweet Italian sausage, removed from its casings and crumbled, or combine sweet and hot sausage
½ cup dry red wine
1½ cups chopped ripe peeled and seeded plum (Roma) tomatoes (see page 33), or an equal amount of whole peeled canned tomatoes

¾ cup canned tomato puree
½ cup chopped basil leaves
3 ounces canned tomato paste
3 tablespoons heavy cream
2 thin slices prosciutto, chopped
½ cup freshly grated best-quality Parmigiano-Reggiano cheese

FOR THE MUSHROOMS

24 (and up to 50) large white button mushrooms, wiped clean
Melted butter or olive oil for brushing
Freshly ground black pepper to taste
4 to 6 ounces each fine-quality low-moisture mozzarella cheese, Muenster cheese, and Parmigiano-Reggiano, grated and combined

MAKE THE FILLING. Combine the leeks, garlic, celery, and carrot in a mixing bowl. Place this mixture in batches in a food processor fitted with the steel blade and pulse until the vegetables are chopped very fine but still have texture. Heat the butter in a 3-quart, heavy-bottomed saucepan over medium heat. Brush a piece of waxed paper, cut large enough to cover the diameter of the pan, with some of the butter. When the pan is hot, stir in the vegetables and place the greased side of the paper directly on top of the vegetables. Reduce the heat to low and "sweat" the vegetables gently for 15 to 20 minutes, stirring occasionally.

WHILE THE VEGETABLES ARE COOKING, heat a 10- to 12-inch deep-sided, heavy-bottomed skillet over high heat and, when the pan is hot, add the ground veal. Break up the meat using a wooden spatula and cook, stirring occasionally, until the veal is no longer pink, about 5 minutes. Using a slotted spoon, transfer the meat to a bowl. Pour out any liquid from the skillet, but don't wipe out the interior. Place the pan back over high heat and deglaze the bottom with the stock, allowing the stock to boil rapidly until reduced by half. Pour this reduction over the veal and add some salt and black pepper. Wipe out the pan and return it to the stove over medium heat.

Add the olive oil to the skillet and, when hot, add the crumbled sausage meat. Brown the sausage as you did the veal, season with salt and pepper, then use a slotted spoon to add it to the bowl of veal. Pour out any fat from the pan and deglaze the pan again, this time using the red wine. When the wine is reduced by half, add it to the bowl with the veal and set it aside.

REMOVE THE WAXED PAPER from the cooked vegetables and stir in the chopped tomatoes, tomato puree, and ¼ cup chopped basil. Add the meat mixture with any surrounding liquid, along with the tomato paste and a good amount of black pepper. Fold everything together well. Bring the mixture to a brisk bubble through the center, then reduce the heat to low and cook the stuffing, with the cover ajar, for 30 minutes. Add the cream and simmer for 10 more minutes. Stir in the remaining ¼ cup chopped basil along with the prosciutto and remove from the stove. Let the stuffing cool, uncovered, then stir in ½ cup of grated Parmesan. Check for seasoning, adding more salt and pepper if needed.

STUFF AND BAKE THE MUSHROOMS. Remove the stems from the mushrooms: Secure each cap in your nonworking hand. Lay your working hand lightly over the exposed mushroom bottom and, using your thumb, gently but firmly push the stem away from you, releasing it from one side of the cap. Turn the cap a half-turn and do the same movement on the other side. The stem should now be separate from the cap and can be easily removed. Save the stems for another use. Use a small spoon to remove some of the mushroom flesh, leaving more room for stuffing.

Preheat the oven to 375°F. and brush a baking sheet with melted butter or olive oil. Using a teaspoon, fill the mushroom caps with the filling, mounding it slightly, and line them up in rows. After filling the mushrooms, sprinkle the tops with black pepper. Lift each stuffed mushroom and sprinkle the filling generously with the combined cheeses, pressing gently to help it adhere.

Bake the mushrooms for 35 to 45 minutes, or until the mushrooms are tender, the filling is piping hot, and the cheese is melted, bubbling, and nicely browned. Serve the mushrooms very hot, with plates and forks.

TIMING IS
EVERYTHING
❧ The stuffed mushrooms can be fully assembled up to two days ahead and kept refrigerated, well covered with oiled aluminum foil. Bring close to room temperature before baking, uncovered, or adjust the baking time accordingly.
❧ The stuffing can be frozen for six months in a heavy-duty, securely sealed and labeled freezer container. Thaw overnight in the refrigerator before gently reheating, adding some additional black pepper and a tablespoon or so of freshly chopped basil. Let cool before filling the mushrooms.

On Entertaining and Confidence

Have you ever left someone's home after sharing a fabulous meal and said to yourself, "I wish my home could smell as wonderful," or "I wish I knew how to entertain with such ease and warmth," or "If only I knew how to cook like that!"? If you let those competitive thoughts or feelings stop you from trying, I'd like you to remember how you felt after attempting the first few rounds of a new sport. Did you feel insecure when watching a person who exhibited extraordinary skill? I doubt it. Usually, we allow those people to inspire us. We use glimpses of proficiency to reinforce the notion that, if we make the act of practicing a priority, then we, too, could become more comfortable and knowing in that particular arena. Well, why should cooking and entertaining be any different?

As with any sport or art, the only way to increase your strength and endurance and to become self-trusting, is to "do" it as often as possible. Making quality home-cooked meals a more regular part of daily or weekly life is the best way to develop "cooking muscles," giving you the ease, confidence, and ultimate ability that you admire in others. And, believe me, it's a lot easier to become a great cook than it is to consistently hit a golf ball down the middle of the fairway!

When new to entertaining, allow yourself to embrace the characteristics exhibited by those you admire, and be more "present" to the best parts of your experience when in their homes. This is a great way to learn more about yourself and about what makes you happy. Rather than setting out to do and be everything for others, ask yourself, "What type of home life would make me feel the most comforted and the proudest to share?" Then make yourself happy. Those around you will gladly come along for the ride! Cooking and entertaining is all about sharing your individual interpretation of deliciousness with those you care about. So, instead of worrying that you're not like someone else, figure out how to bring more of you into your home life, using the proficiency of others to inspire and guide you.

PIGS-IN-A-QUILT

OK, maybe hot dogs rolled in pastry is a retro recipe, but I don't care. Though unfashionable, they are, in fact, one of the most highly chased platters of food by grown men at fancy dinner parties. Personally, I've always found the cocktail-size hot dogs to be way too puny, so I use halved regular hot dogs instead. And I use only best-quality, all-butter puff pastry to make them perfectly cozy before I tuck them into the freezer until needed. This way, there's always something savory waiting in the wings for spur-of-the-moment entertaining. Oh, and just to shake things up a bit, I place a very thin piece of cheese underneath the hot dog before I roll it up. This way, after baking, dribbles of melted cheese ooze out from underneath the pastry. Of course, traditionalists can omit the cheese. Although my husband dips his dogs in deli mustard, use your favorite kind. After all, this recipe is meant to revive for you, a delicious blast from your own past.

🌢 YIELD: 12 SERVINGS

Twelve 5-inch hot dogs, patted dry, rounded ends sliced off, and cut in half widthwise
Up to 8 ounces thinly sliced Jarlsberg or Muenster cheese, cut into 2 × 3-inch strips (optional)
Dijon mustard for spreading

½ recipe chilled Quick Puff Pastry (page 48), or 1 pound store-bought frozen puff pastry, thawed
Unbleached all-purpose flour for dusting
Glaze: 1 egg mixed with 2 teaspoons water
Sesame seeds for sprinkling (optional)
Accompaniment: your favorite mustard for dipping

PLACE THE HALVED HOT DOGS in a bowl on one side of your work surface. If using the cheese, place the strips in another bowl next to the hot dogs. Put a few tablespoons of Dijon mustard in a small bowl. Line a large shallow tray or baking sheet with waxed paper and place it on the other side of your work surface.

PLACE THE UNROLLED PASTRY (or the thawed pastry sheet) on the lightly floured surface. If working with unrolled pastry, use a floured rolling pin to roll the dough out into an 11 × 16-inch rectangle. If using an already rolled sheet of pastry, use the rolling pin to elongate and widen it until it reaches the same size. Place the rectangle of pastry horizontally in front of you and, using a long, sharp chef's knife, cut it in half widthwise (horizontally). Now, make four vertical cuts, creating 12 squares of pastry.

Place one pastry square in front of you and use your rolling pin to widen it slightly so it measures 4 × 4 inches. Cut the square in half (forming two rectangles) and brush each pastry strip lightly with some mustard. Place a strip of cheese over the mustard, then put a hot dog on the bottom short side of each strip. Working with one strip at a time, roll the pastry up (going away from you), enclosing the hot dog and cheese. As you roll up, pull down gently to help create a taut roll. When you reach the top, roll over the edge and press down on the seam to seal the pastry. Place the filled pastry on the prepared baking sheet and continue this process until you've finished. Cover the sheet with plastic wrap and refrigerate the pigs-in-a-quilt for 2 hours or freeze for 1 hour (or longer) before baking.

PREHEAT THE OVEN TO 425°F. Line a baking sheet with parchment paper. Prepare the glaze and strain it into another small bowl, making it easier to apply. Place the glaze next to your work surface, along with a pastry brush. Put some sesame seeds in a bowl next to the glaze, if using. Place the chilled pastries seam side down on the baking sheet and brush the tops and sides with the glaze. Sprinkle the tops with sesame seeds and place the pastries in the preheated oven. Immediately reduce the temperature to 400°F. and bake for 20 to 25 minutes, or until the meat is piping hot, the cheese is visibly bubbling, and the pastry is golden and crisp.

Serve the pigs-in-a-quilt on a tray, and place a bowl of your favorite mustard in the center with either a small butter knife or a demitasse spoon.

TIMING IS EVERYTHING
🐖 The pigs-in-a-quilt can be fully assembled and stored in the freezer for three months. Place them in a single layer on a shallow baking sheet and freeze until solid. Lay the frozen pastries in a labeled heavy-duty plastic container with a tight-fitting lid, separating each layer with a sheet of waxed paper. Transfer the pigs-in-a-quilt directly from the freezer onto a prepared baking sheet and, after glazing and immediately applying seeds, bake them in a preheated 400°F. oven for 30 to 35 minutes.

SERVED WITH CRINKLE POTATO CHIPS page 92,
AND HOMEMADE SPICY KETCHUP page 92

Garlic-scented
CRINKLE POTATO CHIPS
with Homemade Spicy Ketchup

Get ready to caution (more than once) to "slow down, dinner is coming." There is absolutely no way to resist these crisp, extra-long slices of fried potatoes. Serve the spicy ketchup slightly warmed or at room temperature with a spoon, so people can dress these oversized slices. The ketchup recipe can be doubled.

🍠 YIELD: 6 TO 8 SERVINGS

FOR THE SPICY KETCHUP

2 cups bottled chili sauce (I use Heinz)
1½ tablespoons Asian chili paste (available in Asian markets and some well-stocked supermarkets)
3 tablespoons unsulphured molasses
3 tablespoons packed brown sugar
3 tablespoons apple cider vinegar
¾ teaspoon Worcestershire sauce
Freshly ground black pepper to taste

FOR THE POTATO CHIPS

4 large Idaho potatoes
2 to 4 quarts flavorless cooking oil or highly refined peanut oil
8 garlic cloves
1 generous cup flat-leaf Italian parsley leaves, stems removed and the leaves very dry (optional)
Kosher or sea salt to taste

PREPARE THE KETCHUP. Combine all the ingredients except the black pepper in a small, heavy-bottomed, nonreactive saucepan. Over medium heat, bring the mixture to a bubble through the center, then reduce the heat to low. Simmer the ketchup gently, uncovered, until it has thickened and the flavors have blended well, about 10 minutes. Stir in a generous amount of black pepper and set aside. You should have about 2 cups ketchup. The ketchup tastes best when either served tepid (warm to the touch) or at room temperature.

PREPARE THE POTATOES. Fill a large bowl with ice water. Scrub the potatoes and either peel them or dry the skins thoroughly. Cut the potatoes into ⅛-inch slices using a handheld crinkle cutter or a sharp chef's knife, and immediately place the slices in the ice water to prevent them from oxidizing (turning brown) and also to remove some of their surface starch.

If using an electric deep-fat fryer, pour in the oil to the designated line and turn to the highest setting (or follow the manufacturer's instructions). Otherwise, fill a 4- to 8-quart heavy-bottomed saucepan half-way with oil. Attach a deep-frying thermometer securely onto the side of the pan (don't allow the tip to touch the pan's bottom). If desired, insert a frying basket into the oil. Heat the oil to 350°F. Working with one batch at a time, take a large handful of potato slices from the water and dry them very well on paper towels.

Fry each batch at 350°F. until softened, limp, and only beginning to turn golden, 4 to 6 minutes per batch. Remove the potatoes from the oil by lifting the handle on the frying basket, and carefully shake off any excess oil. Drain the potatoes on paper towels. (Alternatively, use a long-handled slotted utensil such as a wire spider to remove the potatoes from the oil.) Pile the potatoes into a large roasting pan lined with more paper towels and let the slices sit in the roasting pan at room temperature until you're ready for the final frying before serving. Set the pot of oil aside.

WHEN ALMOST READY TO SERVE, place a large, shallow baking sheet in the oven and preheat the oven to 325°F. Reheat the oil until it reaches 375°F. Make a deep slit in the garlic cloves without opening them up, and fry them in the hot oil until they're golden and have flavored the oil, about 3 minutes. Remove them using your slotted utensil and set them aside. Fry the potatoes for the second time, in batches, until they're golden and crisp, 3 to 5 minutes. Drain each batch on paper towels, then transfer them to the preheated baking sheet. Add the garlic to the hot oil, just long enough to reheat fully, then add to the platter of potatoes. Add the parsley to the hot oil, if using, and cook it for 10 seconds (the leaves will turn bright green). Use a triple-mesh wire sieve to retrieve the parsley and, after shaking it to remove any excess oil, add the parsley to the platter of potatoes. Use your hands to help the parsley and garlic filter down through the pile of potatoes. (At first, when you remove the parsley from the oil, it might seem limp, but it will become crisp very quickly. Don't overcook the parsley or the leaves will taste acrid.)

Sprinkle the potatoes with salt and serve them hot with the spicy ketchup.

TIMING IS EVERYTHING
❧ *The potatoes can be sliced early in the day and kept in a large bowl of ice water until ready to fry. The potatoes can be fried (for the first time) up to 4 hours in advance of the final frying. After the first frying, keep the limp slices at room temperature, covered loosely, until ready to refry and serve.*

HERE'S THE SCOOP:
On Pairing Cocktail Food with Your Menu

Before you decide on the foods to serve before dinner, choose your dinner menu. Although there are no hard-and-fast rules that apply here, it's best to try to avoid redundancy in flavors so that each can be thoroughly enjoyed. For instance, you wouldn't serve pigs-in-a-quilt before a smoked entree like ham. If you're having mashed potatoes as a side dish, I wouldn't suggest making homemade potato chips, no matter how delicious they are. Also, when you want to serve more than one starter, choose foods with contrasting color and texture. A pile of chilled, poached jumbo shrimp with a spicy cocktail sauce next to a crock of intensely flavored smoked trout spread with a basket of hot garlic toasts would be wonderful. On the other hand, pairing a gorgeous wheel of brie cheese encased in challah dough with a platter of stuffed mushrooms bolognese would seem too heavy and rich. So try to partner something substantial with a starter that's light. Remember, dinner is on its way.

POACHED JUMBO SHRIMP
with Spicy Cocktail Sauce

Shrimp cocktail is so easy and is always such a crowd pleaser. When poaching shrimp, remember to follow the instructions carefully to prevent overcooking, which leaves shrimp tough and rubbery. And if kids will be eating this, set aside some cocktail sauce before adding the horseradish, since it can be too assertive for some palates. YIELD: 6 SERVINGS

FOR THE POACHED SHRIMP
1 pound jumbo shrimp, shelled and rinsed, tails intact and shells reserved, and each shrimp deveined (see page 20)
1 quart (4 cups) Shrimp Stock or Roasted Vegetable Stock (page 22)
1 tablespoon kosher or sea salt

FOR THE COCKTAIL SAUCE
⅓ cup ketchup
⅔ cup bottled chili sauce (I use Heinz)
2 teaspoons Asian chili paste (available in Asian markets and some well-stocked supermarkets)
2 teaspoons strained fresh lemon juice
Prepared horseradish to taste (plain, not the beet-stained kind)
Lemon wedges

POACH THE SHRIMP. If you don't already have stock, use the reserved shrimp shells to make some using the directions on page 20. Otherwise, freeze these shells to use another time. To cook the shrimp, bring the stock to a rolling boil and reduce the heat to low. Fill a large bowl with ice water, then stir in the salt to help it dissolve. Place a large medium-mesh wire sieve over another mixing bowl, close to the stove. Rinse and drain the shrimp. Raise the heat under the stock to high and, when it begins to bubble again, stir in the shrimp. Reduce the heat to low and cook the shrimp, stirring occasionally, for 2½ to 3 minutes, uncovered, until the shrimp lose their translucency and turn pinkish white. Pour the stock with the shrimp into the sieve, allowing the stock to fall into the bowl beneath. Immediately plunge the shrimp into the other bowl of salted water and swish them around to help them cool. Drain the shrimp well, place them in a bowl, and chill them until just before serving.

MAKE THE COCKTAIL SAUCE. Combine the ketchup, chili sauce, chili paste, and lemon juice. Stir in the grated horseradish. Chill the sauce until ready to serve the shrimp. Surround the bowl of sauce with the shrimp and accompany with lemon wedges.

TIMING IS EVERYTHING
The sauce can be assembled and the shrimp can be poached one day ahead and kept refrigerated, separately, well covered.

BRIE EN CROÛTE
with Sautéed Onions, Garlic, Mushrooms, and Crisp Pancetta

Earthy yet majestic, Brie en Croûte is the perfect addition to a buffet table. This recipe represents yet another way I've discovered to use my challah dough. Traditionally, brioche is used to enclose the cheese, but I think challah dough is easier to make, much easier to handle, and even better-tasting than brioche—especially this cheesy, chive-laced version. Make sure to let the fresh baked Brie rest for an hour before serving so that the cheese will be seductively warm and runny. If you serve it too soon, or too late, the cheese won't be the right temperature, and thus the right consistency. Oh, and don't line your serving platter with a paper doily since this will make it more difficult to serve. ❧ YIELD: 12 TO 14 APPETIZER SERVINGS OR 20 TO 22 WHEN PART OF A BUFFET*

¼ pound pancetta, thinly sliced

3 tablespoons extra-virgin olive oil

1 large yellow onion, sliced into thin wedges

2 garlic cloves, chopped

1 tablespoon minced fresh thyme

Kosher or sea salt and freshly ground black pepper to taste

⅓ to ½ cup thinly sliced fresh chives (if unavailable, mince the deeper green part of a scallion)

10 ounces mixed mushrooms, wiped clean and sliced or diced

¼ cup dry white wine

Egg glaze: 1 egg mixed with 1 egg yolk and 1 tablespoon water

1 recipe dough Six-strand Braided Challah (the savory version, page 226), fully risen and well chilled

1 wheel (2 pounds) plain, peppered, or herbed Brie cheese, well chilled

Unbleached all-purpose flour for shaping

Cornmeal and assorted seeds—sesame, poppy, caraway

Up to 2 tablespoons freshly grated Parmigiano-Reggiano cheese (optional)

COOK THE PANCETTA in a 12-inch, deep-sided skillet over medium heat and, when crisp on both sides, drain on paper towels. Dump out the fat but don't wipe out the pan. Place the skillet back over high heat and, when hot, add 1 tablespoon of the olive oil. When the oil is hot, add the onion and garlic and cook, stirring frequently, until tender, very fragrant, and golden, about 6 minutes. Stir in the thyme and cook a minute more, just to heat the herb and release its flavor. Season the onion with salt and pepper and stir in the chives. Scrape the cooked onion into a bowl.

Put the pan back over high heat and add the remaining 2 tablespoons olive oil. When the oil is hot, add the mushrooms and cook, stirring occasionally, until they are tender and golden, 4 to 5 minutes. Add the wine and, as the liquid bubbles furiously, scrape up any caramelized residue from the pan, and cook until the wine evaporates. Season with salt and pepper, then add the

mushrooms to the sautéed onion. Roughly chop the cooked pancetta into small pieces and fold into the vegetables. Let the topping cool completely at room temperature.

To ASSEMBLE, mix the glaze and strain it into a small bowl, making it easier to apply. Line a baking sheet with parchment paper and sprinkle the paper lightly with cornmeal and assorted seeds if desired. Place the sheet close to your work surface, next to the glaze and your cooled topping.

Turn the cold dough out of its bowl onto a lightly floured work surface and knead it, gently, a few times to make it easier to cut. Cut off two-thirds of the dough and reserve the remaining third for another recipe. Divide the larger piece of dough in half. Then divide one half into two pieces, one being twice the size of the other. You'll now have three pieces of dough of all different sizes—small, medium, and large. Cover the dough as you work with one piece at a time.

ROLL THE MEDIUM-SIZE PIECE of dough into a circle that is 1½ inches larger than the wheel of cheese and ¼ inch thick. To check the size, place the wheel in the center of the round after rolling. Remove the cheese and set it aside. Place that bottom round to the side as well. Roll the largest piece of dough out to a circle that's about 3 inches larger than the first one, dusting the pin and your work surface with flour as needed to prevent sticking.

Place the cheese in the center of the smaller round of dough. Using a soft pastry brush, paint the exposed border of dough surrounding the cheese with the egg glaze. Lift this glazed border and press it onto the sides of the cheese so it adheres. Mound the cooled topping on top of the cheese and place the second (larger) circle of dough over the topping. Lift the wheel and, using your working hand, tuck the draping dough underneath. Sit the enclosed cheese on the prepared baking sheet and use a sturdy rubber spatula to shove any slack dough underneath until uniform-looking all the way around. Brush the exposed top and sides of the dough with the egg glaze.

Roll out the remaining smallest piece of dough into a thin 9-inch round. To create a lattice design, cut the round into even ⅓-inch-wide strips and, one by one, place the dough strips 1 inch apart on top of the glazed surface, stretching them slightly before setting them in place so each strip reaches across the top and all the way down the sides of the encased cheese. Shove the ends of the strips underneath the cheese and brush the strips with glaze. Place another layer of strips on top of the first at an angle, creating a diamond lattice pattern. Tuck these ends underneath the enclosed cheese, as well. To give extra dimension to the design, gently apply pressure (using both index fingers) to the top strips just where they surround the bottom ones. Brush the lattice once more with the egg glaze. Let the filled dough rise, uncovered, for 1 hour. (Reserve the remaining glaze.)

Preheat the oven to 375°F. with the rack on the center shelf for the last 30 minutes of the rise.

To bake, glaze the exposed dough once more and, if desired, sprinkle the top with one or an assortment of seeds. Sprinkle the top lightly with kosher salt and bake until uniformly golden brown all over, 35 to 45 minutes. If desired, sprinkle the top with the Parmesan cheese for the last 10 minutes of baking. Remove from the oven and place the sheet on a wire rack. Let the cheese rest this way for 1 hour before presenting, whole, on a platter. To serve, cut into wedges.

TIMING IS EVERYTHING

The Brie en Croûte can be fully baked several hours ahead of serving and reheated on its baking sheet in a preheated 375°F. oven for 15 minutes. Let it sit for 20 to 30 minutes before you serve it.

Garlicky Roasted
RED PEPPER AND FETA SPREAD

A great combination. Garlic, roasted peppers, salted feta cheese—all blended with the added punch of cumin and red pepper flakes. The best part (other than the taste) is that this dip gets even better after sitting around in the refrigerator for a day or so before serving, making it a great choice to have on hand for impromptu weekend guests. And for best flavor, texture, and longevity, always buy fresh feta cheese sold in blocks and steeped in water. ❧ YIELD: 3 CUPS

1 teaspoon cumin seeds, or ½ teaspoon ground cumin

1 scant teaspoon red pepper flakes, or less for tamer spread

½ teaspoon aromatic dried oregano, crumbled

1½ teaspoons unsalted butter

½ cup walnuts

3 medium red bell peppers or pimientos, roasted, skinned, seeded, and sliced (see page 24)

1 tablespoon extra-virgin olive oil

3 garlic cloves, minced

1 generous cup (8 to 10 ounces) best-quality salted feta cheese, well drained

Kosher or sea salt and freshly ground black pepper to taste

¼ generous cup chopped cilantro

Suggested accompaniments: warmed triangles of soft pita bread and diagonally sliced seedless cucumbers

HEAT A 10-INCH heavy-bottomed skillet over medium heat and, when hot, add the cumin. Cook, stirring constantly, until fragrant and light golden, about 2 minutes for seeds (1 minute for ground). Stir in the red pepper flakes and oregano, and cook them for just a few seconds. Immediately transfer the spices to a bowl and let cool until just warm. Don't wash out the skillet. Grind the spices to a powder using either a spice grinder or a mortar and pestle (please don't put your face directly over the ground spices, since the fumes can make you cough furiously). Place a doubled sheet of paper towels on a plate on the counter. Melt the butter over medium heat in the same skillet used to toast the spices and, when bubbling, add the walnuts. Stir the nuts constantly until light golden and fragrant, about 2 minutes. Pour them onto the paper towels to drain.

Place the well-drained peppers, ground spices, toasted walnuts, olive oil, garlic, and half the cheese in the bowl of a food processor fitted with the steel blade. Pulse the mixture until pretty smooth. Add some pepper, the remaining feta, and the cilantro. Pulse until well mixed but not soupy. Taste for seasoning, adding salt if necessary. Transfer the dip to a decorative crock and store in the refrigerator, well covered, for at least 4 hours and as much as two days before serving.

About 30 minutes before serving, take the dip out of the refrigerator. Serve the dip surrounded by pita bread and cucumbers.

TIMING IS EVERYTHING

❧ *The dip can be fully assembled up to two days ahead and kept refrigerated, well covered.*

A Crostini You'll Never Forget . . .
OVEN-ROASTED TOMATOES,
Peppers, Bocconcini, Olives, and Capers on Garlic Toast

If you're looking to impress someone, you should know that this platter of roasted tomatoes, adorned with all the savory goodies listed in this recipe title, is unbelievably gorgeous, very delicious, and truly dazzling to guests. Hot garlic toasts, piled high in a basket, provide the perfect invitation to dig in and pile it on.

🥄 YIELD: 8 OR MORE SERVINGS

12 ripe plum (Roma) tomatoes, peeled (see page 33)
Garlic Confit Oil (page 23) or extra-virgin olive oil
Kosher or sea salt and freshly ground black pepper to taste
Up to 1 teaspoon *herbes de Provence*, crumbled
4 large yellow bell peppers, roasted, peeled, and seeded (see page 24)

4 to 8 ounces bocconcini (small balls of fresh mozzarella cheese), drained and halved
½ cup oil-cured or Kalamata olives, pitted and neatly halved (see page 184)
1 rounded tablespoon capers, drained
Red pepper flakes (optional)
¼ to ½ cup chiffonade of fresh basil (see below)
Garlic Toast (page 45)

PREHEAT THE OVEN TO 425°F. Halve each peeled tomato lengthwise, and use a short, flexible serrated knife to cut out and discard the central membrane and the seed cavity, keeping the flesh intact. Line a large shallow baking sheet with aluminum foil (shiny side up) and brush the foil with the oil. Sprinkle the surface lightly but evenly with some salt, pepper, and *herbes de Provence*. Place the prepared tomatoes on the sheet, rounded sides up, in neat rows and brush the tops with some more oil. Season the tops with salt and pepper and roast the tomatoes for 20 minutes, or until they've become blistered on top with slightly charred edges. Remove from the oven and place the sheet on a wire rack to cool. Once cool, brush the tomatoes lightly with more oil. Set the sheet aside, uncovered, until ready to assemble your platter.

HERE'S THE SCOOP:
On Creating Ribbons of Fresh Basil

Creating a chiffonade of fresh basil is easy and it can be done ahead, if stored properly. Gently rinse and dry your basil leaves. Stack the leaves underside down and roll the stack up widthwise (as if you're making a cigar). Using a sharp chef's knife, thinly slice the leaves, then unravel the slices into thin ribbons. Use them now or store them in the refrigerator for up to 24 hours, wrapped in a piece of paper towel and stored in a plastic bag. Also, when you're preparing a sauce that uses a hefty amount of freshly chopped basil, although you shouldn't chop it ahead, you can create a chiffonade in advance. Simply run your knife over the ribbons just before adding it to your sauce.

About an hour before serving, assemble the platter. Arrange the tomato halves on a large round serving platter, cavity sides down and slightly overlapping. Cut each roasted pepper into as many small squares, rounds, or hearts as possible using a 1-inch fluted cutter. (Save scraps for another use.) Place the roasted peppers, bocconcini, olives, and capers decoratively on top of the tomatoes and sprinkle the top very sparingly with red pepper flakes, if using. If using Garlic Confit Oil, squeeze several of the cooked cloves of garlic out of their papery skins and scatter them around the tomatoes. Drizzle everything lightly with more oil, grind on more black pepper, then strew the ribbons of basil either over the top or around the edges, in a border. Serve with freshly made garlic toasts. Store any leftovers in the refrigerator, covered. Bring close to room temperature before serving for best flavor.

TIMING IS
EVERYTHING
Although the platter should be assembled an hour or two before serving, the tomatoes can be roasted early on the day of serving and kept at room temperature. All the remaining components of the dish, except the basil, can be accomplished two days ahead and refrigerated, seperately, well covered.

(CLOCKWISE FROM TOP LEFT) RED PEPPER AND FETA
SPREAD page 99, GARLIC TOASTS page 45, SMOKED TROUT
SPREAD page 106, MATZOS page 258, SAVORY MUSHROOM
SPREAD page 104, CRINKLE POTATO CHIPS page 92,
LOTSA-ONIONS CREAMY DIP page 107

No, It's Not Chopped Liver . . .
SAVORY MUSHROOM SPREAD

It always amazes me how this meatless spread really does look like perfectly pre-pared chopped liver. I'll often include it when I want to serve something savory to my vegetarian friends and family members before dinner. Having said that, you certainly don't have to be a vegetarian to enjoy this wonderful mixture, made from an abundance of sautéed mushrooms, onions, garlic, and firm-cooked eggs.

❦ YIELD: ABOUT 2 CUPS (RECIPE CAN BE DOUBLED)

½ pound each button and shiitake mushrooms, wiped clean

2 extra-large eggs

Kosher or sea salt and freshly ground black pepper to taste

4½ tablespoons Garlic Confit Oil (page 23) or extra-virgin olive oil

1 large yellow onion, sliced into very thin wedges and separated into strips

6 garlic cloves, minced

¼ cup minced fresh chives

Suggested accompaniments: Matzos (page 258), Garlic Toast (page 45), or warmed crackers

CUT OFF AND DISCARD the stems of the shiitake mushrooms and trim away any tough bottoms on the stems of the button mushrooms. Chop the mushrooms into small but textural pieces and combine them in one bowl.

Place the eggs in a 2-quart saucepan and add enough cold water to cover by 2 inches. Place the pan, uncovered, over medium heat and, as soon as the water begins to bubble, sprinkle in a generous teaspoon of salt. Bring the water to a full boil, then cover the pan and remove it from the hot burner. Let the pan sit undisturbed for 15 minutes. Drain and immediately run the eggs under cool water, just until they're cool enough to handle. While still very warm, crack and remove the shells. Place the eggs in a large mixing bowl.

HEAT A 12-INCH heavy-bottomed skillet over high heat and, when hot, add 1½ tablespoons of the oil. When the oil is very hot but not smoking, stir in the onion. Cook over high heat, stirring frequently, until the onion is reduced and beginning to turn golden, about 8 minutes. Stir in half of the garlic, reduce the heat to medium-high, and continue to cook, stirring occasionally, until the onion is deeply caramelized, about 10 minutes more. Season with salt and black pepper, then transfer the onion to a bowl. Put the skillet back on the stove without wiping out the interior.

Heat the same pan over high heat with the remaining 3 tablespoons oil. When the oil is hot, add the mushrooms and cook them, stirring frequently, over high heat until they begin to release their juices. Stir in the remaining garlic and continue to cook until the mushrooms turn golden and give off a very savory aroma. Season with salt and pepper, then stir in the cooked onion and the chives. Heat the vegetables just for a minute, then use a wooden spatula to scrape up any caramelized bits of onion and mushroom from the bottom of the skillet. Transfer the sautéed mixture to the bowl of a food processor fitted with the steel blade.

PLACE THE COOKED EGGS on top of the sautéed mixture in the processor and add a good dose of salt and black pepper. Pulse the vegetables and eggs together until finely chopped but not pureed (the mixture will look exactly like a batch of chopped chicken liver). Transfer the spread to a decorative bowl or crock and smooth the top. Sprinkle salt and pepper on top, then let the spread cool, covered with a doubled sheet of paper towels, at room temperature. Once cool, for best flavor, chill the spread for several hours (or up to two days), leaving the paper towels in place and wrapping over it with plastic wrap or aluminum foil.

Let the dish sit at room temperature for 30 minutes before serving with garlic toast or matzos your favorite store-bought crackers, warmed on a shallow baking sheet in a preheated 350°F. oven for 5 to 10 minutes.

TIMING IS
EVERYTHING
❧ *The spread can be fully assembled two days ahead and kept refrigerated, well covered.*

SMOKED TROUT SPREAD
with Crunchy Cucumbers and Crisp Garlic Toast

I can't count how many times I've served this fabulous spread, always to rave reviews. If smoked trout is either not available or not in your budget, use an equal amount of well-drained best-quality canned salmon instead. Either way, leftovers are equally delicious when slathered on your morning toast!

❧ YIELD: ABOUT 3 CUPS

2 cups firmly packed skinned and flaked smoked
    trout (1 generous pound fillets)
½ cup packed minced scallions (white and 1½ inches
    of green), plus 2 additional tablespoons for garnish
¾ cup mayonnaise
2 garlic cloves, minced
1 teaspoon strained fresh lemon juice

1 teaspoon freshly ground white pepper
2 rounded tablespoons chopped flat-leaf Italian
    parsley
Freshly ground black pepper to taste
Suggested accompaniments: seedless cucumbers
    sliced ¼ inch thick on the diagonal, endive spears,
    Garlic Toast (page 45), and/or Matzos (page 258)

TIMING IS
EVERYTHING

❧ *The trout spread can be fully assembled but not garnished up to two days ahead of serving and kept refrigerated, well covered.*

PLACE THE TROUT, ½ cup scallions, the mayonnaise, garlic, lemon juice, and white pepper in the bowl of a food processor fitted with the steel blade. Pulse the mixture until finely chopped but not mousselike. Add the parsley and a generous amount of black pepper and pulse just until incorporated. Transfer the spread to a decorative crock and refrigerate it, covered, for 4 hours or up to two days before serving.

Just before serving, grind on a bit more black pepper and apply a border of the remaining minced scallions around the sides of the dish. Surround the spread with cucumber slices and crisp matzos or stand some endive spears, pointed ends up, in a short glass. For an additional, highly aromatic accompaniment, present a linen-lined basket filled with hot garlic toasts. Any leftover spread is good for several days if kept chilled and covered securely.

LOTSA-ONIONS CREAMY DIP

Be prepared to chase your family out of the kitchen so they don't eat all of this dip before your guests arrive (especially when you're busy frying homemade potato chips!). Although I've listed Bovril, which is a thick meat extract found in most markets, as an optional ingredient, it's highly suggested, since it lends an interesting depth of flavor and a slightly deeper hue to the overall dip. Having said this, when serving my kosher or vegetarian friends, I leave this ingredient out and they love it anyway. ❦ YIELD: 2½ CUPS

2 generous tablespoons dehydrated minced onion
1 tablespoon extra-virgin olive oil
1 cup packed finely chopped yellow onion
1 large shallot, minced
Kosher or sea salt and freshly ground black pepper
   to taste
½ cup thinly sliced fresh chives, plus extra for garnish

8 ounces whipped cream cheese, close to room
   temperature
½ cup sour cream
½ teaspoon Bovril (optional)
Suggested accompaniments: Crinkle Potato Chips
   (page 92) or a favorite store-bought brand and/or
   an assortment of crudités

HEAT A 10-INCH heavy-bottomed skillet over medium-high heat and, when hot, add the dehydrated onion. Cook the onion, stirring constantly, until golden but not overly dark. Immediately pour the onion into a bowl, then put the skillet back on the stove.

Heat the same skillet over medium-high heat and, when hot, add the olive oil. When the oil is hot, stir in the chopped fresh onion and sauté, stirring occasionally, until it begins to turn golden, about 5 minutes. Stir in the shallot and cook until the onion is a bit more golden, 3 to 4 minutes. Season well with salt and black pepper, and stir in the toasted onion and the chives. Remove the pan from the stove and let the onions cool.

MEANWHILE, MASH THE CREAM CHEESE with the sour cream until somewhat blended, using a rubber spatula. Add the Bovril, if using, and salt and pepper to taste and mix well. Fold in the cooled vegetable mixture thoroughly. Cover the dip and chill for at least 2 hours and up to 24 hours before serving. To take the chill off, remove the dip from the refrigerator 20 to 30 minutes before serving.

Serve surrounded by freshly fried potato chips and/or an assortment of crudités. (If using store-bought chips, warm them on a shallow baking sheet in a preheated 350°F. oven for 10 minutes.)

TIMING IS
EVERYTHING
❦ *As the recipe directs,
the dip should be made in
advance so the flavors
can meld. For best taste,
however, it's best not to
exceed 24 hours.*

A Quartet of Recipes Starring Chewy Dates

Perfectly sweet and seductively chewy, dates are irresistible with cheese, nuts, and cured ham. So here I've provided four different great ways to serve them during the cocktail hour. And since dried dates easily cross the line from savory nibble to sweet miniature dessert, don't hesitate to serve any of these versions as a delicious addition to a cheese course to conclude a special meal. Without a doubt, dried dates with the best flavor and texture are those large, supple, unpitted Medjool found either in Middle Eastern markets or in health food stores.

SAGA-STUFFED DATES

Wrapped in Prosciutto

 YIELD: 32 PIECES (RECIPE MAY BE HALVED)

⅓ cup Saga Blue cheese, rind removed and the cheese brought to room temperature

¼ cup whipped cream cheese, at room temperature

Freshly ground black pepper to taste

16 large, best-quality dried dates

¾ to 1 pound thinly sliced prosciutto

TIMING IS
EVERYTHING
 The dates can be fully assembled one day ahead and kept refrigerated, well covered. For best flavor and texture, remove from the refrigerator 30 minutes to 1 hour before serving.

COMBINE THE SAGA BLUE and cream cheese, and season with black pepper. Stuff the dates following the instructions given in the following recipe.

Trim off any excess fat from each piece of prosciutto using kitchen scissors. If the slices are very long, cut them in half widthwise. Lay a stuffed date at one end of a slice of prosciutto and roll it up, enclosing it completely. Place in a single layer on a serving platter.

DATES STUFFED
with Roquefort Cheese and Topped with Walnuts

❦ YIELD: 32 PIECES (RECIPE MAY BE HALVED)

16 large, best-quality dried dates
⅓ cup creamy Roquefort cheese, at room temperature
¼ cup whipped cream cheese, at room temperature
Freshly ground black pepper to taste

1 tablespoon unsalted butter
½ cup walnuts, finely chopped
Kosher or sea salt to taste

TIMING IS
EVERYTHING
❦ *The dates can be filled with cheese one day ahead and kept refrigerated, well covered.*
❦ *The nuts can be pan-toasted a few hours ahead. Just before serving, rewarm them for 5 minutes on a shallow baking sheet at 350°F., wrapped loosely in an aluminum foil pouch.*

SLIT EACH DATE lengthwise and remove the pit. Slice each date into two equal lengthwise pieces. Using a sturdy rubber spatula or a fork, combine the cheeses until well mixed, then season to taste with black pepper. Use a small spreader to fill each date half with the cheese, spreading it out flush with rim of the fruit.

Place a doubled piece of paper towel on a plate and set it aside. Melt the butter in a small 8-inch skillet over medium heat and, when hot and bubbling, add the chopped walnuts. Sauté the nuts, stirring constantly, until light golden, being careful not to scorch them. Transfer the nuts to the paper towels to drain. Keep the nuts warm until ready to assemble and serve.

JUST BEFORE SERVING, dip each stuffed date, cheese side down, in the sautéed nuts and place them right side up on your platter. Sprinkle the tops lightly with salt and serve.

DATES WITH PROSCIUTTO
and a Pile of Shaved Parmesan Cheese

❧ YIELD: 10 TO 12 SERVINGS

12 large, best-quality dried dates
¾ pound thinly sliced prosciutto

A generous wedge (about 12 ounces) best-quality
Parmigiano-Reggiano cheese

HALVE THE DATES and trim the prosciutto, as directed on page 108. Shave curls of cheese from the flat narrow sides of a wedge of Parmesan cheese, using either a sturdy vegetable peeler or a handheld cheese shaver. Arrange the dates pitted sides up around the border of your platter. Drape the pieces of prosciutto gently on top of one another just inside the border of dates, leaving an empty round space in the center. Fill this space with the shaved cheese, mounding it in a pile. Invite your guests to fill each date with some shaved cheese and wrap it in a piece of prosciutto. (An alternative to shaving the Parmesan is to chip the cheese into small irregular shards using a short, sharp knife. Pile these in the center, as described.)

TIMING IS EVERYTHING
❧ *The platter can be assembled (without positioning the cheeses) early in the day of serving and kept refrigerated, well covered. Remove from the refrigerator 30 minutes to one hour before serving, and pile the cheese in the center just before serving so it maintains its height.*

WHOLE DATES
Stuffed with Shards of Parmesan Cheese

❧ YIELD: 8 TO 10 SERVINGS

12 large, best-quality dried dates

1 small wedge (about 8 ounces) best-quality
Parmigiano-Reggiano cheese

MAKE A LENGTHWISE SLIT in each date and remove the pit but keep both halves attached at the spine. Mound some small shards of cheese in each date, filling it from side to side. Line the dates up on your platter in a single layer, cheese side up, and serve.

TIMING IS EVERYTHING
❧ *The stuffed dates can be assembled early on the day of serving and kept refrigerated, well covered. Let sit out for 30 minutes to 1 hour before serving.*

COLD SEAFOOD SALAD page 124

CHAPTER FOUR
SUBSTANTIAL
and SATISFYING
SALADS

IN THIS CHAPTER, you'll find a vast array of savory main-dish salads featuring beef, chicken, fish, sautéed vegetables, fruits, nuts, and cheese. And because I know that it's so easy to get into a rut when it comes to choosing dressing every night, I've also provided lots of delicious salad dressings to help bring more diversity to your side salads. These dressings can all be made ahead and kept refrigerated so you'll have one less thing to think about at the end of a hard day. When serving hearty salads as a main dish, all that's needed to complete the picture is a loaf of great bread or a basket of fresh biscuits. And several of these salads are prepared in stages, so do take advantage of the steps that can be done in advance.

A Sea of Salad Dressings

Are you in a salad dressing rut? Most of us are. Let's face it: even the best vinaigrette can become a real bore if you make only one kind. To help shake things up a bit I've provided lots of concoctions. For best flavor, bring salad dressings close to room temperature before using. After use, store any extra dressing in a sealed jar or a well-covered bowl to use throughout the week. For the best texture in salads, pair the right dressing with the appropriate greens. For instance, vinaigrettes are the best choice when serving tender, young greens like mesclun. Stronger leaves like romaine, iceberg, radicchio, cabbage, and even endive can stand up to creamier, more weighty dressings.

And finally, don't limit these dressings to just salads since, with the exception of the creamy ones, they can also be used as flavor-packed marinades. Don't marinate fish for longer than 12 hours (four hours is preferable), however, or the texture will suffer. Poultry and pork can be marinated for 12 to 24 hours, and beef, lamb, and veal for 24 hours.

VINAIGRETTES

Classic Shallot Vinaigrette

Mix 1 heaping teaspoon Dijon mustard (regular or whole-grain) with 1/3 cup red or white wine vinegar or strained fresh lemon juice, 1 large minced shallot, and 1/2 teaspoon kosher salt. Whisk in 3/4 to 1 cup extra-virgin olive oil. Add black pepper to taste. Makes about 1 cup.

Robust Italian Vinaigrette

Mix 2 heaping tablespoons Dijon mustard with 1/2 cup red wine vinegar, 4 minced garlic cloves, 1 rounded teaspoon kosher salt, 1/4 teaspoon red pepper flakes, and 3 tablespoons pickling liquid from Giardiniera salad or jarred hot cherry peppers (found either on the condiment shelf or in the refrigerated section of your supermarket). Whisk in 1 cup plus 3 tablespoons olive oil (ideally a mixture of pure and extra-virgin). Stir in 1 rounded teaspoon crumbled aromatic dried oregano and black pepper to taste. Refrigerate for few hours, well covered, so the flavors can come together. Let the dressing sit out for 30 minutes to 1 hour before using. Makes about 2 cups.

Scallion Vinaigrette

Mix 1 heaping tablespoon Dijon mustard with 1/2 cup red wine vinegar, 2 minced garlic cloves, and 1 teaspoon kosher salt. Whisk in 1 cup olive oil (pure and extra-virgin), and when homogenous, add 1/2 cup minced scallions (white and 1 1/2 inches of green) along with a generous amount of black pepper and 1 teaspoon crumbled dried oregano. Makes about 2 cups.

"The Bomb" Mustard Vinaigrette

Whisk 1/2 cup Dijon mustard with 1/3 cup red wine vinegar, 3 minced garlic cloves, 1 minced shallot, and 1/2 rounded teaspoon kosher salt. Whisk in 3/4 cup olive oil (pure and extra-virgin) and season with freshly ground black pepper to taste. If desired, stir in 3 tablespoons drained capers and/or chopped fresh basil. Season liberally with black pepper. Makes about 1 2/3 cups, without the optional additions. (This dressing is called "The Bomb" by my kids. Apparently, this means "the best" in early 21st-century American adolescent lingo.)

Hazelnut Vinaigrette

Mix 1/3 cup sherry vinegar with 1/4 cup coarse-grained Dijon mustard, 1 teaspoon sugar, and 1 rounded teaspoon kosher salt. Whisk in 1/2 cup each hazelnut oil and pure olive oil. Add black pepper to taste. Makes about 1 1/2 cups.

Sherry Vinaigrette

Mix 2 generous tablespoons Dijon mustard with 1/2 cup sherry vinegar, 1 generous teaspoon kosher salt, and 2 minced large shallots. Whisk in 1/2 cup each pure olive oil and cold-pressed walnut oil. Add black pepper to taste. Makes about 1 1/2 cups.

Raspberry Vinaigrette

Mix 1 generous teaspoon Dijon mustard with 1 minced large shallot, 1/3 cup raspberry vinegar, 1 1/2 tablespoons sugar (or to taste), and 1 teaspoon salt. Whisk in 1/2 cup plus 1 tablespoon pure olive oil (not extra-virgin). Add black pepper to taste. Makes about 1 cup.

Gorgonzola Vinaigrette

Mix 1 generous tablespoon Dijon mustard with 1/2 cup sherry vinegar, 1 generous teaspoon kosher salt, and 2 minced large garlic cloves. Whisk in 1 cup olive oil (pure and extra-virgin). Stir in 1/2 rounded cup finely crumbled aged Mountain Gorgonzola cheese, 2 tablespoons minced scallions, and black pepper to taste. Makes about 2 cups.

HAZELNUT
VINAIGRETTE

PEANUT-
SESAME-SOY
DRESSING

RASPBERRY
VINAIGRETTE

SCALLION VINAIGRETTE

THOUSAND ISLAND
DRESSING

CLASSIC SHALLOT
VINAIGRETTE

TANGY FRENCH
DRESSING

GREEN GODDESS DRESSING

Lemon-Lime Vinaigrette

Mix 2 tablespoons each red wine vinegar, strained fresh lemon juice, and strained fresh lime juice. Add 1 heaping teaspoon Dijon mustard, ½ rounded teaspoon kosher salt, ½ teaspoon freshly ground white pepper, ½ teaspoon crumbled aromatic dried oregano, and a generous amount of black pepper. Whisk in ½ cup olive oil (pure and extra-virgin) until homogenized. Makes about 1 cup.

Tangy French Dressing

In a blender or food processor fitted with the steel blade, blend ⅓ cup red wine vinegar, 2 tablespoons ketchup, 1 generous teaspoon Asian chili paste, 1 tablespoon sugar, 1 teaspoon kosher salt, ½ teaspoon sweet paprika, 2 minced garlic cloves, black pepper to taste, and 1 cup flavorless oil, preferably safflower oil. Makes about 1½ cups.

Honey Dijon Dressing

Whisk together 3 generous tablespoons Dijon mustard and 2 tablespoons mild-flavored honey. Add 1 minced large shallot, ½ generous teaspoon kosher salt, and ⅓ cup red wine vinegar. Whisk in ¾ cup olive oil (pure and extra-virgin). Add ground black pepper to taste. Makes about 1¾ cups.

Sesame-Ginger Dressing

Whisk together ½ cup unseasoned rice vinegar and 1 tablespoon strained fresh lemon juice, 1 heaping teaspoon wasabi paste, 1 tablespoon soy sauce, 1 tablespoon minced fresh ginger, and ⅓ cup minced scallions. Whisk in 1 cup of oil (equal amounts of pure olive oil and cold-pressed peanut oil). Stir in 2 to 4 tablespoons dry-toasted sesame seeds and 1 tablespoon toasted sesame oil. Makes about 2½ cups.

Peanut-Sesame-Soy Dressing

Using a blender or a food processor fitted with the steel blade, puree 1 cup smooth peanut butter, ½ cup simmering water, 3 tablespoons strained fresh lemon juice, 4 tablespoons unseasoned rice vinegar, 2 tablespoons mild-flavored honey, and 2 tablespoons soy sauce, preferably tamari. Add 1 tablespoon each minced garlic and minced fresh ginger, along with 1 tablespoon toasted sesame oil and blend again. Makes about 2¼ cups.

CREAMY DRESSINGS

Mayo-All-the-Way

Mix 2 cups of your favorite mayonnaise with 1 scant cup of minced shallots and ½ cup minced chives or scallions. (If using scallions, use the white part and 1½ to 2 inches of the green.) Add black pepper to taste and enough milk to thin the dressing just to a thick pouring consistency. Makes about 3 cups.

Creamy Ranch Dressing

Mix 1 cup mayonnaise with ⅔ cup plain yogurt, ⅓ cup sour cream, ¼ cup minced yellow onion, 2 minced garlic cloves, ½ teaspoon kosher salt, and ¼ cup each minced flat-leaf Italian parsley and chives. Add black pepper to taste. Makes about 2¼ cups.

Thousand Island Dressing

Mix 1 cup mayonnaise with ½ cup bottled Heinz chili sauce, ⅓ generous cup each minced yellow onion and drained and minced bread and butter pickles. Add 1 tablespoon pickle juice and black pepper to taste. Makes about 2⅓ cups.

Green Goddess Dressing

In a blender or a food processor fitted with the steel blade, blend 1 cup mayonnaise with ½ cup sour cream, 2 tablespoons red wine vinegar, 1 tablespoon Dijon mustard, 4 mashed good-size anchovy fillets, and 2 minced large garlic cloves. Add 1 generous cup green herbs without their stems (flat-leaf Italian parsley, dill, chives, and fresh basil) and black pepper to taste, and blend until the herbs are well incorporated and the dressing takes on a greenish hue. Makes about 1½ cups.

Creamy Blue Cheese Dressing
Use a wide blending fork to blend 1 cup mayonnaise with 8 ounces (1 generous cup) good-quality crumbled Gorgonzola cheese. Use a whisk to mix in ⅓ cup half-and-half (or whole milk), ¼ cup white wine vinegar, 2 teaspoons Dijon mustard, 2 minced garlic cloves, ¼ teaspoon kosher salt, and black pepper to taste. Makes about 2¼ cups.

HERE'S THE SCOOP:
On Nonperishables That Are Great for Salads

Keeping a pantry shelf lined with nonperishable jarred and canned ingredients will make it extra easy for you to embellish a bowl of mixed greens in a colorful, textural, and, of course, flavorful way. Try to always have at least one jar or can of the following:

- **Anchovy fillets.** Those packed in glass jars seem to have the best texture. Canned ones are usually mushy.
- **Beans.** Keep an assortment of canned cooked beans; after opening, rinse and drain well before adding to salad.
- **Capers.** Although tiny capers are chic, I love the chubbier ones packed in balsamic vinegar. Salt-packed capers are also good, but rinse and drain well before using them. Capers are fun to throw into salads (but know your audience, since their flavor is quite assertive).
- **Canned vegetables** (assorted). Vegetables like corn and plain and pickled beets are handy.
- **Giardiniera salad.** These are mixed assorted vegetables in a spicy pickling liquid.
- **Hearts of palm.** Drain, dry, and cut canned hearts into rounds. Trim off any tough parts.
- **Marinated artichoke hearts.** Save the marinade and add some to a vinaigrette to taste.
- **Mustard.** Have an assortment of kinds, with different textures.
- **Oils.** Cold-pressed oils, especially those derived from nuts, are highly perishable and should be kept refrigerated once opened. Purchase these in small bottles since, once opened, their flavor loses its spark quickly. And because these oils congeal when chilled, steep the bottle in a drinking glass half full of very hot tap water for 6 minutes or until it returns to pouring consistency. Alternatively, leave the bottle out of refrigeration for several hours on the day you plan to use it.
- **Olives.** Have an assortment of green and black olives, each with a different degree of saltiness.
- **Roasted peppers.** Available in both red and yellow. Choose a brand that provides large, firm peppers.
- **Vinegars.** Have an assortment of flavored vinegars. Fruit-based or herb-filled vinegars should be kept refrigerated once opened.

SERVED WITH PANE DI CASA page 233

THE AMAZING COBB SALAD

Boy, Mr. Cobb was sure having a good day when he invented his amazing chopped salad at the famous Brown Derby Restaurant in Hollywood. Here, I've provided my rendition, and when fully assembled and presented, this salad is just so amazing to look at (before it's tossed) that you'll never regret taking the time to chop the ingredients. Since most of the ingredients are do-ahead, this salad makes a perfect choice for a luncheon or a light dinner.

🍃 YIELD: 6 GENEROUS SERVINGS AS A MAIN COURSE

1 large head romaine lettuce and 1 head iceberg lettuce, cleaned, spun dry, and coarsely chopped

4 extra-large eggs, hard-boiled and peeled while still warm, then chopped

1 medium red onion, minced

¼ cup chopped scallions (white part and 1½ to 2 inches of green)

1 large or 2 medium ripe but firm Hass avocados, peeled, diced, and tossed with 1 tablespoon strained fresh lemon juice

2 large red bell peppers (or mix red and yellow), roasted, skinned, seeded, and chopped (see page 24)

One 5.75-ounce can jumbo black olives, drained, pitted (see page 184), and chopped

1½ cups cherry tomatoes, halved through the stem end (quartered, if large)

1 pound fresh beets, boiled with skins until tender, then peeled and diced, or one 15-ounce can cooked whole beets, drained and diced

2 cups (8 ounces) sugar snap peas, parboiled for 2 minutes, refreshed, and chopped

8 ounces aged Mountain Gorgonzola cheese, crumbled (or chopped Jarlsberg cheese)

12 ounces smoked bacon, fried until crisp, then drained and chopped, or diced Black Forest ham

1½ pounds cooked skinless, boneless turkey or chicken, diced

Suggested dressing: Mayo-All-the-Way (page 116)

PUT THE GREENS in a large, wide salad bowl, preferably one with a diameter of at least 16 inches. One by one, place each listed ingredient next to the other on top of the greens (split any larger quantity into two portions and place them at different spots on top). Use all of the ingredients, even if you have to push them up tightly against each other.

After presenting the salad (and you're satisfied with several minutes of the inevitable "oohs and ahhs"), bring the bowl back into the kitchen and mix the salad with enough of the dressing to coat the ingredients without overdoing it. Place generous portions of salad on each plate and pass the extra dressing at the table, along with a good peppermill. (Alternatively, toss the undressed salad and present several different dressings for your guests to choose from. For more dressings, see pages 114–117.)

TIMING IS EVERYTHING

🍃 *With the exception of the greens, eggs, and bacon, all of the ingredients, including the dressing, can be assembled one day ahead and kept refrigerated in separate, well-covered bowls.*

🍃 *The salad can be assembled (not dressed) 30 minutes before serving and left out at room temperature, covered.*

MESCLUN WITH
Dried Figs, and Butter-toasted Walnuts, and
PAN-FRIED CHÈVRE

Savory butter-toasted walnuts bathed in the sweetness of chewy dried Calimyrna figs and perched on top of a pile of greens dressed in a fruity vinaigrette are just sensational. The breaded, pan-fried chèvre not only makes this meal more substantial but also offers a very impressive presentation. If they are seasonally available, toss a handful of juicy pomegranate seeds into the salad when adding the dressing. If you don't feel like breading and pan-frying cheese, omit that step entirely and simply place a generous slice of creamy Saga Blue or the decadent French cheese called Epoisses to one side of the salad just before serving.

🌿 YIELD: *6 SERVINGS AS A MAIN COURSE*

FOR THE PAN-FRIED CHÈVRE

1 large egg

2 tablespoons water

¾ cup Dried Bread Crumbs (page 29)

⅓ cup freshly grated Parmigiano-Reggiano cheese

Kosher or sea salt and freshly ground black pepper to taste

1½ pounds (24 ounces) mild-flavored chèvre (fresh goat cheese) logs, well chilled

Olive oil or Clarified Butter (page 195), as needed

FOR THE SALAD

2 tablespoons unsalted butter

1 generous cup walnuts

1 generous cup diced dried but supple Calimyrna figs

Kosher or sea salt to taste

1 pound (14 to 16 cups) mesclun, rinsed and spun-dry

1 small red onion, sliced into thin wedges (optional)

Suggested dressing: Raspberry Vinaigrette (page 114), close to room temperature

PREPARE THE CHEESE. Mix the egg and water in a shallow bowl. Whisk the bread crumbs and Parmesan cheese together on a plate, and place next to the egg. Season the crumbs with salt and black pepper. Place a sheet of waxed paper on a shallow tray and place it next to the crumbs. Take the logs of chèvre out of the refrigerator and unwrap them. Using unflavored dental floss, cut the chèvre into generous 1-inch-thick slices. Dip each slice in the beaten egg, coating on both sides, then coat each slice evenly in the crumb mixture. As each slice is coated, place it on the prepared tray. When finished, cover the plate with plastic and refrigerate for at least 1 hour and as much as 24 hours before continuing.

PREPARE THE SALAD. Melt the butter in a 10-inch skillet over medium heat. When the butter is hot and bubbling, add the walnuts and sauté them, stirring constantly, until light golden, about 2 minutes. Add the figs and cook them with the nuts until the figs are warmed through, about 4 minutes.

Remove the pan from the heat and sprinkle the nuts and fruit lightly with salt. Cover the pan loosely to keep the contents warm.

Just before you're ready to serve, pan-fry the cheese. Place a wire cooling rack on a shallow baking sheet and place the sheet close to the stove. Heat a 12-inch heavy-bottomed nonstick skillet over high heat and, when hot, add a thin layer of olive oil, or melt a few tablespoons of clarified butter. When the fat is hot, add the breaded chèvre, in a single layer, without crowding. Fry on both sides until golden and hot through, turning once. When golden, transfer each slice to the wire rack. (Don't use paper towels, as any oozing cheese will stick to it.)

ASSEMBLE THE SALAD. Combine the mesclun and the onion, if using, in a large mixing bowl and add enough dressing to coat the greens lightly. Sprinkle lightly with salt and gently mix in the dressing. Divide generous portions of the greens among six dinner plates and scatter each serving with an equal amount of sautéed nuts and figs. Place two slices of fried cheese to one side of each salad and serve immediately. Pass a peppermill at the table.

TIMING IS EVERYTHING
❧ *The cheese can be breaded one day ahead and kept refrigerated, well covered.*
❧ *The dressing can be made and chilled and the greens can be cleaned and dried two days ahead, and kept refrigerated in a jumbo plastic bag lined with paper towels. For best flavor, let the dressing sit at room temperature for 1 hour before using.*

SERVED WITH PLAIN BAGUETTE page 247

TENDER GREENS WITH PEARS,
Apples, Grapes, Gorgonzola, and Grilled Chicken

*If you've never put sweet fruit into a savory salad, I urge you to try this recipe.
The contrast between the cool, crisp fruit and the creamy cheese, savory chicken,
toasted nuts, and tender greens makes this salad unusually good.*

❧ YIELD: 6 TO 8 SERVINGS AS A MAIN COURSE

FOR THE DRESSING AND MARINADE

2 large shallots, minced
4 heaping tablespoons honey Dijon mustard
1 teaspoon kosher or sea salt
½ cup thawed frozen apple juice concentrate
⅔ cup white wine vinegar
1 cup pure olive oil
Freshly ground black pepper to taste
1 to 2 tablespoons Asian chili paste (available in
   Asian markets and some well-stocked
   supermarkets)
4 large boneless, skinless chicken breasts

FOR THE SALAD

2 tablespoons unsalted butter
1 generous cup walnuts, coarsely chopped
Kosher or sea salt and freshly ground black pepper
   to taste
Olive oil or vegetable spray
1 pound (14 to 16 cups) mesclun, rinsed and spun-dry
1 generous cup red seedless grapes
2 large unpeeled, cored, and cubed ripe pears (about
   1½ cups)
1 large unpeeled Granny Smith apple, julienned
   (about 1 cup)
12 ounces Gorgonzola cheese (preferably a high-
   quality creamy type, like dolcelatte dolce), chilled
   and cut into medium dice

MARINATE THE CHICKEN. Use a whisk to combine the shallots, mustard, salt, juice concentrate, vinegar, olive oil, and black pepper in a nonreactive bowl. Pour 1 cup of the prepared dressing into another nonreactive bowl and stir in the chili paste to create the marinade. Chill the remaining dressing until needed. (The dressing improves if assembled several hours before serving.) Rinse and pat the chicken dry, and place in a nonreactive dish. Season the chicken on both sides with black pepper and pour the marinade over the pieces, coating well on both sides. Cover the dish and refrigerate for up to 24 hours.

PREPARE THE SALAD. Place a doubled sheet of paper towels on a plate and set aside. Melt the butter in a 10- to 12-inch heavy-bottomed skillet over medium heat and, when hot and bubbling, stir in the nuts. Cook, stirring constantly, until fragrant and light golden, about 2 minutes. Pour the nuts onto the prepared plate and shimmy them to remove the excess butter. Remove the paper, leaving the nuts on the plate, and sprinkle them lightly with salt. Set the nuts aside.

SERVED WITH PANE DI CASA page 233

TIMING IS
EVERYTHING
❧ *The chicken can be
marinated one day ahead
and kept refrigerated. You
can grill the chicken
2 hours ahead and serve it
at room temperature. Slice
just before serving.*
❧ *The greens can be
cleaned and spun-dry two
days ahead and kept
refrigerated in a jumbo
plastic bag lined with
paper towels.*

Take the chicken out of the refrigerator 30 minutes before grilling. Heat an outdoor gas grill on high or heat a charcoal grill to the gray ash stage (see page 180). Alternatively, heat a large stove-top grill-pan until very hot, with your overhead exhaust fan turned on. When hot, oil the rack to your grill or your grill pan and, after letting the oiled surface heat for a minute or so, lay the marinated chicken pieces on the hot surface (discard the marinade). Grill the chicken until golden on each side and the meat is cooked through but still succulent, 6 to 10 minutes. Remove the chicken to a plate and let it rest for 5 minutes, tented loosely with aluminum foil.

SLICE THE CHICKEN into diagonal strips and sprinkle the pieces lightly with salt. Place the greens in a large mixing bowl and lightly coat with some of the reserved dressing. Add the grapes, pears, apples, and half of both the cheese and the toasted nuts. Toss the mixture gently but thoroughly, then divide the salad among individual serving plates and scatter the remaining cheese and nuts lightly over the top. Arrange several slices of grilled chicken either on top or around the salad and serve immediately, with any additional dressing passed separately at the table.

COLD SEAFOOD SALAD
with Oil-Cured Olives in a Lemon-Lime Vinaigrette

Not to be sexist, but in my experience men who love seafood go ga-ga over this salad. The flavors are really clean and fresh-tasting and the textures are diverse. This seafood salad really should be made in advance for all the flavors to come together perfectly. ❧ YIELD: 6 SERVINGS AS A MAIN COURSE

FOR THE SEAFOOD

4 cups Shrimp Stock (page 20), Roasted Vegetable Stock (page 22), or water

Kosher or sea salt to taste

1 pound large shrimp, shelled and deveined (reserve shells for stock; see page 20)

½ pound cleaned calamari (young squid)

½ pound bay scallops, rinsed, drained, and any sinew removed

FOR THE SALAD

1 medium red bell pepper, seeded and chopped

½ cup chopped celery

½ cup chopped red onion

2 generous tablespoons minced scallions (use the white and 1½ to 2 inches of tender green)

2 large garlic cloves, minced

One 6-ounce jar marinated artichokes, drained and each half sliced in half, with 2 tablespoons of the marinade reserved

1 cup drained sliced hearts of palm

1 cup canned chickpeas, rinsed and drained well

½ cup oil-cured olives, preferably herb-marinated, pits removed

6 ripe plum (Roma) tomatoes, cored and cut into small chunks

2 rounded tablespoons each chopped flat-leaf Italian parsley and cilantro

Kosher or sea salt and freshly ground black pepper to taste

1 pound total green and red frisée lettuce, cleaned, dried, and torn into manageable pieces (chicory can be included)

Suggested dressing: Lemon-Lime Vinaigrette (page 116)

Lemons and limes, to serve

Balsamic vinegar, to serve

PREPARE THE SEAFOOD. Bring the stock (or water) to a full boil in a 2½-quart saucepan over medium heat. Meanwhile, fill a large bowl with ice water, then swish in a good pinch of salt. Place a large medium-mesh wire sieve over another bowl close to the stove. Line a third bowl with doubled paper towels. Stir the shrimp into the boiling stock, reduce the heat to very low, and cook the shrimp, uncovered, stirring occasionally, for 2 minutes or until they lose their translucency and are tender but not overcooked. Pour the stock and shrimp into the sieve so the liquid falls into the bowl beneath. Refresh the shrimp by immediately plunging the sieve into the salted ice water, swishing the shrimp around to facilitate cooling. Drain the shrimp and place in the bowl lined with paper towels. Don't dump out the ice water bath.

Cut the calamari bodies into ¼-inch circles and the tentacles in half through the top band of flesh that connects them. Snip any extra-long legs in half with kitchen scissors, adding them to the rest. Pour the stock back into the same saucepan and bring it to a simmer. Add more ice to the water bath and place the tray, lined with fresh paper towels, next to the bowl. Add the squid to the simmering stock and reduce the heat to very low. Cook the squid until no longer translucent, 30 to 60 seconds (stirring frequently for even heat exposure). Avoid overcooking. Drain and refresh the squid using the same procedure as with shrimp. Don't dump out the ice water bath. Add the squid to the bowl of shrimp.

POUR THE STOCK BACK into the same saucepan and bring to a simmer. Add more ice to the water bath. Replace the paper towels in the tray next to the ice bath. Add the scallops to the simmering stock and reduce the heat to very low. Poach the scallops just until opaque, about 1 minute. Avoid overcooking. Drain and refresh the scallops using the same procedure as the squid and, after blotting dry with paper towels, add them to the bowl of cooked seafood.

If using stock (not water), bring it to a rolling boil and let it boil for 2 minutes. Skim off any residue from the top of the liquid, then strain the stock through a fine-mesh sieve. Let the stock cool, then refrigerate it for up to 2 days (to use for rice or soup), or freeze it for future use.

PREPARE THE SALAD. Combine the cooked seafood with all the vegetables, chickpeas, olives, and herbs except the lettuce. Stir the dressing, then pour some over the seafood salad without overdoing it. (Reserve between ⅓ and ½ cup of dressing.) Add salt and black pepper and fold the ingredients, combining well. Add 2 tablespoons reserved artichoke marinade to the reserved dressing. Refrigerate the salad and dressing separately, well covered, for at least 3 (and as many as 24) hours.

Just before serving, taste the seafood mixture for seasoning, adjusting as needed. Stir the reserved dressing, pour over the greens, and dress lightly and evenly. Mound some greens on individual dinner plates and spoon a generous portion of the seafood salad on top. Garnish with parsley and/or slit and twisted slices of lemon and lime. Pass a peppermill at the table, as well as a carafe of balsamic vinegar.

TIMING IS EVERYTHING

❧ The greens can be cleaned and spun-dry two days ahead and kept refrigerated in a jumbo plastic bag lined with paper towels.

❧ The dressing can be made one day ahead and stored in the refrigerator, well covered. For best flavor, let the dressing sit at room temperature for 30 minutes before using.

❧ The seafood salad should be made at least 3 hours (and as much as one day) ahead and kept refrigerated, covered.

EVERYTHING-CRUSTED TUNA SALAD
with Wasabi Mayo, Mixed Greens, and Crisp Chinese Noodles

Talk about sensory stimulation—this incredible salad has it all! Crunchy, tender, spicy, smooth, and savory. The fried noodles are such fun to make, and they're also a great-tasting nibble when heaped in a basket and served with cocktails. Since they can be made a day ahead, including them isn't too much trouble, but feel free to skip them and prepare the salad anyway—it'll still taste divine. Speaking of do-ahead steps, the tuna can be breaded a day ahead and kept refrigerated. Oh, and since the tender Japanese greens called mizuna are available only from spring through summer, use more baby arugula at other times.

🥢 YIELD: 6 SERVINGS AS A MAIN COURSE

FOR THE CHINESE NOODLES

2 cups unbleached all-purpose flour, plus more for dusting

1 rounded teaspoon salt

2 rounded tablespoons each beige and black sesame seeds

1 rounded tablespoon pan-toasted dehydrated minced onions (see page 107), cooled and finely ground

1 tablespoon dehydrated minced garlic, finely ground

A few grinds of black pepper

About ⅔ cup cool tap water

3 to 4 quarts flavorless vegetable oil or highly refined peanut oil for frying

FOR THE WASABI MAYO

1 cup mayonnaise

2½ to 3 tablespoons wasabi paste, or to taste

2 teaspoons toasted sesame oil

2 tablespoons minced pickled ginger

1 teaspoon pickled ginger juice

Freshly ground black pepper to taste

FOR THE TUNA

⅓ rounded cup each mixed black and beige sesame seeds, pan-toasted dehydrated chopped onions (see page 107), and instant mashed potato flakes

2 teaspoons freshly grated lemon zest (optional)

1 slightly rounded tablespoon kosher or sea salt

A generous amount of freshly ground black pepper

1 egg white, whisked with 1 teaspoon toasted sesame oil and 1 teaspoon soy sauce

Two 1½-pound pieces of impeccably fresh tuna, skin removed

FOR THE SALAD

1 pound mixed greens (mesclun, mizuna, and baby arugula), cleaned and spun-dry

1½ generous cups (about 12 ounces) bean sprouts, well drained

1½ cups (8 to 12 ounces) peeled daikon (Asian radish), thinly sliced or cut into small dice

½ cup chopped salted cocktail peanuts (optional)

Suggested dressing: Peanut-Sesame-Soy Dressing or Sesame-Ginger Dressing (page 116)

Make the Chinese noodles. Whisk together the flour, salt, sesame seeds, onions, garlic, and pepper in a medium mixing bowl. While mixing with your working hand, add only enough water to create a moist (not wet), shaggy mass of dough (you'll probably use all of it). Turn the dough out onto a lightly floured wooden board and knead it using a firm, brisk, and deliberate push-fold-and-turn motion until the dough is firm, smooth, and elastic. If the dough ever feels sticky, add a little additional flour. Cover the dough with a clean, dry kitchen towel and let it relax for 30 minutes for easier rolling.

Pour in enough oil to half-fill a wide, heavy-bottomed 8-quart pot and attach a deep-frying thermometer securely to the side of the pan. Don't allow the mercury tip to touch the bottom. Heat the oil over medium-high heat to 375°F. If using a frying basket, let it heat in the oil. (If using an electric deep-fryer, make sure it's large enough to later accommodate each tuna piece. Pour oil to the designated line and heat according to the manufacturer's instructions for frying fish.) Line a large wire-mesh rack and a deep roasting pan with paper towels and place them near the stove, but at a safe distance.

TIMING IS
EVERYTHING

⚜ *The fried noodles can be made one day ahead and left at room temperature, covered well with aluminum foil. Strain the cool oil and leave it in a clean pot, covered, for the tuna.*

⚜ *The mayo can be made, the tuna can be coated in crumbs, and all of the salad ingredients (including the dressing) can be assembled one day ahead, and stored in the refrigerator, well covered.*

⚜ *The greens can be cleaned and spun-dry two days ahead and kept refrigerated in a jumbo plastic bag lined with paper towels.*

UNCOVER THE DOUGH and, using the blade of a pastry scraper, cut into four equal pieces. Keep the rest of the pieces covered as you work with one piece at a time. On a lightly floured board, roll out a piece of dough into a very thin (about 1/16-inch-thick) rectangle. As you roll, occasionally turn the dough over and dust both the board and the dough with flour. When very thin, lay the dough out in front of you with one of the short ends closest to you. Dust the top lightly with flour, spreading it out evenly with your hand, and roll up the dough (going away from you) into a loose jelly roll. Using a sharp knife, slice the roll into 1/4-inch slices. Lift each slice and let it unravel, draping it over the inside of your nonworking hand. When finished, if the oil is not yet hot enough, lay those noodles to the side in a loose pile, covered with a clean kitchen towel. Roll and cut the remaining dough this way. When the oil reaches the desired temperature, carefully ease a single pile of raw noodles into the hot oil and immediately (and gently) stir and separate them, using a long two-pronged fork. The noodles will quickly "balloon up," and little blisters will appear on their surfaces. Fry the noodles until they're golden on the bottom, about 2 minutes (a little longer in an electric fryer), then carefully turn them over with the long fork to fry on the other side, about 2 minutes more. When done, the noodles should be golden, light textured, and perfectly crisp. Don't let them get overly dark, or they can taste burnt. Using either the fry basket or a long-handled wire-mesh tool such as a spider, transfer each batch of cooked noodles from the oil to the paper-lined rack. Shake to remove excess oil, then pile them in the prepared roasting pan. Turn off the heat under the oil but leave it on the stove with the thermometer attached for later.

MAKE THE WASABI MAYO. Combine all the ingredients, and chill until ready to serve.

SEASON THE TUNA. Combine the sesame seeds, onions, potato flakes, lemon zest (if using), salt, and black pepper on a shallow baking sheet or tray. Mix the egg white mixture using a fork, and strain it into another small bowl. Rinse and dry the tuna and use a pastry brush to coat the flesh on all sides with the egg white. Turn the fish in the crumb mixture, pressing with your hands to help them adhere well. Leave the tuna on the crumbs, cover it with plastic wrap, and refrigerate the fish for at least 4 hours, or up to overnight.

Let the fish sit out of the refrigerator for 30 minutes on a warm day or 1 hour in a cool kitchen before frying. Reheat the oil in the 8-quart pot until it reaches 360°F. Place a wire rack near the stove and line the rack with paper towels. Uncover the tuna and pat on more crumbs, coating the meat as heavily as possible. Working with one tuna piece at a time, carefully lower the fish into the hot oil and fry until golden and crisp on all sides, 2½ to 3½ minutes, for medium-rare. (The thicker the piece, the longer the cooking time—avoid overcooking.) Using a slotted utensil, carefully lift the tuna out of the pot, pressing it close to the side of the pan as you lift to prevent it from falling off and splashing into the hot oil. Drain the fish on paper towels and let the oil come back up to temperature before frying the remaining piece. Serve the tuna within 20 minutes of frying, cut into 1-inch-thick slices.

ASSEMBLE THE SALAD. Place the salad ingredients into a large salad bowl and add enough of your chosen dressing to coat the greens lightly, without overdoing it. Place generous portions of salad on each of six dinner plates and arrange two or more overlapping slices of tuna to one side of the greens. Mound a handful of fried noodles on top of the greens and serve right away, with the wasabi mayo passed at the table.

HERE'S THE SCOOP:
On Food Snobbery

I've always found it funny when I hear people profess never to use dehydrated onions or garlic because "they're not fresh." That's like saying "I don't eat raisins, I only eat grapes." Or "I won't eat croutons, I only eat fresh bread." Or "dried mushrooms are fake mushrooms." Dried foods, like fruits and certain vegetables, have an intensity of flavor that's possible only once the water is removed. Actually, there are times when using fresh vegetables is the absolute wrong thing to do. Take these Chinese noodles, for example. If I used fresh onions in the dough, within minutes of frying they'd give off moisture and gases, rendering the crisp noodles limp and chewy (not what the kids had in mind). Here, pan-toasted dehydrated onions are ground to a powder to add the perfect onion flavor without complications. So don't be afraid to embrace dried ingredients. In cooking, it's always best to be open-minded and to appreciate the virtues of as many ingredients as we can. That way, we have more players to choose from.

STEAK WITH GRILLED VEGETABLES,
Tomatoes, Cheese, and Greens

If you're a meat eater who likes to entertain, there's hardly a quicker, simpler, or more satisfying route to a delicious meal than steak with grilled vegetables. If you don't feel like taking the time to marinate the meat, purchase a more naturally tender (albeit expensive) cut, like sirloin strip or porterhouse, and simply brush the meat (and the vegetables) evenly with good olive oil and season both sides generously with black pepper. Just before cooking, apply an even sprinkling of kosher salt. After cooking, don't slice these more tender cuts of beef on the bias — instead, use a straight up and down motion. Feel free to use either the suggested dressing or the unused marinade for the greens. If you choose bone-in steaks, purchase more than called for in the recipe, since the net weight of meat will be less on these. ❧ YIELD: 6 SERVINGS AS A MAIN COURSE

2½ pounds flank steak

Freshly ground black pepper to taste

Suggested accompaniments: "The Bomb" Mustard Vinaigrette (page 114), adding 2 tablespoons drained capers; Garlic Bread (page 45)

4 large or 6 medium portobello mushrooms, stems removed and caps wiped clean

2 sweet onions (like Vidalias), peeled and sliced ½ inch thick, keeping slices intact

2 each red and yellow sweet bell peppers, halved and seeded

2 or 3 large ripe beefsteak tomatoes, cut into ⅓-inch-thick slices

1 generous pound fresh mozzarella cheese, drained, patted dry, and cut into ½-inch slices

Kosher or sea salt to taste

Assorted black and green olives (optional)

½ pound (8 cups) cleaned, spun-dry, and stemmed arugula leaves

1 generous cup Parmigiano-Reggiano cheese shavings

Robust Italian Vinaigrette (page 114)

SCORE THE STEAK by making long, shallow diagonal slits on both sides using a sharp knife. Place the meat in a 13 × 9-inch nonreactive dish and apply a generous amount of black pepper to both sides. Pour enough of the Robust Italian Vinaigrette over the meat to coat it well on both sides. Cover the dish and refrigerate for at least 4 hours or overnight. Alternatively, if the meat is refrigerator-cold, leave it out at a comfortable room temperature for 1 hour before proceeding.

Liberally brush some of the remaining marinade on both sides of the mushroom caps, the onion slices, and the halved peppers and place them in another large dish. Refrigerate the vegetables for several hours or overnight, or leave them on your counter for an hour or so before cooking. Reserve any remaining dressing for basting.

If the meat and/or vegetables have been refrigerated, let them sit at room temperature for 30 minutes to 1 hour. Preheat a gas grill to high or heat an ample layer of charcoal in a charcoal grill until hot (see page 180). Regardless of the type of grill used, brush the hot surface with some oil (a branch of rosemary dipped in olive oil is a very fragrant way to do this) and let the newly oiled surface heat for a few seconds. If your grilling surface is large enough to grill the meat and vegetables together, do so; if not, then grill the meat first, since it needs to rest before being sliced.

Lift the meat out of the marinade, letting any excess drip back into the dish. Lay the meat on the hot grill and cook until the meat is caramelized on the outside but still rosy within, or to your liking. (Press down on the top of the cooked meat, using your finger. If it feels like your cheek, it's medium-rare. If it feels like your chin, it's medium, and if the meat feels as firm as the tip of your nose, it's well done.) Brush the meat with some reserved (never used) marinade after turning. (When grilling, the cooking time will vary, depending on the intensity of your heat source.) Set aside.

Brush the vegetables with some of the reserved marinade. Grill them, turning as necessary, until tender and their edges are charred-looking, but not burnt.

Place the grilled vegetables decoratively on a large serving platter, along with the sliced tomatoes and mozzarella cheese. Sprinkle on some salt, then scatter an assortment of olives all around, if using. Mix the arugula with the Parmesan in a separate bowl. Sprinkle the meat with salt, then slice the steak on the bias. If the platter is large enough, heap the slices next to the vegetables; if not, place on a separate platter. Serve everything together, letting people help themselves. Pass the dressing at the table, with a loaf of hot garlic bread.

TIMING IS EVERYTHING
🌿 *The meat and vegetables can be seasoned, and the dressing can be made, one day ahead and kept refrigerated, well covered.*

Stove-Top Variation

If cooking on the stove, line a large, shallow baking sheet with aluminum foil (shiny side up) and place it on the center shelf of the oven. Preheat the oven to 425°F. for at least 30 minutes. Turn on your exhaust fan. Preheat a large stove-top grill pan over medium-high heat until very hot. Sear the steak over high heat for 3 minutes per side, or until deeply caramelized. At this point the meat will be almost but not quite done, depending on overall thickness. Remove the pan from the heat and, using tongs, transfer the seared meat to the preheated baking sheet. Cook the meat 2 to 5 minutes, depending on how you like it. Let the meat rest on a warmed platter, loosely tented with aluminum foil, for 10 minutes before slicing and serving.

PUREE OF ASPARAGUS
SOUP page 134,
PARMESAN-SCENTED
CROUTONS page 138

CHAPTER FIVE
Hearty and Robust . . .
MAIN-DISH SOUPS, STEWS, and PASTA

T HE COMFORT PROVIDED in this chapter might not always be instantly attained, but I can promise you that the recipes are worth any effort that's required. Having said that, I think you'll be surprised when you see that some of the stews and soups here don't require lengthy simmering. Depending on the ingredients involved, you can have a saucy, soothing simmered dinner on the table in a matter of minutes. And if you take advantage of my timing strategy, provided alongside each recipe, you'll be able to get that much more done, without the last-minute frenzy associated with weeknight meals.

The pasta recipes are hearty yet (with the exception of one) totally vegetable based, making them a great choice when serving vegetarians or those who are kosher. And although most of the soups are on the large side, it's for good reason. Since soup freezes so perfectly, choosing to "cook big and freeze" helps the cook maximize the overall "take" from time spent in the kitchen. Then, on days when you're tired or when time feels nonexistent, a truly wonderful homemade dinner is just around the corner.

Whether your meal features soup, stew, or pasta, all that's needed is a crisp salad and a great piece of bread to complete the picture.

It's Spring!
PUREE OF ASPARAGUS SOUP
with Roasted Red Pepper Coulis

If you love asparagus, this soup is destined to make you very *happy. Please use homemade stock, which is basically salt free. This way you can season it yourself, according to how it's being used. But if using canned broth, add more salt only after tasting the fully assembled soup base.* ❧ YIELD: ABOUT 3½ QUARTS

FOR THE SOUP

3 large bunches asparagus (3½ pounds), rinsed well and hard bottoms cut off and discarded

Kosher or sea salt

6 tablespoons unsalted butter

3 cups thinly sliced leeks (about 3 large; whites and light green)

4 garlic cloves, minced

1 medium Idaho potato, peeled and diced

6 cups Chicken Stock (page 16) or Roasted Vegetable Stock (page 22), or doctored best-quality canned broth (see page 19)

1 teaspoon dried thyme or 1 generous tablespoon fresh

¼ cup thick crème fraîche or heavy cream (optional, but highly recommended)

Freshly ground black pepper

FOR THE RED PEPPER COULIS

2 large red bell peppers, roasted until very tender, peeled, seeded, and coarsely chopped (see page 24)

¼ cup Garlic Confit Oil (page 23) or extra-virgin olive oil

½ teaspoon red pepper flakes (optional)

2 garlic cloves, minced

3 cooked garlic cloves (from Garlic Confit, page 23; optional)

Kosher or sea salt and freshly ground black pepper to taste

Suggested accompaniment: Garlic and Parmesan-scented Croutons (page 138)

Minced chives for serving

MAKE THE SOUP. Tie each bunch of asparagus in two places with kitchen twine. Bring a large pot of water to a rapid boil and add some salt. Submerge the asparagus bundles and boil them until crisp-tender, about 4 minutes. Meanwhile, put a large bowl of ice water on your counter and, when the asparagus are done, transfer the bundles to the ice water. When cold, remove the asparagus from the water and pat them dry. Remove the strings. Cut off their tips and reserve separately. Cut the remaining stalks into 2-inch lengths and set them aside.

Melt 4 tablespoons of the butter in a 4-quart heavy-bottomed saucepan over medium heat. Tear off a sheet of waxed paper and brush one side with some of the melted butter. Stir the leeks and garlic into the saucepan, coating them evenly with butter. Lay the greased side of the paper directly on top of the vegetables, lower the heat, and let them sweat gently until wilted, about 10 minutes. Discard the paper and stir in the reserved asparagus stalks, the diced potato, stock, and thyme. Bring the liquid to a full boil over medium heat, then cover and reduce the heat to low. Simmer the vegetables until tender and the stock is nicely flavored by the asparagus, about 20 minutes.

PLACE A LARGE WIRE SIEVE over a large bowl. Strain the soup through the sieve and reserve the solids. Puree the solids, in batches with some of the liquid, in a food processor fitted with the steel blade, or in a heavy-duty blender, until very smooth. (If using a blender, it's not safe to fill the container more than half full with a hot substance, so if necessary do this in several small batches.) As each batch is processed, empty the puree into another bowl and continue until you've finished. You'll end up with one bowl of puree and another of stock.

After rinsing and drying the saucepan, pour the pureed vegetables back into the pot and add the crème fraîche or cream, if using, along with enough stock to create the desired thickness. (I usually use all of it.) Freeze any remaining stock for another use, but label it "chicken stock, flavored with asparagus." Season the soup well with salt and black pepper to taste.

MAKE THE RED PEPPER COULIS. Place the roasted peppers in either a blender or a small food processor fitted with the steel blade. Add the oil, red pepper flakes, if using, fresh garlic and garlic confit, if using. Puree the mixture until smooth, then add salt and pepper. Transfer the coulis to a bowl or funnel it into a plastic squeeze bottle, snipping the tip so the opening is $\frac{1}{4}$ inch wide.

To serve, reheat the soup slowly over low heat until piping hot. When almost ready to serve, melt the remaining 2 tablespoons butter in a 10-inch heavy-bottomed skillet over medium heat and, when hot and bubbling, add the reserved asparagus tips. Cook the tips, stirring occasionally, until hot and the edges are beginning to caramelize, about 8 minutes. Place one or two croutons in the bottom of either warmed wide soup plates or deep crocks and ladle the soup on top. Add a generous spoonful of asparagus tips, then spoon in or decoratively squiggle on some of the red pepper coulis. Scatter just a few minced chives on top and serve the soup right away.

TIMING IS EVERYTHING

🍃 The soup base can be fully assembled two days ahead and kept refrigerated, securely covered.

🍃 The soup can also be frozen for several months when stored in heavy-duty labeled freezer containers. Under these circumstances, however, add the blanched tips directly to the assembled soup base at the end, without sautéing them.

🍃 The coulis and the croutons can be made up to two days ahead. Keep the coulis chilled, but bring it to room temperature before serving. Keep the croutons at room temperature in an airtight tin.

You Won't Find This in a Can . . .
VEAL AND VEGETABLE BARLEY
Soup Simmered with Marrowbones

To put it simply, this is one of the best soups I've ever eaten. Rich, soothing, and chock-full of vegetables, tender pearl barley, succulent braised veal, and just for some decadence, simmered veal marrowbones. Although the recipe can be halved, I would never do that. Since it takes just as many pots, pans, and utensils to make a smaller batch, I always make a big one and stash some in the freezer. When serving, make sure to provide those at the table with a cocktail fork to retrieve every drop of the marrow. ❧ YIELD: ABOUT 12 GENEROUS QUARTS

6 quarts (24 cups) Beef or Veal Stock (page 18), or doctored best-quality canned broth (see page 19)

5½ pounds trimmed veal shank (osso bucco), cut into 1-inch cubes, bones reserved

5 or 6 extra 2-inch veal marrowbones (optional)

Kosher or sea salt and freshly ground black pepper to taste

Pure olive oil

1½ cups pearl barley, rinsed and drained

6 tablespoons unsalted butter

2 large leeks, cleaned and thinly sliced (white and light green parts)

2 large yellow onions, chopped

4 garlic cloves, minced

6 carrots, peeled and diagonally sliced ½ inch thick

4 celery stalks, trimmed and diagonally sliced ½ inch thick

2 rounded tablespoons minced fresh thyme

3 tablespoons extra-virgin olive oil

1½ pounds button mushrooms, wiped clean and sliced

Two 28-ounce cans peeled plum tomatoes, drained and snipped into chunks

Freshly grated Parmigiano-Reggiano cheese (optional)

BRING THE STOCK to a full simmer in a 12-quart heavy-bottomed saucepan. When it begins to bubble, turn it off and keep the lid on so it stays hot. Trim any excess fatty sinew off the meat and the extra bones, if using, and dry both well. Sprinkle the meat and bones with some salt and black pepper. Heat a 12- to 14-inch heavy-bottomed skillet over high heat and, when hot, add enough olive oil to coat the bottom of the pan. When the oil is hot, sear the veal and bones (in several batches) without crowding over high heat until very golden on all sides. Transfer each batch to a tray as you brown them. (Add more oil to the pan as necessary to maintain a thin even layer, and always heat the new oil before adding more meat.) Remove the pan from the heat, but don't wipe out the pan.

Bring the stock back to a boil over medium-high heat. Add the seared veal and bones and the drained barley, and cover the pot. When the liquid comes back to a full bubble, reduce the heat to low and simmer the meat until just tender, 1 to 1¼ hours.

WHEN THE MEAT HAS COOKED for about an hour, prepare the vegetables. Pour out any fat from the pan used to brown the meat, and melt the butter over medium heat. When the butter is hot and bubbling, stir in the leeks and onions. When nicely coated with butter, reduce the heat to low and cover the vegetables directly with a sheet of waxed paper. Let the vegetables sweat this way, stirring occasionally, until softened and any caramelized meat residue is released from the pan, about 8 minutes. Lift the paper, stir in the garlic, and put the paper back on top. Cook gently for 3 more minutes, then uncover and stir in the carrots and celery. Cover again and cook for 3 more minutes. Stir in the thyme with some salt and pepper to taste, and discard the paper. When the meat is just tender, stir the vegetables into the simmering broth and bring the liquid back to a full bubble. Reduce the heat to low and cover the pot. Simmer for 20 minutes.

Meanwhile, clean the pan used for the meat and vegetables, then put it back on the stove over high heat. When the pan is hot, add the olive oil and, when the oil is hot, stir in the mushrooms. Cook the mushrooms over high heat, stirring occasionally, until any released liquid evaporates and they turn golden, about 12 minutes. Season with salt and pepper. When the vegetables in the soup pot are just tender, add the sautéed mushrooms along with the cut-up tomatoes. Bring the liquid back to a simmer, then cook gently for 10 more minutes. Season once more and allow the soup to cool off the stove so it can be degreased.

TIMING IS
EVERYTHING
❧ *The soup can be made entirely up to two days ahead. Once it's been cooled and defatted, place the amount you plan to serve in a clean pot and keep refrigerated, well covered. The remaining soup can be frozen very successfully for several months in heavy-duty freezer containers.*

ONCE COOL, use a large spoon to skim off any accumulation of fat from the top of the soup and discard it (there will be quite a bit). Depending on how many people you're feeding, ration the amount you plan to reheat for this meal into a clean saucepan and place the rest in heavy-duty freezer containers for future meals. To serve, reheat the soup gently over low heat, covered, until piping hot. Adjust the seasoning as needed, then ladle the soup into bowls. If desired, pass some grated Parmesan cheese at the table.

SERVED WITH BRAIDED CHALLAH page 226

Three-Cheese
FRENCH ONION SOUP
with Garlic and Parmesan-scented Croutons

Who doesn't love onion soup? During the winter months, this soup makes a perfect hearty lunch or casual dinner for family or close friends. Use the best-quality stock in this recipe, since it, along with the right onions, is crucial for this soup to reach its full flavor potential (for more on onions, see page 139). Don't limit the use of these croutons to this recipe—they're also great with savory spreads. Make sure that your bowls are ovenproof. And do shred the cheese, if possible, since grated cheese, which is more granular, seems to almost disappear after broiling instead of melting into big gooey spoonfuls of "yum." ❧ YIELD: 8 SERVINGS

FOR THE CROUTONS

16 slices (½ inch thick) best-quality French bread

⅓ cup Garlic Confit Oil (page 23) or extra-virgin olive oil mixed with 1 large garlic clove, minced

About 2 tablespoons freshly grated Parmigiano-Reggiano cheese

Freshly ground black pepper to taste

FOR THE SOUP

6 tablespoons unsalted butter

8 heaping cups thin-sliced yellow onions (about 4 extra-large Spanish onions)

Up to 11 cups Beef or Veal Stock (page 18), or doctored best-quality canned broth (see page 19)

Kosher or sea salt and freshly ground black pepper to taste

Scant ½ cup unbleached all-purpose flour

1 tablespoon fine cognac

4 generous tablespoons snipped fresh chives (optional)

About 4 generous cups shredded cheese (mix Gruyère, Jarlsberg, and Muenster)

MAKE THE CROUTONS. Preheat the oven to 375°F. Place the bread slices on a wire rack over a shallow baking sheet and bake the slices until light golden on both sides, about 20 minutes, turning once. Remove the sheet from the oven and brush each slice evenly on both sides with the oil, then sprinkle the tops only with a little Parmesan cheese and some black pepper. Place back into the oven and bake the slices for 5 minutes more, then turn the oven off and let the croutons sit there until perfectly crisp, 5 to 8 minutes. Let the croutons completely cool on their rack before storing them in an airtight tin until needed.

MAKE THE SOUP. Melt the butter in a large 12- to 14-inch deep-sided skillet over medium heat. When the butter is hot and bubbling, stir in the onions and cook until deeply caramelized and greatly reduced in volume, 20 to 25 minutes, stirring occasionally. If at any time some onions start to stick, add a little stock to that area and, as it bubbles up, use your spoon to release those onions. Add some salt and pepper to taste. (To speed up this process, divide the butter and onions between two skillets.) Scrape the onions into a 6-quart, heavy-bottomed saucepan, then remove any clinging onions from the pan by deglazing with about ½ cup of stock. Simmer the liquid until it becomes syrupy, then add it along with any onion bits to the saucepan of cooked onions.

PLACE THE SAUCEPAN over medium-high heat. When the onions begin to sizzle, stir in the flour and cook this pasty mixture, stirring constantly, until the flour is well distributed and some of it begins to form a thin toasted layer on the bottom of the pan. When stirring, try not to mash the onions so they retain their texture. Add 10 cups of stock to the onions and bring the liquid to a full boil, stirring frequently. Reduce the heat to low and cook the soup, with the cover ajar, until the broth has thickened a bit and any raw taste of flour has disappeared, about 30 minutes. Season again with salt and pepper, then add the cognac. Raise the heat to high and cook the soup for 1 minute just to meld flavors and to remove any sharp taste of alcohol. Remove the pan from the heat.

To serve, preheat the broiler with the rack on the upper third shelf. If using chives, combine them with the cheese. Line up your warmed ovenproof bowls, mugs, or crocks on a large shallow baking sheet. If your sheet can't accommodate all of the crocks, divide them between two sheets. When the soup is piping hot, ladle it into the crocks, dividing the onions and stock evenly among them, to about ½ inch below the rim. Place one or two croutons on top of the soup (depending on their size), overlapping slightly and pushing them down a bit to help them absorb the top layer of soup. Mound ½ cup of shredded cheese evenly over the tops and run them under the broiler. (If using two sheets, leave the first one on the bottom rack so it stays in a hot environment. After broiling the first batch, switch the positions of the sheets to broil the rest.) Serve the soup right away.

TIMING IS EVERYTHING

❧ *The croutons can be made two days ahead and, once completely cool, stored at room temperature in an airtight tin. Leftovers are fine for several days.*

❧ *The soup can be fully simmered as much as one day ahead and, once completely cool, covered and refrigerated. If serving within a few hours, leave the soup out at a comfortable room temperature before reheating gently, but fully.*

HERE'S THE SCOOP:
On Choosing and Using the Right Onions

Using the right onions in French onion soup is just as essential as using great stock. Only use "storage onions" in this soup, since they have the most pronounced flavor, which after cooking, will leave them sweet without being cloying. These onions come in a variety of sizes and colors, but the ones I prefer are the extra-large yellow Spanish onions. After being harvested, Spanish onions are held for a few weeks in big perforated bins (a process called curing). Because of this, the onions can be stored for several months without losing their taste or texture.

Sweet onions, however, are a different story. These come in lots of varieties, but the ones that are probably most familiar to you are the Vidalias or Maui Sweets. Just as the name implies, sweet onions have a high sugar content and are not cured; they are shipped right after being harvested. Because of their sweetness, though they are perfect for eating raw on a burger, these onions don't have strong enough flavor to stand up to cooking. They actually become either overly sweet or completely passive in a cooked dish.

Apple-Scented, Curried
BUTTERNUT SQUASH SOUP
with Sautéed Mushrooms, Peas, and Poached Chicken

Savory with just the perfect hint of sweetness from the apples and crunch from the toasted pumpkin seeds, this soothing soup is destined to sway even the most devout curry-haters. The easiest way to remove the skin from the squash is with a strong vegetable peeler. If you're serving vegetarians or if you're short on time, just omit the poached chicken and substitute vegetable stock for the chicken stock. If you have some leftover cooked basmati rice in the fridge, reheat it in the microwave (add 1 tablespoon of water for every cup of rice) and place a generous spoonful in the bowl just before ladling in the piping hot soup. ❧ YIELD: ABOUT 6 QUARTS

FOR THE POACHED CHICKEN

1 large yellow onion, scrubbed but not peeled, root end removed, and quartered
2 celery stalks, cleaned and sliced, with leaves
2 carrots, scrubbed and sliced
1 parsnip, scrubbed and sliced
3 parsley sprigs
1 tablespoon black peppercorns
Two 3-pound chickens, halved down the back, reserving the necks and giblets (no liver)

FOR THE SOUP

½ cup (1 stick) unsalted butter
1 large yellow onion, chopped
4 large leeks, cleaned and thinly sliced to measure 6 generous cups (whites and light green parts)
4 large garlic cloves, minced
Kosher or sea salt and freshly ground black pepper to taste
3 large jalapeño chiles, seeded and minced (if desired, leave in some seeds for extra heat)

2 large butternut squash (about 5 pounds), peeled, seeded, and cut into cubes
2 medium-large Golden Delicious apples, peeled, seeded, and diced
2 Idaho potatoes, peeled and diced
2 generous tablespoons curry powder (preferably Madras)
3½ quarts (14 cups) Chicken Stock (page 16), or doctored best-quality canned broth (see page 19)
3 tablespoons extra-virgin olive oil
2½ pounds button mushrooms, wiped clean and sliced
10 ounces frozen peas, thawed
1 cup (8 ounces) thick crème fraîche or sour cream

FOR THE GARNISH

2 tablespoons unsalted butter
1 cup raw hulled pepitas (Mexican pumpkin seeds)
Salt to taste

POACH THE CHICKEN. Place the poached chicken ingredients into a 6-quart heavy-bottomed pot and cover with cold water. Cover the pot and bring the water to a boil over medium-high heat. Reduce the heat to very low and gently cook the chickens just until tender, about 30 minutes. Using a slotted utensil, remove the chickens to a large bowl to cool enough to handle. Set the saucepan with the poaching liquid aside.

MAKE THE SOUP. Melt the butter in a 10-quart, heavy-bottomed saucepan over medium heat and brush one side of a sheet of waxed paper with some of the butter. Stir the onion, leeks, and garlic into the butter and lay the greased side of the paper directly on top of the vegetables. Reduce the heat to low and sweat the vegetables until softened and somewhat reduced, 10 to 15 minutes. Remove and discard the paper. Season the vegetables with salt and black pepper, then stir in the jalapeños, squash, apples, potatoes, and curry powder. When well combined, add the stock (not the poaching liquid) and bring to a boil. Turn the heat down to low and simmer the vegetables, covered, until very tender, 35 to 45 minutes.

Meanwhile, heat a 12- to 14-inch deep-sided skillet over medium-high heat and, when hot, add the olive oil. When the oil is hot, add the mushrooms and cook them, stirring occasionally, until all their released juices evaporate and they turn golden around the edges. Season the mushrooms with salt and pepper, then remove the skillet from the heat.

WHEN THE SIMMERING VEGETABLES are perfectly tender, uncover the saucepan and season the mixture with salt and pepper. Working in batches, ladle the soup into a large wire sieve positioned over a large bowl, and puree the solids with some of the liquid in a food processor fitted with the steel blade or in a heavy-duty blender. (If using a blender, it's not safe to fill the container more than half-full with a hot liquid, so do this in several small batches.) When smooth, empty each batch of puree into another bowl and continue until you've finished processing all of the solids. (You'll end up with one large bowl of puree and another of stock.)

To finish the soup and replenish your stock supply, separate the chicken meat from the skin and bones, and tear the meat into bite-size chunks. Set aside. Return the chicken bones, including the skin and all other parts, to the pot of poaching ingredients (feel free to throw in any stray chicken backs or necks from the freezer as well) and bring the liquid back to a boil. Reduce the heat to low and simmer the liquid for an hour or two, occasionally pressing down on the solids. When done, strain and chill the liquid, covered, so the fat can rise and be removed. Freeze the chicken stock in labeled containers for another day.

Meanwhile, wipe out the pot used to simmer the soup and pour in the pureed vegetables. Add enough of the stock to reach the desired consistency, divide any excess stock into 1- or 2-cup portions, and freeze to use as a cooking liquid for rice. Stir the peas, cooked chicken, sautéed mushrooms, and crème fraîche into the soup and adjust the seasoning.

TIMING IS
EVERYTHING

❧ *The chicken can be poached and the meat removed from the skin and bones one day ahead and kept refrigerated, well covered.*
❧ *The soup can be fully assembled two days ahead and kept refrigerated, securely covered. The soup can also be frozen for several months when stored in labeled heavy-duty freezer containers.*

MAKE THE GARNISH. Line a plate with a doubled sheet of paper towels and set it aside. Melt the butter in a 12-inch heavy-bottomed skillet over medium heat, and when hot and bubbling, add the pepitas. Raise the heat to medium-high and toast the seeds, stirring constantly, until nicely colored, about 4 minutes. If the seeds start jumping or coloring too fast, reduce the heat and keep stirring to prevent overexposure to heat in any one spot. When satisfied with their color, immediately pour the seeds onto the paper towels. Shimmy the plate to help remove any excess butter, then transfer the seeds to a bowl and sprinkle them with some salt. Stir the seeds to disperse the salt. Keep the seeds at room temperature until serving. (To keep leftovers tasting fresh, store them in a sealed container in the refrigerator and warm them briefly in a low oven or in the microwave.)

Serve the soup piping hot, garnished with some toasted pepitas. Pass extra toasted seeds at the table.

SERVED WITH BAKING POWDER BISCUITS page 256

Steaming Hot and Crisp on Top . . .
LAMB POT PIES

Whenever I serve these piping hot pot pies to my family, everyone at the table is initially quiet, since we're all so busy plowing through the crisp pastry, uncovering all sorts of savory goodies inside. Usually, it's not until we reach the half-way mark in our individual dishes that we come up for air and chat as normal. If you're in the mood for beef or veal instead of lamb, just substitute an equal amount of cubed chuck or veal shoulder and use all beef or veal stock in the sauce. And, speaking of stock, although it's OK to use store-bought puff pastry on top, use homemade stock in the sauce, since it really will help make these pot pies better than all others. ❧ YIELD: 6 SERVINGS AS A MAIN COURSE

3½ to 4 pounds lamb stew meat (from the shoulder or neck), cut into 1½-inch cubes

2 cups dry red wine

1 yellow onion, cut into wedges

Kosher or sea salt and freshly ground black pepper to taste

Pure olive oil for browning the lamb

8 cups Lamb Stock (page 18), or combined Beef and Chicken Stock (pages 18, 16)

1 pound new potatoes (about 2 large), peeled and cut into ½-inch dice

4 carrots, peeled and diagonally sliced ½ inch thick

8 ounces fresh pearl onions (or use frozen pearl onions, thawed)

1 tablespoon extra-virgin olive oil

10 ounces button mushrooms, wiped clean and sliced ¼ inch thick

½ cup (1 stick) unsalted butter

2 cups packed, thinly sliced leeks (white and light green parts)

½ cup plus 1 tablespoon unbleached all-purpose flour

1 tablespoon minced fresh thyme, or 1½ teaspoons crumbled dried

¼ cup thick crème fraîche or heavy cream

1 generous cup frozen peas, thawed

1½ cups whole cherry tomatoes, stems removed

1 recipe Quick Puff Pastry (page 48), or 1 pound frozen store-bought puff pastry, thawed

Glaze: 1 egg mixed with 1 teaspoon water and strained

Sesame seeds for sprinkling (optional)

PLACE THE MEAT in a large nonreactive dish and pour in the red wine. Scatter the onion wedges over the top, separating them into strips. Use your hands to help coat the meat with the wine and to disperse the onion. Cover the dish with plastic wrap and refrigerate for 4 to 24 hours, occasionally stirring to redistribute.

Place a medium-mesh sieve over a mixing bowl. Pick the meat out of the wine and drain the pieces on a large doubled sheet of paper towels. Pat the meat dry, then sprinkle the pieces with salt and black pepper. Pour the wine through the sieve and discard the onion. Reserve the wine. Heat a heavy-bottomed, deep-sided 12-inch skillet over high heat and, when hot, add a thin layer of olive oil. When the oil is hot, brown the lamb in batches until deeply browned on all sides (be patient and don't crowd the pan). Transfer each batch of browned meat to a tray as you continue to brown the rest. When finished, dump out any oil from the pan, but don't wipe out the interior. Deglaze the pan over high heat with the reserved wine, reducing it to a syrupy ½ cup, and reserve.

Bring the stock to a boil in a 4-quart heavy-bottomed saucepan. Stir the reduced wine into the stock along with the browned meat, and bring the liquid to a brisk bubble. Reduce the heat to low and simmer the meat, covered tightly, until meltingly tender but not dry, 1 to 1½ hours. Using a large slotted utensil, transfer the meat to a big bowl. Bring the stock to a rolling boil over high heat, uncovered. Add the diced potatoes and set your timer for 10 minutes. After 4 minutes have elapsed, add the carrots and cook them with the potatoes until the timer sounds. Meanwhile, position a medium-mesh wire sieve over an empty 2-quart bowl. When the timer goes off, pour the stock into the sieve, allowing it to capture the vegetables. Place the drained vegetables in the bowl with the cooked meat. Leave the stock in the bowl for now.

If using fresh pearl onions, boil them for 7 minutes, then drain them and run them under cold water to stop the cooking process. Slice off the root end of each onion and slip off their skins.

Heat a 12-inch heavy-bottomed, deep-sided skillet over high heat and, when hot, add the extra-virgin olive oil. When the oil is hot, add the sliced mushrooms and cook them over high heat until tender and starting to turn golden, about 4 minutes. Stir in the pearl onions and cook until any released liquid from the mushrooms totally evaporates and the onions are turning golden, about 5 minutes, stirring occasionally. Empty the onions and mushrooms into the bowl with the meat and other vegetables. Put the pan back on the stove without wiping out the interior.

Melt the butter in the same 12-inch skillet over medium heat and, when hot and bubbling, stir in the leeks. Reduce the heat to low and cook the leeks until tender and fragrant, about 5 minutes. Raise the heat to high and stir in the flour. Cook the vegetable-based roux, stirring constantly, for 1½ to 2 minutes. Add only 6 cups of the hot stock and bring it to a brisk boil, uncovered (freeze the rest for another recipe). Reduce the heat to low and simmer the sauce until thickened, about 5 minutes. Stir in the thyme and crème fraîche and simmer 3 more minutes. Pour the sauce over the meat and vegetables. Fold in the peas and cherry tomatoes, and season again with salt and pepper.

Spoon the meat and vegetable mixture into six individual ovenproof crocks, dividing equally. Let the contents cool completely. Meanwhile, roll out your puff pastry ⅛ inch thick on a lightly floured surface. Cut out six rounds to fit the top of your crocks and cut out a decorative ⅓-inch-wide vent in the center of each round using a tiny pastry cutter (or a thimble). Apply a round of pastry to the top of each filled crock and press the edges of dough onto the outer sides of the rim, helping the dough to adhere. Refrigerate the dishes, covered with plastic wrap, until ready to bake.

Preheat the oven to 400°F. Assemble your egg glaze. Remove the pot pies from the refrigerator and uncover them. Place the crocks on a large, shallow baking sheet. Brush the pastry with the egg glaze and sprinkle the tops with sesame seeds, if using. Bake the pot pies until the pastry is golden, very crisp, and the filling is visibly bubbling through the vents, 35 to 45 minutes. Serve them right away.

TIMING IS
EVERYTHING

The pot pies can be fully assembled and topped with pastry one day ahead and kept refrigerated, covered with plastic wrap. Don't apply the glaze, however, until just before baking.

HERE'S THE SCOOP:
On the Power of Repetition, When Ordering Meat from the Butcher

I can't tell you how many times I've said to myself, "Why didn't I just remind the butcher that I wanted stew meat and not leg meat?" (Or vice-versa.) The distinction between the two is important. Trust me, when you cook stew meat gently, for 1½ hours, you will be rewarded with heaven on a plate. However, when your butcher accidentally slips you leaner meat from the leg and you cook it the same way, you will surely end up with perfect squares of brown sawdust, swimming in a lovely sauce. Conversely, if you're expecting to season, skewer, and quickly cook cubed beef on the grill, and the butcher mistakenly gives you a more connective stew meat cut, like chuck, be prepared to serve little tennis balls disguised as meat for dinner.

Butchers, like all of us, are busy. When you order your meat for a specific purpose (i.e., pan-sautéing, braising, pan-searing, and/or oven-roasting), it's a good idea to reiterate your desires to him or her before leaving the market, meat in hand. This way, you're less likely to learn at the table that someone made a mistake.

*145

SAVORY CHICKEN AND SAUSAGE STEW
with Herbs and Many Mushrooms

A truly satisfying combination of fragrant herbs, sautéed mushrooms, and chicken and sausage pieces that are browned and then stewed in an intense sauce. If you want a cool-weather entree that's earthy and soothing, this stew is a perfect choice. And because both chicken and sausage have little if any connective tissue, they need only a short simmering time to become perfectly tender and succulent.

☙ YIELD: 8 SERVINGS AS A MAIN COURSE

1 rounded cup dried porcini mushrooms

Two 3½-pound chickens, each cut into 8 serving pieces (see page 148)

Kosher or sea salt and freshly ground black pepper to taste

Pure olive oil for pan-searing

2 pounds sweet Italian sausage, cut into 1-inch pieces using kitchen shears or a sharp serrated knife

4 tablespoons (½ stick) unsalted butter

1 large yellow onion, chopped

5 large garlic cloves, minced

2 tablespoons extra-virgin olive oil

½ pound button mushrooms, wiped clean and thinly sliced

½ pound shiitake mushrooms, wiped clean, stems removed and the caps thinly sliced

⅓ cup unbleached all-purpose flour

1½ cups Chicken Stock (page 16)

2 teaspoons chopped fresh rosemary

1 tablespoon chopped fresh thyme, or 1 teaspoon crumbled dried

3 tablespoons chopped flat-leaf Italian parsley for garnish

Suggested accompaniments: Mashed potatoes (drizzled with truffle oil, if you like), rice pilaf, or lightly buttered egg noodles

PLACE THE DRIED MUSHROOMS in a bowl and cover them with 1⅔ cups of very hot water. Set aside for about 20 minutes or until the mushrooms become supple. Using your hand, lift out the mushrooms and squeeze them gently to release any liquid back into the bowl. Coarsely chop the reconstituted mushrooms, then strain the mushroom liquid through a fine-mesh sieve lined with a doubled layer of dampened cheesecloth. Measure out 1 cup of the liquid and discard the rest.

Use poultry shears to cut each chicken breast half in half again widthwise and use a cleaver to hack the thighs in half, for a total of 12 pieces per chicken. Whack off the bony leg tips and use your poultry shears to snip off the wing tips. Freeze any scraps or bones for your next batch of stock. (Your butcher can prepare your chickens for you, but remember to ask for the bony pieces for stock.) Rinse and dry the chicken pieces and sprinkle them all over lightly with salt and black pepper.

HEAT A 6-QUART heavy-bottomed saucepan over medium heat and, when hot, add a thin layer of olive oil. When the oil is hot, add the chicken pieces in batches, skin side down, and brown them well on both sides. Use tongs to remove each batch to a tray while you brown the rest. When done, add the cut-up sausage pieces, in batches, to the hot pan and brown them well. Add the sausage to the tray of chicken. Spill out any oil from the pan but don't wipe out the interior.

Place the pan back over medium heat and add the butter. When the butter is hot and bubbling, stir in the chopped onion and garlic. Stir the vegetables, releasing the caramelized bits of chicken and sausage from the bottom of the pan. Cook until the vegetables are softened, stirring frequently, 3 to 6 minutes. Set aside for now.

HEAT A SEPARATE 12-INCH deep-sided skillet over medium heat and, when hot, add the extra-virgin olive oil. When the oil is hot, add the sliced fresh mushrooms and let them cook, stirring frequently, until tender and golden, about 5 minutes. Stir in the chopped porcini mushrooms, season with salt and pepper to taste, then remove the skillet from the heat and set it aside.

Sprinkle the flour over the sautéed onion and cook over medium-high heat, stirring constantly, until the flour is cooked and beginning to turn a nutty color, 4 to 5 minutes. Stir in the stock and the reserved mushroom liquid and, when well combined, add the rosemary and thyme. Bring the sauce to a brisk bubble, then reduce the heat to low and let it simmer until nicely thickened, about 3 minutes. Add the mushrooms to the sauce with another dose of black pepper. Transfer the seared chicken and sausage to the pan (don't pour in any accumulated fat from the tray). Use a large spoon to fold everything together. Cover the pot tightly and bring the ingredients to a full simmer, then turn the heat down to low and simmer the stew until the meat is tender but not dry, 20 to 30 minutes. (After 15 minutes, gently stir to help give all the ingredients even exposure to bottom heat.) Uncover the pot and, if needed, season the stew again with salt and pepper. Stir in the chopped parsley and serve the stew piping hot with mashed potatoes (drizzled with truffle oil, if you like), a rice pilaf, or lightly buttered egg noodles.

TIMING IS EVERYTHING
🖛 *The stew can be fully cooked a few hours ahead and, about 20 minutes before serving, reheated very gently (with the cover ajar) until piping hot. Just before serving, fold in the parsley.*

HERE'S THE SCOOP:
On the Right Way to Cover a Warm Mixture

The best way to cover a cooked mixture, even when barely warm, is to first place a clean kitchen towel over the pot and pull it taut before applying the lid. The towel will catch any accumulated condensation from rising steam that could then drip down into the food, diluting the flavors.

HERE'S THE SCOOP:
To Cut a Chicken into Serving Pieces and Clean Up Right!

Many recipes call for either a whole chicken that's cut into eight serving pieces or one that is butterflied. The following information will instruct you on how to do this yourself.

When finished cutting any raw meat, it's imperative that you wash your work surface, all utensils, and your hands thoroughly before using them to prepare other foods. Plastic cutting boards can be cleaned with soap and water and then run through the dishwasher. Wooden boards should be rinsed thoroughly with water, then scrubbed with kosher salt using a damp kitchen towel. Pour over the board a homemade sanitizing solution made by mixing 1 tablespoon liquid chlorine bleach with 1 gallon of warm (not hot) water. Pour this over the board in the sink. Rinse the board well, then squeeze the juice from half a lemon over it. Dry the board as best you can, then let it continue to air-dry on your counter. To get the chicken ready, rinse and dry the bird well. Pull out any excess fat from the opening of the cavity and trim away the excess skin.

❧ To CUT UP WHOLE CHICKEN

1. To section a chicken, first remove the legs. Position the chicken, breast up, on your work surface. Hold one drumstick by its bony tip and gently pull it away from the body, stretching the piece of skin between the leg and body. Use a sharp carving knife to make a slit in the skin only, without severing the meat.

2. Firmly grab the top of the leg and bend it away from the body, all the way back and down until you hear a "pop," which means that the hip bone has been released from its socket. Keep bending the leg until the tip of the bone is sticking straight up. Hold the chicken up by the dan-gling leg and simply cut the leg off, running the blade under the exposed thigh bone. Repeat this with the other leg.

3. To separate the drumstick from the thigh, place the whole leg, skin side down, on your work surface with the chubby part of the drumstick on top. Use your fingertips to locate the small but discernible empty space between the top of the meaty drumstick and the beginning of the thigh. Remove your finger just as you position the blade of your knife in this narrow space. Make one downward stroke, pushing the blade away from you going through this space, then pull the knife handle back toward you, which should separate the drumstick from the thigh. (If the first downward motion feels difficult, don't force it. This means the blade is in the wrong place. Use your finger to relocate the space and place the blade there.)

4. To remove the wings, hold the chicken up by one of the wings, allowing the body of the chicken to fall to the side. This will expose the chicken's armpit. Make an incision (about 1/3 inch deep) into this spot and, while holding the wing, bend it back and down, while twisting to release the wing bone from its socket. Keep bending the wing until the round white bone tip is fully exposed. Run the blade under and around this bone, releasing the wing into your hand. Do this with the other wing.

5A & 5B. To remove the backbone, use either a sharp knife or a pair of poultry scissors to cut along each side of the backbone, removing any thin, irrelevant fleshy side areas along with the back. Place the back into a dou-bled heavy-duty plastic bag and store in the freezer for making stock. If your recipe instructs you to remove the wing tips, bony leg tips, or cartilage, freeze these with the chicken back.

6. To split the whole breast into two halves, first fix the skin so it's covering the breast meat neatly. Place the breast, skin side down, on your work surface with the tip of the breast at the top, facing away from you. You'll see on the center of the bottom rim, nearest you, a whitish, translucent piece of cartilage lying directly over the breastbone. Use the blade of your knife to slit the cartilage, trying not to splinter the bone underneath.

7. Bend both sides of the breast back and away from each other, splitting the cartilage open and exposing the breastbone. Use your hand to pry the breastbone out, releasing it completely. Run your thumb under the cartilage that lies in between the breast halves, then pull it out. Cut directly down the center of the breast, separating it into two equal halves.

8. You now have eight pieces of chicken, ready to be seared, stewed, or fried.

❧ To BUTTERFLY WHOLE POULTRY so it lies perfectly flat, use poultry shears to cut up (or down) each side of the backbone, removing it completely. Turn the bird skin side down with the wings closest to you. Remove the breast bone and cartilage as described above. Either cut off the bony wing tips or bend them underneath the breast to protect them from burning. The bird should now lie perfectly flat and, when opened fully, should resemble a butterfly.

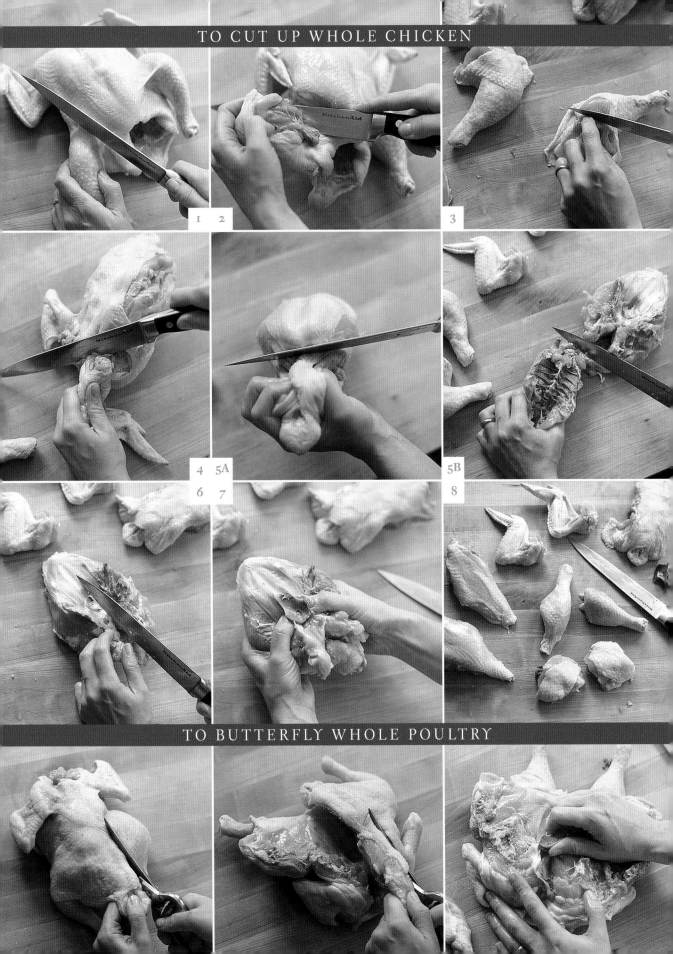

1 2

3

4 5A
6 7

5B
8

TANGY BEEF SHANKS,

Braised with Carrots, Onions, and Prunes

This wintry dish features generous slices of beef shank, which are meatier than veal shanks (called osso bucco). So, instead of presenting each person with an entire slice of shank meat, with the marrowbone in perfect position as you would with braised veal, it's perfectly proper to simply nudge individual portions of the cooked beef off the bones as you serve. However, each person should be served a marrowbone (or two) next to a generous piece of braised meat, along with some tender cooked carrots and a few deliciously sweet prunes.

❧ YIELD: 8 SERVINGS AS A MAIN COURSE, WITH GENEROUS LEFTOVERS

3 large yellow onions, peeled and chopped
    (about 6 cups)

8 garlic cloves, minced

1 green bell pepper, seeded and chopped

2 carrots, thinly sliced, plus 8 cups diagonally
    cut 2-inch carrot chunks

2 celery stalks, cleaned, trimmed, and sliced

½ cup (1 stick) butter or ½ cup extra-virgin oil,
    or a combination

8 large ripe tomatoes, peeled, seeded, and cut into
    chunks to measure 8 generous cups (see page 33),
    or use an equal amount of drained canned plum
    tomatoes

One 29-ounce can tomato puree

One 6-ounce can tomato paste

8 slices beef shank (cut 1½ inches thick), preferably
    from mid-calf section

Kosher or sea salt and freshly ground black pepper
    to taste

1½ cups unbleached all-purpose flour

Extra 2-inch marrowbones as desired (optional)

About ¼ cup flavorless vegetable oil

1½ cups Beef Stock (page 18) or doctored best-quality
    canned broth (see page 19)

½ cup cider vinegar

½ cup packed dark brown sugar

¼ cup strained fresh lemon juice

2 cups packed bite-size pitted prunes, or 1½ cups
    dark raisins, or a combination

Suggested accompaniments: Mashed potatoes or
    freshly cooked egg noodles, tossed with melted
    butter and cooked peas

COMBINE 4 CUPS of the chopped onions with the garlic, green pepper, sliced carrots, and celery in a bowl. Add the vegetables, in separate batches if necessary, to a food processor fitted with the steel blade. Pulse the mixture until the vegetables are finely chopped but remain distinguishable. Heat the butter or oil in a 10-quart, heavy-bottomed nonreactive saucepan. Tear off a piece of waxed paper and brush one side with melted butter or oil. When the fat is hot, stir in the minced vegetables and place the greased side of the paper directly on top of the vegetables. Reduce the heat to low and sweat the vegetables, stirring occasionally, for 20 minutes, then remove and discard the paper. Stir in the tomato chunks, tomato puree, and tomato paste and turn the heat up to medium. Bring the mixture to a brisk bubble, then reduce the heat to low and simmer the sauce, covered, for 30 minutes.

MEANWHILE, BROWN THE BEEF. If the slices are larger than 4 inches in diameter, use a sharp knife to cut off the meat from one side of the central bone. Season the meat with salt and black pepper. Place the flour on a plate and season it with salt and pepper. Heat a 12- to 14-inch heavy-bottomed nonreactive skillet over high heat and when hot, add a thin layer of vegetable oil. While the oil heats, dredge (coat) a few shanks and some of the extra marrowbones, if using, on all sides with some seasoned flour. Coat only as many beef slices and bones as can be browned at one time without crowding. In batches, brown the floured beef and bones in a single layer in the hot oil, turning once. Once deeply colored, transfer each batch to a tray so you can dredge and brown the rest. If needed, add more oil while browning.

Pour out any excess oil from the skillet, but don't wipe out the interior. Return the skillet to medium-high heat and add the stock and vinegar. As the mixture bubbles up, use the flat edge of a wooden spatula to release any caramelized meat and flour from bottom of the skillet. Boil the liquid until reduced by almost half, then strain through a fine-mesh sieve directly into the simmering sauce.

Place the browned beef and the bones in the simmering sauce along with any beefy juices, and spoon the sauce over the meat. Bring the sauce back to a full simmer over medium-high heat, then reduce the heat to low and simmer the stew, tightly covered, for 1 hour. Uncover the pan and add the brown sugar, lemon juice, and the 8 cups carrot chunks. Using oven mitts, hold the pot handles and gently "shimmy" the pot to help the ingredients mingle more thoroughly. Cover the pan again and let the stew cook for 1 hour more. Add the remaining 2 cups chopped onions and simmer for 30 more minutes. Add the prunes with some salt and pepper to taste and simmer for just 10 minutes more. Remove the pot from the heat and allow the mixture to come to room temperature, uncovered. As the mixture cools, spoon off and discard the grease that accumulates on top.

To SERVE, reheat the stew over low heat until piping hot. Place an ample portion of braised beef with some carrots and a generous ladle of sauce into individual wide soup plates next to a serving of either hot mashed potatoes or freshly cooked egg noodles tossed with butter and cooked peas. Make sure each person gets at least one marrowbone, which should be accompanied by a small cocktail fork.

TIMING IS EVERYTHING
🌭 *For best flavor, this entire dish should be cooked at least one (and up to two) days ahead and, after defatting and cooling, kept refrigerated. Bring the stew close to room temperature before reheating very gently, either on the stove over low heat or in a 350°F. oven, until piping hot throughout. This stew also freezes perfectly for several months in large, tightly shut rectangular freezer containers.*

SERVED WITH BAKING POWDER BISCUITS page 256

A VAT OF MUSSELS,
Bathed in a Spicy Persillade

This recipe is a perfect choice when you want something soothing in a hurry. Before you go to the market, read the sidebar for some important information on handling shellfish before you cook them. And don't hesitate to substitute either the little Manila clams (also called vongole or cockles) or the larger littleneck clams for the mussels. Just cook these hard-shell clams over high heat a few minutes longer. ❧ YIELD: 4 TO 6 SERVINGS AS A MAIN COURSE

½ cup extra-virgin olive oil or Garlic Confit Oil (page 23)
Kosher or sea salt
⅓ generous cup chopped flat-leaf Italian parsley, or mixed parsley and thinly sliced chives
⅓ cup dry white wine
10 to 12 garlic cloves, minced
1 teaspoon red pepper flakes
4 pounds mussels, cleaned (see page 153)

½ cup Chicken Stock (page 16) or doctored best-quality canned broth (see page 19)
4 tablespoons melted butter (optional, but highly recommended)
Freshly ground black pepper to taste
Suggested accompaniments: "Spaghettied" Zucchini (page 202) or 1 pound freshly cooked and buttered store-bought linguine, and a loaf of crusty bread

MAKE THE PERSILLADE: Combine the olive oil, ½ teaspoon salt, parsley, wine, garlic, and red pepper flakes in a bowl and set aside.

Heat a 6-quart heavy-bottomed saucepan over high heat and, when hot, add the mussels and a light sprinkling of salt. Cover the pot tightly and allow the mussels to cook until they are opened slightly, about 4 minutes. Remove the lid and pour in the persillade and stock and stir to combine well. Cover the pot and bring the liquid to a boil, then reduce the heat to low and simmer the mussels until fully opened and meat is cooked, about 5 minutes more. Stir in the melted butter, if using, then grind on a good amount of black pepper. Ladle the hot mussels either into individual bowls, with some of the broth spooned on top, or over cooked "spaghettied" zucchini or pasta. Place extra bowls on the table to accommodate the shells, and provide each person at the table with a soup spoon (and a hunk of delicious crusty bread) to enjoy every bit of the savory sauce.

TIMING IS
EVERYMTHING
❧ *The persillade can be made early in the day of cooking. Store it in the refrigerator, but bring close to room temperature before using.*

SERVED WITH PLAIN BAGUETTE page 247

HERE'S THE SCOOP:
On Handling Live Clams and Mussels

Before leaving the fish market, make sure that the bag holding the seafood (which is usually plastic) remains open and is also perforated in several places. When you get home, keep shellfish on the bottom shelf of your refrigerator, which is the coldest spot.

After being removed from salt water, shellfish stay the healthiest (and therefore the tastiest) for the longest amount of time if their salty water residue is allowed to remain and is not rinsed off. So don't clean bivalves more than several minutes before using them. This is especially true of mussels and soft-shell clams (also called steamers).

Thankfully, because mussels today are usually cultivated, they are much easier to clean, and out of an entire batch, you'll find only a few specimens with some scraggly beards attached. To remove these, place the mussels in a large well-perforated colander in the sink and run cold water over them, using your hands to continually toss them, exposing them all to large amounts of water. Pull out and discard any protruding beards, then shake off any excess water. The mussels are now ready to be cooked.

Hard-shell clams, although there are no beards to deal with, can be very dirty. To clean them, scrub them with a wire-bristle clam brush or rub them against each other while rinsing under cold water. Soft-shell clams need only to be rinsed well before cooking. Discard any that have broken shells, and if the shell is opened before cooking, tap on it and wait a few seconds for it to close. Although soft-shell clams are always semi-opened, if you see one that is wide open, touch the neck of the clam and you should see it retreat. If you don't see signs of life, throw it away since one bad clam or mussel can ruin the taste and aroma of the entire dish. Finally, if after cooking there are clams or mussels that have remained shut, don't try to pry them open since they were probably dead at the outset.

PASTA PESTO—
Any Way You Like It!

If you always have in your refrigerator or freezer one or all of the pestos provided in Chapter One, it will take just minutes to pull together a really delicious meal. Whether serving this hot or at room temperature, I always thin the pesto with some hot, well-concentrated stock that, in addition to adding a layer of flavor helps the pesto better coat the strands or tubes of pasta. As a last resort, substitute an equal amount of pasta cooking water. When reheating, always add more stock, since this really renews the texture. And don't be shy about mixing different types of pestos. Doing this is a great (and easy) way to spice up a familiar flavor.

🍃 YIELD: 4 TO 6 SERVINGS AS A MAIN COURSE

2 tablespoons kosher salt
1 pound any pasta
1 cup Roasted Vegetable Stock (page 22) or Chicken Stock (page 16), or doctored best-quality canned broth (see page 19)

1 generous cup prepared pesto of your choice (pages 26–28) or a combination, at room temperature
Freshly grated Parmigiano-Reggiano cheese for serving

TIMING IS EVERYTHING

🍃 *All three pestos can be made months ahead and stored in the refrigerator, well covered with olive oil and tightly shut.*
🍃 *You can combine the cooled pasta with the pesto one day ahead, and keep the dish chilled. Bring the pasta close to room temperature before adding your hot stock and any embellishments, and then serve.*

BRING AN 8-QUART POT of water to a rapid boil and add the salt. Stir in the pasta and cover the pot to quickly bring the water back to a boil. Uncover and cook the pasta according to the directions on the box until cooked through but al dente. Meanwhile, bring the stock to a boil in a 12-inch deep-sided skillet over medium heat. When the pasta is cooked, drain and add it directly to the skillet along with the pesto. While still cooking over medium heat, toss the pesto and stock through the pasta. Serve piping hot with a bowl of grated Parmesan cheese at the table.

To serve the dish at room temperature, cook the pasta in the boiling water as previously described. After cooking, drain the pasta and immediately plunge it into a bowl of ice water to make the strands less absorbent. When cool, lift the pasta out of the water and blot it dry on a tray lined with paper towels. Place the pasta in a mixing bowl and toss with the pesto. Let the pasta sit out, covered, at a comfortable room temperature for a few hours. When ready to serve, bring 1 cup of stock to a boil and toss it with the pasta. Serve it soon.

Embellished Pasta Pesto
After the pasta, pesto, and stock are well combined, add one or more of the following: pitted and sliced oil-cured olives, Oven-Roasted Tomatoes (page 100), minced marinated sun-dried tomatoes, rinsed and well-drained capers, thinly sliced or chopped roasted peppers (see page 24), pan-toasted walnuts or dry-toasted pine nuts (see page 271), halved small balls of fresh mozzarella (called bocconcini), sautéed mushrooms, or a chiffonade of fresh basil leaves (see page 100).

Feel the Difference . . .
FRESH PASTA
Made the Old-Fashioned Way

If you've made pasta before, you already know how much fun the process is. However, if you've always used a hand-cranked pasta maker, I hope you'll try this completely hand-driven method. I learned to make pasta this way in Italy, using a three-foot rolling pin. If you don't have a pin this long or a wooden table or countertop that's large enough to roll the dough out in halves, then simply use a shorter pin (a minimum of 20 inches long) and a slightly smaller board, and divide the dough into quarters. After rolling the dough out, to determine if it's thin enough, slide your hand underneath it at random spots. If the outline of your hand seems pretty clear, you're there. If the dough feels a little too thick in one spot, use the pin to roll over that area only. Keep the dough floured at all times to prevent it from sticking to the pin, or to itself, when applying pressure after each new revolution. If you are new at this, I suggest that you make pasta on a dry day, since this will help the dough to be more obedient, texture-wise.

 YIELD: 1½ POUNDS PASTA; 6 TO 8 SERVINGS AS A MAIN COURSE

3 cups pasta flour (finely ground semolina), plus
  more for dusting and rolling
6 extra-large eggs, made tepid by submerging in a
  bowl of very hot tap water for 10 minutes
1 generous tablespoon extra-virgin olive oil or Garlic
  Confit Oil (page 23)

1 scant teaspoon salt
A few grinds of freshly ground black pepper
½ cup minced fresh herbs such as basil, parsley,
  and/or chives (optional)

PLACE THE PASTA FLOUR in a mound on a large wooden work surface. Press the bottom of a small bowl in the flour to make a deep, wide well. Crack the eggs into the well, then add the olive oil, salt, pepper, and herbs, if using. Using the fingers of both hands, break up the eggs, combining them with the flavoring ingredients without disturbing the flour. Use your fingers to gently and repetitively splash the eggs, rapidly moving your fingers down, up, around, and down again. As you continue to splash the eggs, pull in some flour from the walls of the well, incorporating that flour completely before bringing in more. When all of the flour is incorporated, you'll have an irregularly shaped, shaggy mass of dough. Use a dough scraper to help release any bits of dough from your board and fingers, and incorporate the bits into the dough before you begin to knead.

Knead the dough with the heel of your hands and your fingertips, continually pushing down, pulling up, and turning the dough until it's smooth and supple, yet very firm and elastic, with a texture that's similar to your earlobe. If at any time the dough feels sticky, dust your work surface with a bit of flour—not too much flour, however, or the dough will slip and slide on your work surface, preventing the necessary traction. When done, dust the dough with flour, cover loosely with plastic wrap, and let rest for 30 minutes to 1 hour. Use your scraper to clean off the board so it's perfectly smooth.

Use your scraper to divide the dough in half, and keep one half covered while working with the other. (If your wooden surface is smaller than specified, divide the dough into quarters.) If wearing jewelry on your fingers (even a smooth wedding band), take it off. Sprinkle a generous layer of flour on your wooden board. Flatten the dough into a rectangular shape and sprinkle the top with more flour. At first, roll the dough as if you're rolling out pie pastry, keeping a rectangular shape. When the dough looks about 1/4 inch thick, spread an even layer of flour on top, being more generous than you think necessary.

Now the rolling process changes—you'll be stretching the dough, not just rolling over it. The dough should be positioned vertically in front of you. Place the pin at the top of the dough (at the short side that's farthest from you). Roll down toward you about 2 inches, wrapping that top lip of dough over the top of the pin. Roll down one more revolution, enclosing another section of the dough around the pin. Place your hands lightly on the top center of the pin and rock the pin back and forth in short spurts, while simultaneously applying medium downward pressure and sliding your hands toward each opposing end of the rolling pin. With each rocking and hand-sliding motion, both the dough wrapped around the pin and the area directly below the pin will become thinner. When your hands reach the ends of the pin, come back to the top center and roll the pin down one more revolution toward you (enclosing another section of dough). Repeat the rocking and sliding movements until you reach 1 or 2 inches up from the bottom of the sheet of dough. To finish this first round of dough stretching, make a final full revolution, quickly and firmly, over the bottom lip of dough. Roll up and down three or four times on this bottom section, so it's even with the rest.

At this point, the pin should be close to you, with the entire sheet coiled around it. Turn the pin, switching sides, and unroll the sheet of dough going away from you (so that what was the top short side is now the bottom short side). Flour the dough and, starting at the top end (as before), roll and stretch the dough coming down toward you, as just described. Do this a total of two or three times until the dough is very thin. Let the pasta sheet sit, uncov-

ered, on your work surface until it feels drier but is still able to bend without breaking—depending on the weather, this can take 10 to 30 minutes. Because space will probably be an issue, don't roll out the second half of the dough until you've cut and hung the first sheet. Dust the dough with flour and keep it covered with plastic wrap.

To cut the dough into lasagna noodles, divide the sheet of pasta in half widthwise using a ruler and a sharp chef's knife or a pasta wheel. Square off any irregular ends. Cut long, wide strips (about 3 inches wide by 7 inches long), lift each strip, and drape it over a wooden rod on a pasta rack so it can dry. To cut strands (linguine, wider fettuccine, or wider pappardelle ribbons), spread a thin but even layer of flour over the still-supple sheet of pasta. Roll the dough up into an evenly shaped log. Using a sharp knife (preferably a straight-edge cleaver), cut the log into thin or wide slices. One by one, lift and unravel each slice as you drape it within your nonworking hand. Hang the strands on the pasta rack so they can dry. When dry, slide the noodles off the rods and into a deep roasting pan where they can stay covered with aluminum foil until ready to cook.

To use a hand-cranked pasta machine, follow the manufacturer's instructions on your particular appliance. (I don't suggest rolling the dough through the last setting though, as it produces pasta that's too thin.)

To COOK THE PASTA, fill an 8-quart pot, preferably with a built-in strainer, with cold water and bring it to a rapid boil over high heat. Make sure that your sauce is almost finished and piping hot. Add 2 tablespoons of salt to the boiling water, then stir in the pasta. Cover the pot and bring the water quickly back to a rapid boil. Remove the lid and stir again. If fully dried, it should be perfectly cooked in 4 to 5 minutes. (Start timing as soon as you stir the pasta into the boiling water.) Drain the pasta, allowing a little of the cooking water to adhere to the strands, and immediately either add it to the pan containing your sauce or transfer the cooked pasta to a warmed serving bowl and ladle the sauce on top. Using tongs, toss the strands, coating them evenly.

If serving cooked pasta with a saucy entree, like a stew, that's being served separately, toss the cooked pasta with some melted butter or hot olive oil and salt and pepper to taste. If cooking lasagna noodles, cook a few at a time, undercooking slightly. Then immediately slip them into a bowl of cold water to remove some of their surface starch and to stop the cooking process. Carefully remove them from the water, lay them flat on sheets of waxed paper, and blot them dry with paper towels.

TIMING IS EVERYTHING
* The dough can be made one day ahead and kept in the refrigerator, covered in plastic wrap. Let the dough sit out at room temperature for about an hour before rolling it out.
* Although the noodles can be made and dried several days ahead, for the freshest flavor, the pasta should be eaten within 48 hours. Leave freshly dried pasta at room temperature in a covered roasting pan. Any extra pasta can be frozen in sealed, heavy-duty freezer bags. Drop them into boiling water straight from the freezer. Cooking time will vary at this point, so check frequently to prevent over- or undercooking.

FETTUCCINE ALLA PANNA
with Poached Shrimp and Green Peas

Tender long strands of pasta are flecked with an abundance of fresh chives and coated with a piping hot cream sauce that's infused with Parmesan cheese and lightened with shrimp stock. The only things that could make this dish even more satisfying are some fresh shrimp and peas, so, I added them!

♦ YIELD: 6 TO 8 SERVINGS AS A MAIN COURSE

½ cup (1 stick) unsalted butter

1 large leek, cleaned and thinly sliced (white and light green parts)

1½ cups heavy cream

1½ cups Shrimp Stock (page 20)

¾ cup freshly grated Parmigiano-Reggiano cheese, plus more for passing at the table

Kosher or sea salt and freshly ground black pepper to taste

1 recipe Fresh Pasta (page 155), made with ½ cup chives and cut into fettuccine, or use 1½ pounds store-bought fettuccine

1 generous pound large or jumbo shrimp, shelled, deveined (see page 20), and halved lengthwise (shells reserved for stock)

10 ounces fresh or frozen peas

FILL AN 8-QUART POT with cold water and bring to a rapid boil over high heat. When boiling, reduce the heat to low and let the water simmer until you're ready for it.

Melt all but 1 tablespoon of the butter in a 2- to 3-quart, heavy-bottomed, deep-sided skillet over medium heat and, when hot and bubbling, stir in the leek. Reduce the heat to low and lay a sheet of waxed paper directly on top of the leek and sweat it until softened and slightly reduced, about 6 minutes. Discard the paper. Add the cream and 1 cup of the stock, and bring the mixture to a boil over medium heat. Reduce the heat to low and let the sauce reduce to about 2 cups. Stir in the Parmesan cheese and bring the sauce back to a full simmer, stirring occasionally to help the cheese melt evenly.

AS THE SAUCE SIMMERS, turn the heat up under the pot of water and, when it begins to rapidly boil, stir in 2 tablespoons of salt. Stir in the pasta and cover the pot so it can come back up to a rapid boil. Remove the lid and cook the pasta until done to your liking, stirring occasionally and checking often to prevent overcooking. As the noodles cook, heat a 12- to 14-inch heavy-bottomed, deep-sided oven-to-table skillet over low heat with the remaining ½ cup shrimp stock and remaining 1 tablespoon of butter.

To finish the sauce, turn the heat under the cream sauce up to medium, then stir the shrimp into the simmering sauce and wait 1 minute. Stir in the peas, then reduce the heat to low and let the mixture cook very gently, just until the shrimp and peas are perfectly tender and the sauce is piping hot, 1 to 3 minutes. (The cooking time will vary depending on the size and temperature of your shrimp.) Season well with salt and pepper to taste.

Drain the pasta, allowing some of the cooking water to adhere to the strands, and drop them into the skillet with the stock and butter. Toss. Pour the shrimp sauce over the top and serve at once, with extra grated cheese. Alternatively, if you don't have a large enough skillet to accommodate the pasta with the shrimp sauce, heat the ½ cup stock with the butter in a small saucepan and, after draining the noodles, put them into a large warmed serving bowl along with the stock, and toss together. Pour the sauce over the top and serve, topping with extra grated cheese, if desired.

TIMING IS EVERYTHING
❦ *The sauce base can be assembled, up until adding the cheese, 1 hour ahead and kept on a turned-off burner.*

You Won't Miss the Meat . . .
LOADED-WITH-VEGETABLES
LASAGNA

Every bit as substantial and satisfying as a version made with meat, this vegetable lasagna has layers chock-full of perfectly cooked vegetables. Since the entire recipe can be fully assembled up to two days ahead, you're likely to forget the effort required and just bask in all the compliments you'll undoubtedly receive. ❧ YIELD: 8 TO 10 SERVINGS AS A MAIN COURSE

About 1¼ cups Garlic Confit Oil (page 23) or extra-virgin olive oil

1 cup chopped yellow onion

3 garlic cloves, minced (optional)

3 medium zucchini, cut into small dice (5 cups)

1½ teaspoons aromatic dried oregano, crumbled

Kosher or sea salt and freshly ground black pepper

2 pounds ricotta cheese

1½ cups freshly grated Parmigiano-Reggiano cheese, plus more for serving

12 garlic cloves, peeled, halved, boiled for 2 minutes, and drained

6 medium-large portobello mushrooms, wiped clean and stems removed

3 large eggplants, cut into ⅓-inch-thick lengthwise slices

¾ pound 3 × 7-inch lasagna noodles (about 14 sheets; page 155), or use store-bought

1 recipe Ultra-Speedy Marinara Sauce (page 33)

1 recipe Oven-Roasted Tomatoes (page 100)

1½ generous cups (12 ounces) each grated or shredded mozzarella and Muenster cheese

Fresh basil sprigs for garnish

HEAT A 12-INCH heavy-bottomed, deep-sided skillet over medium-high heat and, when hot, add 1 tablespoon of the oil. When the oil is hot, stir in the onion and garlic, if using. Cook, stirring frequently, until tender, about 4 minutes. Raise the heat to high and stir in the zucchini along with 1 additional tablespoon of oil and 1 teaspoon of the oregano. Sauté the zucchini until it's tender but not mushy and is starting to turn golden around the edges, 4 to 5 minutes. Add some salt and pepper to taste, then scrape the vegetables into a bowl. Add the ricotta cheese, 1 cup of the grated Parmesan cheese, and salt and pepper. Set aside.

Clean out the skillet used for the zucchini and put it back on the stove over high heat. When the pan is hot, add 4 tablespoons of the oil and, when hot, add the poached and halved garlic cloves. Cook the garlic, stirring constantly, until golden. Use a perforated utensil to remove the garlic to a bowl, then immediately add the mushrooms to the hot oil. Cook the mushrooms until tender and golden, about 5 minutes. Remove the pan from the heat and set it aside.

Preheat the broiler with the oven rack as close as possible to the heat source. Line two large, shallow baking sheets with aluminum foil (shiny side up). Brush the foil with some oil and sprinkle with salt and pepper. Working in batches, brush both sides of each slice of eggplant lightly but evenly with some oil and lay them in a single layer on the prepared baking sheets. Sprinkle the tops with salt and pepper, then broil the eggplant until golden on both sides, turning once, about 3 to 4 minutes per side. When each batch is done, transfer the cooked slices to a tray and repeat with the remaining slices.

Bring an 8-quart pot of water to a rapid boil. Set up a bowl of ice water and a tray lined with waxed paper nearby. Add some salt to the water and half the lasagna noodles. Stir the pasta as it cooks until it's almost (not quite) tender. Remove the noodles to the bowl of ice water to stop the cooking process. Add the remaining noodles to the pot. While these cook, remove the already-cooked noodles from the ice water, then lay them on the prepared tray lined with waxed paper and pat them dry. Continue until you've cooked, drained, and dried all the pasta.

Use a 15 × 10-inch pan that's 3 inches deep to assemble the lasagna. If using a glass pan, preheat the oven to 375°F.; if using a metal pan, preheat to 400°F. Brush the interior of the dish with oil.

TIMING IS EVERYTHING

 The lasagna can be fully assembled two days before baking and kept chilled. Bring the dish close to room temperature or lengthen the "covered" baking time accordingly.

SPREAD A VERY SHALLOW LAYER of marinara sauce over the bottom of the dish, then place a layer of cooked noodles over the sauce. Spread a generous layer of the cheese filling over the noodles (about half), then layer half of the roasted tomatoes over the cheese. Layer half of the eggplant over the tomatoes, pressing down lightly to help compact the layers. Spread an even layer of sauce over the eggplant, about 1/3 inch deep. Repeat these layers, but this time after the eggplant goes on, ladle on a more generous layer of sauce, about 2/3 inch deep. Now scatter all the cooked mushrooms and the garlic over the sauce and top this with the remaining cheeses. Sprinkle some pepper over the top along with the remaining 1/2 teaspoon oregano. Grease the shiny side of a large sheet of foil and place it greased side down loosely over the top.

Bake the lasagna for 1 hour, then remove the foil and bake until piping hot at the center, and the cheese is light golden and bubbling, 15 to 20 minutes more. Remove the dish from the oven and let sit for 10 minutes before cutting the lasagna into generous portions. Garnish with fresh basil and pass some grated Parmesan at the table.

FIVE-CHEESE BAKED PASTA
with Cherry Tomatoes, Chives,
and a Savory Crumb Topping

In addition to being a creamy and outrageously luscious entree, there's hardly a better accompaniment to liven up a simple roast or piece of grilled meat, chicken, or fish. Regardless, I suggest serving this pasta dish with a salad of perky greens like frisée, radicchio, and romaine, lightly dressed with a sharp Sherry Vinaigrette (page 114) to cut some of the richness in the sauce.

☙ YIELD: 6 SERVINGS AS A MAIN COURSE

3 tablespoons unsalted butter, melted, plus ½ cup (1 stick) butter for the sauce

⅓ cup Dried Bread Crumbs (page 29), ground a bit coarse

Freshly ground black pepper to taste

2 tablespoons freshly grated Parmigiano-Reggiano cheese

2 tablespoons kosher salt

1 pound store-bought medium shell pasta

4 tablespoons unbleached all-purpose flour

4 cups whole milk

White pepper to taste

½ teaspoon cayenne pepper (optional)

8 ounces each Havarti, sharp Cheddar, and Jarlsberg cheese, grated (or shredded) and combined

2 generous cups (1 dry pint) small cherry tomatoes, stems removed

½ rounded cup thinly sliced chives (if unavailable, mince the deeper green part of a scallion)

3 ounces Gorgonzola cheese (preferably a high-quality creamy type, like dolcelatte dolce), chilled and cut into medium dice (about ½ rounded cup)

Olive oil for brushing

BRUSH THE INTERIOR of a 3-quart oven-to-table baking dish with 1 tablespoon of the melted butter. Heat the remaining 2 tablespoons of melted butter in a small saucepan or skillet over medium heat and, when hot and bubbling, stir in the bread crumbs. Sauté the crumbs, stirring constantly, until they absorb the butter and become a bit more golden, about 1 minute. Remove from the heat and add some black pepper to taste. When cool, stir in the Parmesan cheese and set the pan aside for now.

Fill an 8-quart pot with cold water and bring it to a rapid boil over high heat. Add the salt, then stir in the pasta and let it cook for only half the time recommended on the package. Drain the pasta and place it in a large mixing bowl.

If using a glass baking dish, preheat the oven to 375°F.; preheat to 400°F. if using an earthenware or metal pan.

Melt the remaining 1 stick of butter in a 3-quart heavy-bottomed saucepan over medium heat and, when hot and bubbling, stir in the flour. Cook the roux, stirring constantly with a wooden spoon, for 1 to 2 minutes, just to remove any raw taste. Whisk in the milk, dispersing the roux throughout. Bring the liquid to a simmer, uncovered, stirring frequently. Stir in some white and black pepper, along with the cayenne, if using. Turn the heat down to low and let the sauce cook gently until lightly thickened, 3 to 5 minutes. Stir the mixed grated cheeses into the sauce and let the cheese melt over low heat, stirring frequently, until homogenous.

Pour the hot cheese sauce over the partially cooked pasta and fold in the tomatoes and chives. Add more black pepper to taste, then pour the pasta mixture into the prepared baking dish and dot the top evenly with the diced Gorgonzola cheese. Sprinkle the crumb mixture over the top. Tear off a sheet of aluminum foil and brush the shiny side with olive oil. Place the foil greased side down over the dish.

Bake the pasta for 40 minutes. Uncover the dish and continue to cook for another 20 minutes, or until piping hot throughout and the top is golden and crisp.

TIMING IS EVERYGHING

This dish can be assembled fully one day ahead and kept refrigerated, well covered. Bring the dish close to room temperature before baking or lengthen the "covered" baking time accordingly.

HERE'S THE SCOOP:
On How to Know If It's Really Hot

How many times have you been disappointed with the internal temperature of a baked dish? It's easy to mistake the bubbling around the sides of the dish for an indication that it's ready to be served. Unlike microwave heat, which cooks from the inside out, regular oven heat penetrates food from the outside in. So when steam and bubbles are visible on the outside of a dish, that only means that the oven has begun to do its work. If it's bubbling at the very center of a mixture, you can be sure it's hot enough to be served. If you're uncertain, stick the blade of a table knife into the center of the dish, then place it, flat side down, on the inside of your wrist. If it's really hot, you're good to go.

ROAST CHICKEN page 168,
PANE DI CASA page 233

CHAPTER SIX

It's No Big Deal . . .

GREAT GRILLED, ROASTED, and PAN-FRIED MEAT, POULTRY, and FISH

IF YOU'RE LOOKING to quickly fill your home with aromas that will get your family and friends to the table in a hurry, this is certainly a great chapter for you! Just to name a few of the choices, there's a sizzling platter of steak, chicken, or shrimp fajitas, and an enticing pile of succulent baby back ribs, and broiled swordfish steaks dressed in bubbling browned butter, flecked with tender nuggets of candied garlic, strips of roasted peppers, and piquant capers. There's a huge prime rib roast worthy of the most special gatherings, and a gorgeous pair of scampi-scented stuffed and roasted lobsters, which are perfect for a romantic evening just for the two of you. There's detailed information on how to build and maintain heat in a charcoal grill, and a great indoor pan-searing/ oven-roasting method for chops and butterflied poultry that yields fabulous results. This way, summer-fun food is always doable, no matter what the season. Regardless of which method you use, I trust that the food in this chapter will help you all to come to the table happy.

Everyone Should Know . . .
HOW TO MAKE
A GREAT ROAST CHICKEN

Of all the recipes in this book, this one for roast chicken is the most special to me. This was the first "real" meal that I successfully cooked for my husband, Jon, when we first got married. And although it's been over twenty-five years, this recipe continues to produce the best roast chicken that I and my family have ever had. Feel free to apply the same seasoning and cooking technique to smaller Cornish hens and larger capons. Simply adjust the amount of seasoning, basting butter, and, of course, the roasting time. Lastly, although you might be tempted, please don't throw away the cooked carcasses or any unused skin after carving. Instead, refrigerate them until morning, then make a wonderful pot of stock according to the directions on page 16. If you'd like to serve this with gravy, see the end of the recipe. ❧ YIELD: 4 TO 6 SERVINGS AS A MAIN COURSE

FOR THE CHICKEN

Two 3½- to 4½-pounds chickens

Flavorless vegetable oil or pure olive oil

Kosher or sea salt and freshly ground black pepper to taste

Poultry Seasoning (page 36) or see the end of this recipe

¾ cup (1½ sticks) unsalted butter

3 garlic cloves, minced

8 scallions, trimmed and left whole (use the white and 2 inches of the tender green), if not planning to stuff the birds

3 to 4 cups of your favorite stuffing, at room temperature (optional)

2 cups assorted aromatic vegetables (thinly sliced carrot, yellow onion, and celery)

Vegetable spray or oil

½ cup dry white wine or Chicken Stock (see page 16)

2 teaspoons minced fresh thyme, or ½ teaspoon dried

CLEAN AND SEASON THE CHICKENS. Remove the giblets from each cavity, reserving only the necks and gizzards for the gravy. Save the livers and hearts for another recipe or discard them. Thoroughly rinse and dry the chickens, trimming away any excess fat from the cavities. Place the chickens on two large overlapping sheets of aluminum foil on your counter. Pour a cup or so of oil into a bowl and place it next to the chickens. Working with one bird at a time, sprinkle the insides of each cavity with some salt and black pepper. Sprinkle the poultry seasoning very generously on both sides of each chicken. Use your hands to scoop up a liberal amount of oil and rub it onto the birds, evenly distributing the seasoning. When done, the birds should look deeply colored and glistening. Bend the bony tips of the wings down, securing them underneath the chickens. Transfer the birds, cradled in the foil, to a tray or a

large bowl and cover them with greased plastic wrap, oiled side down. Refrigerate the birds until 30 minutes before you plan to roast. If you intend to make gravy, now is the time to start your gravy base—see the end of the recipe.

MELT THE 1½ STICKS of butter in a small saucepan over medium heat. When the butter is hot and bubbling, add the garlic. Reduce the heat to low and let the garlic sizzle for a few minutes until it's very fragrant. Remove the pan from the stove and let the garlic settle at the bottom of the pan.

If not using stuffing, insert the trimmed scallions into the cavity of each chicken, green ends out. Secure the legs using kitchen twine by wrapping it around the knobby ends, crisscrossing the ends, and tying a knot. If planning to stuff the birds, just before roasting, spoon the stuffing loosely into the cavity. Use about ½ generous cup stuffing per pound of meat. Place any additional stuffing in a buttered baking dish to roast along with the chickens. To truss a stuffed bird, thread a 10-inch length of kitchen twine through a trussing needle and tie a knot at the bottom end of the string. Starting at the top of the cavity, sew through both side flaps of thin fleshy skin until you reach the bottom of the opening. Pull the string, securing the cavity shut, and use the remaining string to wind around the knobby ends of the drumsticks (while pulling) to bring them together. Tie a knot to secure the legs, and snip off any loose ends of string.

PREHEAT THE OVEN TO 400°F. Strew the carrot, onion, and celery on a large shallow baking sheet. Spray a large roasting rack (even if it's nonstick) with vegetable spray and place it over the vegetables. Place the seasoned birds, breast side up, side by side on the prepared roasting rack with a 2-inch space between the birds. Spoon the garlic butter over each bird, leaving most of the garlic behind.

Put the chickens into the oven and reduce the temperature to 375°F. Roast the birds until golden and crisp, 1¼ to 1½ hours for unstuffed birds (about 15 minutes longer if stuffed), basting occasionally with the pan juices using a bulb baster. As the chicken skin becomes crisp and golden, check frequently for signs of doneness (wings and legs should wiggle freely at the joints and an

TIMING IS
EVERYTHING
❧ If impeccably fresh, the chickens can be seasoned (not stuffed) two days ahead and kept refrigerated, well covered with oiled plastic wrap. Always stuff poultry minutes before you plan to cook. If not using stuffing, however, the scallions can be inserted ahead when you apply your seasoning.
❧ The garlic butter can be assembled a few hours ahead and kept at a comfortable room temperature. Reheat just before using.

instant-read theremometer will read 170°F. when inserted into the thigh and 165°F. [no higher] when inserted into the breast meat). Cook stuffed birds until an instant-read thermometer inserted deep into the cavity reads 165°F. When done, remove the chickens from the oven and lift out the roasting rack holding them. Let the birds rest, loosely tented with aluminum foil, over a platter or a carving surface for 10 minutes so the juices can be reabsorbed. (Bake additional stuffing, covered, for 30 minutes and uncovered for 15 minutes more, or until the top is golden and crusty.)

IF YOU DON'T HAVE the preassembled poultry seasoning, take out a jar of onion powder, garlic powder, Lawry's seasoning salt, and sweet paprika, along with a peppermill and a bottle of vegetable oil. Place a sheet of plastic wrap around the center of each bottle, including the oil, which will help keep the jars clean as you season the birds. Grind a generous amount of black pepper into a small bowl. Starting with the onion powder, sprinkle each listed seasoning liberally all over the birds on both sides, being the least generous with the Lawry's. Lubricate the chickens as directed, and follow the remaining instructions.

PAN GRAVY
🍴 YIELD: ABOUT 2¼ CUPS

3 cups Chicken Stock (page 16) or doctored canned broth (see page 19)
Necks and gizzards from the chickens (no heart or liver)
2½ tablespoons unsalted butter
1 large shallot, minced
2 medium button mushrooms, wiped clean and coarsely chopped
3 tablespoons unbleached all-purpose flour
½ cup dry white wine, or use more stock

TO MAKE THE GRAVY, bring 2½ cups of the stock to a brisk simmer in a 1-quart heavy-bottomed saucepan over medium-high heat. Add the necks and gizzards. When the liquid comes back to a full bubble, reduce the heat to low and simmer the chicken parts, covered, until the meat is tender, about 25 minutes for the necks and 40 minutes for the tougher gizzards. When each is done, remove them from the stock. Set the stock aside and let the necks and gizzards become cool enough to handle. When cool, use a fork and your fingers to pull any meat off the necks, then shred or chop it. Chop the gizzards as well, and combine both. Reserve the stock and wipe out the saucepan.

Melt the butter in the same saucepan over medium heat. When bubbling, add the shallot and mushrooms. Sauté the vegetables, stirring frequently, until softened, about 2 minutes, then stir in the flour. Cook the vegetable roux over medium heat, stirring constantly, for 1 minute, then whisk in the reserved 2 cups of stock. Bring the liquid to a full bubble, then reduce the heat to low and let the sauce cook until thickened and rich-looking, 10 to 15 minutes, stirring often. Lay a doubled paper towel over the top of the pan, then apply the lid. Set the sauce aside.

When the chicken is done, reheat the gravy base over low heat until simmering. Pour off all but 2 tablespoons of the drippings from the baking sheet. (Keep all those vegetables and browned bits clinging to the bottom of the pan.) Set the baking sheet on the stove directly over medium-high heat and, when things start to sizzle, pour in the wine. Using a gravy whisk or the flat edge of a wooden spatula, combine the vegetables, drippings, and wine or chicken stock. Simmer the liquid until reduced by half. Position a fine-mesh sieve over the simmering sauce base and carefully pour the contents of the baking sheet into the sieve, mashing down on the vegetables. Stir the thyme, along with the reserved minced neck and gizzard meat, into the gravy. Season the sauce with some salt and pepper and let it simmer over low heat for 3 to 5 minutes. Keep the sauce warm while you carve the chickens.

HERE'S THE SCOOP:
On Carving Up a Roast Chicken

Cut the twine that binds the leg tips and, if the chickens were stuffed, cut and remove the string that secures the cavities shut. Use tongs to remove the scallions and place them on a platter or use a spoon to scoop out the stuffing and place it in a warmed serving bowl. Cover the stuffing loosely with foil to keep it warm. Position one chicken so the cavity is in front of you. To remove the legs, first making an incision in the skin where one of the thighs meets the breast. Use your nonworking hand to grasp the leg tip while you use the knife to separate the leg from the body. When you reach the hip joint, use the tip of the knife to nudge a final separation. To detach the drumstick from the thigh, lay the leg on your cutting board (skin side up) and place your index finger on the top of the drumstick just where it meets the thigh. Use your fingertip to locate the small empty space, indicating the joint. Place the knife blade in this spot and drive the blade through. Place the drumstick and thigh on a serving platter and do the same thing on the other side.

To slice the breast meat, first lift off the top skin covering the breast in one piece and place it to the side, keeping it dry. Use the knife to cut each breast half off the carcass in one piece, driving the blade in from the top to one side of the chest bone. Depending on how chubby the breast is, slice the slab of meat into two or three pieces and put them on the platter. Do this on the other side. Slice the skin into crisp strips and drape them over the breast meat.

To remove the wings, cut them off where they meet the carcass. Then turn each carcass over and run your thumb under the two nuggets of dark meat that sit to either side of the backbone, releasing them. Put these on the platter. Repeat this with the remaining chicken.

Pan-Seared and Oven-Roasted . . .
HERB-SCENTED DOUBLE RIB LAMB CHOPS

You won't find lamb chops better than these: thick with a very dark exterior, a rosy-red interior, and a savory flavor that leaves nothing to be desired. This recipe illustrates perfectly the concept of how uncomplicated food can provide a big dining experience. Make sure your exhaust fan works, and serve your chops on plain sturdy plates so their beauty can shine.

❧ YIELD: 6 SERVINGS AS A MAIN COURSE

Garlic Confit Oil (page 23) or extra-virgin olive oil
1½ tablespoons minced fresh thyme
2 rounded teaspoons minced fresh rosemary
Freshly ground black pepper

Kosher or sea salt to taste
12 double rib lamb chops (1½ to 2 inches thick), trimmed of excess fat (or use chops from the loin)

TIMING IS EVERYTHING

❧ *The chops can be seasoned (but not salted) up to two days ahead and kept refrigerated, well covered.*

❧ *The chops can be pan-seared up to an hour before finishing them in the oven. Leave them on a tray at a comfortable room temperature. Lengthen the roasting time, however, by a few minutes to compensate for the cooler temperature of the chops when entering the oven.*

LINE A LARGE 17 × 13-inch shallow baking sheet with aluminum foil shiny side up, and place the baking sheet on the rack in the upper third of the oven. Preheat the oven to 425°F., preferably for 30 minutes or longer.

Turn on your exhaust fan. Pour about ½ cup of the oil into a bowl and stir in half the minced herbs and lots of black pepper. Use a pastry brush to apply an even layer of the seasoned oil to all sides of the lamb chops, then season again very generously with pepper. Sprinkle the chops generously, on one side only, with salt.

PLACE ONE OR TWO large well-seasoned cast-iron skillets, or a large stove-top grill pan, on the stove over high heat. (Or straddle an extra-large grill pan over two burners.) As a last resort, use one or two heavy-bottomed nonstick skillets. When very hot, lay the chops in the pan salted side down in a single layer without crowding. Brown on the first side for 3 full minutes. Sprinkle the unsalted side with salt, then use tongs to turn the chops and brown them for another 3 minutes. Since double-rib chops will have a wide, thin layer of top fat, after browning them on both sides, stand the chops on this fatty side to brown and crisp it. If doing this in batches, remove each batch of chops to a tray so you can sear the rest.

When all the chops are seared, transfer them to the preheated baking sheet and sprinkle them with the remaining minced herbs and a bit more salt. Roast the double chops until done to your liking: 7 to 9 minutes for medium-rare, 6 minutes for thinner loin chops. Serve hot.

SERVED WITH SAUTÉED
SPINACH page 201

HERE'S THE SCOOP:
On Stove-Top Grilling

Outdoor grilling requires high heat, so when you'd like to get the same results indoors, you need to crank the heat up as high as it goes. Once the food hits the hot pan, the only way to prevent a large amount of billowing smoke from forming (thus an uninvited visit from your local fire guy) is to make sure that you have a properly functioning exhaust fan. And don't wait until the food begins to sear to turn it on. The exhaust fan should be turned on while the pan is heating.

The best pan to use is a heavy, well-seasoned cast-iron pan (with or without grill lines) or a large, high-quality rectangular grill pan that can fit over two burners, increasing the size of your cooking surface. If the food to be grilled is not coated with a wet marinade, it's better to lubricate the dry food with some great olive oil, rather than oiling the grill pan. Conversely, when grilling food that's been marinated, it's best to pat the excess off and, just before placing the food on the pan, either swab the hot surface evenly (but very lightly) with pure oil or remove the pan from the heat and spray it lightly with some vegetable spray. Let the oiled surface become very hot, then add the food to be seared. It's not advisable to sear food longer than 3 minutes per side, since even the best exhaust fan can give out, leaving you with lots of smoke. That's why you finish cooking in the oven, on either a preheated baking sheet or under a hot broiler.

MEAT, POULTRY, AND FISH ❧ 173

GRILLED CHICKEN PESTO
Topped with Marinated Tomatoes

Tender grilled chicken is flavored here with a lemon-spiked basil pesto and served topped with a piquant mixture of fresh tomatoes, garlic, and herbs. Since the dressing for the tomatoes is so flavorful, you really can get away with less than summer-ripe specimens. And, although homemade pesto is fabulous, feel free to substitute your favorite store-bought refrigerated brand. So, although this dish, on paper, screams "summer," if you have a stove-top grill pan (and a good exhaust fan), it's just as doable any other time of the year.

❧ YIELD: 6 TO 8 SERVINGS AS A MAIN COURSE

FOR THE CHICKEN

8 large skinless, boneless chicken breast halves
Kosher or sea salt and freshly ground black pepper
    to taste
1 cup Basil Pesto (page 27), or use a favorite
    store-bought brand
¼ cup strained fresh lemon juice

FOR THE TOMATO TOPPING

⅓ cup extra-virgin olive oil, plus more for brushing
Strained juice from 1 juicy lemon (about 2
    tablespoons)

1 tablespoon red wine vinegar
2 garlic cloves, minced
2 generous teaspoons Dijon mustard
1 teaspoon kosher or sea salt
Freshly ground black pepper to taste
¼ cup each freshly chopped basil leaves and cilantro
16 ripe plum (Roma) tomatoes, cut in half through
    the middle and seeded (skins intact)

6 basil sprigs for garnish (optional)

To FLATTEN THE chicken breasts, position each breast half, boned side up, on your work surface. Put your nonworking hand on top of the breast to keep it in place. Use your working hand to position the blade of a sharp carving knife horizontally, parallel to your work surface, with the blade placed half way up the flesh on one long side. Carefully, while keeping the blade absolutely parallel, drive the knife into the flesh, moving the blade up and away from you and then down and toward you, leaving about ½ inch of flesh attached at the opposite end. Open the breast and lay it flat. If, after opening, you see that you didn't go in far enough, use the blade to slice a little deeper.

Lay one opened breast half (cut side up) in the center of a sheet of waxed paper and place another sheet of paper on top. Using a smooth, heavy meat mallet, give the chicken several firm taps (not whacks) starting at the center and going out toward the edge of the meat. The aim is to thin the meat slightly and to level the outer surface. Run your hand over the top layer of paper and, if not level, give those higher areas several more soft taps with the mallet. Do this same procedure with the remaining chicken. When finished, remove the paper from each piece and stack the chicken in a 13 × 9-inch nonreactive dish.

Sprinkle the chicken pieces on both sides, lightly but evenly, with salt and black pepper. Mix the pesto with the lemon juice and pour this over the chicken. Using clean hands, rub the pesto all over both sides of each piece. Cover the dish and chill until 30 minutes before ready to cook.

ASSEMBLE THE TOMATO TOPPING. Use a whisk to combine the ⅓ cup of olive oil, the lemon juice, vinegar, garlic, mustard, salt, pepper, and chopped herbs in a medium-size nonreactive bowl. Add the prepared tomatoes and fold the mixture together, combining well. Cover the bowl and set it aside.

To cook the chicken using a gas grill, preheat the grill to high, covered. If using a charcoal grill, follow the instructions on page 180 to heat the coals and get the grill hot. If cooking indoors, turn on your exhaust fan and heat your stove-top grill pan(s) over high heat until very hot.

Grill the chicken, uncovered, turning once, until cooked through but not dry, 4 to 6 minutes total. Remove the chicken breasts to a serving platter and let them rest for a few minutes, loosely covered with aluminum foil.

Serve the chicken either hot or at room temperature, using a slotted spoon to top with the marinated tomatoes. Garnish each plate with a pretty basil sprig. Alternatively, the chicken and the bowl of dressed tomatoes can be passed separately at the table.

SERVED WITH FOUGASSE WITH
GARLIC CONFIT   page 237

TIMING IS
EVERYTHING
* The chicken can be marinated up to 24 hours ahead and kept in the refrigerator, well covered.
* The dressing for the tomatoes can be assembled early in the day, but to preserve best color and texture, don't add the tomatoes until just before grilling the chicken.
* You can cook the chicken an hour ahead and serve it at room temperature.

Meat that Falls off the Bone . . .
OVEN-BARBECUED
BABY BACK RIBS

Succulent and incredibly tender, ribs are right up there with roast chicken as one of the most beloved American comfort foods. If you always have a few jars of homemade barbecue sauce tucked in the refrigerator, it's really a snap to put this dish together. If using the larger pork ribs, ask the butcher to crack them for easier separation after cooking. I rarely serve individual portions—instead, I just cut the roasted racks in half, pile them high on a large platter, and stick some sturdy tongs alongside. Although I suggest allowing a minimum of half a rack of baby backs or five of the larger pork ribs per person, I suggest you cook an additional rack for every two people at the table. (Most of us have no shame when it comes to eating ribs.) ❧ YIELD: 6 TO 8 SERVINGS AS A MAIN COURSE

1 very large yellow onion, coarsely chopped
4 carrots, trimmed, scrubbed, and thinly sliced
4 celery stalks, trimmed and thinly sliced
1 tablespoon black peppercorns
4 or 5 whole racks baby back pork ribs, or at least
    5 of the larger spareribs per person
    (10 to 12 pounds total)

Freshly ground black pepper to taste
Vegetable oil spray
The Best Barbecue Sauce (page 30), at room
    temperature

FILL ONE OR TWO wide 6- to 8-quart pots two-thirds full with cold water and bring to a boil. Add the onion, carrots, celery, and peppercorns to the water (dividing them between two pots, if using) and simmer the vegetables for 45 to 60 minutes. Sprinkle the ribs generously all over with black pepper and submerge them in the boiling broth. Cover the pot and, when the broth comes back to a boil, reduce the heat to low and simmer baby back ribs for 30 minutes and the larger ribs for 45 minutes. Remove the pot from the heat and set it on a strong wire rack. Let the ribs sit in the hot liquid, uncovered, until they're almost cool. If time is an issue, however, you can go directly to the next step without letting the ribs cool.

Preheat the oven to 400°F. Spray two large, shallow baking sheets with vegetable spray, then line them with parchment paper. Transfer the ribs to the prepared baking sheets. (Discard the liquid and vegetables.) Brush the ribs liberally on both sides with barbecue sauce and place them, meat side up, in the oven. Roast 35 to 45 minutes, or until the ribs are sizzling and the sauce is only slightly charred looking, basting with more sauce after the first 20 minutes. (If you'd like the ribs a bit more crusty-looking, jack up the heat to 425°F. for the last 20 minutes.)

CUT EACH RACK OF RIBS in half and pile them on a large warmed serving tray. Alternatively, when serving children, use a sharp knife to cut between the ribs, separating them completely. Serve them hot with a bowl of additional barbecue sauce to be passed at the table.

TIMING IS EVERYTHING

❧ *The ribs can be poached several hours ahead and allowed to sit, submerged in the broth, until you're ready to apply the sauce and roast.*

HERE'S THE SCOOP:
About Cooking and Serving Ribs

For the most succulent ribs, let the ribs sit (and actually become cool) in the poaching liquid. While simmering, many of the flavor compounds end up in the broth, but when the ribs are left in the poaching liquid for an hour or more, the meat reabsorbs moisture, making them even more succulent and flavorful.

Now, about those sticky fingers. Let's face it, eating ribs can be messy (if you're doing it right). I suggest setting a bowl of lemon water in front of each place setting before the meal begins. Although customary to do this after the meal, it's nice to allow people to clean up as desired, since they usually won't finish eating at the same time. Just squeeze some fresh lemon juice into very hot tap water (the water will be the perfect temperature when needed), and float a slice of lemon on top. And always have an extra set of napkins waiting in the wings.

SERVED WITH SKILLET CORNBREAD page 254

Oh So Saucy and Slightly Charred . . .
THE BEST BARBECUED CHICKEN
(with or without a Grill)

Rain or shine, on the grill or in the oven, this recipe promises to give you fabulous barbecued chicken. If your family is anything like mine, you'll be turning to this recipe often. So set aside some time to make a big batch of the barbecue sauce on page 30, then reap the benefits all year long. Actually, this butterflied chicken is pretty terrific even without the sauce!

❧ YIELD: 6 SERVINGS AS A MAIN COURSE

½ cup extra-virgin olive oil or Garlic Confit Oil
   (page 23), or more as needed
4 garlic cloves, minced
Freshly ground black pepper to taste
1 rounded tablespoon minced fresh thyme
1 scant tablespoon minced fresh rosemary

Two 3½-pound chickens, rinsed well, dried
   thoroughly, and butterflied (see page 148)
Kosher or sea salt to taste
About 1½ cups The Best Barbecue Sauce (page 30)
   for basting, plus more for serving

TIMING IS
EVERYTHING

❧ *The chickens can be butterflied and seasoned one day ahead and refrigerated, well covered.*

POUR THE OLIVE OIL into a bowl and add the garlic, lots of black pepper, and half the minced herbs, reserving the rest for later. If possible, allow the garlic to steep in the oil for a couple of hours, covered, at room temperature. Position a small wire-mesh sieve over another bowl and strain the oil, pressing on the garlic to extract as much flavor as possible. Use the garlic pulp in another recipe or discard it. Line a large baking sheet with waxed paper and lay the butterflied birds perfectly flat on it. Sprinkle both sides of the chickens lightly with salt and generously with pepper. Brush the chickens liberally with the garlic-flavored oil.

To cook the chicken using an outdoor grill, either heat a gas grill to the highest setting, covered, or heat a charcoal grill (and replenish coals as needed) according to the instructions on page 180.

LAY THE SEASONED BIRDS skin side down on the grill. Cook the chicken, uncovered, over direct heat for 3 to 5 minutes or until the skin becomes golden. Turn the chickens skin side up (being careful not to tear the skin) and sear them on the other side. If using a gas grill, lower the heat to medium-low; if using a charcoal grill, move the chickens to the side, over indirect heat. Sprinkle the remaining herbs and some salt over the skin and cover the grill. Cook the chickens until almost cooked through, 30 to 35 minutes. Uncover and, using a long basting brush, baste the skin side of the birds liberally with barbecue sauce. Lower the lid and raise the heat in a gas grill to high,

or transfer the birds back over direct heat in a charcoal grill. Cover and cook for 5 to 10 minutes more, or until the chicken is perfectly tender and somewhat charred looking without becoming burnt. (Alternatively, if not using barbecue sauce, cook the chickens for 40 to 45 minutes over indirect heat, after the initial sear.) Remove the chickens from the grill and allow them to sit undisturbed for 5 minutes before cutting them into sections.

To divide the chickens into quarters and serve, use a sharp carving knife to cut each bird in half vertically down the length of the breast. Slide the knife blade in between the thigh and breast, completely separating the leg from the breast. Do this on the other side and then again, with the remaining chicken. Serve the chicken hot or at room temperature, passing a fresh bowl of warmed barbecue sauce at the table.

Oven-Barbecued Variation

Line a large (preferably dark) baking sheet with 1-inch sides with aluminum foil shiny side up, and place it in the center of the oven. Preheat the oven to 400°F. for 30 minutes or longer. When ready to sear, turn on your exhaust fan. Place either a large well-seasoned cast-iron skillet, a heavy nonstick pan, or a large stove-top grill pan on the stove over medium-high heat. (Or straddle an extra-large grill pan over two burners.) When hot, raise the heat to high and, depending on the size of your cooking vessel, lay one or both of the seasoned chickens in the pan, skin side down. Sear the skin until golden and starting to crisp, 4 to 5 minutes. Carefully turn the bird(s) and brown them on the other side. As each chicken is browned, remove it to a tray, skin side up.

Transfer the chickens to the preheated baking sheet, toe-to-toe (working quickly, so the oven doesn't cool down). Sprinkle the remaining herbs and some salt on top of the skin and shut the oven door. Reduce the temperature to 375°F. and roast the chickens for 40 minutes. Using a pastry brush, apply a liberal coating of barbecue sauce to all exposed areas of the chickens and push them back into the oven and shut the door. Raise the oven temperature to 450°F. and continue to roast until the chickens are perfectly tender and somewhat charred looking without becoming burnt, 8 to 12 minutes. Alternatively, if not applying sauce, cook for a total of 45 to 50 minutes at 375°F.

HERE'S THE SCOOP:
On the Safest Way to Heat a Charcoal Grill

By far the safest and most effective way to quickly heat a charcoal grill is to use an inexpensive chimney starter (available in most well-stocked hardware stores). Get the biggest one you can find, and if you have a large grill, get two starters so you can heat twice as many coals at once.

To heat charcoal, fill a chimney starter to the top with chunks of hardwood charcoal (not chips, which burn too fast). Place some rumpled-up newspaper on the bottom of the cylinder (underneath the grate holding the coals). Stand the starter either directly on the cold coal grate or prop it securely on a completely heatproof surface (an inverted galvanized bucket works perfectly). Using a long lit match or a hand-held igniter gun, light the newspaper, which will quickly ignite the coals. Let the coals become red-hot throughout (all the way to the top) before carefully spilling them out onto the coal grate, creating a thick, even layer of red-hot coals. Sprinkle some unlit coals over the hot ones (being careful not to smother them). Place the grill over the coals and cover it so the grate gets hot. (Have the vents wide open to encourage a steady flow of oxygen, which will feed the heated coals.)

When you are ready to use direct or indirect heat, the coals will be very hot, but will no longer be producing flames. The tops of the coals should be the color of white ash and the bottoms of some should still be red-hot. If cooking for an extended period of time over indirect heat, leave the lid down and the vents open only halfway, which slows the fire down. During this time you might need to replenish the grill with hot coals. To do this, heat additional coals in the chimney starter, placed on a heatproof surface, as previously described and, when hot, remove the food from the grill to a covered platter. Carefully lift the grill grate and pour in the freshly lit coals. To help red-hot coals to quickly calm down, cover the grill and close the vents halfway. Wait a few minutes, then place the food back over indirect heat and apply the lid. Continue cooking as directed. (Be sure to keep children and pets away from hot coals and heated chimney starters.)

Just for the Two of You . . .
STUFFED LOBSTERS ALLA SCAMPI

Eating lobster is a truly sensual, hands-on experience (especially when it's just the two of you). So, to help remove inhibitions, dim the lights, light the candles, and place two finger bowls filled with tepid lemon water on the table. Oh, and if not using lobster bibs, don't wear silk! Remember to have an extra set of napkins close by.

❧ YIELD: 2 SERVINGS AS A MAIN COURSE (CAN BE DOUBLED)

½ cup lightly packed finely crushed buttery crackers (I use Ritz), from about half of 1 sleeve of crackers

5 tablespoons unsalted butter

½ cup finely chopped scallions (white and 1½ inches of green)

4 garlic cloves, finely minced

¼ rounded teaspoon red pepper flakes (optional)

1 teaspoon strained fresh lemon juice

½ teaspoon kosher or sea salt

Freshly ground black pepper to taste

1 rounded tablespoon chopped flat-leaf Italian parsley

Optional stuffing embellishments: ⅓ pound large shrimp, shelled, deveined, and coarsely chopped (see page 20); or 6 ounces jumbo lump crab meat; or 4 thin slices of pancetta (unsmoked bacon), fried until crisp, drained, and crumbled

2 lobsters (1½ to 2 pounds each), split for roasting and claws cracked (see page 182)

Suggested accompaniments: lemon wedges, nutcrackers, and Clarified Butter (page 195) or melted whole butter

CRUSH THE CRACKERS into fine crumbs either using a food processor fitted with the steel blade or by placing the crackers in an opened heavy-duty freezer bag and rolling over them with a rolling pin. Place the crumbs in a bowl. Melt the butter in a 10-inch heavy-bottomed skillet over medium heat and, when bubbling, add the scallions, garlic, and red pepper flakes, if using. Sauté the vegetables until softened, 2 to 3 minutes, then stir in the lemon juice, salt, and black pepper. Stir about half of this mixture into the crumbs along with the parsley and more pepper to make the stuffing. Set aside. Transfer the remaining scampi butter to a small bowl. If adding shrimp, heat the same skillet over medium heat with 2 teaspoons of the scampi butter. When hot, raise the heat to high and stir in the coarsely chopped shrimp and cook, stirring constantly, until they just lose their raw look, about 1 minute. Transfer the shrimp to a bowl and season them with salt and pepper. If using the crab meat, just place it in a bowl and season the meat. If using the crumbled bacon, stir this into the prepared seasoned crumb mixture.

Line a large shallow baking sheet with aluminum foil shiny side up. If very wet, pat the split lobsters dry and place them, opened and flesh side up, on the baking sheet. Brush the flesh and cracked claws liberally with the reserved scampi butter, spreading the lobsters open so the flesh is completely exposed. Make sure to snip through the tip of the fan-shaped tails with scissors to help

❧ *The cracker crumbs can be made days ahead and stored in a sealed plastic bag.*
❧ *The stuffing can be made early in the day and kept at a comfortable room temperature, covered.*
❧ *The lobsters can be killed and stuffed a few hours ahead (preferably not longer than 3 hours) and kept refrigerated, covered.*

keep them from curling in the oven. Sprinkle the flesh lightly with salt and liberally with pepper, then fill the cavities with the sautéed shrimp or the crab meat, if using. Top this, generously, with the seasoned crumbs.

POSITION THE OVEN RACK on the upper third shelf and preheat the oven to 400°F. for at least 30 minutes. Roast the lobsters until the meat is tender and the stuffing is hot throughout, 15 to 18 minutes, depending on their size. If the lobsters are done before the exterior is golden and crisp, run them under the broiler, taking care not to let the crumbs burn.

To serve, place one whole lobster on an individual plate and serve immediately, with lemon wedges and hot melted butter. (Don't forget the lobster bibs, nutcrackers, cocktail forks, finger bowls, and extra napkins!)

HERE'S THE SCOOP:
To Split a Live Lobster for Roasting

I know that this page will inevitably get some emotional responses, especially if you've seen the movie *Annie Hall*. You can, of course, ask your fishmonger to split the lobsters for you. Regardless of who does the deed, I think we'll all agree on one point: if you plan to eat stuffed lobsters, someone's got to kill them first. And since it's always best to cook lobsters soon after being split, I thought you'd like to know how to do this yourself, just in case your fish market is closing early on a day when you'd like to cook and serve fresh lobsters for dinner.

Make sure that your live lobsters are very lively, at purchase, and that they come home with rubber bands on their claws (for obvious reasons). Keep the lobsters in a paper bag in the coldest part of the refrigerator, which is the bottom shelf, until you're ready to split and stuff them. Actually, if they're really feisty, right before you're ready to work with

them, stick the bag in the freezer for about 5 minutes, which will relax them.

Working with one lobster at a time, turn it on its back horizontally in front of you on your work surface. (If you're right-handed, have the tail to your left and the claws to your right; reverse this, if left-handed.) Using your nonworking hand, fold the tail in toward the center, preventing it from snapping back and forth. Plunge the blade of a very sharp 8-inch chef's knife into the body, just above where the fan-shaped tip of the tail meets the middle (after folding). Immediately after inserting the blade, pull the knife handle down firmly, driving the blade through the body and the head. Pull the blade out and twirl the lobster around so the tail is on the opposite side.

Although there will be some jerky movements, due to severed nerve endings, the lobster is now officially dead. Use the blade of the

knife to cut down the center of the tail, then use kitchen scissors to snip through the fan-shaped tip of the tail. Bend both sides of the lobster away from each other (at either side of the incision), so the lobster is now butterflied with the tail meat fully exposed. Use your fingers to pull out and discard the stomach, which is a small, rough, spongy material located just underneath the head. Now lift out and remove the thin translucent, slightly darkish vein that travels down one inner side of the split tail. Snip off the rubber bands from the claws and, using the dull side of your chef's knife, whack the top of the claws once or twice, cracking the hard shells and trying not to separate the claws from the body. (Keep your face back, when whacking, since the lobster juice squirts upward.) You're now ready to season, stuff, and cook your lobsters.

BROILED SWORDFISH
with Browned Butter, Candied Garlic, Roasted Peppers, and Capers

Even if you've always claimed to dislike garlic, you might just change your mind after trying this recipe. When raw garlic is parboiled, the taste and consistency change dramatically, becoming almost potato-like. And when cooked slowly in melted browned butter, the sugars in the garlic rise to the surface, becoming candied and utterly delicious. This, combined with capers and sliced roasted peppers, creates a topping for the fish (or grilled veal chops, for that matter) that's as vibrant to look at as it is satisfying to eat. Be sure to keep the swordfish well chilled until applying heat. This way, the flesh will be better able to withstand a few more minutes of intense heat exposure, ensuring the sexiest caramelized appearance after cooking. ❧ YIELD: 6 SERVINGS AS A MAIN COURSE

⅓ cup extra-virgin olive oil

6 garlic cloves, minced, plus 24 additional whole peeled cloves

1 rounded teaspoon red pepper flakes (optional)

½ cup minced flat-leaf Italian parsley or cilantro

2 tablespoons strained fresh lemon juice

Freshly ground black pepper to taste

6 swordfish steaks (6 to 8 ounces each), skin and any dark flesh removed

Kosher or sea salt to taste

⅓ rounded cup black oil-cured olives

½ cup (1 stick) unsalted butter, plus 2 optional tablespoons

2 each red and yellow bell peppers, roasted, skinned, seeded, and sliced into thin strips (see page 24)

⅓ cup capers (preferably those packed in balsamic vinegar), drained

2 tablespoons balsamic vinegar (or use the brine used to soak the capers)

COMBINE THE OLIVE OIL, minced garlic, red pepper flakes (if using), ¼ cup of the parsley or cilantro, the lemon juice, and a generous amount of black pepper in a nonreactive bowl. Rinse and dry the fish, then lay the pieces in a 13 × 9-inch nonreactive dish in a single layer. Sprinkle both sides lightly with salt and generously with pepper. Using a pastry brush, paint both sides of the fish liberally with the seasoned olive oil. Cover the dish and keep the fish chilled until ready to cook.

Fill a small saucepan two-thirds full with water and bring it to a boil. Add the whole garlic cloves and boil them for 2 full minutes. Drain the garlic and, using a small paring knife, remove any tough ends. Set the poached garlic aside. To pit the olives, place them, one at a time, on your work surface and lay the blade of a chef's knife flat on top. Push down on the blade firmly, without overdoing it. You'll feel (and almost hear) a dull "pop" as the olive meat releases from its stone. Slit the olive down one side, then open it to lift out the stone. Slice the olives in half.

Melt the ½ cup butter in a 10- to 12-inch nonreactive skillet over medium heat, and when hot and bubbling, reduce the heat to low. Continue to cook the butter, occasionally swirling the pan, until the milk solids turn light golden brown. Add the parboiled garlic cloves and cook, stirring occasionally, until the garlic turns golden, being careful not to allow them to burn. Add the sliced peppers, drained capers, and olives and swirl the pan so they intermingle with the garlic. Add the balsamic vinegar and put the pan on a cool burner for now.

If using a gas grill, preheat it to high, covered. If using a charcoal grill, follow the instructions on page 180 to heat the coals and get the food grate hot. If cooking indoors, position the oven rack as close as possible to the heat source and preheat the broiler. (Do not preheat the broiler pan.)

Remove the fish from the refrigerator. If grilling, cook the seasoned fish uncovered, turning once, until the exterior develops golden patches and the flesh is cooked through but remains succulent, about 8 minutes. If broiling, place the swordfish side by side on a cold broiler pan and cook the pieces until starting to turn golden on first side, about 4 minutes. Turn the fish and broil until the exterior of the second side is golden and the interior is cooked, about 6 minutes on the second side.

To serve, place the fish either on a warmed serving platter or on individual plates, and reheat the sauce until it starts to sizzle. Add the last 2 tablespoons of butter, if desired, and the remaining ¼ cup of herbs and, when the new butter is just melted and the mixture is hot, spoon the sauce over the fish and serve.

TIMING IS EVERYTHING

* The fish can be seasoned up to 12 hours ahead and kept refrigerated, well covered.

* The sauce can be made 2 hours ahead and kept on a cool burner, uncovered, until ready to reheat and finish, just before serving.

Crispy Breaded
PAN-FRIED LEMON SOLE
with Herbed Tartar Sauce

If your kids claim to "hate fish," try this recipe, which has always been a favorite of my three children. When pan-frying, since the fillets are large, I suggest using two nonstick skillets, which speeds up the cooking process substantially. By the way, this same breading method can be applied to skinned, boned, butterflied, and flattened chicken breasts or to pounded veal cutlets. But when using meat instead of fish, instead of using all bread crumbs, combine equal amounts of freshly grated Parmesan cheese and the crumbs for a truly savory coating.

🍂 YIELD: 6 SERVINGS AS A MAIN COURSE

FOR THE FISH

1½ cups unbleached all-purpose flour
Kosher or sea salt and freshly ground black pepper
   to taste
6 extra-large eggs
2 tablespoons thinly sliced fresh chives or minced
   flat-leaf Italian parsley (optional)
1 large garlic clove, minced (optional)
3½ rounded cups finely ground Dried Bread Crumbs
   (page 29)
6 large lemon sole fillets (generous 8 ounces each)

FOR THE TARTAR SAUCE

¾ cup mayonnaise
¼ cup Dijon mustard
¼ generous cup minced yellow onion
¼ generous cup minced drained gherkin pickles
2 rounded tablespoons drained capers, minced
1 teaspoon strained fresh lemon juice
2 rounded tablespoons each thinly sliced fresh chives
   and minced flat-leaf Italian parsley
Freshly ground black pepper to taste

Flavorless vegetable oil
Unsalted butter (optional)
Lemon wedges for serving

PUT THE FLOUR on a shallow rectangular tray or baking sheet and season it lightly with salt and black pepper. Use a fork to beat the eggs in a 13 × 9-inch dish and, if desired, stir in the minced herbs and garlic. Place the eggs next to the tray of flour. Place the bread crumbs on another shallow rectangular tray and position this on the other side of the eggs. Line one or two more large shallow trays with waxed paper. Rinse the fillets and dry them well. Sprinkle them lightly on both sides with salt and pepper.

Working with two fillets at a time, coat each one on both sides in the seasoned flour and shake off the excess. Lay the fillets side by side in the beaten eggs, then turn them over to coat both sides well. Lift both fillets out of the eggs and let any excess drip back into the dish. Lay the fish on top of the crumbs, then turn them both to coat the other side. Turn the fillets in the crumbs several times, while using your working hand to press the crumbs

SERVED WITH AROMATIC
SAFFRON RICE page 200

gently onto both sides, until they are heavily coated. Lay the breaded fillets on the prepared trays. If using one tray, fill the tray, then cover that layer with waxed paper. Lay the remaining breaded fish on top. After each batch of two fillets, rinse and dry your hands before continuing. Cover the breaded fillets with plastic wrap and refrigerate for at least an hour.

TIMING IS
EVERYTHING

❧ *The fish can be breaded one day ahead and kept refrigerated, covered with plastic wrap.*

❧ *The tartar sauce can be made two days ahead and kept refrigerated, covered.*

❧ *The fish can be fried up to 30 minutes before serving. To reheat, place the fillets, on their wire racks, on two shallow baking sheets and place the sheets in a preheated 375°F. oven on the upper- and lower-third shelves. Heat just until the fish is hot throughout, about 5 minutes, making sure not to overcook it.*

MAKE THE TARTAR SAUCE. Use a rubber spatula to combine the mayonnaise, mustard, onion, pickles, capers, lemon juice, herbs, and black pepper in a bowl. Refrigerate the sauce, covered, until needed.

Place two large wire cooling racks close to the stove. Heat one or two 12- to 14-inch nonstick skillets over medium-high heat and, when hot, add enough vegetable oil to coat the bottom of the pan to a depth of ¼ inch. When the oil is hot but not smoking, add a tablespoon of butter to the pan, if desired, and let it sizzle and melt without allowing it to color.

Add two breaded fish fillets to the hot oil, and fry them until golden brown and crisp on both sides, turning once, about 4 minutes per side (see below). Transfer each fillet directly to the wire rack and use paper towels to gently blot off any excess oil from the top. Continue to fry the remaining fish. If at any time the bottom of the pan accumulates too many overbrowned crumbs, dump out all the oil, wipe out the skillet, and heat fresh oil before frying the next batch. Serve the fish hot with the tartar sauce and lemon wedges.

HERE'S THE SCOOP:
On Turning Large Pan-Fried Foods Safely

To avoid getting inadvertently burned when turning a large fillet or cutlet when pan-frying, it's important to use the right type of turning spatulas. You'll need two long (preferably perforated) metal spatulas, each with an elbow bend. Use metal, even when cooking in a non-stick pan, since these are sturdiest.

To turn food safely after it's browned on one side, use your working hand to insert one spatula under the food at one end, going as far across the bottom as possible. Using your nonworking hand, lay the second spatula on top of the food with the handle positioned on the opposite side. Lift the bottom spatula holding the food, and carefully turn it over, using the second spatula to ease it back into the hot oil. Always bring the food as close as possible to the oil before releasing it to prevent hot oil from splashing.

Because Variety Is the Spice of Life . . .
STEAK, CHICKEN, AND SHRIMP FAJITAS

What fun! The look of this assembled dish is big, the flavors are bold, and the temperature, when served, is sizzling hot. Although not necessary, using a well-seasoned cast-iron fajitas pan or a large round paella pan "feels" the most authentic, especially when entertaining. I think you'll love the homemade Fajitas Seasoning on page 37. If you don't have this, however, just use your favorite brand of fajitas seasoning. If you're pressed for time, feel free to use the Fajitas Seasoning to flavor any protein you use, scaling up the olive oil and garlic accordingly.

❧ YIELD: 6 SERVINGS AS A MAIN COURSE

FOR THE MARINADE

⅔ cup olive oil (pure and extra-virgin mixed)

¼ cup strained fresh lime juice

2 tablespoons tequila (or thawed frozen orange juice concentrate), or increase the lime juice to ⅓ cup

8 garlic cloves, minced

2 large jalapeño chiles, seeded and minced (if desired, leave in some seeds for extra heat)

Up to 3 canned chipotle peppers in adobo with 2 tablespoons of the sauce (optional)

1½ tablespoons Fajitas Seasoning (page 37) or see the end of this recipe

FOR THE FAJITAS

Your choice of protein, up to 3 pounds of one or a combination: skirt steaks, flank steak, boneless and skinless chicken breasts (sliced lengthwise into 1-inch-thick strips), shelled and deveined jumbo shrimp (see page 20)

Extra-virgin olive oil to sauté the vegetables and for basting

1 very large yellow onion, cut into thin wedges

1 pound poblano chiles, seeded and thinly sliced lengthwise (or use Italian frying peppers)

1 jalapeño chile, stemmed, seeded, and cut into thin julienne (optional)

4 garlic cloves, cut into thin julienne (optional)

2 rounded teaspoons Fajitas Seasoning (page 37)

Kosher or sea salt and freshly ground black pepper to taste

1 pound button or cremini mushrooms, cleaned and sliced

3 tablespoons minced cilantro

Warmed Homemade Flour Tortillas (page 251) or warm a good-quality brand of store-bought flour tortillas

Suggested accompaniments: Pico de Gallo (page 208) and Oh-So-Cheesy Refried Beans (page 84)

ASSEMBLE THE MARINADE. Place the olive oil, lime juice, tequila, garlic, and jalapeños in a blender and process until pureed. If using two types of protein, pour half the marinade into a nonreactive bowl and add 1 large chipotle with 1 generous tablespoon of its sauce to the blender and process until pretty smooth. (If using only one protein, add the full number of chipotles to the blender and use this to flavor the protein.) To flavor a third protein differently, for each 1 pound of beef, chicken, or shrimp, mix ⅓ cup extra-virgin olive oil with 1½ tablespoons of the fajitas seasoning and 2 crushed cloves of garlic. You can also use this mixture, scaled up proportionately, to flavor all 3 pounds of protein. You'll also need some fresh lime juice to be sprinkled over the meat and/or shrimp, just before cooking.

Place the chicken, beef, and/or shrimp in separate nonreactive dishes and pour the marinades over them. Using disposable (nonpowdered) rubber gloves, rub the marinade all over the meats and/or shrimp. Cover the dishes and refrigerate. (For best results, see the timing notes at the end of this recipe.)

TAKE THE SEASONED MEAT or shrimp out of the refrigerator 30 minutes before cooking. Either heat a gas grill, covered, to the highest setting, or heat a charcoal grill according to the instructions on page 180. Alternatively, if not grilling outdoors, place one or two large stove-top grill pans on the stove but don't turn on the heat just yet. Place either two large fajitas pans, or a large paella pan, or a large shallow baking sheet lined with aluminum foil, in the upper third of the oven and preheat to 450°F. If using shrimp, secure them on wooden skewers that have been soaked in water for 15 minutes. Set aside.

Heat a large 12- to 14-inch deep-sided skillet over medium-high heat and, when hot, add 2 tablespoons of extra-virgin olive oil. When the oil is hot, add the onion and raise the heat to high. Let the onion cook, stirring occasionally, until it begins to soften, about 5 minutes. Reduce the heat to medium and stir in the poblanos. If using the jalapeño and garlic, add them now. Continue to cook the vegetables until tender and the onion has only just started to color, about 5 minutes more. Stir in the fajitas seasoning along with some salt and black pepper, and cook for 1 minute just to wake up the spices. Transfer the vegetables to a bowl.

PLACE THE SKILLET BACK over medium heat (no need to wipe it out) and, when hot, add 2 more tablespoons of olive oil. When the oil is hot, add the mushrooms and cook them over high heat until any released liquid evaporates and the mushrooms become golden, 8 to 10 minutes. Add salt and pepper to taste, then fold the cooked mushrooms and the cilantro into the onion and chiles. If the vegetables seem dry, stir in a bit more olive oil so they won't scorch when they are reheated.

Heat the grill pans over high heat with the exhaust fan turned on or prepare your outdoor grill. When your outdoor grill or the stove-top grill pans are very hot, cook the chicken, beef, and/or shrimp (in that order) over direct heat until each is done to your liking, using sturdy tongs and a flat turning spatula to turn them over. (Squeeze some lime juice over the shrimp just before grilling.)

*If using the marinade
with citrus juice, the beef
can be marinated 24 hours
ahead, the chicken 12
hours ahead, and the
shrimp 4 hours ahead. If
using the fajitas seasoning
mixed with only olive oil
and garlic, all three pro-
teins can be seasoned up
to two days ahead.
Having said this, it's
always best to cook raw
shrimp within 24 hours
of purchase.
*The vegetables can be
sautéed 2 hours ahead and
kept at room temperature,
loosely covered.*

While grilling, baste with olive oil as needed. As each protein is cooked, place on a baking sheet and cover loosely with aluminum foil. Brush off or wipe down the grill after each type of meat is cooked.

CAREFULLY REMOVE THE PREHEATED PAN(S) from the oven and pour all of the sautéed vegetables onto the hot surface. Put it back into the 450°F. oven and reheat the vegetables until they're sizzling, 8 to 10 minutes. Simultaneously, rewarm your tortillas, wrapped in foil or in an earthenware tortilla dish, in the oven for 10 minutes (on the center rack) for 3 to 5 minutes.

If the meats have cooled down, place them in the oven (on the bottom rack) for 2 to 5 minutes, just to reheat briefly. Remove the pan(s) from the oven and place the meats over the sizzling vegetables (either split between two fajitas pans or all in one paella pan) and sprinkle the top lightly with salt. (If you used a baking sheet for the vegetables, transfer them to a warmed serving platter and arrange the cooked meats on top.)

To SERVE, bring the platter of food to the table right away, with a stack of warmed flour tortillas enclosed in a covered dish or wrapped in a linen napkin and tucked into a bread basket. Serve the fajitas with Pico de Gallo and Oh-So-Cheesy Refried Beans.

If you don't have the preassembled fajitas seasoning: Use 2 teaspoons each ground cumin, garlic powder, black pepper, salt, chili powder, and packed light brown sugar. Add ½ teaspoon crumbled aromatic dried oregano.

SERVED WITH HOMEMADE FLOUR TORTILLAS   page 251,
AND PICO DE GALLO   page 208

Served with Chive-Studded
Yorkshire Pudding page 216

A TRULY REGAL ROAST PRIME RIB
with a Garlic and Herb Crust and a Red Wine Sauce

For a special occasion, there's nothing like serving a gorgeous prime rib roast with a rich homemade red wine sauce. And for a perfect partner to both the meat and the sauce, turn to page 216 for an outrageously delicious Yorkshire Pudding. If you'd like to make a quicker sauce that's also great-tasting, make the "beefed-up jus," given at the end of this recipe. Be sure your beef is labelled USDA Prime, and ask for the first four ribs closest to the loin.

❧ YIELD: 10 TO 12 SERVINGS AS A MAIN COURSE

FOR THE ROAST

20 cloves garlic, minced or pressed through a garlic press
1 rounded tablespoon kosher or sea salt
Freshly ground black pepper to taste
2 tablespoons chopped fresh thyme, or 1½ teaspoons dried
2 rounded teaspoons chopped fresh rosemary
Extra-virgin olive oil to lubricate the meat
One 4-rib roast (8½ to 9½ pounds), well trimmed, with a thin layer of fat remaining on top (ask the butcher to cut the meat off the bone, crack the ribs, and tie the meat back in place)

FOR THE SAUCE BASE

4½ tablespoons Clarified Butter (page 195)
2 large shallots, minced
8 ounces fresh button mushrooms, wiped clean and chopped (about 1 cup)
4 tablespoons unbleached all-purpose flour
3 cups Beef or Veal Stock (page 18) or doctored canned broth (see page 19)
1 cup dry red wine
1 generous teaspoon tomato paste
Kosher or sea salt and freshly ground black pepper to taste

Ingredients for Chive-studded Yorkshire Pudding (page 216; optional)
2 tablespoons port wine (preferably vintage, but a high-quality ruby port is perfectly acceptable)
1 tablespoon whole butter or thick crème fraîche (optional)

SEASON THE BEEF. Place the garlic on your work surface and sprinkle it with the salt, black pepper, and herbs. With the blade of a sharp chef's knife, press the mixture together, scraping and mixing until it starts blending together. Drizzle on up to 2 tablespoons of extra-virgin olive oil and continue to scrape, press, and mash the garlic mixture until it becomes pastelike. Sprinkle the meat all over generously with pepper. Rub the garlic-herb paste all over the exposed meat (bottom and sides included). Pour some olive oil on top and pat it all over until the entire seasoned surface really glistens. Apply more pepper to the top, leaving the roast visibly heavily seasoned and well lubricated. Cover the meat with oiled plastic wrap, greased side down, and refrigerate it for up to 24 hours before roasting.

PREPARE THE SAUCE. Early on the day of serving, start your sauce. Melt the clarified butter in a 2-quart saucepan over medium heat and, when hot, stir in the shallots. Sauté the shallots until they turn translucent, about 2 minutes, then add the mushrooms. Raise the heat to high and cook the vegetables until the mushrooms are tender and most of their released liquid evaporates, 4 to 5 minutes, stirring frequently. Stir in the flour and cook the vegetable roux, stirring constantly, for 1 to 2 minutes. Whisk in the stock and wine, and bring the liquid to a full bubble. Reduce the heat to very low and simmer the sauce, uncovered, until the flavors concentrate, the texture thickens, and the volume reduces to about 2½ cups, which will take between 1 and 1½ hours. As it simmers, occasionally skim off any accumulated foam from the top of the sauce.

REMOVE FROM THE HEAT and let the sauce cool for a bit, then pour it through a fine-mesh sieve that's positioned over another clean saucepan. Press hard on the solids to extract all of their goodness, then discard them. Place a doubled sheet of paper towel over the saucepan and apply the lid. (This prevents a skin from forming on the top of the sauce and also keeps any condensation from falling into the sauce and diluting the flavor.) Set the saucepan aside.

To roast the meat, first bring it close to room temperature. Place the seasoned roast, bone side down, on a sturdy shallow baking sheet and preheat the oven to 450°F. for at least 30 minutes. Sear the meat at 450°F. for 30 minutes. While searing, if planning to make Yorkshire pudding, see the next step as soon as the meat enters the oven. After the initial sear, insert a meat thermometer into the top center of the meat so the tip reaches the center of the eye. (If the tip sits on bone, your reading won't be accurate.) Reduce the oven temperature to 325°F. and roast the meat until the internal temperature reaches just above 120°F. (for medium-rare), which will take about 1¾ hours after the initial sear. (This will take longer if the meat was initially cold.) Remove the meat from the oven and transfer it to a warmed serving platter. Tent the meat loosely with aluminum foil and set it aside, allowing it to rest, before carving.

IF MAKING YORKSHIRE PUDDING, assemble the batter as soon as the meat goes into the oven and let it sit out, covered, while the meat cooks. When the meat leaves the oven, increase the temperature to 450°F. and follow the instructions on page 216 for baking Yorkshire pudding. If not making Yorkshire pudding, freeze your rendered beef drippings in a labeled 1-cup heavy-duty freezer container. That way, you can make Yorkshire pudding, flavored the traditional way, whenever you choose.

To FINISH, first reheat the sauce, uncovered, over low heat until it's hot. Let it simmer gently until ready to serve. Cut any strings off the roast and discard them. Lift the meat off the ribs and place it on your cutting board (you may need to use a knife to help release it). Place the bones to the side. Cut the meat into ¼-inch-thick slices and overlap them on a warmed serving platter. Slice the ribs into individual sections and place them around the meat. Pour any juices from the carving board over and around the meat.

STIR THE PORT INTO the simmering sauce base and bring it back to a full simmer. Reduce the heat to low and simmer gently for 1 minute. If desired, stir in the butter or crème fraîche and heat through without simmering. Adjust seasoning and pour the sauce into a warmed gravy boat and pass it, along with the meat, straight away. Accompany the meat with Yorkshire pudding, if desired.

A Beefed-Up "Jus" Sauce (Embellished Natural Juices)

Instead of serving the red wine sauce, after carving the meat, pour the juices from the carving board into a saucepan and add 2 cups of beef or veal stock. Bring the liquid to a boil, reduce the heat to low, and simmer the stock for 1 or 2 minutes. Adjust the seasoning by adding salt and pepper to taste. Pour half of the broth over the meat and serve the rest in a warmed sauceboat. If desired, stir in a tablespoon or so of butter or crème fraîche, after removing the pan from the stove, to enrich the texture. Taste for seasoning, though, since added fat (although wonderfully rich) tends to be muting to seasoning.

HERE'S THE SCOOP:
On Clarified Butter

Clarified butter is a great choice for certain cooking procedures. Its clarity and nutty flavor make it the perfect dip for cooked lobster and steamed clams. Nevertheless, its flavor and texture are not as rich as full butter, and clarified butter is not recommended as a substitute when baking.

To clarify butter, slowly melt 1 cup (2 sticks or more) of unsalted butter in a heavy-bottomed saucepan (preferably with a spout) over low heat, without stirring, until totally liquefied and the milky residue that's fallen to the bottom of the pan becomes light golden and gives off a nutty aroma. Remove the pan from the heat and let the butter settle for 15 minutes. Using a fine-mesh skimmer or a small shallow spoon, remove the white foamy substance that sits on top of the butterfat. When no milky solids remain on top, pour the pure yellow butterfat through a fine-mesh skimmer or a fine-mesh sieve into a bowl, leaving any toasted residue behind. Expect to lose up to a quarter of your original volume after straining. Store clarified butter in a perfectly clean, well-sealed container in the refrigerator for up to one year.

CHAPTER SEVEN

GREAT THINGS ON THE SIDE

Make a Meal Feel BIG and Abundant

To me, a great meal is like an emotionally moving painting. Whether on canvas or on the family table, every component is strategically placed to work as an ensemble, to create a good feeling and to satisfy those present. So, side dishes are every bit as important as the entree, since here is where a cook has the opportunity to transform a shared meal into a lush scene that's truly memorable.

The side dishes featured in this chapter are so satisfying that you might even get a child who claims to hate vegetables to happily partake. There are long, whimsical spaghetti-like strands of zucchini, sautéed fresh carrots, spinach that's perfectly punctuated with sautéed garlic, several rice pilafs, and a creamy mashed-potato casserole that's loaded with chives, grated Parmesan cheese, and garlic-laced cream. There are fried strips of sweet potatoes, crisp hashed browns that are as great with dinner as they are with breakfast, and a corn pudding that (if you're like me) you'll find yourself dreaming about long after the meal ends. And if that's not enough, there's also a crisp chive-laced Yorkshire pudding, to serve with an elegant rib roast.

Simmered and Sautéed . . .
FRESH CARROTS
with a Garlicky Persillade

If you never thought that carrots would be a good partner for an intense garlicky persillade, you're in for a treat. This dish is the perfect accompaniment to any simple grilled, broiled, roasted, or pan-seared meat, fish, or poultry.

❦ YIELD: 6 SERVINGS AS A SIDE DISH

Kosher or sea salt and freshly ground black
    pepper to taste
3 pounds carrots, peeled and sliced diagonally
    ½ inch thick
¼ cup extra-virgin olive oil
3 garlic cloves, minced

¼ cup lightly packed chopped flat-leaf Italian parsley
½ cup Chicken Stock (page 16) or Roasted Vegetable
    Stock (page 22) or doctored canned broth
    (see page 19)
2 generous teaspoons sugar
3 tablespoons unsalted butter

FILL AN 8-QUART POT three-fourths full with cold water and bring to a rolling boil. Add 1 tablespoon salt to the water, then add the sliced carrots and boil them, uncovered, until crisp-tender, about 5 minutes. Meanwhile, place a large bowl of ice water near the stove and, when ready, drain the carrots and add them directly to the ice bath. Use your hands to swish them about to immediately halt the cooking process. When cold, drain the carrots and pat them dry with paper towels. Set them aside.

Combine the olive oil with the garlic and parsley. Add some salt and a generous amount of black pepper. Set this aside.

WHEN READY TO SERVE, place the cooked carrots, stock, sugar, and butter in a 12-inch heavy-bottomed deep-sided skillet over medium-high heat, and bring to a boil. Reduce the heat to medium and simmer the carrots very briskly, uncovered, until the stock evaporates and the carrots are perfectly tender and starting to caramelize around the edges, about 10 minutes, stirring occasionally. Stir in the garlic-herb mixture and cook the carrots until piping hot and sizzling, 2 to 3 minutes. Add salt and pepper to taste and serve the carrots right away.

TIMING IS
EVERYTHING
❦ *The carrots can be blanched two days ahead; after patting them dry, refrigerate them, wrapped in paper towels, and store in a heavy-duty plastic bag.*
❦ *The garlic-herb persillade can be made one day ahead and refrigerated, covered. Bring to room temperature before using.*

AROMATIC SAFFRON RICE

This fragrant rice dish gets its distinctive qualities from several things: aromatic basmati rice, which is further enhanced when simmered in a combination of chicken stock and clam broth that's imbued with the color, flavor, and aroma of crushed saffron threads. The result is a rice dish that's unusually good, and remarkably easy. ❧ YIELD: 6 SERVINGS AS A SIDE DISH

½ teaspoon Spanish saffron threads

2 tablespoons extra-virgin olive oil

1 large yellow onion, chopped

1½ cups basmati rice or long-grain converted rice

2 cups Chicken Stock (page 16) or Roasted Vegetable Stock (page 22) or doctored canned broth (see page 19)

1 cup (8 ounces) bottled clam juice

2 tablespoons softened unsalted butter (optional)

2 tablespoons chopped flat-leaf Italian parsley

Kosher or sea salt and freshly ground black pepper to taste

TIMING IS EVERYTHING

❧ *If you must hold cooked rice before serving, uncover the pot and fluff the rice with a fork. Place a clean folded kitchen towel over the pot and apply the lid. The lid will keep the rice warm while the towel prevents any accumulation of condensation from dripping into the pot, adversely affecting the texture.*

HEAT A 2½-QUART, heavy-bottomed saucepan with a tight-fitting lid over medium heat and, when hot, add the saffron threads. Stir the saffron constantly for about 15 seconds, allowing the threads to toast without letting them scorch. Add the olive oil and, when it's hot, stir in the onion. Cook, stirring frequently, until the onion is tender, reduced, and the color is very yellow, 5 to 8 minutes.

Stir the raw rice into the onion and raise the heat to high. Sauté the rice, stirring constantly, for 2 minutes to lightly toast the grains, then stir in the stock and clam broth and let the liquid come to a full bubble through the center. Cover the pan and reduce the heat to low. Let the rice cook, undisturbed, for 14 minutes for basmati rice and 17 minutes for long-grain converted rice.

After the allotted time, remove the pan from the heat and uncover. Stir in the softened butter, if using, along with the parsley, and salt and black pepper to taste. Re-cover the pan and let sit for 1 minute so the rice can settle and absorb any trace of remaining liquid. Serve piping hot.

HERE'S THE SCOOP:
On Buying Saffron

Don't buy powdered saffron, since the quality is often inferior to the threads, which are the deep red stigmas from a purple crocus. Powdered spices not only lose their flavor quickly but also are much more likely to be adulterated. The flavor intensity of saffron will vary from year to year and with each successive crop, so purchase sparingly and don't go overboard when using it in a recipe, since too much of even the best saffron can easily overwhelm a dish. The best places to purchase saffron threads are either a specialty spice shop or an Indian or Arab ethnic market, since they'll have the best turnover. And when choosing between threads of different origins, pick the Spanish saffron, since those are thought to be the most mellow. Lastly, walk away from saffron threads with lots of yellow stigmas intermingled with the red, which can be an indication of entrepreneurial hanky-panky.

FRESH SPINACH SAUTÉED
with Lotsa Garlic

If you like spinach, I think you'll love it when it's prepared this way. After clean-ing and trimming, the fresh spinach leaves are wilted in extra-virgin olive oil and then laced with both cooked and raw garlic. Serve this spinach dish with any roasted or grilled meat, poultry, or fish. And don't hesitate to keep any leftovers, since they can be reheated and added to the center of an omelet with some Gruyère cheese. ❧ YIELD: 6 SERVINGS AS A SIDE DISH

8 garlic cloves, peeled and left whole, plus 3 large
    garlic cloves, minced
½ cup Garlic Confit Oil (page 23) or extra-virgin
    olive oil
8 cups firmly packed stemmed, cleaned, and
    well-dried spinach leaves (use three 10-ounce
    packages)

Kosher or sea salt and freshly ground black
    pepper to taste
1 tablespoon softened unsalted butter (optional)

BRING A SMALL SAUCEPAN of water to a rolling boil. Add the whole garlic cloves and boil them, uncovered, for 2 minutes. Drain the garlic. Heat ¼ cup of the oil in a 12- to 14-inch heavy-bottomed, deep-sided skillet (or use a 6-quart pot) over medium heat and, when hot, add the drained garlic. Cook the garlic in the hot oil until golden on all sides, stirring frequently with a slot-ted spoon. Use the spoon to remove the browned garlic to a plate, then drag the skillet or pot to a cool burner and immediately add the remaining ¼ cup oil.

Reheat the pan with the oil over high heat and, when hot, add the spinach in batches. As one batch begins to wilt, use tongs to turn the leaves in the oil, then add more. After all the spinach has been turned in the oil, let the leaves become nicely wilted and manageable, about 2 minutes over medium heat. Stir in the browned garlic and the raw garlic, along with some salt and black pepper to taste. Reduce the heat to low and place the cover ajar. Continue to cook the spinach just until the leaves are tender and piping hot throughout, 3 to 4 minutes. If desired, stir in the butter to enrich the dish. Serve the spinach very hot.

TIMING IS
EVERYTHING
❧ *The spinach can be stemmed and cleaned two days ahead and kept in large heavy-duty plastic bags in the refrigerator.*
❧ *The poached garlic can be browned 2 hours ahead and left at room tempera-ture until ready to finish the dish.*

"SPAGHETTIED" ZUCCHINI
Simmered in Browned Butter and Broth

Did you ever think you'd be able to twirl anything other than cooked noodles around your fork? Well, when trimmed zucchini is forced through a manually operated device called a turning slicer, what comes out are long spiral strands that are every bit as twirlable as pasta once they are cooked. I bought my appliance years ago in France, but you can get yours right here in a Japanese grocery store, a well-stocked kitchen store, or through the sources on page 313. It's important to use green zucchini and not yellow summer squash, since the internal flesh of the latter isn't stable enough to be forced through the turning device. Having said this, there are some other vegetables that seem very happy to be turned into spaghetti, so check "Here's the Scoop" on page 203.

❧ YIELD: 6 TO 8 SERVINGS AS A SIDE DISH

6 large zucchini (with straight sides), scrubbed
   and dried
5 tablespoons unsalted butter
1 generous cup Chicken Stock (page 16) or Roasted
   Vegetable Stock (page 22)

Kosher or sea salt and freshly ground black pepper
   to taste
Freshly grated Parmigiano-Reggiano cheese
   (optional)

TIMING IS
EVERYTHING

❧ *The zucchini can be cut into strands one day ahead and kept refrigerated in a well-covered bowl or in a large sealed plastic bag.*

TRIM OFF BOTH ENDS of each zucchini so the ends are flat. Working with one zucchini at a time, center both ends of the vegetable on the slicing device so it's firmly secured. Using your working hand, turn the hand crank, which will cause the zucchini to extrude from one end in long, skinny strands. Do this with all the zucchini and pile the strands in a bowl.

Melt 4 tablespoons of the butter in a 12- to 14-inch heavy-bottomed, deep-sided skillet over medium heat. When the butter is melted and bubbling, reduce the heat to low and let the butter cook until the milk solids turn a nutty brown color (like peanut butter), taking care not to let the solids scorch. Stir in the remaining tablespoon of butter and let it melt but not color. Add the zucchini to the skillet and raise the heat to medium-high. Let the strands cook, occasionally tossing them with the butter, until they're somewhat reduced and are beginning to soften, about 4 minutes. Add the stock and salt and black pepper to taste, and bring the liquid to a simmer. Reduce the heat to low and let the zucchini cook, uncovered, until tender but not mushy (al dente), 4 to 5 minutes once the stock has begun to bubble.

When done, adjust the seasoning, if needed. Serve the zucchini piping hot, in wide soup plates. If desired, pass some grated Parmesan cheese at the table.

On Other Vegetables to Be Spaghettied

Other vegetables that like to be turned into spaghetti are carrots and Idaho potatoes. Use thick, large juicing carrots, and follow the same procedure as when using zucchini, but before sautéing, blanch the strands in lightly salted boiling water for 2 to 3 minutes just to soften them. After refreshing them in ice cold water, drain and dry them. Now, cook them as you would zucchini.

(At this point, you could even mix them both!) Potato strands are delicious when deep-fried into a wild nest of savory strands. Before frying, soak the strands in ice water for 30 minutes or so to remove some of their surface starch. To fry, fill a 4-, 6-, or 8-quart saucepan half full with oil and attach a deep-fry thermometer to the side of the pan, keeping the mercury tip deeply submerged with-

out allowing it to touch the bottom. Heat the oil to 375°F. Then take a handful of wet strands and dry them meticulously with paper towels or, preferably, pat them off and then spin them dry in a salad spinner. Fry each batch in the hot oil, stirring occasionally, until golden and crisp, 3 to 4 minutes. Drain on paper towels and serve them quickly, piled in a heap and sprinkled with kosher salt.

VERY CORN PUDDING
with Green Chiles and Cheese

Have you ever dreamed about a dish because it was so soothing and great-tasting? Well, I dream about this corn pudding and I enjoy it so much that I literally have to restrain myself when it's on our dinner table. This recipe is a perfect example of how fresh ingredients can work side-by-side with canned ones to produce a dish that's truly satisfying. ❧ YIELD: 6 SERVINGS AS A SIDE DISH

2½ cups Chicken Stock (page 16) or Roasted Vegetable Stock (page 22), or as a last resort use water
1 teaspoon salt
½ cup coarse (polenta) cornmeal (not instant or prepared)
1 Scotch bonnet chile (habanero), pricked several times with a fork (or substitute a jalapeño chile)
3 tablespoons unsalted butter, plus a bit more for brushing
½ cup minced yellow onion
One 4½-ounce can chopped green chiles, lightly drained

3 generous tablespoons chopped cilantro
Cayenne pepper to taste
Kosher or sea salt and freshly ground black pepper to taste
⅔ cup buttermilk
3 extra-large eggs, lightly beaten
One 15-ounce can cream-style corn
One 7-ounce can whole kernel corn, drained
½ cup medium-ground cornmeal
12 ounces Monterey Jack or Pepper Jack cheese, grated or shredded (about 1½ packed cups)

TIMING IS EVERYTHING

❧ *The pudding can be assembled fully one day ahead; once cool, cover the dish with greased aluminum foil, greased side down, and refrigerate. Bring the pudding close to room temperature before baking, or adjust the baking time accordingly.*

BRING THE STOCK or water to a boil in a 2-quart heavy-bottomed saucepan, then add the salt. Gradually sprinkle the cornmeal into the boiling liquid, whisking constantly to prevent lumps. Add the whole chile and reduce the heat to very low. Cover the pan and cook the cornmeal, stirring with a wooden spoon every 3 minutes, until the liquid is absorbed, the mixture is thickened, and the cornmeal is tender, 10 to 15 minutes. While you stir, use the bottom of the wooden spoon to flatten the chile against the side of the pan, releasing all of its spunk. When cooked, uncover the pan and remove the chile. Stir in 2 tablespoons of the butter, then cover and drag the pan to a cool burner.

Heat an 8- to 10-inch heavy-bottomed skillet over medium heat and, when hot, add the remaining tablespoon of butter. When the butter is hot and bubbling, add the minced onion and cook, stirring frequently, until the onion is softened, about 3 minutes. Stir in the chopped chiles and the cilantro. Season the vegetables to taste with cayenne pepper, salt, and black pepper. Remove the pan from the hot burner.

BUTTER THE INTERIOR of a 2½-quart oven-to-table baking dish. Preheat the oven to 350°F. In a large mixing bowl, combine the buttermilk, beaten eggs, creamed corn, drained whole corn, and the sautéed vegetables. Add the uncooked cornmeal and the cooked cornmeal, stir to combine, then stir in 1 packed cup of the grated cheese, reserving the rest for later. Season the pudding with more salt and black pepper and pour it into the prepared baking dish. Bake the pudding in the center of the oven for 35 minutes. Sprinkle on the remaining ½ cup grated cheese and continue to bake until the mixture is set and the top is turning golden, about 30 minutes more. Serve piping hot.

HERE'S THE SCOOP:
On the Love-Hate Relationship with Cilantro

I'll bet that everyone knows someone who claims that they hate cilantro. Actually, I've known people so passionate about this that they claim that they're physically allergic to it (just so no one slips some into their food). Personally, as a kid who was rarely exposed to this distinctive flavor, I grew up totally disliking the stuff. But after eating enough gua-camole in my early adulthood, I became a real fan of this wonderful herb. I've concluded that cilantro (also called Chinese parsley or fresh coriander) is often an acquired taste. So, if you don't like it, just leave it out and use Italian parsley instead. However, I'd suggest (except if you're honestly allergic) adding a little bit of cilantro to this corn pud-ding, since the texture of this dish is so soothing that it provides the perfect opportunity for you to expand your palate. From my experience as both a cooking teacher and a former cilantro-hater, once a person decides that he or she likes cilantro, it's only a matter of time before they start adding it to different dishes by the handful.

BUTTER-BRAISED LEEKS

To me, braised leeks are right up there with mashed potatoes as one of my favorite side dishes. At first glance, after cooking, the leeks will appear to have retained their long, sleek shape. But if you've done things right, when you use tongs to lift them out of the buttery broth, their texture will have completely surrendered. Use the last spoonfuls of stock to bathe individual portions, and serve the leeks nice and hot. ❧ YIELD: 6 SERVINGS AS A SIDE DISH

7 tablespoons unsalted butter, melted

Kosher or sea salt and freshly ground black pepper to taste

2 tablespoons extra-virgin olive oil, plus more for brushing

8 to 10 medium-large leeks, cleaned (see page 207)

1½ cups Chicken Stock (page 16) or Roasted Vegetable Stock (page 22) or doctored canned broth (see page 19)

2 tablespoons thinly sliced fresh chives or minced flat-leaf Italian parsley

PREHEAT THE OVEN TO 375°F. Cut out a round of parchment paper large enough to cover a 12- to 14-inch heavy-bottomed, ovenproof, deep-sided skillet. Brush one side of the paper with some of the melted butter and sprinkle the greased side lightly with salt and black pepper. Set the paper aside, seasoned side up.

Heat 5 tablespoons of the melted butter in the same skillet over medium-high heat and, when hot, reduce the heat to low and let the milk solids just begin to turn golden, about 2 minutes. Raise the heat to high and stir in the olive oil. When the fat is hot but not smoking, spread each leek open and lay them flat, cut side down, in a snug single layer in the pan. Sear the leeks until light golden, 2 to 3 minutes, then use tongs to turn the leeks over, keeping them intact. Heat the other side just until softened without letting that side brown, about 1½ minutes. (If, at first, the leeks can't fit in a single layer, sear them in batches, which will cause them to shrink. Once seared, they'll be able to fit.) After softening the leeks on their second side, drag the pan off the hot burner and season them with salt and pepper. Turn the leeks over cut sides down, still keeping them intact.

DRIZZLE THE REMAINING 2 tablespoons of melted butter over the leeks. Pour in the stock and place the greased and seasoned side of the parchment paper directly on top of the leeks. Place the pan in the center of the oven and cook until the stock is very reduced and the leeks are meltingly tender, with an underside that's nicely caramelized, 40 to 45 minutes. Discard the parchment paper and, using tongs, divide the leeks among warmed shallow soup plates. Spoon some of the surrounding stock over each portion, sprinkle the leeks with the chopped herbs, and serve right away.

TIMING IS EVERYTHING

❧ *The leeks can be seared several hours in advance. If planning to cook within 2 hours, leave the skillet at a comfortable room temperature. If planning to wait longer, refrigerate the dish, covered, and bring it close to room temperature before proceeding.*

On How to Get a Leek Squeaky Clean

As vegetables go, few have as much flavor potential as leeks. However, they are also one of the dirtiest vegetables around. To clean a leek meticulously, first cut off the coarse stringy roots. Because most of the long dark leaves are tough and woody, cut off all but 1½ inches of that part. (If desired, after a thorough washing, use these in stock.) Using a sharp 8-inch chef's knife, cut down the entire shaft of the leek without cutting all the way through the bottom (outside) layer. The dirtiest part of the leek is where it changes from light green to a darker shade. Open the leek like a book (keeping the layers intact) and, starting at the green end held horizontally to the side, rinse the leek thoroughly under cool water. Look through all the white and green layers, checking for dirt and, after wiping the leek dry, slice it or leave it whole, depending on your particular recipe.

PICO DE GALLO

With tastes and textures that run the gamut from crisp, crunchy, and piquant to buttery and slightly tart, this mixture is the perfect condiment to accompany a pile of warmed corn tortilla chips or a sizzling platter of homemade Steak, Chicken, and Shrimp Fajitas (page 188). ❧ YIELD: ABOUT 4 CUPS

1 pound plum (Roma) tomatoes, coarsely chopped (skin and seeds intact)

½ cup minced white or yellow onion

2 tablespoons minced red onion

2 large garlic cloves, minced

2 to 4 fresh jalapeño or serrano chiles, seeded and minced

1 ripe Hass avocado, peeled, pitted, and cut into small dice

2 to 3 tablespoons strained fresh lime juice, or to taste

3 tablespoons extra-virgin olive oil

½ cup loosely packed chopped cilantro, or to taste

Freshly ground white and black pepper to taste

Kosher or sea salt to taste

TIMING IS EVERYTHING

❧ *The Pico de Gallo can be assembled fully early on the day of serving and kept refrigerated, well covered, until 15 minutes before serving.*

PLACE THE TOMATOES, onions, garlic, and chiles in a 2-quart nonreactive bowl. In another small nonreactive bowl, gently toss the diced avocado with 2 tablespoons lime juice. Add the avocado to the tomato mixture with the olive oil, cilantro, and a generous amount of both white and black pepper. Fold the mixtures together, combining well, then cover the bowl securely and refrigerate for a few hours, allowing the flavors to meld. To serve, let the Pico de Gallo sit out of refrigeration for 15 minutes, then taste for seasoning, adding salt to taste and a bit more lime juice, if desired. Serve with warmed corn tortilla chips or as an accompaniment to homemade fajitas.

SWEET AND SOUR RED ONIONS

If it were up to me, I'd park a bowl of these cooked onions on the table every night. In addition to tasting great piled over a simple burger, they're wonderful with grilled chops, in omelets, or even as a filling for grilled cheese sandwiches. They're also great with cooked sliced boneless steak and chicken, wrapped in warmed flour tortillas. ✿ YIELD: ABOUT 1½ CUPS

3 tablespoons extra-virgin olive oil
2 large red onions, sliced through the stem end into
    thin strips

¼ cup red wine vinegar or balsamic vinegar
2 tablespoons light brown or granulated sugar

HEAT A 12-INCH, heavy-bottomed, deep-sided nonreactive skillet over high heat and, when hot, add the olive oil. When the oil is hot, stir in the onion strips and cook them until softened, 3 to 5 minutes. Add the vinegar and sugar, tossing well to combine. Continue to cook the onions over high heat until tender and the vinegar has been totally absorbed by the onions, 5 to 7 minutes. Reduce the heat to medium and cook the onions, stirring frequently, until the sugar has begun to caramelize and is clinging to the onions, giving them a very enticing golden color, without allowing the onions to burn. Transfer the onions to a bowl and serve them either hot, warm, or at room temperature.

TIMING IS
EVERYTHING
✿ *The onions can be sautéed several hours ahead and kept at a comfortable room temperature, loosely covered. If you'd like to serve them hot, reheat the onions gently, either in the microwave or on the stove over low heat.*

Baked Garlic
MASHED POTATOES
with Lots of Fresh Chives and a Savory Parmesan Crust

Honestly, I can't count how many times I've made this creamy, crusty mashed potato casserole, always to rave reviews. Loaded with poached garlic, minced chives, and a hefty amount of the finest grated Parmesan cheese, these potatoes seem completely at home whether paired with broiled, roasted, grilled, or pan-seared meat or fish. And because the dish can be fully assembled a day ahead and refrigerated, it's a natural choice when entertaining.

❧ YIELD: 10 TO 12 SERVINGS AS A SIDE DISH

5 pounds red new potatoes
3 tablespoons butter, melted
1⅓ cups freshly grated Parmigiano-Reggiano cheese
Kosher or sea salt to taste
2 cups heavy cream
6 large garlic cloves (or 12 small)

¾ rounded cup thinly sliced chives (about 3 large bunches) or, if unavailable, use the light green of scallions, finely chopped
Freshly ground black and white pepper to taste
Cayenne pepper to taste

FILL A 10-QUART POT two-thirds full with cold water and place over high heat. While waiting for the water to boil, peel the potatoes (and, if large, cut them in half) and place them in a bowl of ice water to prevent them from discoloring. Brush some of the melted butter evenly inside a 3½-quart oven-to-table baking dish and sprinkle in ⅓ cup of the grated cheese. Tilt the dish to coat the interior evenly, allowing any excess cheese to fall to the bottom and remain there. Set the dish aside for now. When the water comes to a rapid boil, add about 2 tablespoons salt and the drained potatoes. Cover the pot and boil the potatoes until very tender, 30 to 45 minutes.

Meanwhile, bring the cream to a simmer with the garlic, uncovered, over medium heat. Reduce the heat to low and continue to simmer until the garlic is very tender and the cream has reduced to about 1½ cups, about 10 minutes. (To prevent the cream from boiling over, occasionally shake the pan by its handle.) Add the chives and black and white pepper to taste, then sprinkle in a few dashes of cayenne pepper (go easy here). Turn off the heat and allow the pan to sit on the hot burner.

If your baking dish is glass, preheat the oven to 375°F. and, if metal, preheat to 400°F.

WHEN THE POTATOES ARE TENDER, turn off the heat and reserve 2 cups of hot potato water separately. Drain the potatoes and pile them into a

TIMING IS
EVERYTHING

❧ *The potato casserole
can be fully assembled one
day ahead and, once cool,
kept refrigerated, well
covered. Bring close to
room temperature before
baking, or increase the
"covered" cooking time
accordingly.*

large mixing bowl. Add the hot garlic-infused cream and use a potato masher to make the mixture smooth. If at all dry, add some of the reserved potato water until the consistency is creamy and luscious-looking. Using a rubber spatula, fold in remaining 1 cup grated Parmesan cheese, then add salt and more black pepper to taste.

Transfer the potato mixture to the prepared baking dish and smooth the top, using a long spreading spatula. Brush the top of the potatoes with the reserved melted butter, then use a decorating comb or the tines of a wide serving fork to make decorative lines on the top surface. Season the top with salt and pepper, then let the potatoes cool, loosely covered with doubled paper towels. When cool, grease the shiny side of a large sheet of aluminum foil and cover the dish securely (greased side down). Bake the potatoes, covered, for 30 minutes, then remove the foil and continue to bake until piping hot, golden, and crusty, 30 to 35 minutes more. Serve the potatoes right away.

Crispy and Spicy
HASH-BROWNED POTATOES

Whether served at dinner alongside grilled chops, or at breakfast with freshly cooked eggs, these flavorful hash-browned potatoes taste great. And since the dish can be fully assembled ahead of time, it's a prime candidate to become a family favorite. ❧ YIELD: 4 SERVINGS AS A SIDE DISH

2 cups Roasted Vegetable Stock (page 22), doctored canned broth (see page 19), or water

Kosher or sea salt

2 pounds peeled and diced Idaho potatoes or small unpeeled red potatoes, scrubbed, and halved

1½ teaspoons balsamic vinegar (optional)

About ½ cup extra-virgin olive oil or melted Clarified Butter (page 195) or a combination

1 medium-large yellow onion, chopped

4 large garlic cloves, minced

½ large green bell pepper, seeded and chopped

Freshly ground black pepper to taste

Cayenne pepper to taste

10 ounces button mushrooms, wiped clean and sliced

2 tablespoons chopped flat-leaf parsley or chives

Sweet paprika for sprinkling

TIMING IS EVERYTHING

❧ *The potato dish can be fully assembled early in the day and kept at a comfortable room temperature before baking. Or, for breakfast, assemble the dish the night before and, when cool, cover the top with aluminum foil and refrigerate overnight. Bring close to room temperature before baking, or adjust the cooking time accordingly.*

❧ *Reheat leftover hashbrowns, uncovered, in a 450°F. oven, in a shallow baking dish, redistributing once or twice during baking, until crisp and hot.*

POUR THE STOCK or water into a 12-inch, nonreactive, deep-sided skillet and add about 1½ teaspoons salt. Add the potatoes, cover, and bring the liquid to a rapid boil. Cook over medium-high heat until almost tender, about 8 minutes. Using a slotted utensil, transfer the potatoes to a bowl. Reduce the liquid in the pan over medium heat until only a few syrupy tablespoons remain. Whisk in the vinegar, if using, and pour this liquid onto the potatoes.

Preheat the oven to 450°F., then heat a 10-inch well-seasoned cast-iron skillet (or another heavy ovenproof nonstick pan) over medium-high heat and, when hot, add 2 tablespoons of the oil or butter. When the fat is hot, add the onion and cook, stirring occasionally, until turning golden, about 10 minutes. Stir in the garlic and cook 2 minutes, then add the green pepper and cook 2 minutes more. Season with salt and black pepper and a few dashes of cayenne and add to the bowl of potatoes. Return the skillet to medium-high heat and add 2 more tablespoons of oil or butter. When hot, add the mushrooms and cook, stirring occasionally, until tender and deep golden, about 7 minutes. Season with salt and pepper, then add the mushrooms to the potatoes, along with the herbs and more salt and pepper to taste. Fold everything together, combining well.

Add 2 more tablespoons olive oil or clarified butter to the same skillet, swirling to coat the bottom surface. Add the potato mixture to the skillet and drizzle the remaining 2 tablespoons of fat over the top. Season the surface, adding a light dusting of paprika. Bake for 30 minutes. Remove the pan from the oven and carefully fold the ingredients together to redistribute. Continue baking for another 30 minutes, or until crisp, crusty, piping hot, and golden brown. Serve right away.

CRISPY FRIED SWEETS

(as in Sweet Potatoes)

As their name indicates, sweet potatoes have a higher sugar content than starchy Russets, making them more heat sensitive and less able to get very crisp. But this has never stopped me from making fried sweets, since my family adores them. In this country, the terms sweet potato and yam are used interchangeably, the latter usually referring to the sweeter, moister (and more orange) variety. True yams, which are not usually available in this country, are very starchy and can grow into ridiculously huge specimens. ❧ YIELD: 4 TO 6 SERVINGS AS A SIDE DISH

2 to 4 quarts flavorless cooking oil or highly refined peanut oil

3 pounds sweet potatoes (about 5 medium), preferably a yellow-fleshed variety

2 cups unbleached all-purpose flour

2 teaspoons baking powder

1 teaspoon salt

Pinch of cayenne pepper

Freshly ground black pepper to taste

Kosher or sea salt to taste

IF USING AN ELECTRIC deep-fat fryer, pour in the oil to the designated line and turn to the highest setting (or follow the manufacturer's instructions). Otherwise, fill a 4- to 8-quart heavy-bottomed saucepan half full with oil and attach a deep-fry thermometer to the side of the pan, so the mercury tip is deeply submerged without touching the bottom. Insert a frying basket, if using, and heat the oil to between 280°F. and 300°F. (If not using a frying basket, you'll need to have a long-handled slotted utensil, like a "spider," nearby.)

Peel the sweet potatoes and slice them into medium-thick french fry shapes. In a medium mixing bowl, whisk together the flour, baking powder, salt, a few dashes of cayenne, and some black pepper. Working with one small batch at a time, take a handful of potato sticks and dredge (coat) them in the seasoned flour, knocking off some of the excess. Fry the seasoned potatoes until softened and beginning to color, about 4 minutes per batch. Drain well on paper towels, then pile them into a large roasting pan lined with paper towels. Dredge, fry, and drain all of the potatoes this way, and let them sit in the roasting pan, covered loosely with paper towels, at room temperature until you're ready for the final frying.

When getting ready to serve, reheat the oil until it reaches 350°F. Line a shallow baking sheet with aluminum foil (shiny side up) and place it in the oven, set at 375°F. Fry the potatoes again in small batches until golden and crisp, 2 to 4 minutes per batch. Drain each batch on paper towels, then transfer to the hot baking sheet. When done frying, heap the potatoes on a warmed serving platter and sprinkle the pile with salt. Serve right away.

TIMING IS EVERYTHING

❧ *Sweet potatoes can be peeled a few hours ahead and kept at room temperature, wrapped in paper towels.*

❧ *Although the potatoes will be crispest when fried twice, in close succession, they can have their first, preliminary frying up to 2 hours ahead, and kept at a comfortable room temperature.*

Crazy for Mushrooms . . .
SAVORY BREAD PUDDING

Although my husband swears that this dish is the best stuffing, it's actually not a stuffing at all. It's much fluffier than a baked stuffing, with its golden-brown exterior and wonderfully crisp top. And, this recipe provides a great way to use yesterday's Italian loaf, since its new, slightly drier texture is perfectly suited for bread pudding. You know, that's part of the kitchen dance: utilizing ingredients in ways that will help them to shine perfectly, without ever having to apologize for their new use. ❧ YIELD: 6 TO 8 SERVINGS AS A SIDE DISH

4 cups packed day-old coarse bread crumbs or small cubes (see page 29), preferably from Italian bread with sesame seeds

3 tablespoons extra-virgin olive oil, plus more for brushing the dish

½ cup dried porcini mushrooms

3 tablespoons unsalted butter

1½ cups minced yellow onions

2 generous teaspoons minced fresh thyme

Kosher or sea salt and freshly ground black pepper to taste

10 ounces button mushrooms, wiped clean and chopped coarsely

1¾ pounds shiitake mushrooms, stems removed, caps wiped clean and chopped coarsely

8 ounces portobello mushrooms (1 or 2 large), stems removed, caps wiped clean and chopped coarsely

2 large garlic cloves, minced

1¾ cups heavy cream

4 extra-large eggs, lightly beaten

1 tablespoon white truffle oil (optional)

¼ to ½ cup freshly grated Parmigiano-Reggiano cheese

TIMING IS EVERYTHING

❧ *For best texture, bake the bread pudding soon after assembling. However, you can mix the bread with the sautéed vegetables and combine your custard ingredients up to 2 hours ahead, keeping them separate at a comfortable room temperature.*

PREHEAT THE OVEN TO 350°F. Lightly toast the bread crumbs or cubes on a shallow baking sheet in the oven until dry and light golden, about 10 minutes. Keep the oven set at 350°F. and transfer the crumbs to a mixing bowl. Brush the interior of a 2-quart oven-to-table baking dish with olive oil.

Steep the dried mushrooms in about 1½ cups boiling water until supple, about 20 minutes. Use your hand to lift the mushrooms out of the water, squeezing them gently to release any excess liquid back into the bowl. Chop the reconstituted mushrooms and set them aside. Place a fine-mesh wire sieve over a bowl and line the sieve with a doubled layer of dampened cheesecloth. Strain the mushroom liquid through the cheesecloth into the bowl. Measure 1¼ cups mushroom liquid and set this aside. (If necessary, add some water to reach 1¼ cups.)

MELT 2 TABLESPOONS of the butter in a 12-inch, heavy-bottomed deep-sided skillet over medium heat. When the butter is hot and bubbling, stir in the minced onions and cook them, stirring occasionally, until softened, about 4 minutes. Add half the minced thyme and some salt and black pepper.

Transfer the onions to the bowl of bread crumbs and, without wiping out the pan, put it back over medium-high heat with 3 tablespoons of olive oil. When the oil is hot, stir in all the chopped fresh mushrooms and, when wilted, stir in the minced garlic and let the mushrooms cook, uncovered, stirring occasionally, until golden and any released liquid has evaporated. Stir in the remaining thyme, the chopped reconstituted mushrooms, and salt and pepper to taste. When hot, transfer the mushrooms to the bowl of bread crumbs and onions.

Replace the pan over high heat and add ½ cup of the mushroom liquid. As the liquid bubbles, use the flat edge of a wooden spatula to release any clinging bits of mushrooms from the bottom of the pan and reduce the liquid to a generous ¼ cup. Pour this reduction into the bowl of bread crumbs and vegetables.

Use a whisk to combine the cream with the eggs and the remaining ¾ cup mushroom liquid. Stir in the truffle oil, if using, and season the custard with salt and pepper. When ready to bake, pour the custard over the bread mixture and fold through to combine well. Transfer this to the prepared baking dish and dot the top with the remaining tablespoon of butter. Bake the bread pudding, uncovered, for 25 minutes. Sprinkle the cheese over the top and continue to bake until the top is golden, the pudding is swollen, and the custard is set, about 25 minutes more. Serve piping hot.

HERE'S THE SCOOP:
On Cleaning Mushrooms

All mushrooms inherently contain a varied (but substantial) amount of water. In addition, many mushrooms have a gill-like structure on the underside of their caps, making them absorb any additional liquid they encounter. Because of these qualities, running mushrooms under water leaves them soggy. The best way to clean mushrooms is to wipe them with a dampened paper towel. If dried meticulously, mushrooms can be cleaned and sliced a few days ahead of cooking and stored in a perforated plastic bag in the refrigerator. Also, for best longevity, purchase mushrooms that are as firm, dry, and blemish free as possible. At purchase, the gills on the underside of each cap should also be closed, since when open this indicates that the mushroom has been in the market for several days. The open gills have no negative affect on flavor; however, it means that they won't last as long once you get them home.

Better Than Plain . . .
CHIVE-STUDDED YORKSHIRE PUDDING

Not a pudding at all, Yorkshire pudding is actually a crisp, delicately flavored, flour-and-egg-based thin breadlike custard that originated in the county of Yorkshire, England. It is traditionally served with roast beef, and it uses the drippings from the meat to give it incredible taste. The added color and sassy flavor from both minced chives and cayenne make this an exceptionally flavorful version of an old-time recipe. Yorkshire pudding is meant to be eaten with every bite of meat, napped either with the natural meat juices (called au jus in French) or with another delicious sauce. If you're looking for a fabulous roast beef recipe, turn to page 193. ❧ YIELD: 6 TO 8 SERVINGS AS A SIDE DISH

1 cup unbleached all-purpose flour
½ teaspoon salt
¼ teaspoon cayenne pepper
Freshly ground black pepper to taste
2 extra-large eggs
1 cup milk

⅓ cup packed thinly sliced chives (if unavailable, mince the deeper green part of a scallion)
3 tablespoons beef drippings (optional)
3 tablespoons melted unsalted butter (if not using drippings, use 3 tablespoons each whole and Clarified Butter, page 195)

TIMING IS EVERYTHING

❧ *The custard mixture (milk, eggs, and chives) can be mixed early in the day and kept refrigerated, covered. Stir before using.*

WHEN YOUR ROAST BEEF enters the oven, assemble the batter. Use a whisk to combine the flour, salt, cayenne, and black pepper. In a separate mixing bowl, use a fork to beat the eggs. Mix the milk and chives into the eggs. Pour the seasoned flour into the beaten egg mixture and, using either a batter whisk or a regular whisk, combine the mixture gently but thoroughly. (No dry pockets of flour should remain.) Cover the bowl and let it sit out at room temperature until your roast leaves the oven.

When the meat comes out of the oven, remove it to another tray (or a warmed serving platter) and loosely cover it with aluminum foil. Turn the oven temperature to 450°F. with the rack on the center shelf. Pour all of the drippings into a bowl (a 9-pound roast should yield ½ to 1 cup of drippings). Place a small heatproof bowl on your work surface, and into it place the measured beef drippings and melted butter (if not using drippings, use equal amounts of whole and clarified butter).

PLACE A 13 × 9-INCH GLASS baking dish in the oven to preheat for 5 minutes. Open the oven and add the mixed fat to the dish and shut the door. Allow the fat to heat for 1 minute. Give the batter a brief stir, then open the oven and pour the prepared batter into the hot dish, using a rubber spatula to scrape out all of it (try to be quick, so the oven doesn't cool down). Shut the door and bake the custard for 12 minutes. Reduce the temperature to 400°F. and bake for 5 minutes. Reduce the temperature to 350°F. and bake for 12 to 15 minutes, or until the pudding is golden, crisp, and puffed around the edges and the center is fully set but not overly dark. Remove the dish from the oven and cut the pudding into 6 to 8 equal rectangles, making sure that each person gets a portion of the crisp rim. Serve as soon as you can, surrounding the sliced roast or on an individual platter.

HERE'S THE SCOOP:
On Using Glass Baking Dishes

Glass is a terrific way to transfer heat and get a nice crisp finish on baked goods, and pie crusts are a good example. If you have only a metal pan, you'll need to raise the oven temperature by 25°F. to help duplicate this quick and intense transfer of heat. This will apply to any recipe that you use where you're asked to use a glass pan, unless your recipe specifies otherwise. Conversely, to avoid overcooking, if a metal pan is requested and all you have is glass, you'll need to reduce the oven temperature called for in your recipe by 25°F.

LONG GRAIN AND WILD RICE PILAF
with Pan-Toasted Pecans and Dried Cranberries

If you are looking for a gorgeous side dish to accompany roasted or grilled meat or poultry, this rice pilaf is a terrific choice. The toasted pecans and dried cranberries make this dish more festive, texturally diverse, and a perfect addition to a Thanksgiving menu. Actually, you could substitute sautéed diced chestnuts for the pecans. By the way, for a pilaf with a wonderful earthy taste and crunchy texture, just combine the sautéed vegetables with the cooked wild rice, omitting the white rice all together. That version will serve four.

YIELD: 8 SERVINGS AS A SIDE DISH

1 cup wild rice, well rinsed and drained

1 teaspoon salt

½ generous cup dried porcini mushrooms

5 tablespoons unsalted butter, plus 2 more tablespoons as an optional enrichment

2 garlic cloves, minced

1 large yellow onion, minced

2 large celery stalks, minced

2 teaspoons minced fresh thyme leaves

2 tablespoons chopped flat-leaf Italian parsley

Kosher or sea salt and freshly ground black pepper to taste

1 cup long-grain rice, preferably converted

2 cups hot well-seasoned stock of choice or doctored canned broth (see page 19)

½ cup coarsely chopped pecans, pan-toasted in 2 teaspoons butter and then drained (optional)

½ cup moist dried cranberries (optional)

To COOK WILD RICE that's been scooped from an open bin, soak the kernels in cold water for 10 minutes, then rinse well to remove any debris. (If prepackaged, this is not necessary.) Place the wild rice in a 2-quart saucepan with about 3 cups cold water and bring the water to a boil over medium-high heat, uncovered. Stir in the salt, then reduce the heat to medium-low and simmer the rice, covered, until tender but not mushy, 40 to 45 minutes. Drain the rice and set it aside.

Meanwhile, put the dried porcini in a bowl, cover with 1 cup of boiling water, and let them steep until supple, about 20 minutes. Place a fine-mesh wire sieve over a bowl and line the sieve with a doubled layer of dampened cheesecloth. Lift the mushrooms out of the liquid and coarsely chop them. Strain the mushroom liquid through the cheesecloth into the bowl. Reserve ½ cup of this flavorful liquid.

MELT 3 TABLESPOONS of the butter in a 12-inch, deep-sided skillet over medium heat and, when hot and bubbling, add the garlic, onion, and celery. Cook the vegetables, stirring frequently, until tender, 8 to 10 minutes. Add the chopped reconstituted mushrooms, the herbs, and some salt and black pepper. Drag the pan to a cool burner for now.

Heat a 2-quart heavy-bottomed saucepan over medium heat with the remaining 2 tablespoons of the butter. When the butter is hot and bubbling, stir the raw long-grain rice into the butter. Sauté the grains, stirring constantly, until lightly toasted, 2 to 3 minutes. Add the hot stock along with the reserved mushroom liquid and bring it to a bubble through the center. Stir the rice, then cover the pan tightly, reduce the heat to low, and simmer for 16 minutes without disturbing. (If using an aromatic rice, like basmati or Texmati, simmer for only 13 minutes.)

WHEN THE RICE has about 4 minutes left to cook, reheat the sautéed vegetables over low heat. After 16 minutes, uncover the rice, which should not have absorbed all of the liquid yet. Stir the white rice and cooked wild rice into the sautéed vegetables along with 2 tablespoons of softened butter, if using, and the toasted pecans and dried cranberries, if using. Season again with salt and pepper and cook gently, uncovered, 4 to 5 minutes longer, stirring frequently until piping hot throughout. Serve hot.

TIMING IS EVERYTHING
 The wild rice can be cooked and the pecans toasted early in the day and left at room temperature until it's time to finish the dish.

HERE'S THE SCOOP:
To Revamp Dried Fruit

When small dried fruits like raisins, currants, or cherries feel brittle, you can plump them either by steeping them in hot tea or in some warmed fruit juice for 10 minutes and then draining well, or by steaming them in a steamer basket over simmering water, with the pan tightly shut, for 5 to 15 minutes, depending on their condition. To help dried fruit retain its supple texture longer, store at room temperature in a sealed container or in doubled plastic bags.

BRAIDED CHALLAH page 226

CHAPTER EIGHT
Make a Real Impact
HOMEMADE BREAD, BISCUITS, and MORE

O F ALL THE THINGS I do (and teach) in the kitchen, making homemade bread definitely feels the most rewarding. If you've always thought that perfect bread had to be made by professionals, think again. Actually, when many of my cooking students first come to me, they've never made bread and now they do it regularly and find joy in the entire process. If you love to cook and would like to try your hand at bread making, I hope you'll trust the breads in this chapter to take you where you'd like to go. Whether you love your bread soft and perfectly tender or impeccably crusty on the outside and chewy within, the breads I've provided in this chapter cover quite a lot of territory.

I think you'll be surprised at how few tools are needed to make beautiful plump loaves like country white bread, or a six-strand braided raisin challah that's as impressive to look at as it is delectable to eat. Other artisan breads that will make you proud and eager to share are the voluptuous *pane di casa*, a whimsical *fougasse*, a savory batch of stuffed onion *ficelles*, crusty pizzas and even a stack of crisp matzos. You'll also learn to make delicious cornbread, soothing biscuits, and even a tender stack of homemade flour tortillas to accompany a sizzling platter of fajitas.

Judging from the reactions of my family, friends, and students, I feel sure that the breads featured on the following pages will make you and your family very happy.

A Few Things About Kneading Breads by Hand

The kneading process is not a dainty one, and it requires your hand movements to be both bossy and deliberate. Always keep a pastry scraper to one side of your work surface, which you'll use frequently to remove the dough cleanly off your board as you aggressively develop texture. You'll need to work on an ample-sized wooden surface for proper traction; to keep the board from sliding around, place either a thin rubber mat or a damp kitchen towel under it.

The kneading process is like this: Think of your hands as a car. Your palms are your power source (the gas pedal) and your fingers are your steering wheel. Kneading is a push, pull, and folding motion that begins by driving the palms of your hands into the center of the dough. Next, your fingertips will bring the dough farthest away from you up and over (toward you), then your fingertips will fold one side of dough over the other. You'll quickly repeat this (pushing in, pulling down, and folding over) motion over and over again, using your scraper as needed at the first signs of stickiness. Scrape the dough off the board and place it in your nonworking hand. Spread a light dusting of flour on the board, drop the dough onto the floured surface, rub some flour onto your hands, and continue to work the dough. When finished, the dough will be smooth and supple, and you'll feel "real resistance" at the center, indicating that sufficient elasticity has been developed. Depending on how adept you are at kneading, the process will take between 4 and 10 minutes.

To Make Bread Using a Dough Hook

Although making bread by hand is clearly the process I prefer, you can make very fine bread by first using a paddle attachment and then switching to a dough hook. Here are the instructions to assemble your dough, using a heavy-duty electric mixer.

Place all of your liquid ingredients in the bowl of the machine (including any eggs and the dissolved yeast). If your recipe suggests the use of a specialty flour (like whole wheat, rye, rye meal, cornmeal, etc.), add it to the liquid now. Then add 1 or 2 cups of white flour and, using the paddle attachment, beat the flour into the liquid at a moderate speed. Keep adding more flour ½ to 1 cup at a time, beating well after each addition. (Always turn off the machine before adding more flour.) When the mixture is thick and glutinous, stop the machine and, using a rubber spatula, scrape the dough off the paddle, then scrape it off the sides of the bowl. Use the spatula to lift up one side of the dough, and sprinkle some flour underneath it. Sprinkle more flour on top of the dough and insert the dough hook. Work the dough using the hook, following the manufacturer's instructions, until it's smooth and elastic. If at any time the dough spreads on the bottom of the bowl, keeping the hook from reaching all of it evenly, stop the machine, scrape the dough off the bottom, sprinkle flour underneath and on top of the dough, and continue using the hook.

A word of caution: Overusing a dough hook can cause the dough to overheat, which could damage the yeast. To prevent this, once the dough seems smooth and glutinous (after about 3 minutes of using the dough hook continuously), scrape the dough off the hook and onto a lightly floured surface to finish the kneading process by hand.

On Creating Steam While Baking

You'll notice, when baking artisan breads, that I create steam by tossing a small amount of ice water onto the floor of the oven, just prior to inserting the raw dough onto either hot quarry tiles or onto a preheated pizza stone. If, however, you are worried about damaging your oven, omit the ice water and instead, place the tiles

or stone on the second or third lowest shelf in the oven and, on the rack beneath it, place a heavy-bottomed, oven-proof pan. Allow the pan to preheat along with the tiles. Just before inserting the dough into the hot oven, carefully pour 3/4 cup warm water into the pan. Place the dough onto the hot tiles and follow the remaining baking instructions.

COUNTRY WHITE BREAD

Not at all like that puffed-up Wonder Bread stuff, these loaves produce slices that are perfectly tender yet substantial enough to stand up to the heftiest sandwich, as well as French toast, stuffing, and sweet or savory bread pudding. Since it's always such a comfort to have a loaf or two tucked in the freezer, this recipe makes three loaves. If you are new to making bread, especially by hand, I suggest that you make the Challah Bread on page 226 once or twice (either plain or with raisins) before making this larger dough. After that, this one will be a piece of cake. ❧ YIELD: THREE 9 × 5-INCH LOAVES

About 10 tablespoons unsalted butter, melted

2½ cups milk

¼ cup solid vegetable shortening

2½ teaspoons salt

½ cup sugar or mild-flavored honey, plus a pinch of sugar

2 packages active dry yeast

½ cup warm water

3 extra-large eggs, at room temperature

3 extra-large egg yolks, at room temperature

5 cups bread flour

Up to 5 cups unbleached all-purpose flour, including flour for dusting

USE SOME OF THE MELTED BUTTER to grease the interior of an 8-quart mixing bowl. Set that bowl aside. Warm the milk with the shortening and add 6 tablespoons of the melted butter. Pour the hot milk mixture into another large mixing bowl and add the salt and ½ cup sugar or honey. Let the mixture cool to lukewarm. In a small bowl, dissolve the yeast in the warm water with the pinch of sugar and allow it to become bubbly, about 3 minutes. Meanwhile, stir the whole eggs and yolks into the milk mixture, then add the dissolved yeast. Stir in the bread flour, 1½ cups at a time, then add enough all-purpose flour, cup by cup, to create a somewhat stiff, shaggy mass that's no longer easily stirred.

Use a sturdy rubber spatula to scrape the mass out onto a floured surface and knead it until you've created a dough that's smooth and elastic, adding only as much additional flour as is needed to keep the dough from sticking. Place the dough in the greased bowl and brush the top with more melted butter. Cover the bowl with greased plastic wrap and a clean kitchen towel. Let the dough rise in a warm draft-free spot for 2 hours. Uncover the dough and punch it down with several swift swats with the back of your hand. Turn the dough over in the bowl and knead it gently to redistribute the yeast. Re-cover the bowl and let the dough rise again until very light and billowy, 1¼ hours.

To SHAPE, RISE, AND BAKE the loaves, first brush three 9 × 5-inch loaf pans with melted butter and set them aside. Turn the risen dough out onto a lightly floured surface and knead it gently and briefly. Use your pastry scraper to divide the dough into three equal portions, and cover them while working with one at a time. Roll one piece into an 8 × 10-inch rectangle, with one short end close to you. Starting at the short end that's farthest from you, roll the dough down snugly toward you. After each revolution, use the fingertips on your working hand to press down and connect the interior wall of the roll to the bottom of the dough. When you reach the bottom, pinch the last inch of dough onto the roll so it adheres. Working with one end at a time, press each coiled spiral of dough in toward the center of the log. Pinch the top and bottom outer rims of dough together, elongating this part slightly, and attach it to the bottom seam, rounding off and sealing each end.

Lay the loaf seam side down in a prepared loaf pan and use your hands to gently plump and correct the shape. Cover the loaf with a clean kitchen towel and repeat this same procedure with the remaining dough. Let the loaves rise for 45 minutes in a draft-free spot.

Twenty minutes before the end of the rise, preheat the oven to 400°F. if using metal pans and 375°F. if using glass. Just before placing the loaves in the hot oven, brush the tops with melted butter. Bake the loaves in the middle of the oven, with 1½ inches between them, for 30 to 35 minutes, covering loosely with aluminum foil (shiny side up) for the last 10 minutes if becoming overly brown. Remove the loaves from the oven and turn them out of their pans onto wire racks. Give the bottom of each loaf a good tap on its bottom, which should sound hollow. If not, put them back into the oven (on a shallow baking sheet) for a few more minutes. When done, remove the loaves from the oven and, for the softest crusts, brush the tops with more melted butter. Let the loaves cool completely on wire racks before slicing.

A word about oven space: If all three loaves won't fit in your oven, bake two risen loaves at once while the third rises in the refrigerator, covered. When the first two loaves enter the oven, remove the third from the refrigerator, letting it rise until the desired volume is achieved. Bake as directed.

TIMING IS EVERYTHING

❧ *The dough can be made two days ahead of baking. After the first punch-down, cover the bowl securely with the original greased plastic wrap and then with aluminum foil. Before shaping, let the dough sit out of refrigeration until it becomes room temperature (which can take 4 hours). Shape, rise, and bake as directed.*

❧ *To freeze these loaves, don't apply the last application of melted butter after baking, which tends to create a shriveled look in frozen breads. When fully cool, wrap the loaf in a double layer of aluminum foil, then slip the loaf inside a large heavy-duty freezer bag and freeze it for up to one month.*

A SIX-STRAND BRAIDED CHALLAH

(Sweet or Savory)

This recipe is very special to me and was actually my signature bread at the beginning of my culinary career. Traditionally, in the Jewish religion, braided challah is eaten with dinner every Friday, to celebrate the Sabbath. The woven, knobby shape of the braid is meant to reflect the forever winding and sometimes bumpy road of life. I thought you'd enjoy knowing the easy step-by-step professional formula for making a six-strand braid at home.

Since this dough is so easy to work and tastes so great, I seem to keep finding more and more wonderful things to do with it! Following are the directions to make two voluptuous six-strand braided loaves, with or without raisins. I also give a savory herb and cheese variation, which can be used for braids, regular loaves, or to enclose an entire wheel of Brie cheese, which is a real show-stopper on a buffet table (see page 96). ❧ YIELD: 2 LARGE FREESTANDING BRAIDS, OR TWO 2-POUND BRIE EN CROÛTE, OR THREE 8 × 4-INCH LOAVES

About 11 tablespoons unsalted butter, melted
1 cup milk
⅓ cup sugar, plus a pinch
1 tablespoon mild-flavored honey
2½ teaspoons kosher salt
2 cups mixed light and dark moist raisins (optional)
2 packages active dry yeast
½ cup lukewarm water

4 extra-large eggs, at room temperature
Up to 6 cups bread flour
Medium-ground cornmeal, for sprinkling
Sesame seeds, poppy seeds, caraway seeds, and/or
    kosher or sea salt for sprinkling (optional)
Glaze: 1 egg beaten with 1 egg yolk and 1 tablespoon
    water

USE SOME OF THE MELTED BUTTER to grease the interior of an 8-quart mixing bowl. Set that bowl aside. Warm the milk in a 1-quart, heavy-bottomed saucepan over medium-low heat. Pour the milk into a large mixing bowl and add 8 tablespoons of melted butter (stir it before measuring to incorporate the milk solids). Stir in ⅓ cup sugar along with the honey, salt, and the raisins, if using. Let the milk cool to lukewarm. Dissolve the yeast in ½ cup of warm water with a pinch of sugar and allow it to become bubbly, about 3 minutes. Add the dissolved yeast to the warm milk mixture, along with the eggs. Stir with a wooden spoon to break up the eggs, then stir in enough flour, cup by cup, to create a somewhat stiff, shaggy mass that's no longer easily stirred.

Using a sturdy rubber spatula, scrape the mass onto a floured surface and knead it until you've created a dough that's smooth and elastic, adding only as much additional flour as needed to keep the dough from sticking. Place the dough into the greased bowl and brush the top with more melted butter. Cover the bowl with greased plastic wrap and a clean kitchen towel. Let the dough rise in a warm, draft-free spot until doubled, 2 to 2½ hours. Uncover the dough and punch it down with several swift swats with the back of your hand. Turn the dough over in the bowl and knead gently to redistribute the yeast. Re-cover the bowl and let the dough rise again until very light and billowy, 1 to 1½ hours.

To SHAPE BRAIDED LOAVES, first line two large, shallow baking sheets with parchment paper and sprinkle the paper with cornmeal. Gather your choice of seeds, if using, and place them next to the bowl of glaze. Turn the fully risen dough out onto your lightly floured work surface and divide the dough in half using your pastry scraper. Cover one half while working with the other. (If not working with a double oven, refrigerate half of the dough in its original bowl, covered.)

Divide one half of dough into six equal pieces and roll each piece into a strand about 10 inches long, with tapered ends and slightly chubby centers. (Use extra flour, only as necessary, to keep dough from sticking.) Position the strands vertically in front of you and pinch the ends farthest from you at the top together, attaching them. See the following page for braiding instructions.

WHEN YOU REACH THE BOTTOM of the braid, pinch the ends together to secure them. Tuck the ends on both sides underneath the braid, plumping it nicely. Place the braid on one of the prepared baking sheets and cover it with a clean kitchen towel. Let the dough rise for 30 minutes, preheating the oven to 375°F., for the last 20 minutes of the rise. (If working with a double oven, repeat this same procedure with the remaining half of dough. If not, wait until the first loaf enters the oven to remove the second half from the refrigerator and shape that braid.)

After a 20-minute rise, uncover the braid and brush the dough all over with the egg glaze. Leave the loaf uncovered for the remaining 10 minutes. Just before baking, give the dough another coat of glaze and, if desired, sprinkle the top decoratively with one or more type of the seeds. Sprinkle the top lightly with salt, if desired, and bake the braid(s) until the loaves are golden, feel light, and sound hollow when lifted and tapped on the bottom, 35 to 45 minutes. As the dough bakes it will expand, exposing new, unglazed dough. To prevent uneven browning, check the braids 20 minutes after they enter the oven and, working quickly, brush any whiter parts of dough with some reserved glaze. Quickly sprinkle those sections with some seeds, if using, and continue to bake until done. Cover the top of the braids loosely with aluminum foil (shiny side up) if the loaves begin to become overly brown before being cooked through, uncovering for the last 2 minutes of baking.

TIMING IS
EVERYTHING
❧ *The dough can be assembled through the first full rise and, after punching down, placed in the refrigerator for up to two days for the plain or raisin bread and one day for the savory version. Unless making a Brie en croûte, make sure to allow the time required to bring the dough to room temperature before shaping, rising, and baking.*

Sandwich Loaf

Brush three 8 × 4-inch loaf pans with melted butter. Turn to the Country White Bread recipe (page 224), and follow the shaping and rising procedure. Before baking, brush the exposed dough with either melted butter or the egg glaze. If using the glaze, you can then apply some poppy, sesame, or caraway seeds. Bake in a preheated 375°F. oven for 25 to 30 minutes. Turn the loaves out of their pans and let them cool on wire racks before slicing.

Savory Challah

When assembling the dough, reduce the sugar to 2 tablespoons, omit the honey, and add ½ cup·thinly sliced chives and ½ cup room-temperature freshly grated Parmigiano-Reggiano cheese for braids or loaves, or 1 cup cheese when making a Brie en croûte. If making a Brie en croute, after the first 2-hour rise, punch the dough down, cover the bowl, and refrigerate it for at least 4 hours and as long as 24 hours before shaping. If using this savory version to be braided or baked in loaf pans, the dough should be at room temperature. Follow the previous topping instructions.

READ THE FOLLOWING PROCEDURE CAREFULLY BEFORE BEGINNING, AND KEEP THIS PAGE OPENED AND WITHIN EASY VIEW THE ENTIRE TIME.

Spread the strands, so they all have some space around them, staying connected on top. Number the position of each strand from 1 to 6, starting at the far left. (No matter how the strands are arranged the numbers stay the same.)

1. Take strand #6 and bring it over to become #1.
2. Strand #2 goes over #6 and becomes #6.
3. Strand #1 goes across and over strand #3 and becomes #3.
4. Strand #5 goes over #1 and becomes #1.
5. Strand #6 crosses over #4 and becomes #4.
6. Repeat steps 2 through 6 until you reach the bottom of the strands.

HERE'S THE SCOOP:
On a Kosher Challah, Plain, Sweet, or Savory

I don't keep kosher, so I make challah the way I feel it tastes the best, which is with butter and milk. However, strict Jewish dietary law prohibits combining, in the same meal, any foods containing dairy products and meat. To make a kosher challah, you need to make a few adjustments (unless, of course, you plan to serve the original version at a meat-free Sunday brunch or a fish dinner!).

For a parve challah (able to be eaten with either meat or dairy), you need to substitute another fat for the butter. Use either ⅓ cup nonhydrogenated coconut butter (see my Source List on page 313) or an equal amount of corn oil, plus extra for brushing, or 1 stick melted nondairy margarine. Instead of cow's milk, substitute either water, plain soy or rice milk, or if making a savory ver-

sion, even the reconstituting liquid from dried porcini mushrooms. Because you'll need to omit the cheese in the savory version, you can punch up the flavor in the bread by using a highly flavored cold-pressed oil like basil oil, instead of the other fats previously mentioned, and add up to ¼ cup minced oil-packed sun-dried tomatoes.

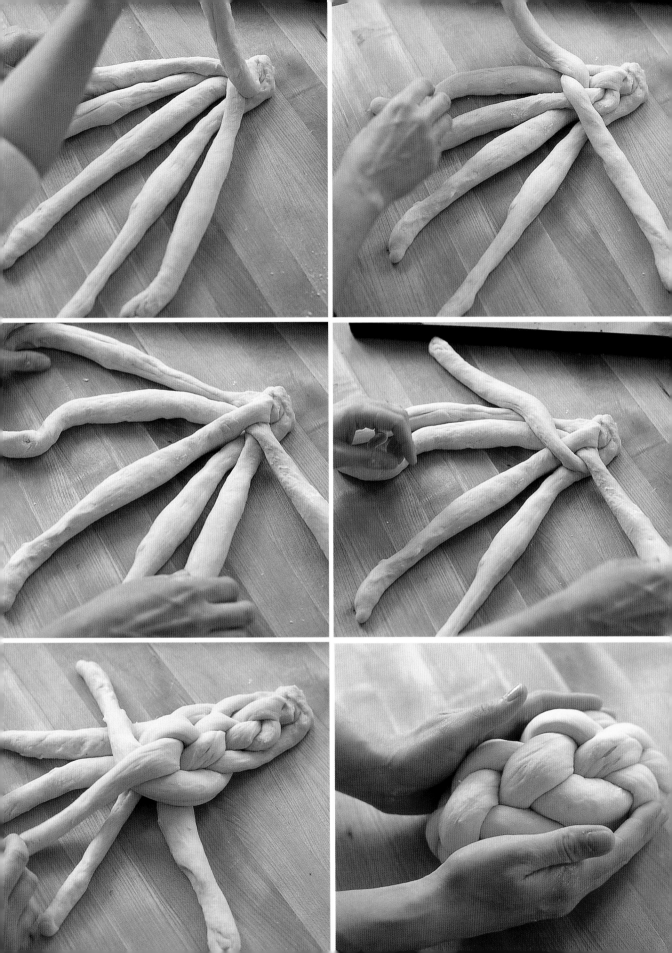

They'll Love Your Buns . . .
FOR HAMBURGERS
& HOT DOGS

You'll get such a kick out of seeing a person's expression when he or she first catches a glimpse of these handsome and truly voluptuous burger and hot dog buns. These round buns can handle a hefty burger with lots of toppings, and the long buns can easily cradle a large, grilled dinner-size hot dog, knockwurst, or generous link of sweet or hot Italian sausage. Regardless of the shape, I love these buns split, with the insides brushed with melted butter that's flavored with sautéed garlic. Just before serving, I broil the seasoned sides until lightly toasted. These buns taste best when enjoyed freshly baked.

❧ YIELD: 10 BURGER BUNS OR 12 DINNER-SIZE HOT DOG BUNS

½ cup (1 stick) unsalted butter, melted
1 cup lukewarm milk
¾ cup warm water
3 tablespoons solid vegetable shortening
2½ teaspoons salt
2 tablespoons sugar, plus a pinch
1 extra-large egg, at room temperature
1 extra-large egg yolk, at room temperature
1 package active dry yeast

Up to 5½ cups unbleached all-purpose flour, sifted
Medium-ground cornmeal
Glaze: 1 egg white beaten with 1 teaspoon water (optional)
Sesame seeds, poppy seeds, caraway seeds, and/or toasted dehydrated onions reconstituted in a little hot water (optional)
Kosher or sea salt to taste (optional)

USE SOME OF THE melted butter to grease the interior of a 5- or 6-quart mixing bowl. Set that bowl aside. Pour the warm milk into a mixing bowl and add ½ cup of the warm water, 3 tablespoons of melted butter, the shortening, salt, 2 tablespoons of sugar, the egg, and the yolk. Mix well. Dissolve the yeast in the remaining ¼ cup warm water with the pinch of sugar and allow it to become visibly active, about 3 minutes. Add the dissolved yeast mixture to the mixing bowl and stir in enough flour, cup by cup, to create a somewhat stiff, shaggy mass that's no longer easily stirred.

Use a rubber spatula to scrape the mass onto a floured surface, and knead it until you've created a dough that's smooth and elastic, adding only as much additional flour as is needed to keep the dough from sticking. Place the dough in the greased bowl and brush the top with more melted butter. Cover the bowl with greased plastic wrap and a clean kitchen towel. Let the dough rise in a warm draft-free spot for 2 hours. Uncover the dough and punch it down with several swift swats with the back of your hand. Turn the dough over in the bowl and knead it gently to redistribute the yeast. Re-cover the bowl and let the dough rise again until light and billowy, about 1 hour.

SERVED WITH CRISPY FRIED SWEETS page 213, AND SWEET AND SOUR RED ONIONS page 209

LINE TWO SHALLOW baking sheets with parchment paper and sprinkle the paper with cornmeal. If using one oven to accommodate both baking sheets at one time, place the racks in the upper- and lower-third shelf positions. If using a double oven, have the racks on the center shelves. Preheat the oven to 375°F. If planning to apply a topping to the buns, make your egg white glaze and strain it into another bowl so it's easier to apply. Place your seeds and/or reconstituted onions in small bowls, if using. After the second rise, uncover the dough and punch it down to deflate it. Turn the dough out onto a lightly floured surface and knead it briefly and gently.

To SHAPE BURGER BUNS, use your pastry scraper to divide the dough into 10 equal pieces and cover them while working with one piece at time. Shape each piece into an irregular round, then pull up the sides, repeatedly, pinching the gathered ends on top to form a small knot. Continue pulling and pinching until the dough is round and taut with a slightly pinched area on top, flouring your fingertips as necessary. Turn the ball of dough on its side and drive the blade of your pastry scraper down through the waist of the round (not through the pinched end), cutting the ball in half. Lay both halves cut side up, gently opening them so they lie flat. Sandwich both cut sides together, then pinch the cut edges together, sealing them shut. Place the squatty round down smoothest side up, and flatten it quite firmly, using your fingers to shove the pinched seam gently under the bun all the way around. When a bit flatter than you think appropriate, lay the bun (smoothest side up) on one of the prepared baking sheets and cover it with a clean kitchen towel while you shape the rest. Let the buns rise for 20 minutes, starting after the last bun has been shaped.

TIMING IS EVERYTHING

❧ The dough can be assembled through the first full rise and, after punching down, placed in the refrigerator for up to two days. Let the dough sit out of refrigeration until it comes to room temperature (which can take 4 hours) before shaping, rising, and baking as directed.

To shape hot dog buns, divide the dough into 12 equal pieces and cover them while working with one piece at a time. For each bun, roll a piece of dough into an 8-inch strand and flatten the strand using either a straight rolling pin or the heel of your hand. Roll both long sides of the dough in toward the center, and when the two sides meet in the middle, pinch them together to seal shut. Working with one end at a time, lift the dough at one short end and fold it over, rounding off that end and attaching that portion of dough to the seam, going about 2 inches down the length of the seam. Do this on the opposite end and pinch the dough, as needed, to correct the shape. When done, the seam should be straight and the bun about 7 inches long. Place the baking sheet horizontally in front of you. Invert the bun onto the prepared baking sheet, seam side down, close to one end of the sheet. Repeat the shaping procedure with the remaining dough, placing them in a vertical line, only ½ inch apart. (They should merge in the oven.) Tear off two large sheets of aluminum foil and scrunch each one into the shape of the buns. Spray them with vegetable spray and tuck these foil buns at either end of the lineup of buns, giving these last buns boundaries. If not applying a topping, cover the buns with a clean kitchen towel and let them rise for 20 minutes, starting after the last bun has been shaped.

If topping hamburger or hot dog buns, as soon as you've finished shaping them, brush the tops of the unrisen buns with the egg white glaze and sprinkle the tops with seeds or the reconstituted dried onions. Cover the buns with a clean kitchen towel and let them rise for 20 minutes. If the remaining melted butter has congealed, rewarm it just until liquefied.

Uncover the risen buns and brush the tops with melted butter (brush gently over the topping). Regardless of their shape, bake the buns in the preheated 375°F. oven until they are golden and feel light, 25 to 30 minutes. If baking in the upper and lower shelves of the oven, switch the position of the baking sheets after half the baking time. Also, check the burger buns after half the baking and, if becoming too pointy in the center, use a flat metal turning spatula to gently push this raised section down a bit, taking care not to split the sides of the bun. When done, remove the buns from the oven and brush them once more with melted butter. Transfer the buns to wire racks so they can cool until just warm. Just before serving, separate the hot dog buns by pulling them off of each other. Serve the hot dogs and burgers with your favorite mustard and relish, a bowl of spicy ketchup (see page 92), and Sweet and Sour Red Onions (page 213), all passed at the table.

That's Some Loaf!
PANE DI CASA

This magnificent sourdough bread was born several years ago, after an inspiring trip to Europe. Instead of shopping, I spent my days traipsing through many different kitchens throughout the regions of Italy and France. A common thread that seemed so meaningful to the French and Italian family table was a big round of crusty bread. So, when I came home (literally, before I even took off my jacket), I headed straight for the kitchen and concocted a yeasty starter, which I let ferment for several days before using it in my bread dough. Since yeast flourishes in a mixture that includes liquid barley malt, that's the preferred sweetener to use in the starter. It's available in some health food stores, or you can order it from the Baker's Catalogue, listed on page 313. If you're really anxious to get started, however, just use a mild-flavored honey. ❧ YIELD: 1 LARGE LOAF

FOR THE STARTER

2 cups filtered or bottled spring water, warmed (not hot)
1 generous teaspoon liquid barley malt or mild-flavored honey
1 package active dry yeast
4 cups unbleached all-purpose flour

FOR COMPLETING THE DOUGH

About 7 tablespoons melted Clarified Butter (page 195) or Garlic Confit Oil (page 23)
Freshly ground black pepper to taste (optional)
½ cup nonfat dry milk
1 tablespoon plus 1 teaspoon salt
2 teaspoons sugar, plus a pinch
1 package active dry yeast
2 cups warm water
1 cup sifted whole wheat flour (optional)
Up to 6½ cups sifted unbleached all-purpose flour
Medium-ground cornmeal
Kosher or sea salt for sprinkling (optional)

MAKE THE STARTER. Combine the water, barley malt or honey, and yeast in a 4-quart mixing bowl. When the yeast is dissolved and appears bubbly, stir in 2 cups of the flour. When combined, briskly stir in another cup of flour and, when smooth, add the remaining 1 cup of flour, ½ cup at a time, stirring briskly after each addition. Alternatively, this can be done in an electric mixer fitted with the paddle attachment. Cover the bowl very securely and place it in a warm, draft-free spot for four days. Uncover the bowl and stir the fermented starter and, if not planning to make bread right away, cover the bowl well and store it in the refrigerator. Let the mixture come to room temperature before using. (See page 234 to learn more on how to keep your starter healthy.)

Once the starter is ready, pour the butter or oil into a small bowl, and use some of it to lightly grease the interior of a 6-quart mixing bowl. If desired, sprinkle with black pepper. Set that bowl aside. Place the dry milk in another mixing bowl with the salt and 2 teaspoons sugar. In a small bowl, dissolve the yeast in ½ cup warm water with the pinch of sugar and allow it to become visibly bubbly, about 3 minutes. Add the dissolved yeast to the mixing bowl along with the remaining 1½ cups of warm water and 4 tablespoons of the butter or oil. Stir in 1 cup fermented starter along with the whole wheat flour, if using, and 2 cups sifted all-purpose flour (or if not using whole wheat flour, add 3 cups white flour). When mixed, stir in more white flour, 1 cup at a time, until the dough leaves the sides of the bowl and is no longer easy to stir.

Use a sturdy rubber spatula to scrape the mass out onto a floured surface, and knead it until you've created a dough that's smooth and elastic, adding only as much additional flour as needed to keep the dough from sticking. Place the dough in the greased bowl and brush the top of the dough lightly with more clarified butter or oil. Cover the bowl with greased plastic wrap and a clean kitchen towel. Let the dough rise in a warm, draft-free spot for 2 hours. Uncover the dough and deflate it using several swift swats with the back of your hand. Turn the dough over in the bowl and knead it gently just to redistribute the yeast. Re-cover the bowl and let the dough rise until very light and billowy, about 2 hours.

To shape the dough into a round or oblong loaf, first rub a generous amount of flour on the interior of a large round or oblong coiled wooden bowl or cloth-lined bread basket. If you don't have this, place a well-floured pastry cloth (or a square of linen) in a low, wide, 2½-quart bowl. Uncover the fully risen dough and turn it out onto a lightly floured work surface. To make a taut round loaf (called a *boule* in French), pull the sides of the dough up and pinch these gathered ends on top. Repeat this over and over again until the dough is round, taut, and smooth on all sides except the top, which will have a slightly pinched appearance. To shape an oblong loaf, after turning the dough out, pat it gently to create a rectangular shape. Fold the long sides in toward each other, pinching in the center to create one central seam. Keep pulling up the sides until the oblong shape is apparent and even. Pinch the ends, elongating them slightly, and attach these ends neatly to the seam on both sides.

HERE'S THE SCOOP:
To Care for Your Sourdough Starter

To keep a fermented starter healthy, you'll need to nourish it. The best way to do this is to use it often, since each time you remove some, you'll feed it with more flour and water. Once refrigerated, if not used in seven days, bring it to room temperature and stir the mixture well. Re-move 1 generous cup and discard it. Briskly stir in 1 generous cup each unbleached all-purpose flour and room-temperature filtered or bottled spring water. When smooth, wipe down the sides of the container and cover it well with plastic wrap and then a tight-fitting lid. (I use a 4-quart plastic bucket with a lid.) Either leave the starter out or refrigerate it, keeping in mind that you'll need to feed a room-temperature starter every day and a refrigerated one every seven days. Always bring it to room temperature before using it.

Place the shaped dough in the prepared basket or bowl, smooth side down (pinched or seam side up), and cover the loaf with a clean kitchen towel. Let it rise until very billowy, 45 minutes to 1 hour.

Immediately after shaping, get ready to bake. Position the rack in the lower third of the oven and preheat to 450°F. for at least 30 minutes. If using a sheet of quarry tiles or a large pizza stone, place it on the rack and sprinkle a baker's peel or a flat cookie sheet with cornmeal. If not using tiles or a stone, brush or spray a large shallow baking sheet with vegetable oil and then sprinkle with cornmeal. Regardless, just before the end of the rise, place four ice cubes in a 1-cup measuring cup and add enough cold water to reach the ¼-cup mark. Place this next to the oven (or see page 223).

Uncover the risen loaf and carefully turn it out, smooth side up, onto the prepared peel or oiled baking sheet. Use your hands to gently plump the shape, if necessary, being careful not to deflate it. If making a round or an oblong loaf, use a very sharp knife to make several ⅓-inch-deep decorative slashes in the top surface. Sprinkle the top with kosher salt, if desired. If baking with tiles, insert the peel all the way to the back of the oven and, with several swift jerks, pull out the peel, leaving the dough on the hot tiles. Immediately toss the ice water onto the oven floor (underneath the tiles) and shut the door. If not using tiles, place the baking sheet directly onto the hot oven rack and toss the ice water underneath it.

Bake the loaf for 30 minutes at 450°F., then reduce the temperature to 375°F. and bake for 10 minutes. Turn off the oven and let the loaf sit there, with the door shut, until it's crisp, golden, and sounds hollow when tapped on the bottom, about 10 minutes. Transfer the bread to a wire rack to cool.

TIMING IS
EVERYTHING

☙ *Allow the starter to ferment for four days at room temperature before using for the first time.*

☙ *The dough can be assembled through the first full rise and, after punching down, placed in the refrigerator for up to two days. Let the dough sit out of refrigeration until it comes to room temperature (which can take 4 hours) before shaping, rising, and baking as directed.*

On Storing Fresh-Baked Artisan Breads

Regardless of shape, to keep the crust of fresh-baked artisan breads crisp, leave them fully exposed on a wire rack when cooling. When completely cooled, however, you can place them in paper (not plastic) bags. Once you've sliced into a large loaf, like the Pane di Casa (page 233), cover the sliced end with aluminum foil and store, cut end down, on a cutting board draped somewhat loosely with more foil. For the next couple of days, uncover and slice as desired. Keep day-old baguettes wrapped in aluminum foil at room temperature. Store rolls to be served the day after baking in a roasting pan covered with aluminum foil, at room temperature.

Refresh day-old bread by baking it on a wire rack set within a shallow baking sheet in a preheated 400°F. oven for 5 minutes. Turn off the oven and let the bread remain there until the crust becomes crisp and the interior is just warmed throughout, about 5 minutes more. Rolls freeze well in doubled heavy-duty freezer bags for up to two weeks. To thaw, remove the bag from the freezer several hours before serving and leave the rolls, in their original wrapping, at room temperature. To re-crisp, follow the instructions given for day-old bread.

FOUGASSE WITH GARLIC CONFIT,
Olives, and Fresh Herbs

This rather large sheet bread has a fun yet rustic appearance and an incredibly earthy taste and aroma from an abundance of garlic-infused olive oil, fresh herbs, and olives. This particular dough is purposely both very light and highly glutinous, which is why I ask an electric mixer to help me build texture using a minimum amount of flour. ❧ YIELD: 1 LARGE (17 × 13-INCH) SHEET BREAD

2 tablespoons minced fresh thyme leaves

2 teaspoons minced fresh rosemary

About ⅔ cup Garlic Confit Oil (page 23) or more, at room temperature

1 package active dry yeast

2 cups warm water

2 teaspoons plus a pinch of sugar

1 tablespoon salt

½ cup nonfat dry milk

1 cup Pane di Casa starter (page 233), fully fermented and at room temperature

3 cups unbleached all-purpose flour

2 cups bread flour, plus more for dusting

Pure olive oil for the baking sheet

Medium-ground cornmeal and sesame seeds for sprinkling (sesame seeds are optional)

About 12 or more garlic cloves from Garlic Confit (page 23), peeled

6 to 10 oil-cured olives, pitted and neatly halved (see page 184)

Kosher or sea salt and freshly ground black pepper to taste

ADD HALF THE MINCED HERBS to the garlic oil and set it aside. Reserve the remaining herbs for later. Dissolve the yeast in ½ cup of the warm water with the pinch of sugar and allow it to become visibly bubbly, about 3 minutes. Using a wooden spoon in the bowl of your electric mixer, combine the dissolved yeast with the salt, 2 teaspoons sugar, dry milk, remaining 1½ cups of warm water, 4 tablespoons of the Garlic Confit Oil, and the fermented starter. Stir in the all-purpose flour and attach the bowl to the mixer fitted with the paddle attachment. Turn the machine on to moderate speed and beat the mixture for 2 minutes. Stop the machine and add 1 cup of bread flour and beat again on medium speed for 1½ minutes. (Always begin beating on low to prevent the flour from flying!) Stop the machine and add another cup of bread flour and beat again for 1½ minutes. Remove the paddle and, using a large, sturdy rubber spatula, scrape any clinging dough off the paddle, adding it back to the bowl. Scrape the mixture up from the bottom of the bowl and switch to the dough hook. Turn the machine to medium or to the setting for kneading dough and let the hook do its work for 2 minutes. Turn off the machine and scrape up from the bottom, once more. Reinsert the hook and let it run for another 2 minutes. (The mixture will not leave the sides of the bowl.)

Remove the bowl from the machine and use the spatula to release any clinging dough from the hook. Scrape the slack but glutinous dough directly

TIMING IS
EVERYTHING
🍂 *The dough can be
assembled and, after the
first punch-down, placed
back in the bowl and
refrigerated for 24 hours
before shaping and bak-
ing. Be aware that this
dough, when very chilled,
can take up to 4 hours
to come to room
temperature.*
🍂 *Reheat the fougasse on
a wire rack set within a
baking sheet in a pre-
heated 400°F. oven for
5 minutes. Turn the oven
off and let the bread sit
there for another 5 min-
utes or until perfectly
crisp and warmed
through.*

into a dry, straight-sided, 6-quart mixing bowl and cover the bowl with greased plastic wrap and a clean kitchen towel. Let the dough rise in a warm, draft-free spot for 2 hours. Lightly flour your work surface and uncover the risen dough. Use your floured fingers to pull the spongy dough away from the sides of the bowl, deflating it. (Repeatedly dust your hand with flour to help keep the dough from sticking.) Turn the dough out onto a floured board and sprinkle the top lightly with flour, patting it on the surface. Using a pastry scraper, fold the dough into fours, pressing lightly with floured hands. Place the dough back in the original bowl and cover it. Let it rise again until very light and billowy, about 2 hours.

Brush the bottom and sides of a large shallow (17 × 13-inch) baking sheet evenly with olive oil and sprinkle with cornmeal. Sprinkle with sesame seeds, if using. Using a floured hand, release the risen dough from the side of the bowl and turn it out, directly into the prepared pan. Pull and stretch the dough into a rectangle that fills the pan three-fourths full (expect this dough to be very sticky, so keep your fingers floured). Use a pastry brush to baste the exposed dough with herbed oil and let the dough rise, uncovered, for 30 minutes. Immediately after setting the dough to rise, position the rack in the lower third of the oven and preheat the oven to 450°F. for at least 30 minutes. If using a sheet of quarry tiles or a large pizza stone, place it on the rack (see page 223).

When ready to bake, place four ice cubes in a 1-cup measuring cup and add enough cold water to reach the ¼-cup mark. Place this next to the oven. Take a sharp knife and make several decorative diagonal cuts in the fougasse dough, making sure the blade reaches the baking sheet. (Because the dough is sticky, cut through each incision several times.) Use your lightly floured fingers to widen the slits substantially (a bit wider than you think necessary), thus push-ing the dough so it covers all of the pan. Let the dough rise for 15 more min-utes, uncovered. Drive your lightly floured fingertips into the puffy dough around the widened slashes, creating a generous number of random dimples. Carefully widen the slashes again so they remain very visible. Insert the peeled Garlic Confit into some of the dimples, alternating with halved black olives, pitted side down. Baste the top of the dough with more garlic oil and strew the remaining herbs, salt, and black pepper over the oil.

Place the baking sheet directly onto the hot tiles (or oven rack) and toss the ice water underneath. Bake until deeply golden, crisp, and sizzling, 25 to 28 minutes. Remove the pan from the oven and immediately baste the exposed crust with more garlic oil. Use the dull side of a knife to release the bread from the sides of the pan, and carefully lift one end up to slide it onto a large wire rack. Let the bread cool until just warm.

To serve, either present the fougasse whole or cut into irregular pieces, heaped into a linen-lined basket. Either way, cut with a serrated knife.

GREAT PIZZA . . .
Any Way You Slice It!

I've been making pizzas for a long time, for occasions that range from my kids' birthday parties to Super Bowl Sundays to fun and informal family dinners. Over the years, I've noticed that certain annoying issues would always pop up. Because I like to pile on lots of toppings, it was often difficult to get the assembled pie to slide off my baker's peel when transferring it to the hot tiles. So, because I didn't want to part with my toppings, I decided to do some snooping at a local pizza shop. I learned there, that commercial pizza makers chill their freshly assembled dough, shaped in wide, domed portions. Then, for an hour or more, before using it to make pizza, the dough sits out, uncovered, at room temperature. The cold, ultra-glutinous dough loosens, making it easier to work with and the dough develops a non-stick skin on the top. This is why their pies don't stick! Now I can top my pizzas as lavishly as I like (and so can you), without the fear of getting stuck at the oven. ☙ YIELD: TWO 15-INCH PIZZAS

FOR THE PIZZA DOUGH

About 4 tablespoons Garlic Confit Oil (page 23) or
    extra-virgin olive oil, or more, as needed
Freshly ground black pepper to taste (optional)
1 package active dry yeast
½ cup lukewarm water for the yeast, plus 2 cups
    warm water for the dough
A pinch of sugar for the yeast, plus 2 teaspoons sugar
    for the dough
1 tablespoon salt
½ cup medium ground yellow cornmeal, for the
    dough (optional), plus more, for the baker's peel
Up to 8 cups unbleached all-purpose flour, including
    flour for dusting and shaping

FOR THE TOPPINGS

About 6 cups freshly grated cheese (preferably a
    combination of fresh low-moisture mozzarella,
    Muenster and Parmigiano-Reggiano cheese)
1½ to 2 cups Ultra Speedy Marinara Sauce (page 33)
Freshly ground black pepper to taste
About ½ cup chopped or slivered fresh basil leaves
    (optional)

To MAKE THE DOUGH, brush the interior of a 5-quart mixing bowl generously with some of the garlic oil and sprinkle with freshly ground black pepper, if desired. Dissolve the yeast in ½ cup of warm water with a pinch of sugar and allow it to become visibly bubbly, about 3 minutes. In a mixing bowl, combine 2 cups warm water, 2 tablespoons of the garlic oil, 1 tablespoon salt, 2 teaspoons sugar, and a few more grinds of black pepper, if desired. Add the dissolved yeast along with ½ cup of cornmeal, if using. Gradually stir in only enough flour, 1 cup at a time, to create a shaggy mass, that's no longer easily stirred.

Use a sturdy rubber spatula to scrape the mass out onto a floured surface and knead it until you've created a dough that's smooth and elastic, adding only as much additional flour as needed to keep the dough from sticking. Place the dough into the greased bowl and turn it over to coat the exterior with the oil. Cover the bowl with greased plastic wrap and a clean kitchen towel and set it aside in a warm, draft-free spot to rise for 2 hours.

Meanwhile, line a large shallow tray or baking sheet with parchment paper and sprinkle the paper lightly with flour. Uncover the dough and deflate it, using several swift swats with the back of your hand. Turn the dough out onto a lightly floured work surface and, using your pastry scraper, divide the dough in half. Use your hands to plump each half of dough and place them, plumped sides up, on the prepared tray. Cover the dough with a clean kitchen towel, then place two large, overlapping and loosely fitting sheets of plastic wrap on top. Refrigerate the dough for 4 to 24 hours, which encourages the gluten to become extra sleepy, making it easier to stretch.

Thirty minutes to 1 hour before you plan to make pizza, remove the dough from the refrigerator and let it sit, uncovered, at room temperature. Position the oven rack in the lower third of the oven and, if using, place a sheet of quarry tiles or a large pizza stone onto the rack. Preheat the oven to 500°F. for at least 30 minutes, before baking. Sprinkle a large baker's peel or a flat cookie sheet generously with cornmeal and spread it out, evenly. (Alternatively, if not using tiles or a stone, brush the interior of two 15-inch perforated pizza pans with olive oil and sprinkle the greased surface with cornmeal. Tilt to coat the pans with meal, then tap out the excess.)

To shape 2 pizzas, first spread about 2 cups of flour on a tray and season it with salt and pepper, to taste. Place this next to your work surface. Remove any protruding rings on your fingers. Uncover the dough and invert each piece of dough, skin side down, in the flour. Leave one piece of dough in the flour, covered and place the other one, floured side down, on your work surface. Flour your working hand and, with spread out fingers, smack the dough, several times, until it's visibly flattened but still round. Lift the dough and drape it (centered) over both floured fists. Stretch dough by pointing your fists upward and gently pulling them away from each other. Try to stretch the dough evenly and, when it becomes thin and feels bottom heavy, lay it on the prepared peel or pizza pan. Use floured fingertips to reposition the dough, stretching it until it completely covers a 15- or 16-inch peel or pizza pan, with 1-inch thick rims. (If the dough resists when stretching, throw a towel over it for 5 minutes and walk away. And, if it should tear, just use your floured fingertips to pinch that spot together.)

If you have a double oven (and you have two peels or pans), stretch the second half of dough, as just described, now. If you can bake only 1 pizza at a time, leave the second half of dough on the original tray, at room temperature, until the first pizza is half baked. Shape the remaining pizza then.

To top the dough, have the sauce, grated cheese and any other toppings, placed to one side of your work surface, in separate bowls. Scatter some of the grated cheese over the dough, excluding the 1-inch border. Spoon or ladle about 1 cup marinara sauce on top of the cheese (not too much or your pizza will be soupy). Spread the sauce over the dough, stopping just before the rim. Scatter more of the grated cheese over the top, then drizzle 1 generous teaspoon of garlic oil over the top. Grind on some black pepper. (If using any of the suggested embellishments in the sidebar on page 243, scatter them over the sauce, before adding the last application of cheese. Allow some of the toppings to be

TIMING IS EVERYTHING:

After the dough completes the first rise at room temperature, you can punch the dough down and place it back in the original bowl and refrigerate it for up to two days before shaping. Keep the bowl well covered. One hour before assembling the pizzas, remove the dough from the refrigerator and follow the remaining instructions.

The sauce can be made well in advance and frozen in small heavy-duty freezer containers or up to three days ahead and stored in the refrigerator.

The mozzarella and Muenster cheeses can be grated, two days ahead and the Parmesan one day ahead. Keep grated cheese refrigerated, in sealed heavy-duty plastic bags.

visible, through the cheese. If using pepperoni, this should be placed on top of the cheese, to be fully exposed to heat.)

To bake, place 4 ice cubes into a 1-cup measuring cup and add enough cold water to reach the ¼ cup mark. Place this next to the oven. Lift the loaded peel and carry it to the oven. Open the oven door, insert the peel all the way back and, with several short swift jerks, remove the peel, leaving the pizza on the hot tiles. Immediately, toss the ice water onto the oven floor, underneath the tiles, and shut the door. Bake until the crust is deeply golden, the toppings are piping hot and the cheese is bubbling, 18 to 20 minutes, depending on the depth of your toppings. (If working with a double oven, repeat this with the remaining pizza.)

When done, slide the peel underneath the pizza and place it on a nonperforated pizza pan. If desired, scatter some fresh basil over the top and, using a pizza wheel, slice the pie into wedges and serve immediately. (If making a second pizza in the same oven, be sure to sweep off any fallen meal from the tiles, before inserting another pizza.)

HERE'S THE SCOOP:
To Go Beyond the Basics

Some topping embellishments (choose one or more of the following): After applying your sauce, scatter on some whole cooked and peeled cloves of Garlic Confit (page 23), sautéed sliced mushrooms, chopped raw garlic, thinly sliced and sautéed yellow onions or leeks, small cubes of floured and pan-fried eggplant, diced parboiled and pan-fried potatoes, pitted and sliced kalamata olives or milder oil-cured olives (see page 184), red and/or yellow peppers, roasted, peeled, seeded and thinly sliced (page 24), thinly sliced pancetta that's fried until crisp and coarsely chopped, diced smoked Black Forest bacon, fried until crisp, sweet and/or hot Italian sausage, removed from its casings and browned in olive oil, crushed red pepper flakes. Now, scatter on the cheese and bake. To add sliced pepperoni, place it, randomly, on top of the cheese.

CRUSTY ONION FICELLES

These long, crusty, and absolutely gorgeous baguettes are stuffed with a double dose of savory flavor from sautéed fresh onions and toasted dehydrated onions. To add a further taste dimension, there's also a heap of minced fresh chives in the dough! So this bread comes out of the oven completely permeated with onion flavor. If you can't find toasted dehydrated onions, then pan-toast the regular kind in a dry skillet, stirring constantly over medium heat until light golden.

🍂 YIELD: 4 THIN BAGUETTES

About 4 tablespoons melted Clarified Butter (page 195) or Garlic Confit Oil (page 23)
1 package active dry yeast
2 cups warm water
2 teaspoons plus a pinch of sugar
½ cup nonfat dry milk
1 tablespoon salt
A few grinds of black pepper (optional)
¾ rounded cup minced chives
Up to 6 cups unbleached all-purpose flour, sifted

3 generous tablespoons Garlic Confit Oil (page 23) or extra-virgin olive oil
2 extra-large yellow onions, sliced into very thin wedges
⅓ cup toasted dehydrated onions, crushed coarsely using a rolling pin
Kosher or sea salt for sprinkling
Up to 1 cup medium-rye flour or more all-purpose flour
Medium-ground cornmeal for sprinkling

LIGHTLY GREASE THE INTERIOR of a 6-quart mixing bowl with some clarified butter or garlic oil and set that bowl aside. Dissolve the yeast in ½ cup of the warm water with the pinch of sugar and allow it to become visibly bubbly, about 3 minutes. Meanwhile, pour the remaining 1½ cups of warm water into a large mixing bowl and add the dry milk, 2 tablespoons melted clarified butter or garlic oil, the remaining 2 teaspoons of sugar, the salt, pepper (if using), and ½ cup of the chives. Add the dissolved yeast and, using a wooden spoon, gradually stir in only enough all-purpose flour, 1 cup at a time, to create a shaggy mass that's no longer easily stirred in the bowl.

Use a sturdy rubber spatula to scrape the mass onto a floured surface and knead it until smooth and elastic, adding only as much additional flour as needed to keep the dough from sticking. Place the dough in the greased bowl and brush the top with more melted clarified butter or garlic oil. Cover the bowl with greased plastic wrap and a clean kitchen towel. Let the dough rise in a warm, draft-free spot for 2 hours. Uncover the bowl and, because this dough will be quite spongy, use your fingertips to help release it from the sides of the bowl. Turn the dough over in the bowl, and knead it gently just to redistribute the yeast. Re-cover the bowl and let the dough rise again until very light and billowy, about 2 hours.

Meanwhile, heat a 12- to 14-inch heavy-bottomed, deep-sided skillet over high heat and, when hot, add 3 tablespoons of Garlic Confit Oil. When the oil is hot, stir in the onions and cook them, stirring frequently, until softened, reduced, and light golden, 10 to 15 minutes. Stir in the dehydrated onions along with some salt and black pepper to taste. Add the remaining ¼ cup chives and transfer the sautéed onion mixture into a bowl so it can cool.

Lay two dry, smooth kitchen towels side by side on your counter and dust them heavily with either medium rye or white flour. Alternatively, you can rise the ficelles in a special baguette pan. If so, grease or spray the interior with vegetable spray and dust with cornmeal, knocking out the excess. (If you have one oven and are not using a four-baguette pan, you'll need to bake the ficelles in two separate batches.)

PLACE THE BOWL OF COOLED ONION filling next to your work surface. Turn the fully risen dough out onto a lightly floured surface and knead it very lightly and briefly just to deflate it. Using a pastry scraper, divide the dough into four equal pieces and cover all the pieces, while working with one at a time. Place one piece of dough in front of you and rotate it under the palms of your hands so it resembles a sausage, elongating it slightly. Flatten the dough widthwise using a rolling pin, then use your fingers to spread one-fourth of the onion filling on top, going down the length of the dough and leaving a ½-inch space at each end. Pull up both long sides of the dough and pinch them together at the top of the filling, enclosing it completely. Keep pulling up the sides and pinching it on top, going up and down the length of the baguette, creating one long, tight central seam and lengthening the baguette shape. Pinch the ends together, sealing them. Pinch these ends to the seam.

Carefully transfer two ficelles to each floured towel, seam side up, or to the prepared baguette pan, seam side down. Cover the ficelles with a clean towel and continue shaping the rest. Let them rise for 45 minutes. (When transferring the baguettes, try not to let them stretch and become too long for your oven!) If baking in two batches, transfer two of the ficelles on one of the floured towels to a tray, cover with another towel, and refrigerate until the first batch comes out of the oven.

POSITION THE RACK in the lower third of the oven and preheat to 450°F. for at least

30 minutes. If using a sheet of quarry tiles or a large pizza stone, place it on the rack. If not using tiles, a stone, or a baguette pan, brush two large shallow baking sheets with vegetable oil and sprinkle the interior with cornmeal. If using tiles or a stone, sprinkle a baker's peel (or a flat cookie sheet) with cornmeal. Just before the end of the rise, place four ice cubes in a 1-cup measuring cup and add enough cold water to reach the 1/4-cup mark. Place this next to the oven. Do this twice, if using a double oven (or see page 223).

Uncover the ficelles and carefully invert two of them, smooth side up, onto the prepared peel (or flat cookie sheet) or baking sheet with several inches in between them. Simply uncover the ficelles if in a baguette pan. Use a very sharp knife to slash the top of each ficelle three or four times on the diagonal, going down the length of the dough. Then, if desired, sprinkle the tops with some salt. If baking with tiles, insert the peel all the way to the back of the oven and, with several swift jerks, pull out the peel, leaving the ficelles on the hot tiles (preferably not touching). Immediately toss the ice water onto the oven floor (underneath the tiles) and shut the oven door. If not using tiles, place the baking sheet directly on the hot oven rack and toss the ice water underneath it. Do the same with the baguette pan, with or without tiles.

BAKE THE FICELLES for 15 minutes at 450°F., then reduce the temperature to 425°F. and bake for 5 minutes. Reduce the temperature to 400°F. and bake for 5 minutes. Turn off the oven and let the ficelles sit there (with the door shut) until they are crisp, uniformly golden, and sound hollow when tapped on the bottom, 5 to 10 minutes. Transfer the ficelles to wire racks to cool. If they've stuck together in the oven, just pull them apart.

If baking a second batch, take them out of the refrigerator when the first batch leaves the oven. Use an oven sweep to clean off the tiles, then preheat the oven to 450°F. for a full 30 minutes. Slash and bake the remaining loaves as previously described.

Plain Baguettes (4 skinny baguettes)

Keep the dough the same, even including the chives, if desired. Omit the onion filling and divide the fully risen dough into four pieces. Shape each one into a log, but don't flatten it. Pull the sides of dough up tautly as previously described, pinching at the top and creating a tight seam down the length of the loaf. The rising, slashing, and baking process is the same as for the onion ficelles.

ONION BIALYS

If you love bialys and you've never had one that's homemade, I hope you'll try this recipe. Topped with onions and baked until crisp, these bialys are so superior to the store-bought kind that you might just end up telling your morning bagel to "step aside." If planning to eat these bialys right after they cool, there's no need to toast them—just slice off the rimmed top and fill them lavishly with your favorite spread. However, if you've stored bialys overnight, it's traditional to split them and toast both pieces. In this case, don't overbake initially, since after splitting, the thinner top can become overly brittle when toasted. Or just broil the pieces, cut sides up, for the perfect crunch. ❧ YIELD: 12 BIALYS

FOR THE DOUGH

2 rounded tablespoons solid vegetable shortening, melted
⅓ cup minced yellow onion
1 package active dry yeast
2¼ cups warm water
Pinch of sugar
1 teaspoon freshly ground black pepper (optional)
2 teaspoons barley malt extract or sugar
Up to 6 cups bread flour
2 to 4 tablespoons unsalted butter, melted
1 tablespoon salt

Medium-ground cornmeal for dusting

FOR THE ONION TOPPING

2 tablespoons flavorless vegetable oil
1 cup minced yellow onion
2 teaspoons poppy seeds
⅓ cup dehydrated onions, pan-toasted and reconstituted in a little hot water
Kosher or sea salt and freshly ground black pepper

MAKE THE DOUGH. Melt the shortening in an 8- to 10-inch heavy-bottomed skillet over medium heat and, when hot, add the minced onion. Sauté the onion until softened, about 3 minutes. Drag the skillet to a cool burner. Dissolve the yeast in ¼ cup warm water with the pinch of sugar and allow it to become visibly bubbly, about 3 minutes. In the bowl of your electric mixer fitted with the paddle attachment, combine the remaining 2 cups warm water, the sautéed onion (scrape in any surrounding shortening), the black pepper (if using), the barley malt or sugar, and the dissolved yeast. Add 3 cups of bread flour and, with the mixer on low, combine the mixture well. Turn the speed up to moderate, and beat for 3 minutes. Stop the machine and scrape down the sides of the bowl. (Alternatively, if you don't have a mixer, use a wooden spoon to beat vigorously in one direction, with the bowl of the spoon never leaving the bottom of the mixing bowl.) Cover the bowl with plastic wrap and a clean kitchen towel, and allow the sponge to rise for 1¼ hours.

Brush a 6-quart mixing bowl with some melted butter and set the bowl aside. Uncover the risen starter and attach the bowl to your electric mixer fitted with a clean paddle attachment. Beat in the salt and 2 more cups bread flour at low speed. When well combined, raise the speed to medium and continue to beat for 3 minutes. Use a sturdy rubber spatula to release the shaggy mass from the paddle, then turn it out of the bowl onto a lightly floured wooden surface. Knead the already glutinous dough briefly, until smooth and very elastic. Place the dough in the greased bowl and brush the surface with more melted butter. Cover the bowl with greased plastic wrap and a clean kitchen towel. Let the dough rise in a warm, draft-free spot for 1 to 2 hours.

MEANWHILE, PREPARE THE TOPPING. Heat the vegetable oil in a 10-inch skillet over medium heat and, when hot, stir in the minced onion with the poppy seeds and sauté the mixture until the onion is softened, 3 to 5 minutes. Stir in the reconstituted toasted onions along with salt and black pepper to taste. Allow the topping to cool.

Position the rack in the lower third of the oven and preheat to 500°F. for at least 30 minutes (or see page 223). If using a sheet of quarry tiles or a large pizza stone, place it on the rack and sprinkle a baker's peel or flat cookie sheet with cornmeal. If not using tiles or a stone, brush or spray two large, shallow baking sheets with vegetable oil and sprinkle with cornmeal. Lay two clean, smooth kitchen towels next to your work surface and sprinkle them with a mixture of cornmeal and flour.

WHEN THE DOUGH HAS FULLY RISEN, turn it out onto a lightly floured surface and knead it gently and briefly. If you have a double oven, use the blade of your pastry scraper to divide the dough into 12 equal pieces. If you don't have a double oven, divide the dough in half and put one piece back in the bowl, cover, and refrigerate it, cutting the remaining half of dough into six equal pieces. Keep the dough covered while working with one piece at a time. Shape each piece of dough into a flat round using either a rolling pin or your hand. Turn the outer rim of the round in, toward the center, to form a 1-inch raised border all around. Using your fingertips, pinch to seal the inside of the folded rim to the bottom of the round. Using the tines of a fork, prick holes in the center. As each bialy is shaped, transfer it (raised sides up) onto the prepared towels and cover with a kitchen towel as you continue to shape the rest.

When all the bialys are shaped, place four ice cubes in a 1-cup measuring cup and add enough cold water to reach the ¼-cup mark. Place this next to the oven. (Do this twice, if using a double oven.) Starting with the first bialy shaped, prick the center again, and use your hand to slightly flatten the rim of

*❧ The dough can be
assembled through the
first full rise and, after
punching down, placed in
the refrigerator for up to
two days. Let the dough
sit out of refrigeration
until it comes close to
room temperature (which
can take 3 hours) before
shaping and baking as
directed.*

*❧ To bake the bialys in
the morning, make the
dough (and the topping)
the night before and shape
the bialys as directed,
placing them on baking
sheets lined with kitchen
towels dusted with corn-
meal. Cover the bialys
with plastic wrap that's
been sprayed with veg-
etable spray and then
with a kitchen towel.
Refrigerate overnight.
The next morning, pre-
heat the oven(s) to 500°F.
Place the cold unbaked
bialys on your prepared
baker's peel or baking
sheet. Prepare and bake as
directed, letting the bialys
sit in a turned-off oven for
an extra 5 minutes.*

each bialy while also gently widening the empty interior. Transfer each bialy to the prepared peel or baking sheet. Spoon an equal amount of onion–poppy seed filling into the center of each one. Sprinkle the tops lightly with salt, if desired.

IF BAKING WITH TILES, insert the peel all the way to the back of the oven and with several swift jerks, pull out the peel, leaving the bialys on the hot tiles. Immediately toss the ice water onto the oven floor (underneath the tiles) and shut the door. If not using tiles, place the baking sheet directly on the hot oven rack and toss the ice water underneath it. If planning to store and toast the bialys, bake for 10 minutes. If planning to eat the bialys right after cooling (without toasting), turn the oven off and leave them in a turned-off oven for 5 more minutes. Transfer the bialys to wire racks to cool thoroughly before storing. (And be sure to use your oven sweep to brush off any fallen meal from the tiles or the stone before baking another batch.) If half the dough is in the refrigerator, take it out as soon as the first batch goes into the oven, and shape the remaining six bialys.

To serve, use a serrated knife to slice off the top of each bialy and either spread on your desired topping or toast both pieces until just golden and heated through before spreading.

Of Course It's Worth It . . .
HOMEMADE FLOUR TORTILLAS

Although not a yeast dough, in many cuisines tortillas are used exclusively instead of regular bread. Over the last decade, because of an obsession with wraps, flour tortillas have also become increasingly popular with Americans. Not only are homemade tortillas simple to prepare but there's absolutely no comparison, in taste or aroma, between these and the store-bought version. Rubbing shortening into the flour before adding the liquid prevents excess elasticity in the dough after kneading. This makes the tortillas exceptionally easy to roll and very tender after cooking on a hot griddle. ❧ YIELD: TEN 8-INCH TORTILLAS

3 cups unbleached all-purpose flour, plus more for
  dusting
1½ teaspoons salt
Up to 1 teaspoon freshly ground black pepper
  (optional)

½ cup solid vegetable shortening
¾ to 1 cup hot water

WHISK THE FLOUR, salt, and pepper (if using) together in a mixing bowl. Using your fingertips, pinch and rub the shortening into the seasoned flour until it becomes mealy. Pour ¾ cup of the hot water into the flour mixture and, using your working hand, combine the wet and dry ingredients. As some of the flour is moistened, push that part to one side of the bowl and pour a little more water over the dry areas. Stop adding liquid when all of the flour is moistened and holds together when gently pinched between two fingers. (The dough should not be wet, just moist enough to be kneaded.) Turn the dough out onto a lightly floured surface and knead it until you've created a smooth dough, about 3 minutes. Wrap the dough in a clean, dry, smooth kitchen towel and let it rest for 30 minutes to 1 hour, allowing it to relax.

When ready to cut, roll, and cook the tortillas, first lay a clean dry, smooth kitchen towel next to your work surface and sprinkle it lightly with flour. Use your pastry scraper to divide the dough into 10 equal pieces, and cover them while working with one piece at a time. Lay a piece of dough on a lightly floured surface and fatten it slightly with the palm of your hand. Turn the dough over to flour the other side and, using a tapered wooden rolling pin, roll the dough into a very thin circle (see page 252). As you finish rolling each tortilla, lay them side by side on the prepared towel. When you run out of space, place either another floured towel or some floured plastic wrap on top of the first batch and lay the remaining tortillas on top.

Open a fresh kitchen towel in a safe spot near the stove. Have another one, folded, next to it. Heat one or two nonstick griddles or seasoned cast-iron

❧ *The dough can be
made 2 hours ahead and
kept at room temperature.
To prevent a skin from
forming, dust the dough
with some flour and cover
it with plastic wrap.*
❧ *The tortillas can be
rolled 30 minutes ahead
of cooking. Keep them
covered.*
❧ *Although tortillas are
best when served shortly
after cooking, they can be
reheated, either stacked in
a special covered tortilla
dish or wrapped in alu-
minum foil (shiny side
down) and placed in a
preheated 350°F. oven
until warm, 5 to 10 min-
utes. Alternatively, reheat
tortillas briefly in a
microwave, in an unsealed
heatproof heavy-duty
freezer bag.*

skillets over medium-high heat. When hot, brush the cooking surface very lightly with vegetable oil. This is the only time that you'll lubricate the surface. Lay one circle of dough on the center of the hot surface and cook the tortilla until the bottom is generously covered with golden brown spots, about 1½ minutes. During this time, use a flat turning spatula to occasionally smack down any bubbling that might occur, due to internal steam. Turn the tortilla over and cook the other side for a minute or so, just to sear it. Transfer the cooked tortilla to the opened towel and cover it with the other one. Continue cooking and stacking the tortillas until finished.

SERVE THE TORTILLAS WARM, either in a shallow, cloth-lined round basket or in an earthenware tortilla warmer with a lid.

HERE'S THE SCOOP:
On Rolling a Perfect Circle of Dough

Whether rolling out tortillas or pie crusts, it can be challenging to create a circle of dough that's both uniformly thin and perfectly round. Here are some simple tips. First, after flattening the dough, use the center of a long, tapered, wooden rolling pin to roll over the dough once, going away from you. Turn the dough a quarter-turn and roll over it again. Repeat this turning and rolling process until the round shape is apparent and the dough has gotten thinner. At this point, roll the pin back and forth and side to side over the round, thinning it as required by your recipe. As you do this, occasionally place the chubby center of the pin over the rim and roll back and forth once or twice. Rotate the circle while continuing to roll over the rim, thinning it and keeping the circular shape. If, while doing this, you create a raised pleat of dough around the edge, place the pin in the center of the round and roll up and down, and side to side, always beginning in the center. This will widen the round in order to accommodate the now-thinner rim.

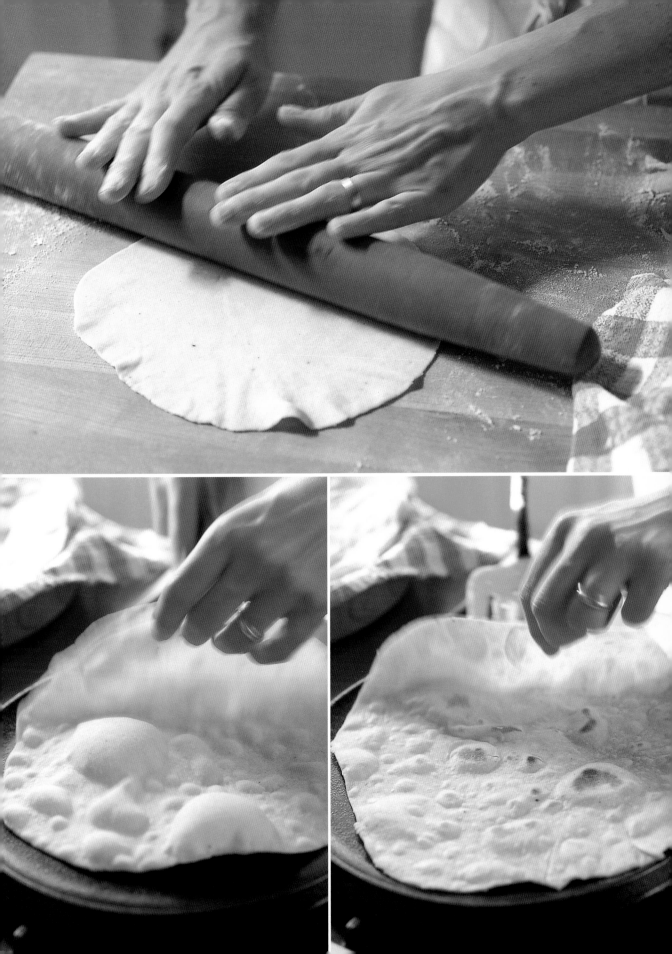

Hot and Crispy . . .
SKILLET CORNBREAD

Because my son Ben loves this cornbread so much when lavished with butter and drizzled with warmed maple syrup, that has become our traditional way of serving it. For instructions on how to season a cast-iron pan, see page 255.

🍂 YIELD: ONE 10-INCH CORNBREAD

5 tablespoons butter, 4 tablespoons of it (½ stick), melted and cooled to just warm

½ cup minced yellow onion

Freshly ground black pepper to taste

2¾ cups Cornbread Mix (page 41), or see the end of this recipe

2 cups buttermilk

2 extra-large eggs, lightly beaten

3 generous tablespoons Clarified Butter (page 195) or solid vegetable shortening

Softened butter and warmed maple syrup

Kosher salt to taste

TIMING IS EVERYTHING

🍂 *Early in the day, place your measured cornbread mix in a bowl and leave on your counter, covered. Combine your wet ingredients (including the sautéed onions but excluding the melted butter) and refrigerate it, covered. Before baking, remove your wet ingredients from the refrigerator to take the chill off. Meanwhile, melt the 4 tablespoons butter and let it cool slightly, and preheat the oven with the pan inside as described. Mix the ingredients, let the batter sit a little (covered), then bake away!*

PLACE A 10-INCH, well-seasoned cast-iron skillet or a heavy nonstick 10-inch round cake pan on the center rack of the oven. Preheat the oven to 425°F. Melt the 1 tablespoon butter in another small skillet over medium heat and, when melted and bubbling, add the minced onion. Sauté the onion until softened and fragrant, 2 to 3 minutes; add some black pepper and remove from heat. Set the pan aside.

Place the cornbread mix in a bowl. Combine the buttermilk, lightly beaten eggs, and the cooled sautéed onion and mix well. Pour the buttermilk mixture into the bowl with the cornbread mix and add the melted butter. Using a batter whisk or a wide blending fork, gently combine the ingredients just until there are no dry pockets. The cornbread batter should sit undisturbed, well covered, for 20 minutes, but not longer than 1 hour, before baking.

PLACE THE CLARIFIED BUTTER or solid shortening in the preheated pan and put the pan back into oven and shut the door. When melted and hot, 45 to 60 seconds, open the oven door and carefully (using oven mitts!) pull the rack holding the skillet toward you. Using a large sturdy rubber spatula, quickly (so the oven doesn't cool) ease the cornmeal mixture into the hot skillet (the batter should sizzle furiously). Push the pan back into the oven and close the door. Bake until firm but not overly dry and a toothpick comes out clean when inserted into the center of the bread, about 20 minutes.

Carefully remove the pan from the oven and run a knife around its circumference. To remove from the pan, place a wire rack or a flat cookie sheet over the top and turn the bread out of the pan. Immediately invert once more onto a warmed serving plate so the bread is right side up. Alternatively, you can also serve the bread straight from the pan. Either way, cut into wedges and serve hot with fresh softened butter that's lightly sprinkled with salt and/or warmed maple syrup for drizzling.

If you don't have the preassembled cornbread mix: Per each batch of cornbread, use a whisk to combine 1½ cups fine or medium-ground cornmeal, 1 cup bleached all-purpose flour, 2 teaspoons baking soda, 2½ tablespoons sugar, and 1½ teaspoons salt. Sift into another bowl, then follow the remaining instructions.

HERE'S THE SCOOP:
On Using Cast Iron Cookware

Cast-iron cookware is great for cooking certain foods but not at all appropriate for others. First the bad news: because unseasoned cast-iron cookware is porous, the interior retains flavor. This means that if not cared for properly, the pan will transfer flavors from one dish to another. And this problem is not limited to food—if soap is used, its flavor will also be detected in your next dish. Cast iron also reacts poorly with acidic foods (like tomatoes, wine, vinegar, or citrus), and gives these foods an "off" color and a metallic taste. Cast iron is also really susceptible to rusting, so it has to be kept meticulously dry after each use. However, the good news is that cast iron is superior for frying because of its ability to retain high temperatures for long periods of time. This material also distributes heat extremely evenly and efficiently, which helps produce food with a crisper, more uniformly golden exterior. And, when the seasoned surface is maintained properly, the pan becomes less flavor retentive (more tolerant of those no-no foods) and also develops a wonderfully deep, dark nonstick interior. (Thus, the original nonstick cookware!) So, if you play your cards right, you just might be able to hand your cast-iron cookware down to your children and eventually to your grandchildren. What a wonderful way to induce a batch of delicious memories.

Before using your cast-iron skillet for the first time, rinse and dry the pan completely (inside and out). Rub the entire surface (inside, outside, bottom, and handle) generously with vegetable oil. Place the skillet into a preheated 375°F. oven for 1 hour. Turn the oven off and leave the pan there for an additional hour. Then use a paper towel to remove any excess oil, allowing only a thin layer to remain. Your pan is now seasoned and ready to use. Every three times you use it, repeat this seasoning procedure, which will give the pan a darker color, making it not only more heat retentive but also less reactive and more nonstick. After each use, don't actually wash the skillet. Just give the interior a thorough wiping, using a wad of paper towel and a good pinch of coarse salt as your abrasive. You can use water, just no soap. And make sure to dry the pan thoroughly. Once clean and dry, apply another thin layer of oil to the entire surface and wipe off any excess before storing.

BAKING POWDER BISCUITS

Whether sitting next to a mound of hot scrambled eggs at breakfast or sharing the spotlight with a succulent roast chicken at dinner, these biscuits are destined to become a family tradition, trusted to bring comfort any time you want.

❧ YIELD: ABOUT EIGHT 2-INCH BISCUITS

2 cups Baking Powder Biscuit Mix (page 42), or
   see the end of this recipe
3 tablespoons cold unsalted butter, cut into small dice
About 1⅓ cups heavy cream

Unbleached all-purpose flour for dusting
2 tablespoons unsalted butter, melted
Softened butter and/or jam

TIMING IS
EVERYTHING
❧ *The unbaked biscuits
can be prepared 24 hours
ahead and refrigerated,
covered well with plastic
wrap. For best texture,
bring the chilled dough
close to room temperature
before baking.*

LINE A THIN, flat cookie sheet with ungreased parchment paper and preheat the oven to 400°F. Place the biscuit mix in either a large mixing bowl or the bowl of a food processor fitted with the steel blade. Add the cubed butter and, if not using a machine, cut the butter into the dry mix, using a hand-held pastry cutter or your fingertips. If using a food processor, pulse the diced butter with the dry mix. Either way, blend until the mixture looks like coarse meal. Pour 1¼ cups of the heavy cream into the bowl of dry ingredients. If making biscuits by hand, use a wide blending fork to gently but thoroughly combine the wet and dry ingredients without overworking the mixture. As some of the flour becomes moistened by the cream, push that section of the dough to one side of the bowl and continue until the dough resembles a moist, shapeless mass. (If the dough seems too dry, add the remaining tablespoon or so of cream.) Turn the mass out onto a lightly floured surface and knead it very gently, about eight or nine times, until it holds together. If working with a food processor, add the cream to the workbowl and give it several quick pulses just until the dry mix is thoroughly moistened and able to be turned out and handled. Dump the contents out and knead gently as directed above.

Using a wooden rolling pin or a lightly floured hand, roll or pat the dough out to a thickness of about 1½ inches. Using a floured 2-inch biscuit cutter, cut out as many rounds as possible, using a straight down, up, and out motion without twisting (which yields severely lopsided biscuits). Lay the rounds on the prepared baking sheet and gather the scraps so you can gently knead them just to smooth the surface. Pat or roll the dough out again and cut out more rounds.

BRUSH THE TOPS of the biscuits with melted butter and place the sheet in the center of the preheated oven. Bake until they have risen high and turned light golden brown, 18 to 20 minutes. Remove from the oven and serve hot, with butter and/or jam.

If you don't have the preassembled biscuit mix: For each batch of biscuits, mix 2 cups unbleached all-purpose flour with 1 tablespoon plus 1 teaspoon baking powder, 1 tablespoon sugar, and ¾ teaspoon salt. Whisk well and follow the recipe instructions above.

HERE'S THE SCOOP:
On Handling Biscuit Dough

Unlike yeast doughs, which require tough and persistent kneading from the cook, hands that touch biscuit dough have to be much more gentle. For the tenderest biscuits, each kneading movement must be light-hearted and superficial, with the goal of making the dough just cohesive enough to be rolled (or patted) out. Homemade biscuits are usually a bit irregularly shaped after baking. Resist the temptation to work the dough aggressively, in the hopes of making the dough smooth. Most people would take a lopsided biscuit over a tough one any day.

Homemade Flatbread Crackers . . .
MY MATZOS

These large, irregularly shaped, slightly blistered flatbread crackers are nothing like the square, factory produced sheets that taste, more than a little, like cardboard. Actually, this recipe produces the only matzos that my kids will eat with gusto. When entertaining, serve these crackers stacked and slightly staggered, whether whole or broken into manageable pieces.

Before you begin, a few words of advice: Read this recipe from beginning to end twice before getting started. Don't use an overly dark baking sheet, which is more heat retentive than heavy aluminum, making it easier for the crackers to scorch. And, don't leave the kitchen (not even once) during baking. After the first minute of baking, peek into the oven often, to check for doneness. Once the center of the cracker becomes darker in color, it's just seconds away from being done. Lastly, remember to sweep off the baking sheet after removing each cracker from the oven, so any floury residue won't cause subsequent crackers to burn.

❦ YIELD: 14 TO 16 LARGE IRREGULAR SHAPED FLATBREAD CRACKERS

FOR THE MATZOS

4 cups unbleached all-purpose flour, plus more for dusting

A few grinds freshly ground black pepper

¼ cup sesame seeds (optional, but highly suggested)

2 teaspoons Kosher or sea salt, plus more for sprinkling

1½ cups warm water

POSITION ONE OF THE OVEN RACKS in the lowest shelf position and remove any other racks. Lay a heavy aluminum or stainless steel baking sheet, inverted (bottom-side up), on the oven rack. Turn on the oven to the highest setting, just below broil, 550°F. Place 2 large wire cooling racks on your counter, side by side. Take out your rolling pin and either a docker or a wide fork. Place a short handled oven-sweep on a small shallow baking sheet, next to the oven.

To assemble the dough, place the flour in a mixing bowl and whisk in some black pepper and the sesame seeds, if using. Stir the 2 teaspoons salt into the warm water and add this to the dry ingredients. Using your hand, mix the water and flour together, until you form a mass that leaves the sides of the bowl. Turn the mass out onto a lightly floured wooden work surface and knead the dough until smooth, 2 to 3 minutes. Using your pastry scraper, divide the dough into 14 to 16 equal pieces. Cover all the pieces while working with one at a time.

Using a rolling pin, roll out one piece of dough, as thin as possible. Never hesitate to add additional flour while rolling, to keep the dough from sticking and turn the dough over, occasionally, as you roll. When the sheet seems ultra thin, run your hand over the surface. If you detect any thicker areas, use the pin to roll over those areas until the sheet feels even. Either use a docker or a fork to prick many holes in the dough, all over. Sprinkle the top of the sheet, lightly, with more salt, then run your hand gently over the sheet to help some of the salt adhere, without pressing down.

Carefully lift the sheet, letting one side drape down as you carry it to the oven (some salt might fall off, which is fine). Open the oven and, while holding the sheet of dough at one end, fan the bottom of it, going away from you, toward the back of the oven and lay the sheet flat on the preheated (ungreased) baking sheet. Do this as quickly as possible, to prevent the oven from cooling down. Shut the oven door and set your timer for 1 minute. Meanwhile, start rolling out another piece of dough. When the timer sounds, turn the cracker over and let it bake for 45 seconds to 1 minute, checking occasionally for doneness.

When done, the crackers should be light golden and slightly blistered. (It's not unusual for several areas to be a bit darker, due to some areas being rolled thinner than others. These darker spots are usually the best-tasting part of the cracker.) If the cracker needs a few more seconds, turn it over and shut the door. Count to 20 and check again. When satisfied, remove the cracker to a wire rack to cool. (At first the cracker will feel a bit bendable but will quickly become very crisp, as it cools). Open the oven and quickly and carefully (watch your forearms) brush any floury residue off the surface of the baking sheet, using the cool sheet to catch the crumbs. Continue rolling, baking and stacking the remaining matzos until the batch is finished. Please be aware that the oven will become progressively hotter with each sheet. So, the baking timing at end of the batch might be shorter, than at the beginning. If the matzos are baking too fast, reduce the temperature to 500°F, to gain more control.

Store the cooled matzos at room temperature stacked in sealed jumbo (2 gallon) plastic bags. If you've rolled the dough thin enough, the crackers will stay perfectly crisp and fresh tasting, until there's not a crumb left. Do not store these crackers in paper bags, which makes them get stale, quickly.

TIMING IS EVERYTHING:

❧ *Make the matzos one or two days before serving, but hide them, since they've been known to disappear very quickly, once spotted. They can stay perfectly good for a week.*

BISCUITS FOR MY SWEET ROSIE

I can't think of a more deserving soul on earth to be presented with a tub of home-made crunchy nibbles than my wonderful dog, Rosebud. I've seen Rosie sit and stare at the filled container and actually drool at the sight of these biscuits. As the list of ingredients indicates, these are not just any *dog biscuits. If I had to guess, I think the component that makes Rosie swoon is the glaze. Flavored with either chicken or beef and mixed with egg, milk, and honey, it's this glaze that makes my dog go ape when she gets one of these biscuits between her teeth. Speaking of teeth, be prepared to hear quite a crunch when your dog bites down on these biscuits, since they're intentionally very hard. This way, in addition to making your pup feel happy to be home, each bite will give your dog's teeth a good cleaning.*

🐾 YIELD: ABOUT NINETY 2½-INCH BISCUITS

FOR THE DOG BISCUIT DOUGH

3 cups unbleached all-purpose flour, plus more for dusting

2 cups whole wheat flour

½ cup coarse rye meal

½ cup cornmeal (coarse or medium-ground)

1 cup cracked wheat or cracked wheat cereal

¼ cup toasted wheat germ

½ cup nonfat dry milk

1½ teaspoons salt (optional)

1¾ cups low- or no-sodium Beef (page 18), Chicken (page 16), or Roasted Vegetable Stock (page 22) (if using salted canned broth, omit the additional salt)

½ cup packed dark brown sugar

¼ cup mild-flavored honey

1 package active dry yeast

¼ cup warm water

Pinch of granulated sugar

FOR THE GLAZE

1 egg, lightly beaten

1 tablespoon milk

1 teaspoon mild honey

1 teaspoon Bovril (beef- or chicken-flavored concentrate)

MAKE THE DOUGH. Position the oven racks in the upper- and lower-third shelf positions and preheat the oven to 325°F. Line two large baking sheets with parchment paper and set them aside for now. In a large mixing bowl, use a whisk to combine the white and whole wheat flours, rye meal, cornmeal, cracked wheat, wheat germ, dry milk, and salt, if using. Heat the stock in a 2-quart saucepan over low heat until tepid (just warm to the touch) and stir in the sugar and honey. Turn off the heat. Dissolve the yeast in the warm water with the pinch of sugar and allow it to become visibly bubbly, about 3 minutes. Pour the sweetened stock into the flour mixture and add the dissolved yeast. Stir until a firm but shaggy dough forms. When the mixture pulls away from the sides of the bowl, turn it out onto a lightly floured wooden surface and knead it, adding more white flour as needed, until the dough is smooth and quite stiff (but not so stiff that it's too hard to roll out).

Cut the dough in half using a pastry scraper and cover one piece while working with the other. Using a straight rolling pin, roll the dough out on a lightly floured surface until it's about ¼ inch thick. Using sturdy cookie cutters in a variety of shapes, cut out as many biscuits as you can and place them on the prepared baking sheets. Gather the scraps and reroll the dough until you've cut out as many biscuits as possible. (Since tenderness isn't the goal, don't worry about overworking the dough.) Fill up both baking sheets, leaving ½ inch between biscuits. If desired, use the tines of a regular fork to decoratively prick the center of each biscuit. (If you fill the sheets before using all the dough, and if you don't have a double oven, you'll need to wrap any remaining dough in plastic wrap and refrigerate it overnight. Allow it to come to room temperature before rolling and cutting more biscuits.)

MAKE THE GLAZE. Combine the egg, milk, honey, and Bovril and strain this through a medium-mesh wire sieve positioned over another bowl. Using a pastry brush, paint some of the glaze over each biscuit. Place the baking sheets in the oven and reduce the temperature to 300°F. Bake the biscuits for 45 minutes, switching the shelf positions of the baking sheets after half the baking time. Turn the oven off and allow the biscuits to sit there, undisturbed, overnight. In the morning, bring on the pooch! Store the biscuits at room temperature, piled either in a tightly covered cookie jar or in an airtight tin with a sticker with your dog's name on it.

TIMING IS EVERYTHING

❧ *Each time you make a batch of dog biscuits, make an additional dry mixture and freeze it in doubled, well-sealed freezer bags.*

CHAPTER NINE
PLEASE, NO DITSY DESSERTS!

PERSONALLY, I'VE NEVER been attracted to tiny, jewellike confections. I'm much more enticed by a big platter of full-sized, gorgeous desserts. So if you're like me, I think you'll find what you need in this chapter, which is chockfull of voluptuous layer cakes and cupcakes stemming from the pancake mix in Chapter One. There are big, fat cookies; chubby filled pastries; and even Mixed-Nut Butter-Crunch Toffee, which I call "the sexiest candy alive." There's also a slab of moist, yummy brownies studded with chocolate chips and swirled with sweetened cream cheese, and a really easy and extra-creamy parfait made with banana-infused mascarpone cheese, layered with crushed chocolate wafer cookies and fresh strawberries. In addition to all of this, there's a fabulous recipe for homemade lavender-scented ice cream served with buttered, sugared, broiled fresh figs. And, speaking of ice cream, wouldn't you love to be able to enjoy the authentic taste and varied textures in a luscious chocolate-covered Tartufo without having to go to the neighborhood Italian restaurant? If so, you've come to the right place.

STRAWBERRIES, BANANA MASCARPONE,

and Crushed Cookie Parfaits

As easy as they are attractive, these creamy, crunchy parfaits can be assembled a couple of hours ahead of serving and refrigerated. Don't apply the caramelized banana garnish, however, until just before serving. Mascarpone is an Italian double or triple cream cheese, available in many well-stocked supermarkets and "gourmet" food shops. Its thick, luscious texture makes it a great partner to pureed ripe bananas. As individual servings go, these are quite generous. So, if you use smaller parfait glasses, you'll have some of the individual components left over. But don't throw them away! Use any leftover berries or banana mascarpone in a smoothie. And save the extra cookie crumbs to top ice cream or to sprinkle on a frosted cake. ❧ YIELD: 6 GENEROUS SERVINGS*

2 dry pints fresh ripe strawberries, rinsed and drained

3 tablespoons seedless raspberry or strawberry jam

1 tablespoon Grand Marnier, Framboise, or Crème de Banana liqueur

3 large or 4 medium very ripe bananas, chilled

¼ cup confectioners' sugar, sifted

4 tablespoons granulated sugar

1½ teaspoons pure vanilla extract

2 generous cups mascarpone (2-pound, 2-ounce tub), well chilled

One 9-ounce box Nabisco chocolate wafer cookies, crushed into small pieces

2 extra-large ripe but firm bananas for garnish

Mint sprigs for garnish

PICK OUT SIX STRAWBERRIES with the most pointed tips and slice the tips off, in ⅓-inch pieces, reserving them for the garnish. Place the rest of the berries in the bowl of a food processor fitted with the steel blade, and add the jam and the liqueur. Pulse the berries until they are chopped but not pureed and the jam is mixed throughout. Pour the berry mixture into a nonreactive bowl and set it aside, covered.

To make the banana mascarpone, puree the cold bananas in the blender or simply mash them well using a wide blending fork. Measure out 1⅓ cups puree and discard the rest. Pour the puree into the blender (or in a bowl) and blend in the confectioners' sugar, 2 tablespoons of granulated sugar, and the vanilla. Place the cold mascarpone in a bowl and whisk in the flavored banana puree to make things homogenous. Cover the bowl and keep it chilled until ready to assemble the parfaits.

TO SERVE, take out a small handheld blowtorch or preheat the broiler with the rack as close as possible to the heating element. Spoon some of the berries on the bottom of a parfait dish, then top them with some banana mascarpone and then with some cookie crumbs. Repeat this until you reach the top of the dish, finishing the top layer with a dollop of banana cream.

Slice the two remaining cold bananas on the diagonal into ½-inch-thick slices and place them flat, side by side, on a wire rack within a shallow baking sheet. Sprinkle the bananas lightly but evenly with the remaining 2 tablespoons of granulated sugar and either torch them or run them under the broiler until the sugar is caramelized. Plant a few slices of the bananas decoratively in the dollop of banana mascarpone and stick one of the reserved strawberry tips at the base of the bananas. Position a mint sprig decoratively on top, and serve.

TIMING IS EVERYTHING

🌿 The berries and the banana mascarpone can be prepared early in the day of serving and kept refrigerated separately, well covered.

🌿 The parfaits can be assembled 2 hours before serving and kept covered in the refrigerator. Don't peel or caramelize the bananas, however, until just before serving.

Lavender-scented
FRENCH VANILLA ICE CREAM
with Broiled Fresh Figs

To me, this recipe screams "Provence!" If you've never cooked with dried laven-der, I think you'll be pleasantly surprised; when used correctly, its gorgeous fragrance lends itself perfectly to a rich frozen custard. Make sure, however, that you use only the edible lavender (available in specialty food shops) and not the kind meant for scented pouches. When making ice cream, make sure to set up correctly to prevent the risk of curdling the custard, which can happen if it's initially overheated. If you don't feel like making ice cream, just serve these buttered, sugared, and broiled figs on top of a scoop of your favorite store-bought vanilla ice cream or some lightly sweetened, thick crème fraîche.

❧ YIELD: ABOUT 1 QUART ICE CREAM; 6 SERVINGS

FOR THE ICE CREAM

Ice cubes or crushed ice for cooling the custard
2½ cups heavy cream
1 cup whole milk
2 large supple vanilla beans
2 teaspoons dried edible lavender
8 extra-large egg yolks, at room temperature
¾ cup plus 2 tablespoons granulated sugar
2¼ teaspoons pure vanilla extract
Pinch of salt

FOR THE FIG TOPPING

6 fresh figs, wiped clean and quartered through the stem end
2 tablespoons unsalted butter, melted
1 to 2 tablespoons granulated sugar (or use light brown sugar pushed through a medium-mesh wire sieve)

MAKE THE ICE CREAM. Place a shallow layer of ice cubes or crushed ice on the bottom of a 6-quart bowl. Add a little water to the ice and sit a 3-quart bowl directly into the ice, pushing it down so it's secured. Place a triple-mesh wire sieve over the smaller bowl.

Pour the cream and milk into a 3-quart heavy-bottomed saucepan. Using a sharp knife, slit the vanilla beans lengthwise through the top skin only. Open the beans and, using the dull side of the knife, scrape down the length of the beans, removing their seeds. (To use the empty vanilla pods to make Vanilla Sugar, see page 35). Whisk the seeds into the cream, dispersing them through-out, then whisk in the lavender. Place the pan over medium-low heat and scald the liquid, but do not let it simmer.

Meanwhile, beat the egg yolks in a bowl using either an electric mixer or a whisk, while gradually adding the sugar, until the mixture is thick yet very light in texture and a pale lemon color. Lower the speed of the mixer to slow and add a ladle of the scalded cream mixture (a little at a time at first to temper the yolks). Slowly add more and more of the hot cream while mixing continuously and, when the bottom of the bowl feels hot, add the rest of the cream in a steady stream. When all of the hot liquid is added, pour the contents of the bowl back into the saucepan, off the heat. Use a rubber spatula to scrape any remaining mixture off the bottom of the bowl and into the saucepan, and place the pan over low heat. Cook the custard, stirring constantly with a wooden spoon, until the mixture is thickened and coats the back of the spoon, about 3 minutes once the mixture becomes hot throughout. (To check the consistency of the custard, always remove the pan from the heat first, to prevent accidental curdling.)

POUR THE COOKED CUSTARD through the sieve over the chilled bowl and discard anything that remains in the sieve or on the bottom of the pan. Stir in the vanilla and salt, and drape a clean kitchen towel or paper towel over the top of the bowl. Let the custard cool to just warm, stirring occasionally, before placing both bowls in the refrigerator to cool the custard thoroughly. (If time is an issue, add more ice to the larger bowl, going up the sides, which will speed up this initial chilling process.)

To churn and store the ice cream, transfer the well-chilled custard to the bowl of an ice cream maker and follow the manufacturer's instructions. After churning, store the ice cream in a sealed container in the freezer.

PREPARE THE FIGS. Preheat the broiler with the rack as close as possible to the heating element. Line a shallow baking sheet with aluminum foil (shiny side up) and lay the quartered figs cut sides up on the prepared sheet. Brush the cut sides of the figs with melted butter and sprinkle them with sugar. Broil the figs until they are warmed through and the sugared surface is bubbling. Use tongs to place the broiled figs on top of individual scoops of lavender ice cream, and serve right away.

Old-fashioned French Vanilla
Omit the lavender and keep everything else the same.

TIMING IS EVERYTHING
* The ice cream can be churned three days ahead and kept frozen.
* To prevent having to struggle with very hard ice cream just before serving, it's wise to scoop out portions several hours or a day ahead, and keep the scoops on a tray lined with waxed paper in the freezer, covered with plastic wrap.

Yes, I'll Share . . .
CHOCOLATE-CHERRY TARTUFOS

If you want to serve a dessert that will make different types of people happy, a great choice is ice cream. Here, two different types of ice cream are molded into individual cups, separated by a thin layer of toasted almonds mixed with chopped glacéed cherries. Then, after being unmolded, the whole thing is drenched in a cherry-scented chocolate ganache. Be careful not to ladle on the ganache when it's even the least bit warm, or it will literally fall off the ice cream as it slides down the sides. Since this ganache is very fluid, it can stay at room temperature for a long time before getting too thick to pour. Glacéed cherries are chewy, like those you'd use in fruit cake. If unavailable, use chopped maraschinos. Be sure to see the end of the recipe for an easy tartufo loaf variation. ❧ YIELD: 8 GENEROUS SERVINGS

FOR THE TARTUFO INTERIORS

Vegetable shortening for greasing

1½ quarts best-quality cherry vanilla ice cream

1 quart best-quality chocolate chocolate chip ice cream

1 generous cup deeply toasted blanched almonds (see page 271), finely chopped

About 3 tablespoons chopped glacéed cherries

FOR THE GANACHE

36 ounces bittersweet chocolate, chopped

12 ounces semisweet chocolate, chopped

2 tablespoons light corn syrup

3 cups heavy cream

2 teaspoons natural-flavored cherry extract (if unavailable, use 1 teaspoon pure almond extract)

2 teaspoons pure vanilla extract

MAKE THE INTERIORS. Use a paper towel to coat the inside of eight 8-ounce baking ramekins or custard cups with shortening. Tear off a large sheet of plastic wrap and fold it over to double it. Make a fist with your working hand and drape the plastic over your fist, covering it completely. Insert your fist into the cup all the way to the bottom. Release the plastic from your hand and push it up against the bottom and sides of the dish, helping it adhere to the shortening. Allow any excess plastic to hang over the edge (make sure you have lots of excess *doubled* plastic visible, which you'll need later to unmold the contents). Wrap the excess plastic around and under the cups for easy handling. Clear a shelf in your freezer. Line a large shallow baking sheet or tray with waxed paper, and place it in the freezer to chill.

Remove only the cherry vanilla ice cream from the freezer so it can reach a spreadable, but not soupy, consistency. Working with one mold at a time, use a small icing spatula or a spoon to spread a generous layer of ice cream about ½ inch thick on the bottom and up the sides of the plastic-lined cups. Place each mold in the freezer while you continue with the rest. Let the first layer of ice cream firm up for about 30 minutes. Meanwhile, remove the chocolate ice cream from the freezer to soften. When it is spreadable, sprinkle the chopped

TIMING IS
EVERYTHING

The tartufos can be assembled fully one week ahead and kept frozen, well covered.

almonds liberally over the first layer of ice cream, along with a few pieces of chopped cherries. (Reserve some of the nuts for the garnish.) Use the spatula to fill the cups with the chocolate ice cream, smoothing the tops. Freeze the cups for at least 2 hours or up to a few days, covered with waxed paper.

MAKE THE GANACHE. Melt the two types of chocolate together either in the top of a large double boiler over barely simmering water while stirring constantly, or in the microwave on medium power for about 4 minutes, occasionally stopping to stir, until perfectly smooth. Stir in the corn syrup. Heat the cream in a small heavy-bottomed saucepan over medium heat until it comes to a boil. Slowly pour the cream into the bowl of chocolate, still over barely simmering water, while stirring constantly. When perfectly smooth, remove from the heat. Whisk in the cherry and vanilla extracts, then push the ganache through a medium-mesh sieve directly into another bowl using a rubber spatula. Set the bowl aside to cool for about 20 minutes.

When the ganache is perfectly cool but still pourable, uncover the tartufos and spoon a generous tablespoon of the ganache over the top of the ice cream, and use the small spatula to cover the top evenly. As the ganache gets cold, it will become more difficult to move around, so spread quickly. Scrape off any excess ganache as you spread, placing it on the edge of an empty bowl. Freeze the tartufos, uncovered, for 30 minutes, then cover the tops loosely with plastic wrap and freeze them for at least 2 hours or up to overnight. If finishing the tartufos today, leave the ganache at room temperature. If planning to continue tomorrow, store the remaining ganache in the refrigerator, well covered. To use the remaining ganache, let it come close to room temperature, then reheat the ganache briefly to thin it to a pourable consistency. Let it sit, however, until *completely* cool.

Work as close as possible to the freezer while finishing the tartufos. Place an empty bowl on a flat work surface along with the reserved chopped almonds, a 3- to 4-ounce ladle, and two long metal spatulas (one wide and the other thin). Line a plate with a piece of waxed paper. Keep the tartufos in the freezer while working with one at a time. Pull the molded ice cream out of its cup, using the overhang of plastic wrap (hold on to the cup with a hot, damp kitchen towel). Invert the ice cream onto the plate and peel off the plastic wrap. Place the tartufo, ganache side down, on the prepared tray in the freezer. Continue until all the tartufos are unmolded and on their tray.

ONE BY ONE, POSITION a tartufo, chocolate-base down, at the end of the long, wide spatula held over the empty bowl. Fill the ladle generously with the ganache and pour it over the top of the ice cream, allowing any excess to fall down over the sides, using the narrow spatula to quickly help spread the ganache evenly on the sides and also to clean up the bottom edges. If there are empty pockets, ladle on more ganache and spread gently until smooth. Sprinkle the wet chocolate tops with some of the chopped almonds, and carefully slide the tartufo off the spatula and onto its original spot on the tray that sits in the freezer, uncovered. Continue with the remaining tartufos, wiping off both spatulas after drenching each one in the ganache. (If, when applying the ganache, the ice cream ever starts to melt, let the excess chocolate fall into the bowl beneath and, when the dripping stops, put the tartufo back in the freezer to firm up. Once firm, ladle on more of the ganache until you're satisfied with the coverage.)

Freeze the tartufos, uncovered, for 2 hours, then cover them with plastic wrap and keep them frozen for up to one week before serving. (The ganache will accommodate 10 to 12 tartufos, but you'll need more ice cream and ramekins to make more than 8. Store any leftover ganache in the refrigerator for up to a week, and rewarm it for a quick topping for either ice cream or a thick slice of plain pound cake, topped with sliced strawberries.)

To serve, remove the tartufos from the freezer and cut them, using a sharp serrated knife, into quarters, wiping off the blade after each cut. Place three to four quarters on each individual dessert plate. Serve right away.

An Easy Tartufo Loaf

If you don't have a lot of time, or 8-ounce cups, just make one big tartufo shaped into a loaf. To do this, coat the inside of a 9 × 5-inch loaf pan with shortening and line it with doubled plastic wrap, leaving an overhang as described in the original recipe. Be sure to reach all four corners. Spread the bottom and sides of the plastic-coated interior with a thick layer of softened cherry vanilla ice cream and sprinkle the ice cream first with chopped almonds and then with chopped glacéed cherries. Freeze until firm, covered loosely with plastic wrap. When firm and the chocolate ice cream has been allowed to soften, use it to fill the vacant center space in the loaf, coming up to about ¼ inch from the top. Freeze the loaf until very firm on a tray lined with waxed paper.

Prepare the ganache as directed in the recipe, reducing the ingredient amounts by half. When the ganache is perfectly cool but still pourable, spread the top (which will become the bottom) of the loaf with the ganache, covering it completely and flush with the top of the pan. Freeze the loaf until the chocolate is very firm, about 8 hours. Rewarm the remaining ganache briefly and allow it to become cool and thick but still fluid. Straddle a large wire rack over an empty bowl placed on your work surface, close to the freezer. Remove the loaf from the freezer and, using the overhang of plastic, unmold and invert the loaf, ganache side down, onto the wire rack. Peel off the plastic and ladle the ganache over the ice cream, coating it generously and completely. Sprinkle the top with some chopped toasted almonds and immediately place the tartufo loaf onto its tray and back into the freezer, uncovered. When the ganache is completely set, cover the loaf with plastic wrap and leave it there until you're ready to cut it into individual slices and serve.

HERE'S THE SCOOP:
On Toasting Nuts

If your toasted nuts are scorched on the bottom, it's because either your oven is too hot or your pan is too dark, which makes it extra heat-retentive. Skinless nuts (whether whole, sliced, or chopped), like almonds, pine nuts, and macadamias, should be toasted gently in a moderate, 350°F. oven on a shallow heavy aluminum baking sheet in a single layer. Don't mix different types of nuts on one baking sheet. Usually, blanched (skinned) nuts will take between 9 and 12 minutes. To avoid scorching nuts, let your nose be your guide. The first savory waft of toasting nuts is usually the best indication that they're almost done. Shake the pan occasionally while toasting to redistribute the nuts and prevent them from being overexposed to heat on any one side.

Toasting nuts with skins is a bit trickier. Because of their skins, unblanched almonds, walnuts, and pecans are more likely to taste bitter if left in the oven too long. So for these nuts, heat them just long enough to release their aroma, 6 to 7 minutes, at 350°F. After this, quickly remove them from their baking sheet to stop the cooking process. Another great way to get terrific flavor from nuts with skins is to pan-toast them over medium heat in a little melted unsalted butter until their color deepens, about 3 minutes, stirring constantly. (Use the ratio of 1 tablespoon butter for every cup of nuts.) Immediately remove them to a plate lined with paper towels to absorb any excess butter. Store leftovers in the refrigerator, since the inclusion of butter makes these toasted nuts perishable.

The Sexiest Candy I've Ever Tasted . . .
MIXED-NUT BUTTER-CRUNCH TOFFEE

If I had to choose, this would be my favorite candy in the whole world. Savory, sweet, and incredibly delicious, this is a great choice when you want to prepare the "sweet part" of your menu a week or two ahead. The candy keeps really well when refrigerated in an airtight tin. If unsalted nuts are not available, reduce the salt in the recipe to ¼ teaspoon. Oh, and you might be wondering why I add baking soda to a candy recipe when there's no obvious need for leavening. The candy mixture needs to be lightened in order to keep you from breaking a tooth on it once it's hardened. When baking soda is stirred into the hot toffee, the soda is activated, producing millions of microscopic bubbles that "interrupt" its hard texture, forcing the candy to shatter (and not crack) when you take a bite. For those allergic to nuts, see the nut-free variation at the end of this recipe.

🍮 YIELD: ABOUT FORTY 1½-INCH SQUARE CANDIES

1¼ cups (2½ sticks) unsalted butter, 4 tablespoons melted

½ teaspoon salt

¼ teaspoon baking soda

1½ teaspoons pure vanilla extract

1½ cups coarsely chopped deeply toasted unsalted macadamia nuts (see page 271)

3 cups finely chopped toasted nuts (blanched almonds, walnuts, pecans, and/or macadamia nuts; see page 271)

⅓ cup water

1½ cups sugar

½ cup light corn syrup

12 ounces semisweet chocolate

USING SOME OF THE MELTED BUTTER, coat a shallow 12 × 10-inch baking sheet and line it with a sheet of parchment paper, allowing some excess paper at both ends. Brush the paper with some more of the melted butter and set the sheet aside on a wire rack. Reserve any remaining melted butter for later. Line two more shallow baking sheets or trays with waxed paper, for holding and chilling the candy once assembled, and set the sheets aside.

Cut each unwrapped stick of butter in half and place on a plate next to your work surface, along with a tiny bowl with the premeasured salt and baking soda, an opened bottle of vanilla, and the coarsely chopped macadamia nuts. Place the finely chopped nuts in another bowl. Place a small bowl half full of boiling water next to the stove and insert a pastry brush in the water. Put your candy thermometer within easy reach. Place a medium bowl of ice water close by and, if by accident any hot sugar syrup should touch your skin, dunk the affected area into this bowl.

PLACE A 2½-QUART heavy-bottomed saucepan on the stove. Place the water, sugar, and corn syrup in the pan and stir gently to combine. Place the pan over medium-high heat and let the mixture come to a rolling boil. Don't stir anymore. If, while the sugar was dissolving, any sugar crystals jumped to the sides of the pan, use the moistened pastry brush to wash the sides down. Cook the syrup until the color turns very light amber. Reduce the heat and add the butter, one half-stick at a time, stirring very gently with the clean stem end of a wooden spoon. Add the next piece of butter only after each preceding piece has melted and become fully incorporated.

When all of the butter has been added and the mixture is well combined, clip the candy thermometer on the side of the pan so the bottom is submerged in the boiling toffee without allowing the mercury tip to touch the bottom of the pan. Raise the heat to medium and boil the mixture until the temperature reads between 295° and 300°F. Remove the thermometer from the pan and stand the bottom in the bowl of boiling hot water. Working quickly but carefully, immediately take the pan off the stove and stir in the combined salt and baking soda, vanilla, and coarsely chopped macadamia nuts (in that order). Immediately, pour the candy mixture onto the prepared greased baking sheet and, using a long, buttered metal icing spatula or a table knife, spread the toffee into a thin even layer about ⅓ inch thick (the toffee won't cover the entire pan). Use a buttered blade of a pastry scraper to frequently push the toffee into a rectangular shape as it cools, giving it a straight edge. Let the mixture set for a few minutes, or until it firms up a bit (not too long, however, or the candy will become too hard to cut).

MEANWHILE, MELT THE CHOCOLATE, stirring constantly, either in a heatproof bowl set in a skillet filled with an inch of very hot but not simmering water over low heat, or in a microwave oven for 1 minute on high, stirring until smooth after heating. As you work with the chocolate, occasionally check the slab of toffee, using the straight edge of your scraper to move it back in line. Once the chocolate is melted, place the bowl next to your work surface.

While the toffee mixture is still warm and pliable, use a buttered pastry scraper to score it into 1½-inch squares. Let the candy set until it's firmer, about 5 more minutes. Score again through the original cuts, making sure that the candy is in separate squares all the way through to the bottom. If stubborn, reapply butter to your pastry scraper and place the blade in your original cut. Using a heavy mallet, whack the top of the scraper, forcing the blade through any sticky, tough spots.

WHEN FIRM AND SEPARATE, make sure the toffee pieces are in their original positions and pour the melted chocolate over the top. Using a long

TIMING IS EVERYTHING

❧ Toast and chop the nuts one or two days ahead of assembling the candy and keep them at room temperature, securely covered. Freeze any extra nuts, or leave them at room temperature and use them within two weeks.

❧ These candies stay well for over a month when covered tightly and stored in the refrigerator.

metal icing spatula, spread the chocolate evenly over the toffee. (It's fine if the chocolate runs down into the grooves.) Scatter 2 cups of the ground toasted nuts on top of the chocolate and press them gently into the chocolate. Reserve the remaining 1 cup of nuts. Lift one end of the parchment paper so the first line of cut candy bends and separates from the next line. One by one, carefully lift each piece away from the rest and, if there are any bare spots, sprinkle them with the nuts. Place the candy, in a single layer, on the prepared baking sheets and refrigerate the pieces, covered with plastic wrap, to let the chocolate harden, 1 to 2 hours. Once set, place the candy into an airtight tin in layers, separated with waxed paper. Although these candies may be stored at room temperature, to best preserve the freshest flavor, store them in the refrigerator.

Nut-Free Butter Crunch

Be sure to purchase chocolate that isn't made in an environment with nuts, since this can cause inadvertent cross-contamination. In this recipe, I use Nestle's brand. For a company that specializes in nut-free chocolates, see my Source List on page 314. Since I suggest the use of Nabisco chocolate wafer cookies, which contain coconut oil, if you are allergic to this you'll need to find another cookie that's safe for you to eat (like Chips Ahoy chocolate chip cookies, also by Nabisco).

For a nut-free version, make the following changes in the original recipe. Instead of using nuts in the toffee, use an equal amount of coarsely chopped salted thin pretzel sticks. Mix 1½ cups each of crushed Nabisco chocolate wafer cookies and Lorna Doone shortbread cookies, and use them to top the melted chocolate. Reduce the salt to ¼ teaspoon. All other instructions are the same.

Want to Feel Like a Good Giver?
MAKE CHOCOLATE CRISPS!

I've been making these chocolate candies with my kids since they were little. Each year, they would give them to their friends and teachers as holiday gifts. They also make wonderful party favors for adults and kids. Regardless of the occasion, it's nice to wrap them in colorful foil papers. I've provided a source for these papers on page 313. ❧ YIELD: 20 TO 40 CHOCOLATE CANDIES, DEPENDING ON THE SIZE OF YOUR CUTTER

24 ounces semisweet chocolate, chopped
1 tablespoon solid vegetable shortening
8 ounces milk chocolate, chopped

1½ rounded cups Rice Krispies cereal, plain and/or cocoa-flavored

LINE THE BOTTOM of a 15 × 10-inch baking sheet with waxed paper, leaving a 2-inch overhang at each end. Line a second tray with waxed paper and place both trays next to your work surface.

To temper the chocolate, melt the semisweet chocolate with the shortening either in the top of a double boiler over barely simmering water or in a bowl that sits in a pan of very hot (but not simmering) water over low heat. Stir the chocolate constantly as it melts, being very careful not allow any water to enter the bowl, which will cause it to quickly stiffen, a process called seizing. Also, don't let the chocolate overheat. (If using an instant-read thermometer, remove the bowl of chocolate when it reaches between 115° and 118°F.) When just about smooth (one or two small pieces of chocolate may remain visible), immediately remove the chocolate from the stove and briskly stir in the milk chocolate. Stir constantly and briskly until perfectly smooth. Check the temperature; the chocolate should be cooled to between 88° and 90°F. in order to be in proper "temper" after setting.

STIR THE CEREAL into the melted chocolate as soon as it's tempered. When well combined, use a large rubber spatula to transfer it to the prepared baking sheet. Use a long metal icing spatula to spread the chocolate mixture evenly within the pan, then lift the pan and rap it once or twice on the counter, removing any air bubbles. Place the sheet in the freezer, uncovered, for no longer than 5 minutes.

Remove the sheet and, using sturdy cookie cutters (rounds, squares, hearts, etc.) in one or a variety of sizes, cut the chocolate into shapes. (If the chocolate is very firm, place a quilted pot holder or a folded kitchen towel on the top of

TIMING IS
EVERYTHING
❧ *When tempered properly, these candies can be stored at room temperature for several weeks.*

the cutter to protect your hand when pressing down.) Gently push the cut chocolates out of the cutter and onto the second paper-lined tray.

If desired, wrap the chocolate crisps individually in colored foil wrappers, or just lay them unwrapped in a tin, separated by sheets of waxed paper. Since these candies are tempered, they can be stored at a comfortable room temperature.

CHOCOLATE CHOCOLATE-CHIP
Brownies, Swirled with Sweetened Cream Cheese

If you love both brownies and cheesecake, then you'll really love this dessert. Personally, I prefer to use my index finger to swirl the sweetened cream cheese mixture into the brownie batter, but you can use the stem end of a wooden spoon or even a table knife. And don't leave out the chocolate chips, since they make these brownies even more interesting texturally, not to mention great-tasting!

 YIELD: ABOUT 22 BROWNIES

2 tablespoons unsalted butter, melted, for brushing

FOR THE CREAM CHEESE MIXTURE
12 ounces cream cheese (1½ 8-ounce blocks), at room temperature
1 tablespoon sour cream
¼ cup each granulated sugar and confectioners' sugar
1 teaspoon pure vanilla extract
1 extra-large egg, at room temperature
Pinch of salt

FOR THE BROWNIES
1 cup unbleached all-purpose flour
3 tablespoons cake flour (not self-rising)

1 teaspoon baking powder
½ teaspoon salt
1 cup (2 sticks) unsalted butter
2 ounces unsweetened chocolate, chopped
6 ounces bittersweet chocolate, chopped
1 teaspoon instant espresso powder
2 teaspoons pure vanilla extract
1½ cups granulated sugar
3 generous tablespoons Lyles Golden Syrup or light corn syrup
3 extra-large eggs, at room temperature
1 extra-large egg yolk, at room temperature
1 cup semisweet chocolate chips

TIMING IS EVERYTHING
 If wrapped securely, the brownies can be stored in the refrigerator for up to three days before cutting and serving.

LINE A 13 × 9-INCH BAKING DISH with aluminum foil (dull side down for a glass dish, dull side up for metal), allowing a 2-inch overhang at each end. Brush the foil with melted butter and set the pan aside. If using a glass dish, preheat the oven to 325° F. If using a metal pan, preheat to 350° F.

MAKE THE CREAM CHEESE MIXTURE. Using an electric mixer, beat the cream cheese with the sour cream, sugars, vanilla, egg, and salt until smooth. Set aside.

MAKE THE BROWNIES. Whisk together and then sift both types of flour, baking powder, and salt. In a 2½-quart heavy-bottomed saucepan, melt the butter with the two types of chocolate over low heat. Remove the pan from the heat and stir in the espresso powder and vanilla. Whisk the sugar and syrup into the melted chocolate until smooth. Add the eggs and egg yolk, one at a time, whisking well after each addition. When smooth, add the dry ingredients. Using a batter-whisk, combine the mixtures until smooth. Fold in the chocolate chips using a large rubber spatula.

Pour half the brownie batter into the prepared baking dish and gently spread it to each corner using a long icing spatula or a table knife. Drop heaping spoonfuls of half the cream cheese mixture, randomly, on top of the chocolate batter. Pour and lightly spread the remaining brownie mixture over the top. Drop spoonfuls of the remaining cheese mixture on top and swirl both mixtures together using either your index finger, the stem end of a thin wooden spoon, or a regular table knife, going through both mixtures until intertwined.

PLACE THE PAN in the oven and bake the brownies until a toothpick inserted into the center comes out with some chocolate adhering to it without being overly wet, about 35 minutes. (If you shake the pan gently, the brownie cake will jiggle just a bit.) Avoid overbaking. Place the pan on a wire rack and let the brownie cake cool thoroughly. Once cool, cover the pan with aluminum foil and let it sit for at least 4 hours (preferably overnight) in the refrigerator.

To cut the brownies, lift the brownie cake out of the pan using the overhang of foil as a handle, and invert it onto another flat tray lined with waxed paper. Peel off the foil, then re-invert, right side up, and discard the waxed paper. Slice the slab into 2-inch squares using a sharp knife. For easier slicing, wipe off the knife after each cut. To best preserve moistness, store sliced brownies in an airtight tin or in a heavy-duty rectangular plastic container, separated by sheets of waxed paper. Either way, because of the perishable cream cheese, store these brownies in the refrigerator. For best flavor, however, bring them to a cool room temperature before serving.

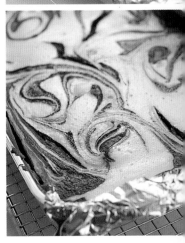

JUMBO BLACK AND WHITE COOKIES

Truly enticing, these cookies are a perfect choice to serve at a school bake fair, after a teenage sporting event, as a take-home party favor at your child's birthday party, or simply lined up on a decorative platter when entertaining casually. Also, since the batter and the glazes can be assembled the day ahead of baking and the cookies can be baked, glazed, and individually wrapped a day ahead of serving, this recipe is a great choice when you want a satisfying dessert that can be worked into a busy schedule. The glazes are also great for dunking the tops of cupcakes.

❧ YIELD: EIGHTEEN 5-INCH COOKIES

4½ cups unbleached all-purpose flour

½ teaspoon baking soda

1½ teaspoons baking powder

1 teaspoon salt

1 cup (2 sticks) unsalted butter, at room temperature

One 8-ounce block of cream cheese, at room temperature

½ cup solid vegetable shortening

2 cups granulated sugar

1½ cups confectioners' sugar (not sifted)

3 extra-large eggs, at room temperature

2 teaspoons finely minced lemon zest

1 tablespoon strained fresh lemon juice

2 teaspoons pure vanilla extract

FOR THE CHOCOLATE GLAZE

3½ cups sifted confectioners' sugar, or more as needed

8 ounces unsweetened chocolate, chopped

6 generous tablespoons light corn syrup, or more if needed

1½ teaspoons flavorless vegetable oil

1½ teaspoons pure vanilla extract

5 to 7 tablespoons boiling water

FOR THE VANILLA GLAZE

3½ cups sifted confectioners' sugar, or more as needed

3 generous tablespoons light corn syrup, or more if needed

1 teaspoon pure vanilla extract

4 tablespoons milk, or more as needed

USE A WHISK to combine the flour, baking soda, baking powder, and salt in a bowl, then sift this into another bowl and set aside. Using an electric mixer, cream the butter with the cream cheese and shortening until homogenous, then add the granulated sugar in a steady stream, beating constantly on a moderate speed until light. Beat in ½ cup of confectioners' sugar and, when well mixed, add the eggs one at a time, beating well after each addition. Add the lemon zest, juice, and vanilla and beat well. Stop the machine and, using a large rubber spatula, scrape down the sides and across the bottom of the bowl. Beat again, briefly. Stop the machine and add all of the dry ingredients. With the machine on a slow speed, stir the mixture until the flour is well mixed, but don't overwork the batter. Run the spatula underneath the batter, incorporating any unmixed fat. Cover the bowl and chill the batter for 1½ to 2 hours or up to overnight.

Position the rack on the center shelf. Preheat the oven to 350°F. (Although it's preferable to bake these cookies on the center shelf, if not working with a double oven, place the racks on the upper- and lower-third shelves.) Line several cushioned cookie sheets with parchment paper. Place the remaining 1 cup of confectioners' sugar on a plate and place it next to your work surface, along with a large triggered ice cream scoop with a liquid capacity of a generous ⅓ cup or a ⅓-cup measuring cup.

SHAPING ONE COOKIE at a time, use the ice cream scoop to retrieve a level portion of the chilled batter and release it into your nonworking hand that's been dusted with confectioners' sugar. Use your index finger to release any clinging batter from inside the scoop and add this to the batter in your hand. Coat your working hand in sugar and gently shape the batter into a ball (the mixture will feel very soft and light). If at any time the dough starts to stick to your hands, dust your hands lightly with more sugar. Place the ball on a prepared cookie sheet. Repeat with the rest of the dough, placing four balls on each sheet. Use your hand to gently flatten the balls evenly, then correct the circular shape as needed.

Bake the cookies in batches for 18 to 21 minutes. If baking two sheets in one oven, switch the shelf positions after half the baking time. When done, the cookies will have widened substantially, and the outer rims will be light golden and the middles will be quite light, but firm. Place the baking sheets on wire racks and let them sit there for 5 minutes before using a thin metal spatula to transfer the cookies to wire racks to cool further. While the cookies bake, keep the remaining batter in the refrigerator. And before applying more parchment and batter to the sheets, run them under cold water to cool them completely, then dry them well. (Alternatively, to make these cookies smaller, use a slightly smaller ice cream scoop with a liquid capacity of ¼ cup. Bake these for between 14 and 17 minutes. This will yield about six more cookies.)

MAKE THE GLAZES. Place 3½ cups of confectioners' sugar in a glass mixing bowl. Melt the chopped chocolate either in the top of a double boiler over barely simmering water, stirring constantly, or in the microwave on high for about 1 minute, stirring after heating until perfectly smooth. Stir the chocolate into the confectioners' sugar along with the light corn syrup, vegetable oil, and vanilla. Stir in 5 tablespoons boiling water. If too thick to spread, add more boiling water, 1 tablespoon at a time. If it ever becomes too thin, stir in some more confectioners' sugar. When right, the mixture should be dark and thick but pourable and very smooth and shiny. Set this aside. Place 3½ cups of confectioners' sugar in a glass mixing bowl and add the corn syrup, vanilla, and milk. Mix until perfectly smooth. If too fluid, add more confectioners' sugar or, if too dry, add a more few drops of milk. When right, the mixture should be bright white, quite thick, and very smooth and shiny. Set it aside.

Tear off two long sheets of waxed paper and lay them, slightly overlapping, on your counter. Place the racks holding the cookies over the paper. Lay another sheet of waxed paper alongside and place the bowls of glaze on the paper next to the cookies. Stick a short metal icing spatula or a regular table knife into each bowl of glaze. Lift one cookie off the rack and hold it over the bowl of chocolate glaze in your nonworking hand. Use the spatula to spread the glaze generously and evenly over only half of the cooled cookie, allowing any excess glaze to fall back into the bowl. Use the spatula to scrape off any glaze from the bottom edge of the cookie. Place the cookie back in its original spot on the rack. Continue this with the remaining cookies until all of them have been half-covered in chocolate.

Repeat this procedure with the white glaze, meeting the chocolate flush in the center. When finished, each cookie should be lavishly coated with the two glazes. Let the cookies sit on their racks, uncovered, until the glaze is completely set (it will feel firm and no longer sticky), which can take a few hours, even on a dry day. When set, the cookies can be wrapped individually in plastic wrap and kept at room temperature. These cookies will stay perfectly tender and very moist for several days.

PEANUT BUTTER AND JAM HEARTS

These fantastic sandwich cookies merge a melt-in-your mouth texture with the most classic American flavor combination of all, making them a real family favorite. The flip side, however, is that these sandwich cookies are delicate and won't transport well. It's also wise to make a few extra cookies "with holes" since these are the most fragile. For best results, allow the baked cookies to cool for the full amount of time specified and use a very thin metal spatula to remove them to a wire rack. You should know that these cookies are also great on their own, without any filling, and can also be cut into other shapes and sizes.

❧ YIELD: 22 TO 26 2½-INCH SANDWICH COOKIES

1¼ cups (2½ sticks) softened unsalted butter,
    4 tablespoons melted
1¾ cups granulated sugar
1 cup store-bought peanut butter (smooth or chunky)

2½ cups unbleached all-purpose flour
12 ounces seedless raspberry jam
½ to 1 cup confectioners' sugar

POSITION THE OVEN RACKS in the upper- and lower-third shelves and preheat the oven to 375°F. Use some of the melted butter to generously grease two cushioned cookie sheets. Reserve any remaining melted butter. Pour ¾ cup granulated sugar on a doubled paper towel that sits on your counter. Use some of the reserved melted butter to generously grease the bottom of the outside of a wide drinking glass, and plant the buttered surface directly in the sugar, pressing down, and leave it in the sugar until needed. Put four wire cooling racks on your counter and place two long overlapping sheets of waxed paper under two of the racks (these will be for the tops of the cookies).

Use an electric mixer with a paddle attachment, or a handheld mixer, to cream the 1 cup softened butter with the remaining 1 cup of sugar until light and creamy. Add the peanut butter and combine well. Turn off the machine and add the flour. With the machine on the lowest setting, mix the dough until fully combined, without overworking it. Form walnut-size balls of dough and place them 1½ inches apart on the prepared cookie sheets. (You should be able to bake 9 to 12 cookies on each sheet, if using a 2½-inch cookie cutter.) Lift the buttered and sugared glass and press down on each ball of dough, flattening it to ¼ inch thick. After flattening each portion of dough, rub the greased glass in the sugar before flattening the next. (If the sugared surface gets clumpy, wipe it off and reapply some melted butter and sugar.) Use a clean pastry brush to gently remove any excess sugar from the tops of the flattened cookie dough.

USE A 2½-INCH HEART-SHAPED cookie cutter to cut out hearts from the flattened dough. Before removing the cutter, use your finger to remove the excess cookie dough, and place these scraps back in the original bowl. Insert a small cutter or a thimble into half (or a few more) of the shaped cookies and rotate the cutter in a circular motion to widen the hole slightly. Lift out the cutter and, using the pointed tip of a short paring knife, pick the dough out of the hole. Put these pieces of dough back into the bowl with the other scraps.

TIMING IS
EVERYTHING

The cookie dough may be made one day ahead and kept refrigerated, covered. The dough can be used chilled, but expect to lengthen the overall baking time accordingly.

When the cookie sheets are full, transfer them to both levels of the oven and bake for 6 to 9 minutes, switching their positions after half the baking time. Check after 6 minutes. When done, the cookies will be slightly more golden around the edges but the tops should be only a light golden color. Remove the sheets from the oven and place the sheets with cookies with holes on the wire racks set over waxed paper. Place the sheets with uncut cookies on the two other racks and let them all cool for 10 minutes. Using a very thin metal turning spatula, carefully transfer the cookies to their wire racks to cool further. (Wipe off the spatula after removing each cookie from the sheet.) Cool, clean, and grease the cookie sheets and repeat the above procedure until all of the cookie dough has been used.

These sandwich cookies can be fully assembled one day ahead and stored at room temperature, as instructed.

ONCE COMPLETELY COOL, assemble the sandwiches. First, generously sift the confectioners' sugar over the cookies with holes. Lift and turn a hole-free cookie flat side up, and spoon a generous teaspoon of jam in the center. Carefully lift a top "sugared" cookie and (gently now) lay it, sugared side up, on top of the jam, applying only the slightest bit of wiggling pressure so the jam plumps up through the hole. Place the assembled sandwich cookie back on its rack while you continue to assemble the rest.

If serving soon, use a thin metal spatula to transfer the cookies to a decorative serving platter. If serving later in the day of baking, or the next day, carefully transfer the cookies to a deep rectangular container (like a large roasting pan) to protect their appearance. Cover the pan securely with aluminum foil and leave it at room temperature.

Chocolate-Filled Hearts

Melt 12 ounces of semisweet or milk chocolate in either the top of a double boiler over barely simmering water, stirring constantly, or in a microwave (uncovered) for 1 minute on high power, stirring after heating until smooth. Apply the chocolate as you would jam to the flat side of a cookie and sandwich them as directed.

CHUBBY FIG NEWTONS

I've always found it such fun to create homemade versions of American classic foods that are usually store-bought. These pudgy, fig-filled cookies illustrate perfectly how it's possible to magnify the voluptuous, enticing quality of a favorite supermarket food, thus making a good thing even better. For the most tender results, use bleached all-purpose flour in this pastry. And do take advantage of the timing strategy given on the opposite page. ❧ YIELD: ABOUT 35 COOKIES

2 cups plus 2 tablespoons bleached all-purpose flour, plus more for dusting
1 teaspoon baking powder
¼ teaspoon baking soda
½ teaspoon cinnamon
½ teaspoon salt
4 tablespoons (½ stick) unsalted butter, at room temperature

4 ounces cream cheese (½ of an 8-ounce block), at room temperature
¾ cup packed light brown sugar
2 extra-large eggs, at room temperature
1½ teaspoons pure vanilla extract
1 recipe Fig Butter (page 288), completely chilled
Confectioners' sugar for dusting

USE A WHISK TO COMBINE the flour, baking powder, baking soda, cinnamon, and salt. Sift this into another bowl. Using an electric mixer fitted with the paddle attachment, or a handheld mixer, cream together the butter and cream cheese and, when homogenous, beat in the brown sugar until thoroughly combined and light. Add the eggs one at a time, beating well after each addition. Add the vanilla and, when combined, use a large rubber spatula to scrape down the sides and up from the bottom of the bowl, releasing any clinging mixture. Beat briefly, then turn off the machine and add the entire dry mixture. Starting on low and proceeding to a moderate speed, mix until just combined. Use the spatula to scrape down and underneath the dough to incorporate any wet pockets. At this point, the mixture will be very soft and pasty, but the batter should be uniform in consistency.

Lay two large, slightly overlapping sheets of plastic wrap on your counter and sprinkle the plastic lightly but evenly with flour. Scrape the pastry batter directly onto the floured plastic and sprinkle the top of the batter lightly, but evenly, with more flour. Lay two more overlapping sheets of plastic on top of the batter and, using your hand, pat it down gently.

Use a straight rolling pin to gently roll the mixture into a 10 × 13-inch rectangle that's about ¼ inch thick. Transfer the sheet of pastry to a large shallow baking sheet and place it in the freezer for at least 4 hours, and up to one week, before using. (If storing for more than 24 hours, further protect the pastry by covering it with another sheet of plastic.)

WHEN READY TO BAKE, position the rack on the center shelf of the oven and preheat to 350°F. (Although it's preferable to bake these cookies on the center shelf, if not working with a double oven, place the racks on the upper- and lower-third shelves.) Line two cushioned cookie sheets with parchment paper and place them next to your work surface. Tear off four sheets of waxed paper and stack them next to your work surface. Lay a pastry cloth on your work surface and rub it heavily and evenly with flour. (The surface should be white with flour, and spread smoothly over the cloth). Remove the Fig Butter from the refrigerator. Place a small bowl of confectioners' sugar next to your work surface. You'll also need a soft pastry brush and a straight rolling pin.

Remove the pastry from the freezer and slide it off the baking sheet (still wrapped in plastic). Turn the pastry so it sits horizontally in front of you. Lift off the top sheet of plastic only, and use the blade of a sharp knife to divide the pastry into four sections (cut from top to bottom, not side to side). Carefully lift one section of dough off the plastic and place it on the prepared pastry cloth. (If, when attempting to lift the pastry, it seems in danger of breaking, lift and invert the pastry onto the cloth.) Cover the remaining pastry with plastic wrap and freeze it for now. Sprinkle the top of the pastry strip evenly with some flour and place a piece of waxed paper on top. Roll the pastry out to widen it to about 5 inches in width, then lengthen it slightly to about 14 inches long. Optimally, the pastry should be about ⅛ inch thick all over.

POSITION THE PASTRY horizontally in front of you and carefully peel off the waxed paper. Brush off any exposed flour, using a soft pastry brush. Scoop out 1 generous cup of the chilled fig filling and, while holding the filling in your hands, elongate it into a log shape (if necessary, sprinkle your hands with a lit- tle confectioners' sugar to prevent the filling from sticking). Lay the filling in a straight line across the pastry, placed one-third of the way up from the long edge closest to you, and pat the filling down slightly to "square" it a bit. Lift the bottom edge of the pastry cloth and drape the bottom third of the pastry over the top of the filling. Brush off any excess flour from the pastry, then con- tinue to lift the cloth, forcing the pastry to roll over the filling, enclosing it com- pletely. Pat down the top of the roll to flatten it slightly, and use your hands to straighten the sides. Carefully lift and transfer the filled roll to a prepared cookie sheet. Correct the shape, which should be long, low, and rectangular. Cover the pastry with plastic wrap and refrigerate it while you shape another strip. (You'll bake two logs on each sheet.)

Before placing another sheet of frozen pastry on your cloth, rub in more flour and use a new piece of waxed paper to cover the dough when thinning it. Continue to roll and fill the remaining strips of pastry until all are placed on the baking sheets, chilling the filled logs as you go.

TIMING IS
EVERYTHING
🌢 The filling can be made up to two weeks ahead and stored in the refriger- ator, securely covered.
🌢 The pastry can be assembled and stored in the freezer for up to one week before using.
🌢 The unbaked cookies can be assembled one day ahead of baking and stored in the refrigerator, covered with plastic wrap.

UNCOVER THE BAKING SHEETS and bake until the pastry is light golden, 24 to 27 minutes. If baking both sheets in one oven, switch the shelf positions half-way through baking. Meanwhile, place two wire cooling racks on your counter. When done, remove the sheets from the oven and, using two long, wide metal spatulas, carefully transfer the logs to wire racks to cool thoroughly.

When cool, place a baked log on a cutting board and, using a sharp serrated knife, trim off any dark irregular ends. Cut the log into 1½-inch squares. (To make uniform squares, cut off one square, then place it on top of the log, beginning at the cut end. Continue cutting, using the first square as your model, until you reach the end. If planning to store (or give) these cookies "stacked," always place the last square cut on top of the remaining log before cutting the next cookie. Line each cookie up on the rack as they are cut.

Place the cooled cookies in a single layer on a serving tray and, if desired, sift some confectioners' sugar over the top just before serving. Store extras in an airtight tin, separated by sheets of waxed paper.

FIG BUTTER

☙ YIELD: 3½ TO 4 CUPS

4½ generous cups dried whole Calimyrna figs (2¼ pounds), stems removed
2 cups water
2 cups orange juice
2 teaspoons pure vanilla extract
1 cup sugar
2 teaspoons minced lemon zest
⅓ teaspoon salt
¾ cup finely ground toasted macadamia nuts (see page 271)

PLACE THE FIGS in a 3-quart heavy-bottomed nonreactive saucepan along with the water and orange juice. Bring the liquid to a brisk bubble, then reduce the heat to low and simmer the figs with the cover ajar until tender, about 20 minutes, stirring occasionally to prevent scorching on the bottom. Drain the figs in a large sieve that's positioned over another bowl to catch the poaching liquid. Place the fruit in the bowl of a food processor fitted with the steel blade, and add 4 tablespoons of the poaching liquid, discarding the rest. Add the vanilla, sugar, lemon zest, and salt and, after pulsing to chop everything into small pieces, turn the machine on until processed fairly smooth. Add the ground nuts and process again until incorporated. Use a rubber spatula to transfer the fig butter to a bowl, and let it cool before storing it in the refrigerator in a well-sealed tub.

Perfect Tender
VANILLA-SCENTED CUPCAKES
or Layer Cakes, with an Italian Meringue Icing

If you're trying to decide on a great dessert for a mixed group of kids and adults, you're in luck! This recipe makes the most wonderful cupcakes and layer cakes. These cupcakes (or cake layers), topped with big swoops of fluffy Italian meringue, taste and feel like you're sinking your teeth into a mound of melted marshmallows. I usually either torch the tips of the meringue or coat an entire iced cake or the tops of cupcakes with shredded coconut. Please read the instructions for making the meringue from beginning to end before getting started. Alternatively, for a vanilla birthday cake or for a batch of cupcakes to tote to school for a child's birthday, try the buttery, sweet, and smooth-as-silk vanilla frosting on page 298. My children really love that, too.

❧ YIELD: 28 CUPCAKES OR TWO 9-INCH CAKE LAYERS

Flavorless vegetable spray or melted unsalted butter
   for brushing cake pans
About 2 tablespoons cake flour for dusting

FOR THE CAKE BATTER
½ teaspoon baking powder
3¼ cups Buttermillk Pancake and Cake Mix
   (page 39) or see the end of this recipe
¾ cup (1½ sticks) unsalted butter, at room
   temperature
¼ cup solid vegetable shortening
1¾ cups granulated sugar
4 extra-large eggs, made tepid by submerging in a
   bowl of very hot tap water for 10 minutes
1½ teaspoons pure vanilla extract
1¼ cups milk, at room temperature or slightly warmed

FOR THE MERINGUE ICING
3 extra-large egg whites, at room temperature
1⅓ cups superfine sugar
⅓ cup water
2 tablespoons light corn syrup
¼ teaspoon cream of tartar
Pinch of salt
1½ teaspoons pure vanilla extract
1 to 2 cups mixed plain and toasted shredded
   sweetened coconut (optional)
Alternative frostings or icings: Silky White Butter
   Frosting (page 298) or chocolate variation (page
   299) and/or chocolate and vanilla glazes (see
   page 281)

IF MAKING CUPCAKES, spray the tops of two nonstick 12-muffin tins and one 6-muffin tin with vegetable spray and line them with paper liners. If making cake layers, brush the interiors of two 9-inch cake pans (2 inches deep) with melted butter and line both bottoms with a round of parchment paper. Grease the paper and dust the bottom and sides with cake flour, tilting to coat the pans evenly, then shake out any excess flour by rapping the pans hard against the sink hard several times. Preheat the oven to 350°F. If using a double oven, keep the oven racks on the center shelf. If using one oven, arrange the oven racks on the upper- and lower-third shelf positions to accommodate all three cupcake tins. Both cake pans should be able to fit on the center rack. (Best results are achieved when cupcakes and cake layers are baked undisturbed in the center of the oven.)

In a medium bowl, whisk the baking powder into the preassembled cake mix and set aside. Use your electric mixer with the paddle attachment or a handheld mixer to cream the butter and shortening with the sugar until light. Add the tepid eggs one at a time, beating well after each addition. When very light, beat in the vanilla. Stop the machine and, using a large rubber spatula, scrape down the sides and across the bottom of the bowl, then beat the mixture once more, briefly. With the mixer on low, add the cake mix, alternating with the milk, beginning and ending with the mix. Mix on low until combined very well, 30 to 40 seconds.

For cupcakes, use a medium-size ice cream scoop or a large spoon to place the batter in the prepared muffin cups, filling them no more than two-thirds full (if you have a few unused cups, fill those half full with very hot tap water). If making cake layers, divide the batter between the prepared cake pans and, using a small icing spatula, smooth the tops. Bake the cupcakes for 20 minutes (if not baked on the center shelf, switch their positions halfway through baking). Bake the cake layers until the top is golden and a tester comes out clean, 30 to 35 minutes. The cake layers will begin to pull away from the sides of the pan and will feel springy at the center when done. Don't worry if the tops look a bit irregular, since they will be used flat bottoms up.

Remove the pans from the oven and, for cupcakes, let them sit in the tins for 5 minutes, then carefully lift each one out and let them cool on wire racks before applying any topping. For cake layers, remove them from the oven and let them sit on a wire rack for 5 minutes, then invert them onto wire racks. Let the cake layers cool completely, keeping them bottoms up, before dividing them and applying your filling and any frosting.

MAKE THE MERINGUE ICING. Place the egg whites in a perfectly clean, dry, nonreactive bowl of an electric mixer. Place the bowl in a skillet with 1 to 1½ inches of hot, not simmering, water over low heat and whisk constantly as the whites become warm to the touch. This will happen almost immediately, if initially at room temperature (be careful not to overheat). Remove the bowl from the skillet and attach it to the electric mixer with the whip attachment.

In a small heavy-bottomed saucepan (preferably one with a spout), combine 1 cup of superfine sugar, the water, and the corn syrup. Stir just to help the sugar dissolve and place the pan over medium heat. Let the mixture come to a full boil, then clip a candy thermometer to the side of the pan without letting the mercury tip touch the bottom of the pan. Continue to boil until the tem-

perature reaches between 238° and 240°F. To test for this, if not using a candy thermometer, place a small bowl of ice water and a teaspoon next to the stove. As the sugar mixture boils, check the consistency every minute by dropping a few drops of the boiling syrup into the ice water. When the syrup forms a mass that is soft and pliable but does not quite hold its shape after being rolled into a ball, the mixture is ready. (This temperature range marks the end of the soft-ball stage and the beginning of the firm-ball stage.) Always remove the syrup from the hot burner as you check to avoid overcooking.

While the sugar mixture is boiling, set the speed of your mixer to moderate and whip the warmed egg whites until frothy and beginning to turn white. Add the cream of tartar and the salt, and increase the speed to medium-high. Slowly add the remaining ⅓ cup sugar while continuing to beat the whites until they thicken substantially and hold soft peaks. When the sugar syrup has reached the correct temperature, carefully pour it down the side of the bowl into the whites, while whipping them constantly. (Take care not to pour directly into the beaters or the syrup will splatter onto the sides of the bowl and immediately harden into candy.) After all the syrup has been incorporated, add the vanilla, then raise the speed to the highest setting and continue to beat the mixture until very thick and the bottom of the bowl is cool. By this time the whites will be very shiny, firm, and spreadable, with the consistency of melted marshmallows. Turn off the machine and remove the bowl.

To DRESS THE CUPCAKES, use a small metal icing spatula or a table knife to apply some of the meringue to the tops of the cooled cupcakes, covering them completely. Apply another dollop of meringue on top and use the tip of the spatula to make swirls or swooping peaks. Either run the flame of a small, handheld blowtorch over the protruding tips of the meringue until caramelized or top the meringue with a generous amount of mixed plain and toasted shredded sweetened coconut. Alternatively, if using either variation of the butter frosting or the glazes, decorate the tops with any of the suggested toppings from "Here's the Scoop" on page 293. Let these cupcakes remain at room temperature, covered either with a cake cover or, once the icing is set, with plastic wrap.

To cut, fill, and stack the cake layers, place each layer (on a cake disk) bottom up on a rotating cake stand and slice the layer in half horizontally using a long sharp serrated knife. After dividing the first, keep the halves together and just move the whole layer to the side. After dividing the second layer, insert a cake disk between the two halves and lift off the top piece. Working with the bottom of one cake layer, cut side up, on the cake stand, spread an even layer of the meringue icing on top using a long icing spatula or a table knife. Don't go overboard, or the layers will slip and slide off each other once stacked. Place the top of that cake layer on top of the icing and press down gently. Spread the top of that layer with more meringue. Place the bottom of the second cake layer on top of the stacked cake layers. Apply more icing, then place the last top layer, which should be the flat, golden bottom of that layer, on top. Use your hand or a cake disk to lightly press down on the top to help the layers adhere and to level the stack. Coat the outside of the assembled cake evenly. If you'd like to pipe on a top and bottom border, see the Silky White Butter Frosting recipe on page 298.

Store the assembled cake or cupcakes on a platter at a comfortable room temperature, covered with a wide, high cake cover, before serving. If using a buttercream frosting, refrigerate leftovers and bring to room temperature before serving.

If you don't have the preassembled cake mix: Whisk together 3¼ cups of cake flour, ¾ teaspoon fine salt, and 1 tablespoon baking powder and sift this into another bowl. Increase the sugar to 2 cups. Expect the top of this cake to not be quite as evenly colored at the one made from the assembled mix (but the tops will become the bottoms, anyway). Bake the cake or cupcakes as previously described.

TIMING IS
EVERYTHING
❧ *The cake layers or cupcakes can be made a day ahead and kept at room temperature, well wrapped in plastic wrap.*
❧ *The cake or cupcakes can be fully assembled early on the day of entertaining and kept out at a comfortable room temperature until ready to serve.*
❧ *Although the meringue icing should be used the day it's made, the vanilla frosting can be fully assembled and refrigerated for up to three days before using it. Bring it to room temperature, then whip it until it's fluffy and of a good spreading consistency.*

HERE'S THE SCOOP:
Kid- and Adult-Friendly Cake Decorating Ideas

❧ Edible flowers: use only unsprayed, organically grown flowers that are known to be safe for human consumption. Eat only the petals of these flowers and, if you suffer from allergies, hay fever, or asthma, avoid them. To order by mail, see the source list on page 313.

❧ Finely ground chocolate wafers, vanilla shortbread cookies, or toasted nuts: after applying a frosting or glaze, sprinkle the tops generously.

❧ Grind one or two cupcakes in the food processor. Sprinkle them on top of frosted cupcakes or the sides of a frosted cake.

❧ Coconut (shredded and sweetened): use toasted or untoasted sweetened coconut alone, or combine both to give a two-toned look to your garnish. To toast, place it in a single layer on a shallow, heavy-aluminum (not dark) baking sheet and bake it in a 300°F. oven for 10 to 20 minutes, stirring occasionally to redistribute. When done, the shreds should be uniformly golden but not at all scorched.

❧ Whole baby Oreo cookies or tiny chocolate chip cookies.

❧ Assorted sprinkles and candies: Jordan almonds (pastels, silver, gold), nonpareils, Necco wafers, M&M's, gummy worms, gumdrops, jelly beans, chocolate kisses, malted milk balls, Junior Mints, chocolate-covered espresso beans, and so on.

DEVIL'S FOOD CUPCAKES
(or Cake Layers)

Once again, my Buttermilk Pancake and Cake Mix on page 39 proves to be the hero. Whether the cocoa-laced batter is baked into two dark cake layers or lots of tender cupcakes, you won't be disappointed. If you ever run out of batter when making cupcakes, just fill the empty cups half-full with very hot tap water and they'll bake just fine. ❧ YIELD: 18 TO 24 CUPCAKES OR TWO 9-INCH LAYERS

About 2 tablespoons unsalted butter, melted, or flavorless vegetable spray

2 tablespoons plain cake flour to dust the pans

2½ cups Buttermilk Pancake and Cake Mix (page 39) or see the end of this recipe

½ cup nonalkalized (not Dutch-processed) unsweetened cocoa powder, sifted before measuring (see page 295)

1 teaspoon baking soda

6 tablespoons unsalted butter, at room temperature

¼ cup solid vegetable shortening

1½ cups granulated sugar

2 extra-large eggs, made tepid by submerging in a bowl of very hot tap water for 10 minutes

1½ teaspoons pure vanilla extract

1¼ cups buttermilk for cupcakes, 1½ cups for cake layers

1½ cups semisweet mini chocolate chips, chopped a bit smaller in a food processor (optional and only for cupcakes)

IF MAKING CAKE LAYERS, brush two 9-inch cake pans (1½ inches deep) generously with melted butter and line each with a round of parchment. Grease the paper, then dust the pans with flour, tilting to coat the interior evenly. Shake out the excess flour by rapping the pans hard on the side of the sink.

For cupcakes, spray the tops of two 12-cup muffin tins (or one 12-cup and one 6-cup tin) with vegetable spray and line the cups with paper liners. (The number of cups needed will depend on whether or not you're using the optional chocolate chips. Also, if you're not using the prepared pancake mix, and instead you're using the dry mixture offered at the end of this recipe, you'll get 24 cupcakes.) If using one oven and making cupcakes, position the racks in the upper and lower positions. If making two cake layers, try to fit them on the center shelf together. If working with a double oven, it's also best to bake the cupcake tins separately in the center of the oven. Either way, preheat the oven(s) to 350°F.

Whisk the pancake mix with the cocoa and baking soda, or assemble the dry mixture at the end of this recipe. Using an electric mixer fitted with the paddle attachment, or a handheld mixer, beat the softened butter and shortening with the sugar, eggs, and vanilla (all at once) until light. Stop the machine and, using a sturdy rubber spatula, scrape up the butter mixture from the bottom of the bowl and beat again briefly. Turn off the machine and, all at once, add the dry mixture and 1½ cups buttermilk for cake layers (or 1¼ cups for cupcakes), and beat on low for 1 full minute to incorporate well. Stop the machine and scrape down the sides of the bowl, then beat on a moderately high speed (setting #6 on a KitchenAid) for 2½ to 3 minutes, until very light and fluffy.

IF MAKING CUPCAKES, fold in the mini chocolate chips (if using) and use a medium-size ice cream scoop or a large spoon to ration the batter among the cupcake tins, filling each cup only three-fourths full (if you have a few unused cups, fill those half full with very hot water). Bake cupcakes for 20 to 22 minutes, or until a tester comes out just clean, without allowing them to become dry. If baking both cupcake tins in the same oven, switch their positions halfway through baking. Remove the tins from the oven and let them sit on a rack for 5 minutes. One by one, carefully lift each cupcake out and let stand on a rack to cool before applying a glaze or frosting to the tops.

IF BAKING CAKE LAYERS, divide the batter between your prepared cake pans and, using a small metal spreader, smooth the top. Bake the layers in the center of the oven for 30 to 35 minutes (cakes will begin to pull away from the sides of the pan and feel springy at the top center). Place two wire cooling racks, preferably nonstick and without a center pleat, on the counter. Place the cake layers, in their pans, on two additional wire racks (any kind) and let them sit for 5 minutes before inverting them, bottoms up, onto the nonstick racks. Cool the cake layers completely this way.

If you don't have the preassembled pancake mix: Whisk 2½ cups of cake flour with 2 scant teaspoons baking soda, ½ teaspoon salt, 2½ teaspoons baking powder, and ½ cup nonalkalized unsweetened cocoa powder. Sift this into another bowl. Increase the sugar to 1⅔ cups.

TIMING IS
EVERYTHING

* Always having the pancake mix on hand is a real time saver.

* The cake layers and cupcakes can be made one day ahead of applying frosting and kept at room temperature, well covered with plastic wrap. Place the cooled cake layers on two separate cake disks (keeping them bottoms up) before covering them.

HERE'S THE SCOOP:
On Choosing the Right Cocoa

Unsweetened cocoa powder is sold two ways: pure ground cocoa (simply labeled "unsweetened cocoa") and the other tagged "Dutch-processed." The latter means that the cocoa has been treated with an alkali in order to remove some of its inherent bitterness. This also changes the color from a deep, dark (almost reddish) brown, (traditional in a devil's food cake) to a softer, more subdued color. Most often, for a non-astringent flavor and for proper leavening, you'll choose the alkalized cocoa, especially when using it in a mixture that has no acid ingredients. In these cupcakes, however, since I use both buttermilk and untreated cocoa (both of which are considered acids), they need to be neutralized in order for the batter to rise properly. The use of baking soda (which is an alkali), in addition to creating the best conditions for proper leavening, takes care of the bitterness in non-treated cocoa along with any extreme tangy taste of the buttermilk, while also allowing me to keep that "devilish" color so prized in this wonderful cake.

Light and Tender . . .
YUMMY MARBLED POUND CAKE

This is my favorite pound cake. Light and tender, it has a crisp crust that's deliberately thick, created by baking it in an oven that's initially a bit hotter than usual. This creates a pound cake with an almost candied exterior, especially when fresh-baked. I add some dried buttermilk to the cake, which adds a wonderful, albeit subtle, dimension to the overall flavor. I suggest making several batches of the dry mixture in advance and storing them in separate sealed plastic bags. That way, it's really a breeze to pull this cake together. ❧ YIELD: ONE 9 × 5-INCH LOAF

1 cup (2 sticks) unsalted butter, softened, plus
   1 tablespoon melted butter for brushing
1⅔ cups plus 1 generous tablespoon whisked cake
   flour (whisk, don't sift, before measuring)
2 rounded tablespoons (one 0.8-ounce packet) dried
   buttermilk
1 teaspoon baking powder
¼ rounded teaspoon salt

4 ounces bittersweet chocolate, finely chopped
1⅓ cups granulated sugar
4 extra-large eggs, made tepid by submerging in a
   bowl of very hot tap water for 10 minutes
2 teaspoons pure vanilla extract
2 teaspoons minced lemon or orange zest (optional)
Confectioners' sugar for dusting

PREHEAT THE OVEN TO 350°F. Brush the interior of a 9 × 5-inch loaf pan with the melted butter, then sprinkle the greased surface with 1 generous tablespoon of cake flour. Tilt the pan to coat it with flour, then knock out any excess.

Whisk together the remaining 1⅔ cups of cake flour with the dried buttermilk, baking powder, and salt and sift this into another bowl. Melt the chocolate either in the top of a double boiler over barely simmering water or in a microwave on high power for 1 minute, stirring until smooth. Using an electric mixer fitted with the paddle attachment, or a handheld mixer, cream the softened butter until lightened. Add the sugar in increments, beating well after each addition. In a 2-cup liquid measuring cup (or other vessel with a spout), beat the eggs with the vanilla and zest, if using. Drizzle the eggs into the creamed butter mixture a little at a time, allowing each addition to be fully incorporated before adding the next. When done, the mixture should be very light. Stop the machine and, using a large rubber spatula, scrape the butter down from the sides and up from the bottom. Beat briefly. Stop the machine and add a heaping ½ cup of the flour mixture. Turn the machine to low, then up to medium and mix until the flour is almost totally incorporated. Continue to stop the machine, add another scoop of the flour mixture, and beat again until almost combined. After adding all the dry ingredients, beat the batter, still on medium speed, for 30 to 40 seconds, or until very smooth and silky look-

TIMING IS
EVERYMORE

*If you love pound cake
(and who doesn't?), why
not keep several sealed
bags of the dry mixture in
your pantry? That way
it's much quicker to get
this cake into the oven.*

ing. Scrape half the batter into another bowl and add the melted chocolate to the first bowl, folding it in until homogenous.

Pour and spread half of the plain cake batter into the prepared loaf pan, then do the same with half of the chocolate batter. Repeat this with the plain batter and then the rest of the chocolate batter, creating four layers in all. Beginning at one end of the loaf, drag a plain table knife through the batter, going up and down in a soft sweeping swirling motion, making loops at the top and then at the bottom while traveling to the opposite end of the loaf pan. (Don't overdo this, however, or you'll actually lose your marbled design.) When done, pull the knife blade straight up and out of the batter, and gently smooth the top using a short metal spreader. Place the pan in the center of the oven and reduce the temperature to 325°F. Bake for 1 hour and 10 minutes, or until a tester comes out clean and the cake is golden. Place the pan on a wire rack and carefully run a knife around the sides of the pan. Turn the cake out of the pan and let it cool on the rack. Just before serving, dust the top with confectioners' sugar, if desired, and cut into thick slices.

Plain Pound Cake

Prepare the batter as directed, omitting the chocolate. Add the entire batter to the prepared pan and smooth the top. Bake for 65 minutes (about 5 minutes less than you would a marbled pound cake). Cool and serve as previously described.

Perfect for a Birthday Cake
SILKY WHITE BUTTER FROSTING

I often use this smooth-as-silk vanilla butter frosting on cakes and cupcakes. I love to spread it inside and out of my kids' birthday cakes. When making cupcakes, I make a batch of both the vanilla and chocolate variation and split the batch between them. Actually, when I'm feeling playful, I'll make a double batch of vanilla frosting and divide it into four or more bowls. Then, I use a craft stick to stir a drop or two of a different pastel food coloring into the bowls, leaving one portion white. This recipe purposely provides plenty of frosting so you'll have enough to be really generous with cupcakes or to accommodate two cake layers (after dividing each one horizontally), and also pipe on a decorative border on both the top and bottom of the assembled cake after frosting the outside. Although the listed meringue powder is optional, I do like the way it flavors and helps to stabilize the frosting.

2 cups (4 sticks) unsalted butter, at room temperature
1 tablespoon pure vanilla extract
½ teaspoon salt
4 cups sifted confectioners' sugar
2 rounded tablespoons meringue powder (available in The Baker's Catalogue, page 313; optional)

Up to 3 tablespoons milk
Pastel food coloring (optional)
Assorted candy decorations: see page 293 for some fun and colorful suggestions

TIMING IS
EVERYTHING

🍃 *Either variation of the butter frosting can be made three days ahead and kept in the refrigerator, well covered. Let it come close to room temperature before rewhipping it until spreadable.*

USE AN ELECTRIC MIXER to beat the softened butter with the vanilla and salt. When the butter is light, add the confectioners' sugar in ⅓-cup increments, stopping the machine before adding more and beating well after each addition. Beat in the meringue powder, if using, then add 2 tablespoons of milk and beat the frosting until it's very light. If not fluffy enough, beat in another tablespoon of milk. Be patient—this could take 3 to 5 minutes with a heavy-duty mixer. If planning to tint the entire frosting with a color, add two to three drops of a pretty pastel color when adding the milk. If planning to make a variety of colored frostings for cupcakes, divide the frosting among several small bowls and stir 1 or 2 drops of pastel food color into each one.

To frost a cake, divide, fill, and stack the layers according to the directions on page 293. Keeping the assembled cake on a rotating cake stand, use a long metal icing spatula or a table knife to apply a thin but even layer of frosting to the sides of the cake, beginning on the bottom and using an upward motion. Run the blade around the sides to smooth them. Apply a thin but even layer of frosting to the top, smoothing it out. Allow the cake to sit uncovered for several minutes to allow the first layer to set. Apply a more generous amount of frosting to the sides, using the same upward motion, then place a large dollop of frosting on the top of the cake and either use the tip of the spatula to make dips and swirls, so the cake is covered with lovely soft peaks, or (when making a birthday cake) smooth the frosting completely so you can apply your decorations and written message. To get the smoothest finish on the top of a frosted cake, once the top is coated evenly, run the clean blade of your spatula over the top just once, then clean off the blade (scrape it onto the side of the bowl containing the frosting) and smooth the top again and again, cleaning the blade after each stroke. (Try not to get obsessive, though. After all, this is a homemade cake).

To PIPE FROSTING onto the cake, insert a star tip into a pastry bag and place the bag in a tall drinking glass. Spoon some of the remaining frosting into the bag, filling the bag only three-fourths full. Use your working hand to twist the bag at the top, then cradle the tip end in your nonworking hand. Apply pressure at the top of the bag while directing the tip over the spot where you want to apply the frosting. Always keep the area being piped directly in front of you and keep the tip 1/4 inch up from the surface of the cake. Pipe a border of frosting around the top and bottom of the cake, then, if desired, decorate the inside of the top and bottom border with your favorite colorful candies.

Chocolate Butter Frosting

Follow the recipe for the vanilla frosting, with the following exceptions: After beating in the meringue powder, beat in 4 ounces each chopped and melted unsweetened and bittersweet chocolate. Omit the milk and, of course, the food coloring. This frosting is a light chocolate brown (similar to mocha), preferred by adults and children who find dark chocolate frosting too rich. This will make enough to frost and fill a 9-inch four-layer cake or 28 cupcakes.

Amaretto-laced Bittersweet
CHOCOLATE AND
TOASTED ALMOND PIE

Regardless of the occasion, before I plan a menu for entertaining, I always phone my guests to ask several questions. "What do you love? What do you hate? And, What won't you eat, either due to an allergy or because of religious reasons?" One year, I learned that one of my Thanksgiving guests was highly allergic to pecans, but he loved chocolate and could eat other nuts. To further complicate things, several others expressed their longing for the rich, nutty flavor and oozing texture of pecan pie. Thus, the creation of this decadent dessert. Who says you can't make everybody happy? ❧ YIELD: ONE 10-INCH PIE

1 recipe Pâte Brisée (page 50), or Toasted Almond
    Pâte Brisée (see page 302)

FOR THE FILLING
4 ounces bittersweet chocolate, chopped
3 tablespoons unsalted butter, melted
1¼ cups dark corn syrup
¾ cup sugar
4 extra-large eggs, at room temperature
1½ teaspoons pure vanilla extract
½ scant teaspoon pure almond extract
3 tablespoons Amaretto liqueur

Pinch of salt
3 cups thinly sliced almonds, deeply toasted
    (see page 271)

FOR THE WHIPPED CREAM
2 cups heavy cream, very well chilled
3 tablespoons sugar
1½ tablespoons dark crème de cacao liqueur
½ teaspoon each pure vanilla and almond extracts

Shaved bittersweet chocolate for garnish

REMOVE YOUR PREPARED pâte brisée from the refrigerator. Roll out the dough to fit a 10-inch pie dish, trimming the overhang so it doesn't exceed 1 inch. Fold this overhang under itself, reinforcing the rim of pastry. Dock (prick) the dough all over with a fork and crimp the edges, making sure the rim of dough does not extend past the edge of the dish. Freeze the unbaked crust, covered with plastic wrap, for 1 hour or refrigerate overnight.

Place a large, shallow baking sheet on the center rack of the oven and preheat the oven to 400°F. Uncover the chilled pie shell and line the pastry completely with aluminum foil, shiny side down. Fill the foil to the top with dried beans (or commercially made pie weights) and place the pan on the hot baking sheet. Bake for 10 minutes (14 minutes if frozen). Carefully lift out the foil, cradling the weights, and set aside. Dock the dough once more. Reduce the oven temperature to 375°F. and continue baking the crust until it starts turning light golden, 8 to 10 minutes. Check occasionally for bubbling, and prick any swollen areas with the fork. Let the crust cool completely on a wire rack before proceeding. (Dried beans are reusable as weights, but should not be used for cooking.)

MAKE THE FILLING. Preheat the oven to 375°F. and line a large, shallow baking sheet with aluminum foil (dull side up), and place the sheet on the center rack of the oven. Melt the chocolate either in the top of a double boiler over barely simmering water or in a microwave on high power for 1 minute. Off the heat, stir the melted butter and chocolate together, then one by one whisk in the corn syrup, sugar, eggs, vanilla and almond extracts, Amaretto, and salt, mixing well after each addition. Fold in the toasted nuts, then pour the filling into the cooled pie pastry. Place the pie on the preheated baking sheet and bake for 15 minutes. Reduce the temperature to 350°F. and bake 10 minutes more. Carefully remove the pie from the oven (on its baking sheet) and, to prevent the rim of crust from becoming over-browned, pull up the aluminum foil from the sheet and drape it loosely around the rim. Continue to bake for 25 more minutes, pulling the foil away from the rim for the last 2 minutes of baking. When done, most of the filling will seem set, but the center will be slightly concave and will jiggle just a little. Transfer the pie to a wire rack and allow it to cool.

MAKE THE CREAM. Place the cold cream in the chilled bowl of an electric mixer or another low, wide bowl. Begin whipping the cream either on medium speed using the whip attachment or with a bulbous whisk. Increase the speed to medium-high and, once the cream begins to thicken, add the sugar, liqueur, and vanilla and almond extracts. Increase the whipping speed to high and continue to beat the cream until quite stiff but not broken. Chill until ready to serve.

JUST BEFORE SERVING, cut the pie into individual wedges and spoon a dollop of whipped cream on top. If desired, scatter some thin wisps of shaved chocolate on top of the cream. (To shave chocolate, run the blade of a sturdy vegetable peeler down the narrow sides of a thick bar of bittersweet chocolate.)

Toasted Almond Pâte Brisée

Assemble the dough as directed on page 50, adjusting the ingredients as follows: Reduce the amount of flour to 1½ cups and whisk in ½ cup deeply toasted and finely ground sliced almonds (see page 271). Add 3 tablespoons dark crème de cacao to the ice water. Wrap the dough and refrigerate it, shaped in a flat disk, for at least 1 hour and up to two days. (This dough, although delicious, is a bit more delicate).

TIMING IS EVERYTHING

❧ Although for best texture, the pie should be filled and baked on the day of serving, the pie crust can be prebaked the day before and kept at room temperature, carefully covered with aluminum foil.

❧ The whipped cream can be made early in the day of serving and kept chilled.

CHOCOLATE LAYER CAKE
Covered in Chocolate Ganache, Chocolate Crumbs,
and Perfect Raspberries

It's hard to believe that this cake, so incredibly light and tender, starts from the Buttermilk Pancake and Cake Mix on page 39. However, since you might not have the mix on hand, I've provided the recipe for a single batch. Since the cake layers are so tender, it's best to make them a day ahead. Doing this will make the cake sturdier and less likely to tear when you apply the frosting. By the way, don't limit the ganache frosting to this cake. You can also use it to lavishly dress "adult" cupcakes and top them, as you would this cake, with perfect raspberries and a light sprinkle of confectioners' sugar. ❧ YIELD: ONE 9-INCH 2-LAYER CAKE

Two 9-inch layers Devil's Food Cake (page 294),
    baked and cooled
10 Nabisco chocolate wafer cookies

FOR THE FROSTING
12 ounces semisweet chocolate, chopped, or
    chocolate chips
1 cup mascarpone, thick crème fraîche, or sour cream,
    close to room temperature
1 generous tablespoon light corn syrup

1½ teaspoons pure vanilla extract
1½ tablespoons Framboise liqueur (raspberry brandy)
    or raspberry-flavored syrup
2 tablespoons unsalted butter, softened

TO ASSEMBLE THE CAKE
3 tablespoons seedless raspberry jam, at room
    temperature
1½ to 2 pints firm but ripe fresh raspberries
Confectioners' sugar for sifting

ONE DAY AHEAD of assembling the cake, bake the layers according to the instructions on page 294. Cool them thoroughly, then cover them with plastic wrap (still on their cake disks) and leave them out at room temperature until ready to proceed.

Uncover each cake layer and, working with one layer at a time, place a smaller 8-inch cardboard cake disk on top. Using a pointed serrated knife, cut off the cake that extends past the disk (it will be only a scant ½ inch all the way around). Do this for the second layer, and place the cake scraps in the bowl of a food processor fitted with the steel blade. Process the scraps into fine crumbs and transfer them to a wide bowl. Grind the chocolate wafer cookies in the processor, then combine them with the cake crumbs. Keep cake layers covered.

MAKE THE FROSTING. Melt the chocolate either in the top of a double boiler over barely simmering water, stirring constantly, or in the microwave, uncovered, for about 1 minute on high power. When perfectly smooth, set the chocolate aside to become just barely warm. Using an electric mixer fitted with the paddle attachment or a handheld mixer on medium speed, beat together the melted chocolate, mascarpone, corn syrup, vanilla, and Framboise. Beat this until the mixture becomes very fluffy and much lighter in color, 3 to 5 minutes at a pretty high speed. Add the butter and continue to beat until perfectly smooth. Remove the bowl from the machine and check for consistency. (Because this cake is very tender, the frosting must be whipped until very light, or the cake can tear when being coated. If at any time the frosting becomes too stiff to spread, sit the bottom of the bowl in hot water, stir until softened, and then rewhip it briefly just to lighten the texture.)

TIMING IS
EVERYTHING

🌿 *The cake layers and the frosting can be made one day ahead. Keep the layers, well wrapped, at room temperature and refrigerate the frosting, securely covered. Let the frosting come to room temperature, then beat it using an electric mixer until light and spreadable.*

Place one cake layer on a cake stand, with a 9-inch cake disk underneath it. Using a long icing spatula or a table knife, spread a thin, even layer of frosting on top of the layer, then spread 1 generous tablespoon of jam over the frosting, swirling the two together gently. Don't go overboard, though, or the layers will slip and slide off each other when stacked. Place the second layer (flat bottom up) on top of the first. To make sure the layers sit level on one another, use your hand or a cake disk to *lightly* press down on the top just to help them adhere. Apply a thin but even layer of icing to the sides of the cake starting from the bottom, using an upward motion. (Don't worry if the exposed cake disk looks messy; this will be completely covered with crumbs later.) Spread a slightly more generous layer of frosting on top, covering the cake smoothly and completely, then swirl on any remaining jam. (Again, be careful not to tear the cake when applying the frosting.)

CAREFULLY TRANSFER the cake to your nonworking hand, holding it underneath. Position the cake over the bowl of mixed crumbs and, using your working hand, grab handfuls of the crumbs and coat the sides and top of the cake, allowing the excess crumbs to fall back into the bowl. Gently pat the crumbs into the frosting so they adhere. Give the entire cake several coats of crumbs, especially the sides, until cake is heavily coated and looks scrumptious. Cover the top of the cake entirely with fresh raspberries, tips up. (Gently push the berries down so they settle in the crumbs.)

Transfer the cake to a decorative serving platter and, if planning to serve the cake within a few hours, leave it out at a comfortable room temperature, covered with a domed cake cover. Just before serving, sift some confectioners' sugar over the berries. Cut the cake into wedges at the table and store any leftover cake in the refrigerator, bringing the cake close to room temperature before serving. (Store any leftover crumbs in the freezer in a doubled and sealed heavy-duty plastic bag and use as an impromptu topping for ice cream, mousse, etc.)

PUMPKIN CUSTARD TORTE
with a Ganache Top, Garnished with Crushed Toasted Pepita Praline and Chocolate Leaves

To put it bluntly, this dessert is drop-dead gorgeous! More important, the flavor and texture combination of the creamy pumpkin custard, bittersweet chocolate ganache topping, and cookie crumb crust is just sensational. And just to gild the lily, the top border is sprinkled with crunchy pepita praline and the top center is decorated with overlapping, lifelike chocolate leaves. The best part is that every component of the torte is completely do-ahead, making it easy to pull together this truly impressive dessert. ❧ YIELD: 10 to 12 SERVINGS

Vegetable oil spray

FOR THE COOKIE CRUST
One 9-ounce box Nabisco chocolate wafer cookies, less about 5 cookies
½ cup walnuts or pecans, finely chopped
5 tablespoons unsalted butter, melted

FOR THE PUMPKIN CUSTARD FILLING
One 8-ounce block cream cheese, at room temperature
½ cup packed light brown sugar
½ cup granulated sugar
⅓ cup maple syrup (pure or pancake syrup)
One 1-pound can of solid-pack pumpkin
1 tablespoon plus ¼ teaspoon Spice Blend (page 38), or see the end of this recipe
6 extra-large eggs, at room temperature
½ teaspoon natural maple extract (omit if unavailable)
1 teaspoon pure vanilla extract (increase to 1½ teaspoons if not using maple extract)
1½ cups heavy cream

FOR THE CHOCOLATE LEAVES
20 to 30 unsprayed lemon leaves (in a variety of sizes) from your local flower shop
16 ounces chopped chocolate (any combination of bittersweet and semisweet)
2 generous teaspoons solid vegetable shortening

FOR THE PEPITA PRALINE
1 cup hulled raw pumpkin seeds
2 teaspoons Clarified Butter (page 195), melted
¼ teaspoon salt
Flavorless vegetable oil for brushing
1½ cups granulated sugar
¼ cup water
½ teaspoon pure vanilla extract

FOR THE GANACHE TOP
8 ounces bittersweet chocolate, chopped
½ cup heavy cream
¼ teaspoon pure vanilla extract
½ teaspoon flavorless vegetable oil

LINE THE BOTTOM of a 10-inch cake pan (2 inches deep) with a round of parchment paper and spray the paper and the sides of the pan with vegetable oil spray. Preheat the oven to 350°F., with the rack in the center shelf position. Fill a tea kettle and turn it on. When the water boils, hold it at a simmer until needed.

PREPARE THE CRUST. Either finely grind the chocolate wafer cookies in the bowl of a food processor fitted with the steel blade or place the cookies in an unsealed heavy-duty plastic bag and roll over them with a rolling pin. Combine 2 cups of the cookie crumbs with the chopped nuts in a medium-sized bowl. Stir in the melted butter until the crumbs are evenly moistened. Turn the crumbs into the prepared cake pan and press them down firmly, covering the bottom evenly without extending up the sides. Refrigerate the pan.

MAKE THE FILLING. Using an electric mixer, beat the cream cheese until very smooth. Add the brown and white sugars and mix well. Add the maple syrup and, when well combined, add the pumpkin and the spice blend. When smooth, add the eggs one at a time, combining well after each addition. Add the maple and vanilla extracts along with the cream. When mixed, remove the cookie crust from the refrigerator and push the custard mixture through a medium-mesh sieve directly into the crust using a rubber spatula, leaving behind any stray bits of cream cheese in the sieve.

Fill a roasting pan with a scant 1 inch of simmering water from the kettle and transfer the pan to the oven. Carefully carry the custard-filled cake pan to the oven and place it in the roasting pan. The water should come one-half to two-thirds of the way up the sides of the cake pan, so pour in more simmering water, if needed. Bake the torte for 1 hour and check for doneness by inserting a knife into the top center. When done, the blade should come out almost clean. The custard should jiggle a little bit, since it will set further when refrigerated, but if it is very loose, bake it longer, checking after every 5-minute interval. When done, carefully lift the cake pan out of the water and place it on a wire rack to cool. Lay a doubled sheet of paper towel, pulled taut, over the torte, then cover it with aluminum foil. Refrigerate the torte for 6 hours, or up to two days.

MAKE THE CHOCOLATE LEAVES. Line a tray with waxed paper and place it in the freezer. Pick out about 20 lemon leaves in a variety of sizes, and wipe each one clean with a dampened paper towel. Use a dry paper towel to dry the leaves meticulously, and lay them on your work surface. Melt the chocolate with the shortening in the top of a double boiler, or in a bowl that sits in a larger pan of barely simmering water, stirring constantly until smooth. Be careful not to allow any water to enter the bowl of chocolate, which would cause it to quickly stiffen, a process called seizing. When smooth, remove the melted chocolate from the stove and dry the bottom of the bowl.

Working with one leaf at a time, turn it so the visibly raised veins (the underside) are facing up. Using a small paintbrush designated specifically for food purposes, carefully paint only the veined side with a generous layer of

melted chocolate. Apply a slightly thicker layer of chocolate at the stem end, which will make it easier to umold the leaves later. Use your finger to carefully wipe off the outer edges of the leaf, and lay it, chocolate side up, in the freezer on the tray. Continue with the remaining leaves and allow them to remain in the freezer for 30 minutes to 1 hour before unmolding them.

To umold, keep all the leaves in the freezer while working with one at a time. Lay a piece of paper towel on the palm of your nonworking hand. Lay the chocolate-coated leaf on the paper towel chocolate side up, and using the thumb and forefinger of your working hand, grasp the small exposed tip of the stem. Invert the leaf chocolate side down, and carefully lift and peel back the stem tip, separating the leaf from the chocolate. (The chocolate should be resting on the paper towel to keep the warmth of your hand from melting it.) Immediately place the leaf back in the freezer and continue umolding the remaining leaves. (Although you won't need all of the leaves for the torte, it's best to make extra to allow for some breakage.)

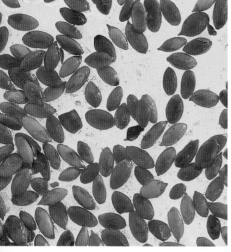

MAKE THE PRALINE. Sauté the pumpkin seeds in the clarified butter over medium heat, stirring constantly until nicely toasted, about 3 minutes. Drain the seeds on paper towels, then place them in a bowl and toss them with the salt. Brush the interior of a shallow (preferably nonstick) baking sheet well with flavorless vegetable oil and set it near the stove. Brush the blade of a long metal icing spatula or a table knife with some oil as well, and place this next to the baking sheet. Place the sugar and water in a small heavy-bottomed saucepan, preferably with a light-colored interior. Stir the mixture just to help liquefy the sugar, without getting any sugar crystals on the side of the pan. Place a small cup of boiling water next to the stove and insert a pastry brush. Bring the syrup to a boil, uncovered, over medium-high heat, and let it bubble until it turns a deep amber color. If, as the mixture bubbles, any sugar jumps to the side of the saucepan, use the wet pastry brush to wash this away. When the correct color is achieved (it should look like a well-brewed cup of regular tea), remove the pan from the heat and stir in the pepitas and the vanilla.

Immediately pour the mixture onto the prepared baking sheet and, using the oiled spatula or knife, spread the praline so it has an even thickness. Place the pan on a wire rack and let the praline cool and harden completely, about 1 hour. When cool, lift off the praline and break it into irregular pieces. Place these pieces in a doubled heavy-duty freezer bag and, using a heavy mallet or a hammer, bust up the praline into very small pieces without pulverizing it.

Alternatively, pulse the praline in a food processor fitted with the steel blade, being careful not to turn it into dust. Transfer the praline to a bowl and set it aside.

MAKE THE GANACHE. Position a medium-mesh sieve over a mixing bowl and set it aside. Place the chopped chocolate in a small bowl. Heat the cream in a small saucepan over low heat and, when it comes to a boil, remove it from the heat and pour it over the chocolate. Let it sit for 1 minute, then stir the mixture until it's very smooth. Stir in the vanilla and vegetable oil, then force the ganache through the sieve using a rubber spatula. Set it aside until just warm.

If very chilled, remove the torte from the refrigerator 10 to 20 minutes before ready to unmold. Run the blade of a sharp knife around the circumference of the pan and place the bottom of the pan on a kitchen towel that's been soaked in very hot water and wrung out. Leave it this way for 3 to 5 minutes. Place a piece of waxed paper on top of the torte and place a flat cookie sheet or a tray over the paper. Invert the pan onto the tray and lift off the cake pan. (If stubborn, reinvert and place the pan on the stove over low heat for a few seconds.) Remove and discard the parchment paper. Carefully center your serving platter on top of the exposed cookie crust and invert it so the custard is facing up. Discard the waxed paper.

If the ganache has become too stiff to pour, rewarm it briefly by placing the bowl either in a skillet of hot water or for several seconds in the microwave. Pour the ganache onto *the center* of the baked custard. Using a long, metal icing spatula, spread the ganache over the custard just shy of the edge of the torte, without letting the chocolate drip down the sides. Using either the jagged edge of a decorating comb or the tines of a fork, make decorative ridges or lines over the entire top, starting at the outer rim. As you do this, the ganache will naturally move toward the outer edge of custard. If the ganache starts to fall over the edge, use your icing spatula (or your finger) to push it back up while smoothing the sides. Decorate the top rim with a border of crushed praline, then lay several of the chocolate leaves, slightly overlapping, in the center in the shape of a flower. Place a small mound of crushed praline in the eye of the flower, then cover the torte with a domed cake cover and refrigerate it until 10 to 20 minutes before serving.

To serve, present the torte whole, then slice it into individual wedges, each accompanied by a chocolate leaf.

If you don't have the preassembled spice blend: Use 1 teaspoon each ground cinnamon, ginger, and freshly grated nutmeg. Add ¼ teaspoon ground cloves.

TIMING IS
EVERYTHING
❧ *The pumpkin custard torte can be baked up to two days ahead and, once cool, covered well and refrigerated.*
❧ *The praline can be made two weeks ahead and stored in the refrigerator in a sealed heavy-duty plastic container.*
❧ *The chocolate leaves can be made one month ahead and kept in the freezer in an airtight tin, separated by sheets of waxed paper.*
❧ *Apply the praline and leaves to the top of the torte no more than 3 hours ahead and keep it refrigerated until 10 to 20 minutes before serving. Don't keep the assembled torte in a hot kitchen, however, or the leaves can start to soften and lose their shape.*

ACKNOWLEDGMENTS

Anyone who's gone through the process of writing a cookbook will tell you that the finished product, especially a highly illustrated book such as this, is the result of a long line of talented, dedicated, hardworking people. I have been unbelievably fortunate to have been able to surround myself with the following individuals who have made this entire process a wonderful one. I'm so grateful to you all.

To Susan Ginsburg, my literary agent: Susan, although you're petite physically, there's nothing small about you. From the very beginning, you've been on my side, always showing me tremendous respect and making me feel that you truly value the philosophy behind my work—so important when being represented. Your support, faith, and friendship mean so much to me.

To Katie Workman: I'll never forget the first day we met, when I offered you a big tin of my homemade mixed-nut butter crunch candy without knowing you were deathly allergic to nuts. Thanks for inspiring me to create the delicious nut-free version that appears in this book. Thank you, too, for welcoming me so warmly into the Clarkson Potter family.

To Adina Steiman, my editor: Adina, I'm so proud to have you attached to this book. You are incredibly intelligent, articulate, clear, and focused, yet your soft-spoken style makes you truly approachable and a pleasure to work with. Your continual show of respect and appreciation of my work has made me feel totally comfortable and trusting when handing you my words. Thank you, for being you.

To Mark Ferri, Paul Grimes, Francine Matalon-Degni, and Andrea Morini, my photography team: It was my lucky day when I chose Mark Ferri (and his team) to photograph the food for this book. Mark, you and your team are all unbelievably talented and special—and not just because you take (and style) wonderful pictures. You always remained open to my visions, making the summer-long photo shoot at my home more than pleasurable. You all became family. Thank you for bringing such humanity to the photographs. I love you all.

To Marysarah Quinn, my art director: One thing I'm sure of is that this book has been designed with love. I'm so proud to be working with you, Marysarah. I knew from our first real meeting, when I felt your innate tenderness emanate, that you were the right person to put this book together. Designing a book like this, with so much text and so many photographs, is very difficult. Not only did you "get it," but your design made the text come alive with inspiration and warmth, and the photographs are arranged in such an enticing and motivating way. It's been such a joy just becoming friends, Marysarah.

To anyone and everyone who had a hand in the formation of this book, thank you all, from the depths of my heart.

SOURCE LIST

Beryl's Cake Decorating and Pastry Supplies
P.O. Box 1584
North Springfield, VA 22151
800-488-2749
www.beryls.com
This is a wonderful source for all sorts of domestic and imported baking supplies. This company, operated by a British-born baker who now lives in the United States, offers an extensive catalog for a small fee.

Bridge Kitchenware
214 East 52nd Street
New York, NY 10022
212-688-4220
www.bridgekitchenware.com
This no-frills, industrial-style New York classic carries 3-foot rolling pins for making pasta, turning slicers (for making spaghetti-like strands from vegetables), along with bakeware and cookware of all types.

Chef's Catalog
P.O. Box 620048
Dallas, TX 75262-0048
800-884-2433
www.chefscatalog.com
A terrific catalog for the serious home cook. They carry top-of-the-line small kitchen appliances, cookware, hand tools, gadgets, and other items used in the kitchen.

Culinary Parts Unlimited
80 Berry Drive
Pacheco, CA 94553
Outside California: 800-543-7549
California residents: 800-722-7239
www.culinaryparts.com
I can't count how many times I've used this terrific source for purchasing new tops, blades, rubber feet, containers, etc., for different small kitchen appliances. This company carries small replacement parts for many of the most popular manufacturers. And if they don't carry it, they're happy to help direct you to someone who does.

Culinary Parts Research Center
800-431-1001
This is a reasearch center that helps consumers to locate specific food products in their local area.

Diamond Organic
800-922-2396
www.diamondorganic.com
For unsprayed organically grown produce and edible flowers.

Indian Rock Produce
530 California Road
Quakertown, PA 18951
800-882-0512
www.IndianRockProduce.com
For unsprayed organically grown produce and edible flowers.

King Arthur Flour Company
The Baker's Catalogue
P.O. Box 876
Norwich, VT 05055-0876
800-827-6836
www.KingArthurFlour.com
A baker's dream catalog. This terrific company sells everything from specialty flours to a wide variety of seeds, salts, sugars (including nonmelting Snow White sugar), meringue powder, powdered vanilla, dried buttermilk, all kinds of bakeware, food storage containers, and handheld kitchen tools.

New York Chocolate and Baking Distributors
56 West 22nd Street
New York, NY 10010
212-675-2253
800-942-2539
Extensive assortment of equipment for all types of cake, pastry, and candy making, including decorating tools, rolling pins, cookie cutters, meringue powder, food colors, pastry clothes, decorative foil wrappers, etc. Available through mail order catalog only, with a minimum purchase.

Omega Nutrition
Bellingham, WA 98226
Vancouver, BC V5L 1P5
800-661-3529
www.omeganutrition.com
infor@omeganutrition.com
For cold-pressed organic oils and nonhydrogenated coconut butter, which can be used as a substitute for butterfat in some dairy-free recipes.

Pensky's, Ltd.
P.O. Box 924
Brookfield, WI 53008-0924
800-741-7787
This company has every spice, seed, and herb you could think of. They also sell an assortment of cocoas and plump vanilla beans.

Peoples Woods
75 Mill Street
Cumberland, RI 02846
800-729-5800
www.peopleswoods.com
A terrific source to purchase lump hardwood charcoal by mail.

Tennessee's White Lily Flour Company
P.O. Box 871
Knoxville, TN 37901
423-546-5511
www.whitelily.com
This Southern company produces a very good unleavened low-protein, all-purpose flour, which is great for quick breads.

Vermont Butter & Cheese Company
Pitman Road
P.O. Box 95
Websterville, VT 05678
800-884-6287
www.vtbutterandcheeseco.com
Although I like homemade crème fraîche, I must admit that this company produces a product that's better. The taste is mild but rich and the texture is thick and very luxurious, which makes it not only able to enrich the taste and texture of dishes but also help to boost the stability of certain mixtures because of its initial thickness.

Vermont Nut-Free Chocolates
316 Route 2
P.O. Box 124
South Hero, VT 05486
888-468-8373
www.vermontfree.com
This company specializes in nut-free chocolates. Although the web site lists only prepared candies in their catalog, when you call them directly you can order semisweet chocolate chips, unsweetened chocolate, and semisweet bars.

Williams-Sonoma
P.O Box 7456
San Francisco, CA 94120-7456
800-541-2233
www.williams-sonoma.com
A luxurious "toy store" for home cooks, this high-end retail store has a wide range of fine-quality cookware, bakeware, stemware, small kitchen appliances, hand-held gadgets, etc.

BIBLIOGRAPHY

Although I've learned so much and been inspired by many books and periodicals over the course of the past twenty-five years, the books mentioned below helped me most while completing this book.

BARNHART, ROBERT K. *The American Heritage Dictionary of Science.* Boston: Houghton Mifflin, 1986.

ETTLINGER, STEVE. *The Kitchenware Book.* New York: Macmillan, 1992.

GREEN, ALIZA. *The Bean Bible.* Philadelphia, PA: Running Press, 2000.

GREENE, JANET, RUTH HERTZBERG, AND BEATRICE VAUGHAN. *Putting Food By.* 4th ed. Lexington, MA: Stephen Greene Press, 1988.

HERBST, SHARON TYLER. *The New Food Lover's Companion.* 2nd edition. Hauppauge, NY: Barron's Educational Series, 1995.

HILLMAN, HOWARD. *Kitchen Science.* Rev. ed. Boston: Houghton Mifflin, 1989.

MARGEN, SHELDON, MD and the editors of the University of California at Berkeley Wellness Letter. *The Wellness Encyclopedia of Food and Nutrition.* New York: Random House, Rebus, 1992.

MCGEE, HAROLD. *On Food and Cooking.* New York: Macmillan, Collier Books, 1984.

MCGEE, HAROLD. *The Curious Cook.* San Francisco: North Point Press, 1990.

UBALDI, JACK, AND ELIZABETH CROSSMAN. *Jack Ubaldi's Meat CookBook.* New York: Macmillian, 1987.

INDEX

CONVERSION CHART
EQUIVALENT IMPERIAL AND METRIC MEASUREMENTS

American cooks use standard containers, the 8-ounce cup and a tablespoon that takes exactly 16 level fillings to fill that cup level. Measuring by cup makes it very difficult to give weight equivalents, as a cup of densely packed butter will weigh considerably more than a cup of flour. The easiest way therefore to deal with cup measurements in recipes is to take the amount by volume rather than by weight. Thus the equation reads:

1 cup = 240 ml = 8 fl. oz.   *$^1/_2$ cup = 120 ml = 4 fl. oz.*

It is possible to buy a set of American cup measures in major stores around the world.

In the States, butter is often measured in sticks. One stick is the equivalent of 8 tablespoons. One tablespoon of butter is therefore the equivalent to $^1/_2$ ounce/15 grams.

LIQUID MEASURES

Fluid Ounces	U.S.	Imperial	Milliliters
	1 teaspoon	1 teaspoon	5
$^1/_4$	2 teaspoons	1 dessertspoon	10
$^1/_2$	1 tablespoon	1 tablespoon	14
1	2 tablespoons	2 tablespoons	28
2	$^1/_4$ cup	4 tablespoons	56
4	$^1/_2$ cup		110
5		$^1/_4$ pint or 1 gill	140
6	$^3/_4$ cup		170
8	1 cup		225
9			250, $^1/_4$ liter
10	$1^1/_4$ cups	$^1/_2$ pint	280
12	$1^1/_2$ cups		340
15		$^3/_4$ pint	420
16	2 cups		450
18	$2^1/_4$ cups		500, $^1/_2$ liter
20	$2^1/_2$ cups	1 pint	560
24	3 cups		675
25		$1^1/_4$ pints	700
27	$3^1/_2$ cups		750
30	$3^3/_4$ cups	$1^1/_2$ pints	840
32	4 cups or 1 quart		900
35		$1^3/_4$ pints	980
36	$4^1/_2$ cups		1000, 1 liter
40	5 cups	2 pints or 1 quart	1120

SOLID MEASURES

U.S. and Imperial Measures		Metric Measures	
Ounces	Pounds	Grams	Kilos
1		28	
2		56	
$3^1/_2$		100	
4	$^1/_4$	112	
5		140	
6		168	
8	$^1/_2$	225	
9		250	$^1/_4$
12	$^3/_4$	340	
16	1	450	
18		500	$^1/_2$
20	$1^1/_4$	560	
24	$1^1/_2$	675	
27		750	$^3/_4$
28	$1^3/_4$	780	
32	2	900	
36	$2^1/_4$	1000	1
40	$2^1/_2$	1100	
48	3	1350	
54		1500	$1^1/_2$

OVEN TEMPERATURE EQUIVALENTS

Fahrenheit	Celsius	Gas Mark	Description
225	110	$^1/_4$	Cool
250	130	$^1/_2$	
275	140	1	Very Slow
300	150	2	
325	170	3	Slow
350	180	4	Moderate
375	190	5	
400	200	6	Moderately Hot
425	220	7	Fairly Hot
450	230	8	Hot
475	240	9	Very Hot
500	250	10	Extremely Hot

Any broiling recipes can be used with the grill of the oven, but beware of high-temperature grills.

EQUIVALENTS FOR INGREDIENTS

all-purpose flour—plain flour
coarse salt—kitchen salt
cornstarch—cornflour
eggplant—aubergine

half and half—12% fat milk
heavy cream—double cream
light cream—single cream
lima beans—broad beans

scallion—spring onion
unbleached flour—strong, white flour
zest—rind
zucchini—courgettes or marrow